ROBERT THE BRUCE

By the same author

The Making of a King: The Early Years of James VI and I
James V, King of Scots
The Life and Times of Edward II
The Crowned Lions: The Early Plantagenet Kings
James VI of Scotland
James I of England
The History of Royal Holloway College, 1886–1986
Beyond the Highland Line: Highland History and Culture
Darnley: Henry Stuart, Lord Darnley, Consort of Mary Queen of Scots

ROBERT THE BRUCE

————|✳|✳|✳|————

Caroline Bingham

CONSTABLE · LONDON

First published in Great Britain in 1998
by Constable and Company Limited
3 The Lanchesters, 162 Fulham Palace Road
London W6 9ER
Copyright © 1998 by Caroline Bingham
ISBN 0 09 476440 9
The right of Caroline Bingham to be identified as the
author of this work has been asserted by her in
accordance with the Copyright, Designs and Patents Act 1988

Set in Monotype Garamond 12pt by
Servis Filmsetting Ltd, Manchester
Printed in Great Britain by
St Edmundsbury Press Ltd
Bury St Edmunds, Suffolk

A CIP catalogue record for this book
is available from the British Library

His faults were those of his
times, his virtues were
all
his own

CONTENTS

PART THREE: FROM WAR TO PEACE

ILLUSTRATIONS

ACKNOWLEDGEMENTS

Caroline Bingham died a few weeks after completing this book, a month before her sixtieth birthday. She had finished writing, revising, and noting the sources, but I have typed her manuscript and prepared it for publication. Fortunately, my mother was able to undertake the research which involved travelling (whether to the British Library or the Highlands of Scotland) before she became ill, and so her scholarship was never compromised. I have done my best to maintain her scrupulously high standards, but if any errors appear, they are entirely mine. There are some omissions; I have only been able to provide a select bibliography, there are doubtless many individuals and institutions Caroline Bingham would have included in these acknowledgements who are unknown to me, and the book is undedicated.

As it is, I must on her behalf thank everyone who has contributed in a professional capacity; I believe the London Library deserves a special mention, as does Mary Stewart and that the staff of the British Library, Public Record Office and Institute of Historical Research were also helpful. Of friends and family, it is impossible to mention so many who gave support, encouragement, and practical assistance in their different ways. I know my mother would want to acknowledge them all with her usual courtesy. On my own behalf I would like to thank everyone who has asked after my progress with 'Caroline's book', and assure them it would never have reached publication without my partner, Liz Mathews.

Finally, there is the omission of a dedication. I considered the possibility of dedicating it, on my mother's behalf, to all those who loved her and miss her, but I'm sure they would agree it is, inevitably, a memorial volume. The very existence of this biography of Robert the Bruce is a tribute to Caroline Bingham. In her determination to finish it, her unfailing humour and undiminished spirit, she showed perseverance and courage worthy of her heroic subject.

FRANCES BINGHAM

INTRODUCTION
HISTORY AND MYTH

'We were a tribe, a family, a people.
Wallace and Bruce guard now a painted field,
And all may read the folio of our fable,
Peruse the sword, the sceptre and the shield . . .'
Edwin Muir, *Scotland 1941*

A WAR OF INDEPENDENCE, a type of conflict that establishes a nation's identity and enforces its right to exist, produces protagonists who are perceived as heroes and villains, who become figures of myth as well as history. Such are the protagonists of Scotland's War of Independence, and part of the purpose of this book will be to examine the interaction between myth and history.

The subject of this book, Robert the Bruce, is a popular and national hero, 'Good King Robert'. As such he is to some extent a 'construct', a mythic figure who is more simply delineated than the complex figure of reality. This is not to say that Robert the Bruce was not a genuine hero, as undoubtedly he was, but that the historic figure is not the same as the hero of popular mythology.

The fact that Robert de Brus, the feudal magnate, was slow to discover himself as Scotland's 'Man of Destiny', and changed his loyalty more than once before he did so, may be an embarrassment to the mythopoeic writer, but historically it is perfectly understandable, because the patriotic cause had to be defined before it could be defended. And it was out of the experience of John Balliol, William Wallace, Robert the Bruce and others that it was defined. The magnates of Scotland had to find their own way out of the classic feudal dilemma: how could a man who was the vassal of two overlords reconcile conflicting loyalties? The excessive demands of Edward I of England in his self-appointed role as overlord of Scotland caused some of them to define their position in society as members of the Scottish nation rather than as members of the international caste of feudal aristocracy. It was through this choice that a national state developed out of a geographical nation.

Edward I was described in the epitaph on his tomb in Westminster Abbey as 'Scottorum Malleus' – the 'Hammer of the Scots' – though the famous epitaph may have been added to the tomb as late as the sixteenth century. In any case, its message is ambiguous, for a hammer is not essentially a weapon but a craft tool. Edward may have intended to batter the Scots into submission, but his hammer-strokes served to forge them into a nation characterized by a particularly strong sense of identity. Part of the hammering process was the reshaping of Robert de Brus, Earl of Carrick, from a member of the international feudal aristocracy into Robert the Bruce, the quintessential patriot king and national hero.

The same process reshaped William Wallace from an ordinary member of the knightly class into the precursor of Robert the Bruce as the liberator of the nation. Wallace has been described as a kind of Scottish Joan of Arc, an obscure person gifted with clarity of vision and a sense of mission who, although serving a confused and undeserving king (John Balliol), gave his nation a sense of its destiny and a belief in itself. The effects of his actions appear to justify this interpretation; but in life he had a mission with more modest aims than the mythic version of his career suggests. Wallace was not the democratic revolutionary or freedom fighter of modern mythology. Nor was he a native Celtic hero rebelling against the Norman invader. Wallace, like his Stewart overlords, belonged to a family which had arrived in Scotland as part of the feudalizing policy of King David I, who had died in 1153. The Stewarts were of Breton origin, and held lands in Shropshire before they received grants from David of lands in Scotland. The Wallaces (the name was probably originally 'le Waleys', meaning 'the Welshman') in all likelihood followed their lord to Scotland from the Welsh Borders. William Wallace was the son of a knight, Sir Malcolm Wallace of Elderslie, and himself became a knight, and as such was firmly embedded in the structure of feudal society. He had no wish to alter the structure, a concept which would have been beyond the imagination of a man of his class and time. He fought against Edward I with the determination to expel the English occupying forces from Scotland,

and to restore John Balliol, whom he perceived as Scotland's rightful King, in order to resurrect Scotland from the status of a conquered territory to that of a feudal kingdom. This was a great enough ambition, and a hard enough task, with a bitter enough end for Wallace himself, to make Wallace a genuine hero without recasting him in a modern mould which would have meant nothing to him.

The other protagonists in the struggle, if they were not perceived as heroes, have also been subjected to the mythopoeic process. Edward I was once an English hero, 'Edward Longshanks', the Crusader Prince who almost fell victim to the poisoned dagger of a Moslem assassin, to be saved by his wife, Eleanor of Castile, who sucked the venom from his wound. Though this fable faded from popular memory, an element of the King's romantic image has survived through his great sorrow for her death, which led him to order the construction of the 'Eleanor Crosses', each one marking the resting place of the funeral cortège bearing her body from the place of her death in Nottinghamshire to her burial at Westminster. To serious English historians, Edward I remained 'the Greatest of the Plantagenets' and 'the English Justinian', though both these verdicts may be questioned in an age in which conquering kings are not automatically admired, and in which the law can be seen as an instrument of manipulation as much as one of justice. By Scottish historians Edward I has been seen as a ruthless legal manipulator and a would-be tyrant, of whom there is nothing to be said in extenuation. The fact that he was misguided enough to make a martyr of Wallace placed him beyond the bounds of excuse, and beyond the hope of revision. His attitudes and actions perhaps may be explained if not excused within the context of his times.

Edward II, the principal antagonist of Robert the Bruce, was perceived by his contemporaries as an unworthy successor of a great king, the weak son of a strong father, a king, furthermore, lacking in kingly qualities, and addicted to unworthy favourites. At the beginning of the reign magnatial resentment centred upon Piers Gaveston and at the end upon the Despensers, father and son. The mythopoeic tendency has concentrated on the relations of Edward and Gaveston, who, chiefly as a result of the work of Christopher Marlowe (and later of Bertolt Brecht and Derek Jarman), have been established in the pantheon of famous homosexual lovers. This interpretation of their relationship has been challenged recently by the historian Pierre Chaplais, who has offered the counter-interpretation that Gaveston was unacceptable to the magnates of England, not because he was the King's lover, but because the King adopted him as his brother, and attempted to endow him with a sort of pseudo-royalty. Whichever interpretation is correct, this relationship laid the foundations of Edward II's troubles. Whether homosexual or quasi-fraternal, it was castigated as unacceptable because it was 'immoderate' and 'extravagant', words of condemnation used by contemporary chroniclers. In an age in which men were permitted to embrace each other or weep for each other without embarrassment, Edward's demonstrativeness towards Gaveston must indeed have been immoderate to have transgressed the conventions; and certainly it was unacceptably extravagant to have bestowed the royal earldom of Cornwall upon this son of a Gascon knight.

A sort of sub-myth is that Edward II abandoned or repudiated his father's ambitions, thus easing the task of Robert the Bruce in reasserting the independence and establishing the nationhood of Scotland. Part of the mythological fabric that this book will attempt to unravel is that into which is woven the picture of Edward II as an inactive king and an uncommitted adversary of Scotland. Hereditary enmity to Robert the Bruce and his supporters was the part of his father's legacy that Edward II did not repudiate or neglect. He returned to it again and again, whenever the internecine troubles of his own realm were in abeyance, and used it as the one unifying cause to which the factions within his kingdom would respond. He contested the field of Bannockburn resolutely before conceding defeat, and for the remainder of his reign steadfastly refused to acknowledge the kingship of Robert the Bruce, or the independence of Scotland, which were only conceded in the minority of his son. To admit the determination of Edward II in fact enhances the achievement of Robert the Bruce, for what would have been the value to the Scots of a victory without a determined enemy?

Finally, the war itself was inspired and dominated by a myth: the myth that the Kings of England were, or ought to be, overlords of the Kings of Scots. Belief in it was the justification for Edward I's dealings with John Balliol, and for the conflict that he and his son waged with Robert the Bruce.

As a modern historian of medieval Anglo/Scottish relationships has explained:

Medieval thinkers had no concept of evolution. To us it is clear enough that the progress of time inevitably brought changes in the relative positions of the two countries, in the degree to which one could impose its will on the other, and in the practical implications of feudal theories. In the middle ages . . . the past was commonly regarded as a witness to unchanging inherent rights and obligations. Thus the records of the past could . . . provide a definite answer to any question of title, and one which was perpetually valid. Hence Edward I . . . traces feudal relationships back to the time of the Trojan war![1]

Thus the mythic antiquity of the overlordship in which Edward desired to believe enabled him to ignore the fluctuating relationships between the two kingdoms in what were to him recent times, and to ignore the validity of treaties that invalidated his own arguments. Therefore it suited him to approve the 'Treaty of Falaise' in 1174, in which William the Lion, King of Scots, having been captured by Henry II, King of England, became the liegeman to Henry, 'for Scotland, and for all his other lands'; for the sake of argument Edward I was obliged to ignore the 'Treaty of Canterbury' of 1189, in which King Richard I of England released or 'quitclaimed' William the Lion of his homage. A century later, on 29 October 1278, in defence of his kingdom's status, Alexander III was able to claim before Edward I that 'Nobody but God himself has the right to the homage for my realm of Scotland, and I hold it of nobody but God himself.'[2]

With Alexander III's death, the seemingly secure condition of his kingdom was suddenly revealed as extremely vulnerable. Throughout the period covered by this book, the relations of the two kingdoms would continue to fluctuate, with the English myth of overlordship in the ascendant when the power of Edward I was at its zenith, and with the Scottish claim to independence triumphant at the end of the reign of Robert the Bruce.

Most biographies of Robert the Bruce begin with the death of Alexander III, a dramatic event which came to be seen as the end of an era of alliance between Scotland and England. The early pages, or chapters, deal with the period of the Guardians, the death of Alexander's granddaughter and heir 'The Maid of Norway', and the adjudication of Edward I in the 'Great Cause' to decide between the thirteen 'Competitors' or claimants to the throne of Scotland.

The familiar version of the complex drama presents Edward I as a ruthless imperialist, his intentions having been veiled during the lifetime of his brother-in-law, Alexander III, a strong ruler, partly revealed in his negotiations for a marriage between the Maid of Norway and his son Edward of Caernarvon, and then unveiled in all their naked aggression as soon as the claim had been settled, and John Balliol, a malleable nonentity, inaugurated as King of Scots.

This plausible interpretation, founded on hindsight, requires the reader to suppose that the Guardians, a group of politically experienced magnates and ecclesiastics, were almost unimaginably ingenuous. But these men knew the King of England well, and had known him for many years. They did not see him as a bloated spider already engorged with the blood of Wales, and preparing to devour Scotland as his next victim. They saw him in familiarly human terms as the reliable ally of the late King of Scots, and potentially as a powerful protector of its child Queen.

In order to set the scene, though admittedly delaying the entry of the protagonist, I shall begin with an impression of the period during which Scotland and England were at peace.

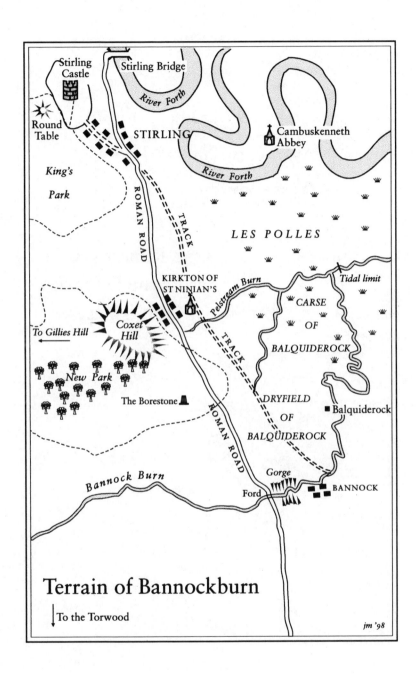

Terrain of Bannockburn

To the Torwood

jm '98

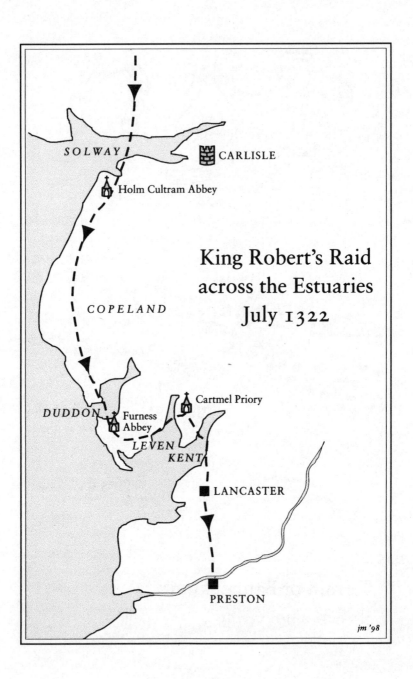

SOLWAY

CARLISLE

Holm Cultram Abbey

King Robert's Raid
across the Estuaries
July 1322

COPELAND

Cartmel Priory

DUDDON   Furness
Abbey

LEVEN
KENT

LANCASTER

PRESTON

jm '98

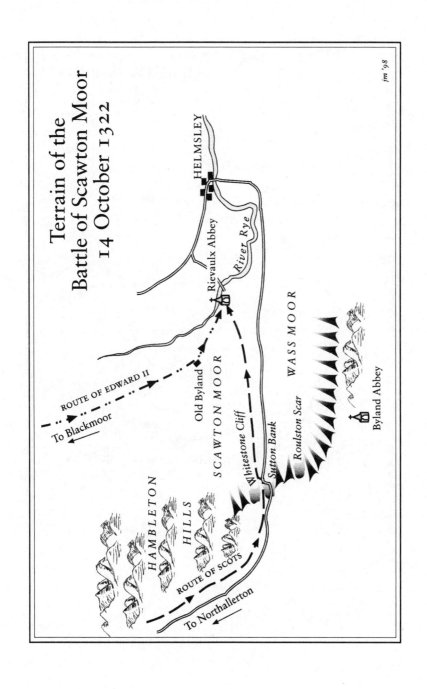

Terrain of the
Battle of Scawton Moor
14 October 1322

HELMSLEY

Rievaulx Abbey

River Rye

ROUTE OF EDWARD II

To Blackmoor

Old Byland

SCAWTON MOOR

Whitestone Cliff

Sutton Bank

Roulston Scar

WASS MOOR

Byland Abbey

HAMBLETON

HILLS

ROUTE OF SCOTS

To Northallerton

jm '98

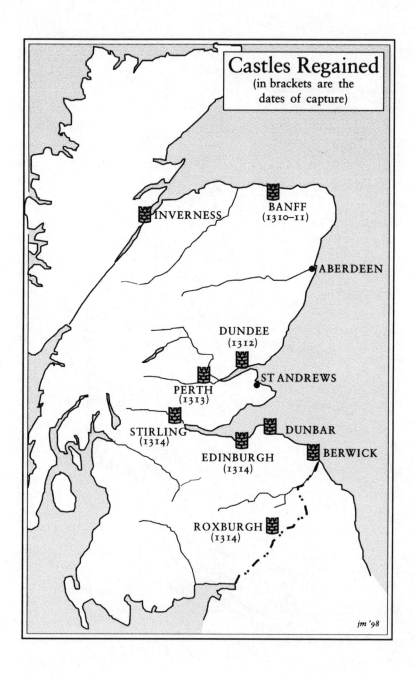

Castles Regained
(in brackets are the
dates of capture)

INVERNESS

BANFF
(1310–11)

●ABERDEEN

DUNDEE
(1312)

PERTH
(1313)

ST ANDREWS

STIRLING
(1314)

DUNBAR

EDINBURGH
(1314)

BERWICK

ROXBURGH
(1314)

jm '98

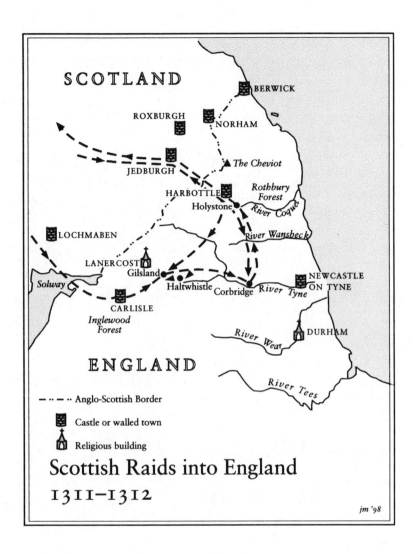

SCOTLAND

BERWICK

ROXBURGH

NORHAM

JEDBURGH

The Cheviot

HARBOTTLE

Rothbury Forest

Holystone

River Coquet

River Wansbeck

LOCHMABEN

LANERCOST

Gilsland

NEWCASTLE ON TYNE

Solway

Haltwhistle

Corbridge

River Tyne

CARLISLE

Inglewood Forest

River Wear

DURHAM

ENGLAND

River Tees

— ·· — ·· — Anglo-Scottish Border

Castle or walled town

Religious building

Scottish Raids into England

1311–1312

jm '98

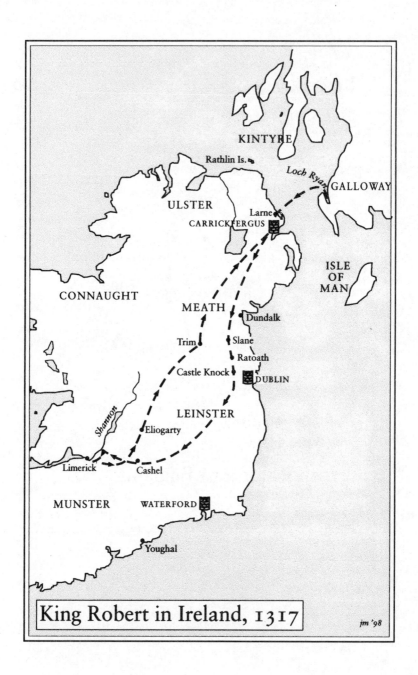

Rathlin Is.

KINTYRE

Loch Ryan

GALLOWAY

ULSTER

Larne

CARRICKFERGUS

ISLE
OF
MAN

CONNAUGHT

MEATH

Dundalk

Trim

Slane

Ratoath

Castle Knock

DUBLIN

LEINSTER

Shannon

Eliogarty

Limerick

Cashel

MUNSTER

WATERFORD

Youghal

King Robert in Ireland, 1317

jm '98

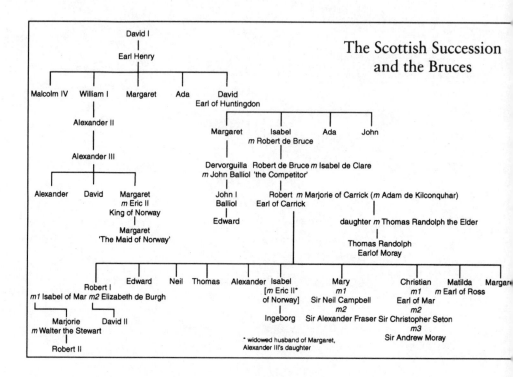

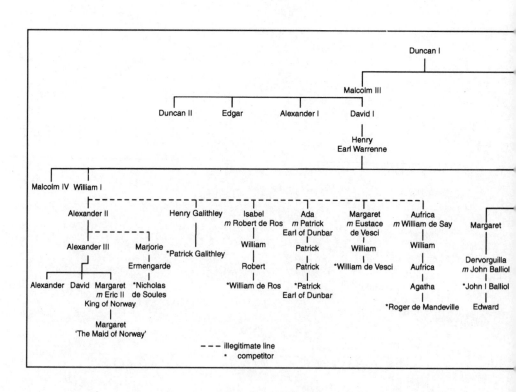

The Competitors for the Crown of Scotland

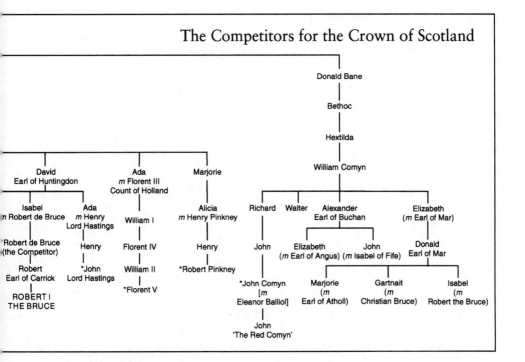

Donald Bane
|
Bethoc
|
Hextilda
|
William Comyn

David
Earl of Huntingdon

Ada
m Florent III
Count of Holland

Marjorie

Isabel
m Robert de Bruce

Ada
m Henry
Lord Hastings

William I

Alicia
m Henry Pinkney

Richard

Walter

Alexander
Earl of Buchan

Elizabeth
(*m* Earl of Mar)

*Robert de Bruce
(the Competitor)

Henry

Florent IV

Henry

John

Elizabeth
(*m* Earl of Angus)

John
(*m* Isabel of Fife)

Donald
Earl of Mar

Robert
Earl of Carrick

*John
Lord Hastings

William II

*Robert Pinkney

*John Comyn
[*m*
Eleanor Balliol]

Marjorie
(*m*
Earl of Atholl)

Gartnait
(*m*
Christian Bruce)

Isabel
(*m*
Robert the Bruce)

ROBERT I
THE BRUCE

*Florent V

John
'The Red Comyn'

PART ONE
A CLAIM TO THE THRONE

——|✳|✳|✳|——

1

———|✳|✳|✳|———

THE ROYAL ALLIES

'Faithful friends know not fickleness in their affection,
and after our long experience we ought with good
reason to praise the faithfulness of your excellency for
the many kindnesses that we have received . . .'

Alexander III of Scotland to Edward I of England, 20
April 1284[1]

IN THE LAST few days before Christmas 1251 the royalty, nobility and
knighthood of the two kingdoms converged on the city of York. King
Henry III of England and his Queen Eleanor of Poitiers rode north
with a great entourage, bringing their daughter, the Princess Margaret
Plantagenet, to be married to Alexander III, King of Scots. Alexander
came south with a much smaller retinue, to be joined at York by his
mother Marie de Coucy, Queen-Dowager of Scots, returning from a
visit to France. Alexander, born on 4 September 1241, was just over ten
years and three months old; his prospective bride was his senior by
exactly a year and a day. Their marriage, like most royal marriages
throughout the centuries, was a political union, to which their personal
feelings were subordinated. Its purpose was the renewal of the existing
alliance between Scotland and England, and the guarantee of continuing friendship between the two kingdoms. The emotions of the princi-
pals were not important enough to be matters of historical record, but
excitement and apprehension were probably common to both of them,
while Margaret probably added reluctance, since she was about to
exchange everything familiar for an unknown future.

King Henry is said by the chronicler Matthew Paris to have gone
to York attended by over a thousand knights, while King Alexander's

following totalled no more than sixty, numbers which indicate the disparity of population between the two countries. Thirteenth-century Scotland is estimated to have had a population of some four hundred thousand, England of perhaps two million.[2] These figures would have been unknown to the people of the time, whose estimates of number were haphazard and mostly exaggerated; large gatherings simply made it obvious that the population of England must be much greater. This was unimportant so long as the two countries were at peace, but it would put Scotland at a serious disadvantage when they went to war.

Peace, however, did not preclude Anglo-Scottish rivalry, and even bellicosity, especially when liquor was flowing, so preparations for the wedding festivities in York included arrangements that Scotsmen and Englishmen of the royal and magnatial followings should be lodged in different streets. Even so, competition for lodgings resulted in an affray in which a man was killed. The total number of people who came to York is not known, but it must have been well over two thousand, assuming the reported numbers of knights to have been correct; for besides the members of the royal households, the magnates also would have had their attendants, and the more prosperous knights would have brought a squire and a servant.

The logistics of feeding and feasting such a multitude were formidable, but the highly organized household of Henry III was equal to the task. Preparations began in the summer, with the slaughter of vast numbers of red and fallow deer in various royal forests, to be converted into salt venison and transported to York. In early December, open season for the hunting of the hind, red and fallow hinds were made captive to be slaughtered at the appropriate date to provide fresh meat. As the autumn progressed poultry and game were ordered from the Sheriffs of the Northern Counties, and provided in prodigious quantities: 1,000 chickens and over 2,000 partridges, 125 swans, 120 peacocks, 290 pheasants, 1,300 hares, 400 rabbits, 70 boar, and many other creatures. Live fish were collected in a stock pond, to be caught by the King's 'piscator' at the last moment. Huge amounts of salmon were made into pâté. Rice, almonds, sugar and spices were ordered to be made into biscuits and pastries, and finally the bailliffs of several northern towns were required to provide a staggering total of 68,500 loaves of bread. It scarcely mattered that much of the bread would be stolen by the time it reached York, for many of the loaves were destined for use as 'trenchers' or disposable plates, which at the end of the feast, well impregnated by rich sauces, were customarily distributed to the destitute. Hundreds of tuns of red and white wine were amassed to wash down the rich food at what must have been one of the feasts of the century.

Henry III, who had a taste for splendour and ceremony, gave his personal attention to the matter of clothes and wedding presents. With the rigours of a northern winter in mind, he ordered a fur cloak for himself, and fur linings and trimmings for many other garments. In the course of several days' festivities, a splendid display of clothes would be required. The King's twelve-year-old son, the Lord Edward (the future Edward I), was to have no fewer than five robes of Cloth of Gold trimmed with different furs; miniver, grosvair and bissis.[3] What the King of Scots would wear was the responsibility of his own household officers; but Scottish prestige would have required that Scotland's King should not be outshone by England's Prince. The eyes of onlookers would be upon them, and critical comparisons could be made.

Alexander was to be knighted by Henry III on Christmas Day, and the English King ordered for him 'a beautiful sword with silk-covered scabbard and a well decorated silver pommel as well as a beautiful belt to suspend it from', and also a pair of silver gilt spurs with silk ties to attach them to his feet.[4] These were the traditional presents to a new-made knight – hence the expression 'to win one's spurs'.

The ceremony of knighthood, at which the honour was bestowed on Alexander and twenty others, was the culmination of the Christmas Feast. At the conclusion in the evening King Henry invited King Alexander to pay him his homage for the kingdom of Scotland. Alexander had doubtless been warned by his advisers to be on his guard, and King Henry's attempt to take advantage of the exaltation of the moment was deftly parried. Alexander replied with a courteous evasion, that he had come to York to be married, and 'not to answer about so difficult a matter'.[5] It was quite appropriate that the Royal Standard during Alexander's minority bore the motto ESTO PRUDENS UT SERPENS ET SIMPLEX SICUT COLUMBA (Be as wise as the serpent and simple as the dove) – a lesson which he had evidently taken to heart.[6]

The wedding of Alexander III and Margaret of England was

celebrated the following day – St Stephen's Day; very early in the morning 'secretly and before it was expected', said Matthew Paris, to avoid the pressure of disorderly crowds. Medieval marriage was a secular contract, blessed by the Church; the marriage performed at the church door, the blessing within. Alexander and Margaret were probably married on the steps ascending to the South Door of York Minister, the entry to the recently completed South Transept,[7] before being conducted into the luminous glory of the interior, to be blessed by the Archbishop, Walter de Fray.

The English royal family stayed in York to celebrate Epiphany (6 January), the traditional conclusion of Christmas festivities. The King and Queen of Scots left for Scotland on 30 December. On the way, they would be entertained by the Sheriff of Northumberland, at the castle of Newcastle-on-Tyne, where two tuns of wine and meat and fish were to be provided at Henry's expense to feast them.[8]

The impressive young King of Scots had been the undoubted cynosure of the festivities at York, for once displacing the Lord Edward, who was accustomed to that position at his father's court. It may have been with envy or relief that the English prince watched him depart; knighted, married and a king, at ten years old. In three years' time Edward would be married to the Spanish bride Eleanor of Castile, who won his lifelong devotion, and knighted by her half-brother King Alfonso X;[9] but he would have to wait twenty-one years before he succeeded his father as King of England. Even then, ambitious as he was, he would grieve for his pious, inept and luxury-loving father, whose authority he had fought a civil war to defend.[10]

Among medieval kings, Henry III was an unusually affectionate father. It distressed him that his daughter was lonely and unhappy during the early years of her marriage. In 1253 she complained to her father that Edinburgh Castle was a cold and uncomfortable place, and that she and her husband were not allowed to live together. Surely they were still too young to do so, though they may have thought themselves a man and a woman at twelve and thirteen years. Henry requested that she might be permitted to visit her mother, but the Scottish government would not let her go.[11] It is sometimes said that anxiety for his daughter provided Henry's pretext for interfering in Scottish affairs, but he scarcely needed such a pretext. As the Queen's father and the King's father-in-law he had a natural claim to be interested in the welfare of the young couple and *ipso facto* the welfare of their kingdom. Besides, the relationship between the two families was long-established. Henry III's sister, Joan of England, had been the first wife of Alexander's father, Alexander II of Scotland. It was the mischance of infertility that Alexander III was not the English King's nephew. Joan died childless and Alexander III was the son of his father's second marriage to Marie de Coucy, daughter of Inguerrand III, Lord of Coucy in Picardy. For the purpose of the next diplomatic marriage this was fortunate, for had Alexander and Margaret been first cousins, though their marriage could have been permitted by papal dispensation, the relationship would have been undesirably close.

Henry's interest in Scottish affairs seems to have been benign and fatherly in intention, and 'neither document nor chronicle suggests that Henry III claimed to interfere by virtue of overlordship,'[12] but the unfortunate result, according to Matthew Paris, was the formation of 'English' or 'native' groups, striving to influence the king.

Alexander III, like the several Kings of Scots who succeeded as minors in later centuries,[13] suffered a troubled minority as the object of a self-perpetuating power struggle, until he reached maturity and emerged from tutelage to impose his authority upon his subjects. This happened probably sooner than they had expected, towards the end of the 1250s. In 1260 Alexander took his wife to England to visit her parents (and took the opportunity to remind her father that most of her dowry was still unpaid!). He was persuaded to leave her in England for the birth of her first child, though it caused some indignation among the Scots that the baby was born in England. The child was a daughter, named Margaret, after her mother, and after Alexander's ancestress St Margaret of Scotland, who had been canonized in 1250, bringing additional lustre to the royal throne of Scotland – for not every royal dynasty could claim to include an officially canonized saint. (The Plantagenets, indeed, had to make do with the Anglo-Saxon king St Edward the Confessor, to whose honour Henry III dedicated the new church of Westminster Abbey, or else extend their veneration to the ambiguous figure of St Thomas Becket, who had won his martyr's crown by resisting the pretensions of Henry II to taking over the Church.[14]) Queen Margaret and her child returned to Scotland in the summer of 1261, by which time Alexander felt his authority firmly enough established to revive his father's ambition of wresting the Western Isles from the possession of Norway.

In the fourth century AD Gaelic-speaking tribesmen from a little kingdom called Dalriada (now County Antrim) crossed the Irish Sea and invaded the islands and the larger landmass beyond. In around 500 they established a kingdom called Dalriada after their homeland, which comprised the Western Isles and the coast of Argyll (Erra-gaidheal – the coast of the gael). Their king, Fergus Mór MacEirc, was the ancestor of the succeeding Kings of Scots; a name which shows the predominance of literary culture. When they ceased to call their new country Dalriada, they called it 'Alba' and themselves 'Albanach'; which Latin-writing histories called the 'Scoti', their kingdom 'Scotia', and these were the names that prevailed. Colonizing the mainland, the Scots came into conflict with the Picts, whose kingdom extended from Shetland to the Forth. The Picts were also Gaelic-speaking, and probably predominantly of Celtic stock, though ancient Pictish upright stones with inscriptions in an undeciphered language hint at an earlier racial element submerged by incoming Celts.

After centuries of conflict and fluctuating fortunes the Picts and the Scots were united under a Scottish King, Kenneth Mac Alpin, c. 850, and the political centre of the united kingdom shifted eastward from Dunadd in Argyll to Dunkeld in Perthshire.

The religious centre of the kingdom was transferred from the Isle of Iona to Scone, which became the place of inauguration of the Kings of Scots, who were enthroned on a sacred stone, the palladrim of their ancestors, brought from Irish Dalriada and believed to have been carried from Egypt by Scota, the daughter of the Pharoah from whom the Israelites had fled, the eponymous matriarch of the Scots.[15]

The move to the east probably assured the survival of the kingdom, for in the next century the Norse invasions stripped the Western Isles from the authority of the Kings of Scots, but did not erase the belief that they were, or ought to be, an integral part of Scotia.

While the Western Isles remained unredeemed, Scotia extended its boundaries to the south, taking in the old British kingdom of Strathclyde in the south-west, and in the south-east the Anglian province of Lothian, which was an outlier of the Anglo-Saxon

Northumbria, won by Malcolm II of Scots by the battle of Carham, 1018.

The recovery of the Western Isles became a priority of the Kings of Scots when their relations with England favoured the enterprise. At the beginning of the 1260s Henry III's embroilment with the baronial opposition led by Simon de Montfort was drawing him inexorably towards civil war, which conveniently prevented him from intervening when Alexander chose to indulge in a trial of strength with the King of Norway. Had he been free of domestic entanglements, he might have interfered, for few powers view the territorial expansion of a neighbour, even though a reliable ally, with equanimity.

Alexander III had attempted to recover the Western Isles from Norway over twenty years earlier, and had initially offered to purchase them. When the Norwegian King Haakon IV refused his offer, Alexander moved from negotiation to force, and prepared a military expedition to annexe the isles. His fleet sailed round the Mull of Kintyre and into the Firth of Lorn. The King had landed on the Isle of Kerrera opposite Oban, where he was attacked by sudden illness and died on 8 July 1249.

In 1261 Haakon IV was still on the throne of Norway – by now he was 'Haakon the Old' – and he remained as determined as ever to retain possession of the Western Isles. Not only did he repel the approaches of the Scottish embassy which visited him in 1261, but he held the Scottish ambassadors in custody over the winter, thereby providing a convenient *causus belli* for the Scots.[16] In 1262 a force commanded by William, Earl of Marr, invaded and devastated the Isle of Skye, and Haakon accepted the necessity to mount a large-scale expedition to defend his possession of the Isles. He prepared for the voyage, which he may have sensed would be his last, by having his son Magnus crowned as his successor before his departure. But his preparations were slow, and the fleet did not sail until 11 July 1263,[17] which left little enough time for the voyage and the gathering of local support before the onset of wild weather at the autumn equinox. Magnus, King of Norway, and Daguld of Guimorra joined King Haakon, but most of the other island chiefs gave their support to King Alexander or reluctantly submitted to a levy of cattle to save their lands from Norwegian devastation. Haakon was short of supplies and his reception was not encouraging. Ewen of Lorn, who held his mainland possessions from

Alexander, resigned his island territories to Haakon and was held in honourable captivity during the ensuing action.[18]

Alexander came to Ayr, and diplomatic exchanges between the two kings held the Norwegians inactive until the storms came. The Norwegian fleet was battered by the gales on 30 September, and on 2 October a Norwegian landing party was defeated at the 'Battle of Largs'. King Haakon had been hustled back to his ship when the fighting began, and the Scottish commander, Alexander Stewart, was left in victorious possession of the beach.

It was a small engagement but an ignominious end to King Haakon's expedition; added to lack of supplies and lack of local support it was enough to make him abandon his plans and sail for Norway. The storms continued and one of his ships went down in the Pentland Firth before the fleet reached Orkney on 29 October. There King Haakon fell ill and died in the Bishop's Palace at Kirkwall, on 16 December.[19]

With the Norwegian menace removed, there was little resistance to Scottish annexation of the Isles. In 1264 King Magnus of Man, threatened with invasion, offered his homage to King Alexander III, and was confirmed in possession of his island kingdom in return for the service of ten galleys.[20] But the following year he died, and the Isle of Man came under direct Scottish rule.

The Manxmen resented their loss of independence, and in 1275 rebelled under the leadership of Godfrey, an illegitimate son of the late king. A Scottish army invaded Man, offered Godfrey the chance to submit peacefully, and when he refused defeated him with great slaughter, and the Isle of Man was discontentedly incorporated into the Scottish realm.

Meanwhile the cession of the Western Isles to Scotland was negotiated with Haakon's successor, King Magnus Lagaboater ('the Law mender'). By the Treaty of Perth of 1266 the Western Isles became subject to Scotland for the sum of 4,000 marks and an 'annual' of 100 marks, to be paid in perpetuity (the payments lapsed in the next century). The Northern Isles of Orkney and Shetland were specifically reserved to the Norwegian crown, although the line of the Norse Earls of Orkney had died out in 1231, and the islands fell increasingly under Scottish domination. They were transferred to Scottish rule exactly two hundred years later, in 1466.[21]

While Alexander III had been successfully pursuing his course of territorial aggrandizement (justified in medieval fashion by reference to the past), England had lurched into civil war. On 14 May 1264 Edward and his father were defeated by the forces of Simon de Montfort at the battle of Lewes, and both were taken prisoner. A contingent of Scots lords (including Comyn, Balliol and Bruce) had gone to the assistance of Henry III and his son, all of whom were captured, and a huge number of their followers were killed. The Abbot of Dryburgh was sent to visit the English King and prince while they were captive, but after Edward had escaped he sent an appeal to Alexander. However, the need for help was pre-empted when Edward and his father turned the tables on the enemies, and defeated Simon de Montfort at the battle of Evesham on 4 August 1265. Montfort was killed, and the mutilation of his corpse was the first indication that Edward would not be a magnanimous enemy.[22]

The battle of Evesham did not immediately end the civil war in England, but it ensured the royalist victory. By 1268 Henry III's authority was sufficiently firmly re-established to entitle Edward to fulfil his ambition to take the cross and join the crusade (of Louis IX, King of France). Although the crusading ideal had been degraded and politicized, and many took the cross with cynical disregard of religious motives, for others to be a crusader remained the highest chivalric ideal, the dedication of military prowess to the service of God. For Edward the inspiration to take the cross probably derived from a mixture of conventional piety, restless ambition and desire for prestige. He collected a following of 225 knights, and other magnates who took the cross at the same time gathered their own contingents, among them Edward's younger brother, Edmund of Lancaster.[23] In the latter's following was an elderly Scottish nobleman, Robert de Bruce, Lord of Annandale, who was accompanied by his son and namesake. The crusaders left England in 1270, and though Edmund and his companions returned two years later, Edward's absence was prolonged until 1274.

Edward was in Sicily when he heard of the death of his father, who died on 16 November 1272. He made no haste to return, but travelled overland in a leisurely manner through Italy, Savoy and France. In Paris he paid homage to King Philip III for the English lands in France, and returned to his own country on 2 August 1274. Preparations for the coronation were well advanced by the time he returned, and he and Eleanor of Castile were crowned together on 19 August.

Alexander III brought his Queen to attend her brother's coronation. He accepted expenses to attend, but was careful to obtain written confirmation that he would not be prejudiced by attending or by performing the service that had been asked of him. It has been suggested that he had been asked to carry one of the State swords in the coronation procession, but he did not do so.[24] Nor did he perform the homage which he owed for the lands he held in England; he was not withholding the homage but ensuring that it should be performed under conditions which were not prejudicial to his status.

In 1274 Alexander had been King for twenty-five years, and had gained great prestige by an enlargement of his kingdom which had taken place with remarkably little bloodshed. The only other military action of his reign would be the bloodier quelling of the Manx revolt the following year. His achievement, developing year by year, was to create a kingdom which was harmonious without being homogenous; the ruling class on whom he depended for advice, military service and local government comprised both the old Celtic nobility and the feudal aristocracy whose roots in the kingdom were more recent, families from whom many of the higher clergy were also drawn. By creating consensus among them and ruling through them, Alexander won and deserved the epithet of 'peaceable King'.

When Edward I was crowned King of England he had the victory over Simon de Montfort to his credit, and had gained the prestige of a crusader prince, but as a ruler he was as yet an unknown quantity. It would not have been surprising if he had admired, or desired to emulate, the achievements of his brother-in-law; but it is an historical irony that Edward I, who was to become one of the great *bêtes noires* of Scotland's history, may have found a role model in Alexander III. (The conquest of Wales was soon to extend his realm, as the annexation of the Isles had extended Alexander's.)

They parted on the best of terms, and the question of the homage Alexander owed for the lands of Tyndale and Penrith in northern England was deferred until a future visit. Alexander returned, but the Queen of Scotland never saw her native country again. Queen Margaret died in Cupar, Fife, on 26 February 1275. The Chronicler of Lanercost, a Minorite friar of generally misogynistic views, grudgingly admitted

'She was a woman of great beauty, chastity and humility – three qualities seldom united in one individual'.[25] Alexander's grief for the wife to whom he had been married since they were children is implied by the fact that he showed no intention to remarry. It seemed that the succession was secure; the Queen had borne him three children: Margaret (born 28 February 1261), Alexander (born 21 January 1264), and David (born 20 March 1273).

Alexander returned to England in 1278. He met King Edward at Tewkesbury on 16 October, and offered to perform the act of homage immediately. Edward declined it, and requested that it should be performed in the presence of the Council, at Westminster, at the end of the month. There the ceremony took place, with the Council as witnesses, on 28 October.

Alexander had brought with him Robert de Bruce, Earl of Carrick, the younger of the two crusaders who had accompanied Edmund of Lancaster and who since his return had acquired the Earldom of Carrick by marriage. Alexander requested that the Earl of Carrick should be permitted to perform the act of homage as his proxy, for no king relished being seen on his knees before another, an attitude too easily misinterpreted. Edward, who himself had knelt before Philip III of France in 1273, accepted Carrick as his brother-in-law's proxy 'as an act of special grace'. The Earl then repeated the words

> I, Robert, Earl of Carrick, by virtue of the power given me by my lord the King of Scotland in the presence of the King of Scotland and by his command, do thus swear fealty to Edward, King of England; 'I, Alexander, King of Scotland, will keep true faith with Edward, King of England . . . in matters of life, limb and earthly honour, and will faithfully perform the services due for the lands and tenements that I hold of the King of England'.[26]

This was the English account of the occasion, recorded in the Close Rolls of the reign. According to the Scottish account in the Cartulary of Dunfermline, Alexander paid homage to Edward with the words 'I become your man for the lands which I hold of you in the realm of England, for which I owe you homage, reserving [the right of] my kingdom' [*salvo regno meo*].

Then William de Middleton, Bishop of Norwich, interrupted with the words 'and let it be reserved to the King of England, if he should have right to your homage for the kingdom'. Alexander's reply was forceful and uncompromising: 'Nobody but God himself has the right of the homage for my realm of Scotland, and I hold it of nobody but God himself' ('*Ad homagium regni mei Scotia nullus ius habei nisi solus Deus nec illud teneo nisi de solo Deo*').[27]

The Earl of Carrick then swore the oath of homage on Alexander's behalf, with his hand on a volume of the Gospels, saying, 'So may God help me, and these holy Gospels, my lord the king of Scotland here will be faithful to you in all matters of life and limb, and of earthly honour, and will keep your counsels secret.' And Alexander reiterated 'for the lands that I hold of you in the kingdom of England' ('*de terris quas de vobis teneo in regno Anglie*').[28]

Alexander could not have stressed his position more clearly and forcefully, and no doubt he was glad that the presence of the King's council had given him the maximum publicity. The Bishop's intervention had presumably been pre-arranged for the purpose of keeping the claim of the English kings on record – it was always a useful political bargaining counter, or threat, if the relations between the kingdoms deteriorated. But Edward accepted Alexander's declaration without protest, and he had shown consideration and courtesy in sparing Alexander the obligation of kneeling to him, and accepted the Earl of Carrick as his proxy.

Only long afterwards did this episode, and the one that had occurred at Alexander's wedding, appear to have been landmarks in Anglo-Scottish relations. Henry III's attempt to take advantage of his youthful son-in-law, and the interruption of the Bishop of Norwich, both demonstrated that the English kings did not wish their ancient claim to overlordship to vanish by default; but in each instance a few words had sufficed to protect the Scots' position, and in the latter instance Alexander was speaking from a position of strength. Edward's behaviour towards Alexander demonstrated that he respected him both as a king and as a man, and he could not have nourished deep plans to subvert his kingdom's independence, for at this date the Scottish succession seemed to be secure.

At the beginning of the next decade Alexander took steps to secure the future in so far as it lay in his power.

The role of his daughter Margaret was to confirm the peace with Norway, established by the Treaty of Perth of 1266. King Magnus Lagaboater had now died, and her marriage was negotiated with his son, King Eric II Magnusson, to whom she was married at Riga in August 1281. According to the Lanercost Chronicle 'the union was very distasteful to the maiden' – as well it might be, since she was twenty and her bridegroom was a boy of 'thirteen winters'. However, 'she comported herself so graciously towards the king and his people that she altered their manners for the better, taught them the French and English languages, and set the fashion of more seemly dress and food'.[29] If she achieved all this, she did so very quickly, for her opportunity was brief. King Eric consummated his marriage when he was fourteen, and in April 1283 Margaret bore him a daughter, and died in childbirth. The baby was Margaret, 'The Maid of Norway'. Meanwhile, King Alexander's elder son Alexander was married on 15 November 1282 to Margueritte, daughter of Guy de Darpierre, Count of Flanders, but the marriage was childless and the young prince died at Ladoies Abbey, Fife, on 28 January 1284, a week after his twentieth birthday. His younger brother David had predeceased him in the summer of 1281. This sequence of deaths left Alexander III with no heir but his Norwegian granddaughter.

When the young prince Alexander died, Edward I sent his condolences to the King of Scots in a letter carried by a friar named Brother John of St Germain, in which Edward assured King Alexander that they remained 'united together perpetually, God willing, by the tie of indissoluble affection'. Alexander replied on 20 April 1284, assuring Edward that 'faithful friends know not fickleness in their affection, and after our long experience we ought with good reason to praise the faithfulness of your excellency for the many kindnesses we have received'.[30] This letter also included the important passage 'We are bound to thank your dear highness . . . that you have regard for our kinship and we would recall . . . to your recollection, that in the providence of God much good may yet come to pass through your kinswoman, the daughter of our beloved the late Queen of Norway, . . . who is now our heir apparent . . .'[31]

The words show a friendliness beyond regard for the formalities of alliance, and though the Latin letter would have been composed by a clerk of the King's Chapel (Chancery), it conveyed the message in the

tone the King desired. The concluding passages indicated that
Alexander would look favourably on a marriage between his granddaughter and a member of the English royal house. Another Anglo-
Scottish royal marriage would have confirmed what was becoming an
old alliance between the two kingdoms; and Alexander's letter stressed
the value of the marriage with the information that the Maid of
Norway had been acknowledged as his heir.

Immediately after the death of his elder son, Alexander III exacted
from the magnates a formal acknowledgement that 'we each and all of
us will accept the illustrious girl Margaret . . . as our lady and right heir
of our said lord King of Scotland, of the whole realm of Scotland, of
the Isle of Man and of all other islands belonging to the said Kingdom
of Scotland, and of Tynedale and Penrith . . .'[32]

All the countries to which she was heir are carefully enumerated but,
as the words make clear, Alexander did not designate her the future
sovereign; her status as heir apparent was dependent on his failure to
beget more children. That he hoped to replace her with a more desirable male heir was shown by the haste with which he sought a new
bride, after ten years of widowhood.

The bride of Alexander's choice was Yolande de Dreux, the young
daughter of a French nobleman, Robert II, Count of Dreux, a descendant of Louis VI of France, and also a vassal of the King of England.
Thus, in choosing a wife in France, Alexander chose tactfully and did
not jeopardize his friendly relations with England. The fact that the
marriage was welcomed by Edward I was demonstrated by his permitting the bride to travel through England to her wedding.

Alexander III and Yolande de Dreux were married on 14 October
1285 in Jedburgh Abbey. Alexander was now forty-three. In his maturity he was described as being 'exceptional in appearance, physically well-
built, thickset and tall in stature, though he could not be called fat. He
had a jovial face, a steadfast heart, a devout spirit.'[33] Yolande, a shadowy
young bride whose date of birth is not known, was described in accordance with the convention that all queens are beautiful as 'the fairest of
women'.

Outwardly the royal wedding was an occasion of splendour and
rejoicing, though there was no concealing the fact that its prime
purpose was to repair the loss of the King's sons. But tragedy had preceded the wedding, and tragedy followed, so that in retrospect it seemed

to have been a doomed union. The *Scotichronicon* recorded the folkloric recollection of it:

> I cannot recall of having read of such a famous feast ever before in Scotland . . . While everything was going on at the royal wedding according to due custom, a kind of show was put on in the form of a procession amongst the company who were reclining at table. At the head of this procession were skilled musicians with many sorts of pipe music including the wailing music of bagpipes, and behind them others splendidly performing a wardance with intricate weaving in and out. Bringing up the rear was a figure regarding whom it was difficult to decide whether it was a man or an apparition. It seemed to glide like a ghost rather than walking on feet. When it looked as if he was disappearing from everyone's sight, the frenzied procession halted, the song died away, the music faded, and the dancing contingent froze suddenly and unexpectedly. Laughter is [always] mixed with grief, and mourning takes over from extremes of joy; after such splendour the kingdom lamented ingloriously . . .[34]

From this it was a short step to the traditional belief that an apparition of death had appeared at the wedding feast of Alexander III, presaging the death of the King and the ensuing misfortunes of the kingdom. In the fourteenth and fifteenth centuries, when the story was written and rewritten, confrontations between the world of the flesh and the world of the spirit were commonplaces of art and literature and popular belief. Twentieth-century readers will rationalize the tale, perhaps imagining a dark-cloaked and footsore pilgrim seeking the abbey's hospitality and fortuitously entering the hall at the tail of the dancing procession, then revealed as an incongruous figure at a wedding feast, swiftly effacing himself and slipping from the room just as the music and dancing ceases . . . Later, this fleeting impression grows into the story that reaches the *Scotichronicon*. This may be true, but it was not a truth recognized by the subjects of Alexander III.

Their world-view, which could easily accommodate a supernatural visitant, and all the miracles, portents and prophecies reported by medieval chroniclers, could equally easily accommodate a rumour that the Day of Judgement was at hand. Over the winter of 1285 the people of Scotland began to believe that the next 18 March would be Judgement Day. Since the world continued to exist thereafter, the rumour might have been forgotten, had it not become associated with the death of Alexander III.

On 18 March 1286 Alexander held a meeting of his council in Edinburgh Castle, and afterwards dined with his councillors. To one of these lords Alexander sent a dish of lampreys, which was presented to him by a squire with the message that he should make merry since this was to be the Day of Judgement. The recipient thanked the King with the words 'If this be the Judgement Day we shall soon arise with full bellies'[35] – an appropriate jest among men who believed in the bodily resurrection at the Last Day but were not taking the immediate prospect very seriously.

It was late when the feast ended, and Alexander decided to cross the Forth to the Manor of Kinghorn, where Queen Yolande awaited him. The weather was wild, and possibly the unusual violence of equinoctial gales had enhanced the popular belief in the impending end of the world; but despite the wildness of the night, the King refused to be deflected from his resolve. Whether it was passion for his young wife or anxiety for the future of the kingdom that impelled him, Alexander braved the storm. The autumn gales of 1266 had blown in his favour at Largs, but the spring gales of 1286 blew against him:

> When he arrived at the village near the crossing, the ferryman warned him of the danger, and advised him to go back; but when the King asked him in return whether he was afraid to die with him 'By no means', quoth he, 'it would be a great honour to share the fate of your father's son'. Thus he arrived at the Burgh of Inverkeithing, in profound darkness, accompanied only by three equerries. The manager of his salt pans, a married man of that town, recognizing him by his voice, called 'My Lord, what are you doing here in such storm and darkness? Often have I tried to persuade you that your nocturnal rambles will bring you to no good. Stay with us, and we will provide you with decent fare and all that you want until the morning light.' 'No need for that', said the other with a laugh, 'but provide me with a couple of bondmen, to go afoot as guides to the way.'[36]

Alexander set off with his three squires and the guides from Inverkeithing along the rough coastal track toward Kinghorn. The King's companions reached their destination, but Alexander was never again seen alive. It was assumed that his horse had stumbled in the darkness and thrown him on to the rocks below the track. In the morning his body was found on the foreshore, with a broken neck.

Alexander III was buried in the south aisle of Dunfermline Abbey, and deeply mourned by his people, who had loved and revered him. In the words of Andrew of Wyntoun's metrical chronicle:

> Scotland menyd hym than full sare
> for wyndyr hym all his legis ware
> In honoure qwyate, and in pes
> For thi cald pessybill Kyng he wes . . .
> He [was] stedfast in Chrystynfay
> Relygyous men he honoryde ay . . .
> He led his lyff in honeste
> Devotyown and chastyte,
> Till lordys, knychtys and sqwyerys,
> That was of plesand manerys
> He was lele, luward and liberal
> And wertuous in governale
> He was gret of almons dede
> Till all he couth wyt had nede.[37]

> [Scotland sorely mourned him then
> For under him all his legemen
> Lived in peace and quiet and honour,
> He was called 'Peaceable King' therefore . . .
> He was a steadfast Christian
> And always honoured clergymen . . .
> He led a life of honesty
> Devoutness too, and chastity.
> And to the lords and knights and squires
> Who bore themselves with pleasing manners
> He was liberal, loyal and loving
> And virtuous in governing
> Great were his charitable deeds
> To all he knew to be in need]
> (English translation by CB)

The English friar who wrote the Chronicle of Lanercost, and who penned the dramatic story of his death, gave a very different report of his character: 'He used never to forbear, on account of season or storm, nor, for perils of flood or rocky cliffs, but would visit none too creditably, matrons and nuns, virgins and widows, by day or by night, as the fancy seized him . . .'[38] But besides being a very schematic morality tale, with its appropriate mention of storms and cliffs, the chronicler's account of Alexander's sexual adventures is almost certainly disproved by the fact that he left no illegitimate children.

For a few months after Alexander's death there was a lingering hope of posthumous issue, while Queen Yolande clung to the expectation that she might be pregnant. The Lanercost Chronicler, who had a low opinion of 'Woman's cunning', accused her of pretending to be pregnant, while 'intending to deceive the nation forever by foisting on herself the child of another', and of ordering a white marble font for the christening of the supposititious baby, or perhaps for the purpose of having it smuggled to her.[39] Had she borne Alexander's posthumous child, no doubt it would have been pursued by the font story, just as centuries later the son of James VII and II and Mary of Modena was pursued by the story that he had been smuggled into his mother's bedchamber in a warming-pan. However, within a few months Queen Yolande's pregnancy either ended in miscarriage or proved illusory, and the gossip concerning it died away.

The magnates of Scotland were obliged to face the unpalatable fact that the sovereignty of Scotland was represented by the least desirable heir imaginable: a female, a minor, a foreigner, the 'illustrious girl Margaret', the Maid of Norway.

2

|❋|❋|❋|

THE LORDS OF ANNANDALE

'E nobis Liberator Rex'

('From us sprang the Liberator King')[1]

THE EARL OF CARRICK, who had accompanied King Alexander III to England in 1278, and acted as his proxy in swearing homage for his English lands to Edward I, was a member of one of the greatest families of the feudal aristocracy of Scotland, an imported military élite which had swiftly rooted itself in the kingdom. In England Norman families boasted of an ancestor who had come over with William the Conqueror; in Scotland of one who had been granted his lands by King David I. These were simplified versions of what had happened in each kingdom, but they enshrined the difference that England had been invaded and conquered and had had an alien aristocracy imposed upon it, whereas Scotland had been infiltrated by feudal tenants of the Crown as a means of extending royal authority. The policy is chiefly attributed to King David I (1124–53), but it was begun by his elder brother and predecessor Alexander I (1107–24). In Alexander I's time Anglo-Scottish relations were close; Henry I was married to Alexander's sister Maud,[2] and Alexander's Queen was Henry I's illegitimate daughter Sibylla. David spent many years in England, and married a great Anglo-Norman heiress, Matilda of Huntingdon. Some, though by no means all, of the men who received grants of land in Scotland came from the honour of Huntingdon (which in fact comprised a large swathe of the English Midlands). Others came from lands granted to David by Henry I, and the duchies of Normandy and Brittany, whence Henry had drawn his own supporters in his reinvigoration of England which enhanced his claim to the throne. The feudalization of Scotland continued in the reign of David I's successors, his elder and younger grandsons, Malcolm IV (1153–65), who was known as 'the Maiden' from his vow of celibacy, and William 'the Lion' (1165–1214). The largest grants, however, had been made in the reign of David I.

Scotland's Norman lords did not displace the existing Celtic aristocracy, for grants to the incomers were made from Crown lands, or from lands which had fallen forfeit to the Crown, or which lacked an heir. There was also intermarriage between the old and the new nobility, which assisted the two social groups to mesh. It was by marriage that the Comyns acquired the earldom of Buchan, and the Umfravilles that of Angus. The different theories at the basis of each group did not prevent their coexisting in a single kingdom, since loyalty was the ideal common to both of them. The basis of Celtic society was tribal, with a local king or prince or chief as the ruler of a group which was at least notionally a kindred. (The fiction of kinship would remain with the later development of Highland clans, even though blood relationship between chief and clansmen was frequently non-existent.[3]) The followers of a Celtic chief owed him unquestioning loyalty, and he, while retaining local autonomy, owed his ultimate loyalty to the High King. This was the nature of kingship in Scotia, and the evolving kingdom of Scotland.

The cement of feudal society was the oath of homage by which loyalty was sworn, with the formula 'I become your man', followed by a declaration of the specific conditions; as the words of Alexander III at the ceremony of homage to Edward I had demonstrated, in theory the King held his kingdom directly from God, the supreme overlord, and the King's tenants-in-chief held their portions of the kingdom from the King. They in turn granted lands to sub-tenants, and theoretically the whole social structure was held together by the concept of loyalty, expressed in the 'vassalic commendation' by which the vassal promised service and the lord promised justice and protection. The structure of both societies was inherently military, for the Celtic kindred provided its leader with a band of warriors, while the feudal tenant owed to his overlord knight-service, and the lord brought to his King's service a specified number of knights. Celtic warriors and feudal knights served in the same army – for instance under King David I at the 'Battle of the Standard' in 1138, when David, intervening in the civil war between King Stephen and the Empress Maud (on behalf of Maud, who was his niece), but hoping also to extend his own frontier to the south, was defeated near Northallerton, in North Yorkshire. The Norman knight did not remain as an undigested element of the Scottish population. Scotland was still evolving, and the Normans were only the latest ingredient of a racial hotchpotch which already included Picts, Scots, Britons, Angles, Norse and Flemings (who were represented both in modest communities and as feudal tenants). No doubt as Scotland's Normans were absorbed into their new country they would have echoed the sentiments of Kipling's Norman knight Sir Richard Dalyrymple.

> I followed my Duke 'ere I was a lover,
> To take from England fief and fee
> But now the game is the other way over
> But now England hath taken me.[4]

Under circumstances that did not introduce them as an army of occupation, Scotland absorbed them without enmity.

It is customary to call the invaders of England and the infiltrators of Scotland 'Normans', but this is a convenient historical shorthand rather than a true definition. A modern historian of the Normans in Scotland pointed out that among those families who settled in Scotland between 1100 and 1250 'it is seldom possible to ascertain their continental home, whether in the Duchy [of Normandy] or in Flanders or in Brittany or elsewhere, and the precise connection which their forebears had with Duke William's Breton, Lotharingian, Flemish, Picard, Artesian, Cennomanian, Angevin, general-French and Norman Conquest'.[5] Scotland's leading feudal families certainly mirrored this diversity – more recent research has identified the origins of many of them. Of the three that occupied the throne of Scotland, deriving their claims through intermarriage through the old royal house, the Stewarts came from Dol in Brittany, the Balliols from Bailleul-en-Vimeu in Picardy, and the Bruces from Brix in the Cotentin peninsular in Normandy.

The history of the Bruces is a paradigm of the history of the feudal aristocracy.

All noble families, Celtic or feudal, sought to establish a prestigious antiquity by claiming a legendary ancestor, a king or hero. Sometimes there was a genuinely historical descent, sometimes a plausible if tenuous link, sometimes a wholly fictitious one. The claim of the Bruces to descend from Lodver, a Norse Earl of Orkney, probably belonged to the second category, though the pedigree which purported to establish the claim (replete with unlikely names) has been dismissed by historians as fictitious.[6] However, it is possible that the mythic ancestry of the Bruces enshrined the truth that they were indeed of Norse descent, as was the ducal house of Normandy, to which they may have been related.[7] However, the Norman Bruces took their name not from the dubious 'Brusee' of the pedigree, but from the town of Bruis (now Brix).

The first member of the family to hold land in Scotland was Robert de Bruce I, who had been created Lord of Cleveland by Henry I. He founded Guisborough Priory to which the Bruces remained so attached that even when the focus of their power shifted to Scotland they did not cease to be benefactors of Guisborough and did not make another ecclesiastical foundation in the Scottish domains. Robert de Bruce was close to David during his years in England, and he received a grant of Annandale when David succeeded to the throne of Scotland.

As a magnate of both kingdoms, he was placed in a difficult position when David I intervened in the English civil war between Stephen and Maud. Despite his personal attachment to King David, he decided that his duty lay with Stephen, and accordingly renounced his fief of Annandale before taking up arms against the King who had granted it to him. He fought for King Stephen in the Battle of the Standard, and his younger son Robert in the army of David I. According to the chronicler Aelred of Rievaulx, father and son met on the eve of battle and each attempted to dissuade the other from fighting. Fortunately, and perhaps surprisingly, neither came to any harm in the next day's conflict.[8]

Robert de Bruce I died in 1141. His eldest son Adam inherited his English lands, but the male line failed in 1271, when the lands were divided between four co-heiresses.[9]

Annandale was inherited by Robert de Bruce II, known as Le Meshin (the younger, the cadet), who had fought for David I at the Battle of the

Standard. Under him the Bruces established themselves in an immensely strong strategic position in south-western Scotland, where they were effectively acting as Wardens of the West many centuries before that title had been created.[10] The town and castle of Annan guarded the ford of the Solway and the road that was the main route from England to Scotland on the west side of the country. It was here that Robert de Bruce II maintained his *caput* or administrative head-quarters, and here that he had the misfortune to incur the ire of St Malachy O'Moore.

Maelmaedhoig Ua Morgair, to give him his Irish Gaelic name, was Archbishop of Armagh and a reformer of the Irish Church. He travelled the country on foot, had no possessions, and was described as 'a brilliant lamp which illuminated territories and churches by preaching and good works'.[11] But he had a fiery temper, as he demonstrated at Annan, where he paused on his way to Rome, having crossed from Ireland and walked through Galloway, probably around 1140. The colourful story of the Curse of St Malachy was recorded by the ever-sensational Chronicler of Lanercost:

> ... a table having been dressed for him ... he sat down ... to refresh himself, and, as the servants were discussing the death of a certain robber that had been taken, who was then awaiting the sentence of justice, the baron [Robert de Bruce II] entered the hall and bade his feasting guests welcome.
>
> Then the gentle bishop ... said 'As a pilgrim I crave a boon from your excellency, that as sentence of death has not hitherto polluted any place where I was present, let the life of this culprit ... be given to me.'
>
> The noble host agreed, not amiably but deceitfully, and ... privily ordered that the malefactor should suffer death ... When the Bishop had returned thanks both to God and to his host, he said 'I pronounce the blessing of God upon this hall, upon this table, and upon all who shall eat there hereafter.'
>
> But, as he was passing through the town, he beheld by the wayside the thief hanging on the gallows. Then, sorrowing in spirit, he pronounced a heavy sentence, first on the lord of the place and his offspring, and next upon the town, which the course of events confirmed ...[12]

The curse upon the town appeared to be fulfilled when a violent flood swept away part of the Mott of Annan (the castle hill), taking a substantial part of the bailey with it. This caused the *caput* of the Lordship of Annandale to be transferred to Lochmaben, reducing the status of Annan, which was presumably what the Lanercost Chronicler meant when he said 'the chief town of that district lost the dignity of a borough through the curse of a just man.'[13]

Robert de Bruce II appeared none the worse for the saint's malediction since he survived until 1171, but his son Robert de Bruce III, who married an illegitimate daughter of King William the Lion, died childless. Whether he predeceased his father is uncertain, but his misfortunes were undoubtedly attributed to the offended saint. He had a younger brother, William, whose son was Robert de Bruce IV, Lord of Annandale.

The fourth Lord was responsible for the royal destiny of his descendants, by his marriage to Isabella, second daughter of the third grandson of King David I. It may be remembered that King David's first and second grandsons occupied the throne of Scotland as Malcolm IV and William the Lion. The third inherited the King's English lands as David, Earl of Huntingdon. Earl David's wife, Matilda of Chester, bore him a son known as John of Scotland, who died without issue, and three daughters, whose descendants would all be claimants or 'competitors' to the Scottish throne.

The son of Robert de Bruce IV and Isabella of Huntingdon was born in 1210 and died in 1295. A life that spanned the greater part of a century was immensely long by medieval standards, and the life of Robert de Bruce V, known as 'the Noble' by his contemporaries, was an adventurous life throughout.

On 4 March 1238 Joan of England, queen of Alexander II, died childless, and the King of Scots nominated Robert de Bruce V as his heir. As a man of twenty-eight years of age, and the son of the King's first cousin, Isabella of Huntingdon, Robert de Bruce was a very suitable choice, and since he was an able, energetic and ambitious man, it might have been well for Scotland had he succeeded to the throne. He is said to have received official recognition by a gathering of magnates in 1238. However, Alexander II naturally preferred the possibility of being succeeded by a son of his own, and with this hope he married Marie de Coucy, on 15 May 1239, who bore the future Alexander III on

4 September 1241. The period during which Robert de Bruce V was heir to the kingdom was brief, but it influenced his view of his status, and his conviction concerning his rights, for the remainder of his long life. Also, when the line of Alexander III was finally extinguished, it convinced him that the right of succession belonged to himself, as the nominee of the previous King, and was vested in his descendants.

In 1240 he married an English heiress with a great name and a small dowry, Isabel de Clare, daughter of the Earl of Gloucester. Her dowry of a single manor in Sussex might have discouraged more acquisitive suitors, but her connections were an investment which linked her husband to the greatest families in the English aristocracy.[14] Thenceforward he was drawn into English politics. He was appointed Governor of Carlisle by Henry III, for whom he fought, and was captured by the baronial forces, at the battle of Lewes. His ransom was arranged by his son, who accompanied him on Crusade in the following of Edmond of Lancaster, leaving England in 1270 and returning in 1272. That Robert de Bruce V was a man of exceptional energy is demonstrated by the fact that he took the cross at the age of sixty, and on his return to Scotland took as his second wife the twice-widowed Christine de Ireby, the daughter of a knight of Cumberland.

On his journey homeward from the Crusade, Robert 'the Noble'[15] paused at the Abbey of Clairvaux, where St Malachy O'Moore was buried. The saint had died there, on his return journey, on foot, from his second visit to Rome, and his tomb in the abbey church was a place of pilgrimage. Robert de Bruce V was said to have made previous pilgrimages thither at three-yearly intervals for some time past.[16] But on his way home from the Crusade he 'made his peace forever with the Saint' by donating 'three silver lamps with their lights' to burn in perpetuity before the saint's shrine. This benefaction, in the opinion of the Lanercost Chronicler, accounted for the pious warrior's survival to the great age that he attained.[17]

Whether Robert the Noble was inspired by the desire to lift the curse of St Malachy from the family, or whether he sought the saint's blessing for his intended marriage, is not clear. But he may have desired the latter in particular, since his marriage to the widowed Christine was resented by his son (as later marriages of parents so often are, for fear that generosity to a new spouse will erode the expected inheritance).

However, whether or not the favour of St Malachy had anything to do with it, the marriage of the elder Bruce proved no threat to the inheritance of the younger, and the younger was swiftly freed from any necessity to wait for his inheritance with impatient resentment.

While the elder Bruce went home to prepare for his marriage, which took place on 3 May 1273, the younger Bruce took upon himself the melancholy task of visiting the Countess of Carrick, to tell her that her Crusader husband had died in the Holy Land.

Marjorie, Countess of Carrick in her own right, was a member of the old Celtic nobility. Marjorie's father Neil, Earl of Carrick, had died in 1256, leaving a great inheritance to an heiress who must have been a very late-born child to have been of marriageable age in 1270. Neil himself was the last male descendant of Fergus, Lord of Galloway, a semi-autonomous ruler of an area which lay on the rim of the kingdom of King David I. Galloway, Gaelic-speaking, and linked by a brief sea passage to Northern Ireland, remained a remote part of the kingdom of Scotland to which it belonged, an area that claimed to possess its own laws, and had a sense of separation which was slow to fade. The Countess of Carrick was also the lady of lands in Northern Ireland which had been granted to her grandfather Duncan, Earl of Carrick, by King John, following the English Conquest of Ulster.

The Countess of Carrick's husband was Adam de Kilconquhar, a member of a cadet branch of the family of the Earls of Fife, who, in accordance with Scottish custom, had become Earl of Carrick in right of his wife. He, together with the elder and younger Bruces, had taken the Cross in the following of Edmund of Lancaster, and his death at the siege of Acre was the news brought by the younger Robert de Bruce.

For a bringer of sad news the meeting with the Countess and its aftermath could scarcely have been more surprising:

> One day, while she was out hunting as she liked to do with her men at arms and ladies in waiting, she met a distinguished and very hand-some young knight by the name of Robert de Bruce, son of Robert surnamed de Bruce the noble lord of Annandale . . . riding across the same stretch of countryside. When greetings and kisses had been given on each side, as is the custom of courtiers, she begged him to

stay for hunting and walking about; when he resisted, she by force, so to speak, with her own hand pulled back his reins and brought the knight with her, unwilling though he was, to her castle of Turnberry. And while staying there, along with his followers for the space of fifteen days or more, he secretly married the Countess, the friends and wellwishers of both knowing nothing about it. They had in no way obtained the royal consent for the marriage, and because of this it was the common talk of the realm that she had all but carried off this young man into marriage by force.[19]

The story is very curious, and, as it is reported, implausible. It is likely enough that Robert de Bruce should have encountered the Countess and attendants out hunting. But why should he have been reluctant to accompany her to Turnberry when he was already on his way to see her? And why, when she had learnt the sombre nature of his visit, should she have enacted the playful abduction of the strong by the weak and taken him to Turnberry 'by force, so to speak'? The story has been dismissed as 'romantic nonsense',[20] but it will bear a different interpretation.

The marriage was certainly a love-match, speedily and impulsively celebrated. But the marriage of the widowed Countess was within the King's gift. Widows and heiresses were from time to time abducted and married by force, but Robert de Bruce was not held guilty of such an offence. The King might forgive him if he were told that it was the widow who had abducted the knight, and the story may contain the kernel of truth that the initiative in the marriage had indeed come from the Countess. If this was the case, it was settled to everyone's satisfaction. King Alexander III gave a sharp reminder of his flouted authority and exacted a fine for a marriage which had taken place without his permission, after which Robert de Bruce was permitted to assume the title of Earl of Carrick, *ius uxorus*, as his predecessor Adam de Kilconquhar had done. It was further evidence that the new Earl of Carrick was restored to the king's grace that Alexander chose to take him to England to act as his proxy at the ceremony of homage to Edward I.

Of its nature, the marriage was one entirely in accordance with the policy of Alexander III, a marriage between the Celtic and the feudal nobility, which kind he relied upon to increase the harmony within the kingdom. It was also an illustration of the fact that these categories were no longer clear cut; the merger of the old and the new aristocracies was already well advanced. Countess Marjorie's ancestor Fergus of Galloway had married the daughter of Henry I of England – one of his nineteen illegitimate children. Robert de Bruce was a descendant of the Royal House of Scotland through his grandmother, Isabella of Huntingdon. Unfortunately, for all its apparent contribution to social harmony, the marraige also contained a latent threat of discord, for the descendants of Fergus of Galloway were divided by an inherited feud. Fergus had had two sons, Gilbert and Uchtred, whose relations were most unfraternal. Gilbert had had Uchtred murdered, and in revenge Uchtred's heirs had despoiled Gilbert of lands which he believed to be his own inheritance. Enmity among the descendants of the brothers had continued, until the two branches of the family were each represented by an heiress: Marjorie, Countess of Carrick, was the great-granddaughter of Gilbert; Uchtred's great-granddaughter was Dervorguilla, Lady of Galloway.[21] (Fergus's old principality of Galloway had included the lands of Carrick; and while Dervorguilla was styled 'Lady of Galloway', her lands comprised the later counties of Kirkudbright and Wigtownshire, representing the partitioning of the inheritance between the sons of Fergus.) Dervorguilla's husband was John Balliol the elder, and they were the parents of the future King John. The marriage of Robert Bruce VI (sixth of his name, though not yet sixth lord of Annandale) aligned Bruce and Balliol on the opposite sides of the ancient feud long before their own families became rivals for the throne of Scotland. The feud did not effect the issue but it embittered the rivalry.

As one of the thirteen Earls of Scotland, Robert de Bruce, Earl of Carrick, was in the highest rank of the peerage, and theoretically took precedence of his father. But the old Lord of Annandale remained the undisputed head of the family, not only because his advancing age gained him respect in a period when the attainment of old age was seen both as a remarkable achievement and a gift of God, but also because he impressively retained his mental and physical vigour. The Lanercost Chronicler approvingly described him as the pattern of Christian nobility:

He was of handsome appearance, a gifted speaker, remarkable for his influence, and, what is more important, most devoted to God and the clergy . . . It was his custom to entertain and feast more liberally than all the other courtiers, and was most hospitable to all his guests, nor used the pilgrims to remain outside his gates, for his door was open to the wayfarer . . .[22]

The Lord of Annandale ruled and administered his lands from the castle of Lochmaben, beautifully sited on its promontory extending out on to the loch, and defended from the landward side by a moat which converted the natural promontory into an artificial island. It is believed to have been a sacred Celtic site, long converted to the purposes of secular defence; the surrounding ruins are those of a late-fourteenth-century castle, which replaced the earlier buildings of the previous century.

A local tradition claims that the eldest son of the Earl and Countess of Carrick was born in Lochmaben Castle, and the arms of the Burgh of Lochmaben proudly proclaim it with the motto 'E Nobis Liberator Rex' (From us came the liberator king). But this is a late claim, and the burgh arms date from the seventeenth century. While it is not impossible that Robert de Bruce VII, the future King Robert, was born in his grandfather's castle, it is far more likely that his birth, on 11 July 1274, was in the castle of Turnberry, on the Ayrshire coast, overlooking the firth of Clyde.[23] However, if the proud claim to have given birth to the 'liberator rex' be extended to south-western Scotland, then it is a true claim that King Robert was a native of his country, with a Celtic ancestry of immeasurable antiquity, and a Norman ancestry naturalized for six generations before his birth (which is further than the majority of people can reckon their ancestry). This family history makes nonsense of the curiosly tenacious myth that King Robert was a scion of an alien aristocracy, who eventually threw in his lot with the native resistance and redeemed his origins by his triumphs as 'the Patriot King'. The truth was different: King Robert was as much a native Scot as William Wallace (the surname of one referred to Brix in Normandy, and of the other to Wales); but the highest-stratum feudal aristocracy was a cosmopolitan caste, its loyalties entangled by landholding in different countries. When concepts of feudal loyalty and nationality clashed, considerations of honour and self-interest clashed with them. All these would come to a head in the career of Robert de Bruce VII.

In the meantime, he arrived in the world as the first-born son of proud parents, who named him with the monotonous tradition of his paternal ancestry, and then went on to produce four more sons and six daughters – a family of great distinction, which produced two kings (Robert I, King of Scots, and Edward de Bruce, acknowledged as High King of Ireland), and one queen (Isabella de Bruce, who married Eric II of Norway, the widower of Alexander III's daughter Margaret). Even more remarkable than these attainments was the mutual loyalty and love of all these siblings, maintained in conditions which would have tested the faith of any family, in any century.

Little is known about the childhood of the future King Robert, but something can be deduced from his territorial and family background, and from his later abilities and interests. In his mother's lands of Carrick, Gaelic was still spoken. In one of the heroic exploits attributed to Robert the Bruce, John Barbour describes the fugitive King as being accompanied by a 'Foster Brother', who is a fellow in misfortune, and is killed in a chance encounter. The existence of a foster brother implies that the young Robert de Bruce was placed in fosterage in accordance with Celtic practice, and would have spent his earliest years with a family whose children would have been his foster brothers and sisters. It was a relationship which was regarded as imposing the deepest obligations of kinship. In such a close relationship with a Gaelic-speaking family the young Robert would have acquired the language which enabled him to communicate with his Gaelic-speaking subjects, both as a fugitive and a king, and command their loyalty. It was a valuable accomplishment, for Gaelic was spoken throughout the north-west of Scotland, the central Highlands, the south-west and the Western Isles.

The language of the feudal aristocracy of Scotland (and also of England) was French. It was the language of the books they read, or had read aloud to them, the romances and *chansons de gestes* which entertained them and influenced their views of chivalric behaviour; and it was a language of diplomacy sometimes used as an alternative to Latin (for instance in Scoto-Norman relations).

Annandale had been settled by speakers of the dialect of Northern English which evolved into the Lowland Scots vernacular in which John Barbour wrote 'The Brus', and which later became the language of the Renaissance poets Robert Henryson, William Dunbar and Gavin Douglas. Gradually it became the predominant language of the kingdom, driving Gaelic further and further into retreat, until it became the mother tongue of an ever-dwindling minority.

The young Robert de Bruce, talking to his family and his parents, and their retainers, and living with his foster parents, would have grown up automatically trilingual in French, Gaelic and Lowland Scots. He would also have acquired the acquaintance with Latin which would come with frequent attendance at Mass and awareness of the liturgy, and with attention to chants, even if these were always composed by the clerics. With Latin as the principal language of liturgy and legality, and most diplomacy, a king or magnate who was obdurately ignorant of it would be at a disadvantage. A man as intelligent as the future King of Scots had probably a working knowledge of it, even if the clerks of his Chapel (chancery) wrote his diplomatic correspondence.

The linguistic attainments of a medieval magnate might be acquired by ear, and his literacy be in many instances superficial, even non-existent, but the *miles literatus*, the lettered knight (or magnate or other layman), was becoming less of a rarity. That reading was habitual to Robert is shown by the fact that he had a book with him even when he was a fugitive with only a handful of followers. Barbour's account of the King reading aloud to his fellow fugitives to keep their spirits up is a very civilized little vignette.

While the Bruce family evidently thought literacy important, the young Bruce's father and grandfather probably would have considered the most important part of his education to be his acquisition of the essential martial arts of horsemanship and skill in arms. These martial arts were learnt by all noble youths and practised with consuming enthusiasm and in a passionately competitive spirit. On superb horsemanship, and on skill with lance, sword, axe or mace, depended victory in battle or escape and survival in defeat, or reputation in the tournament, in which knights competed to maintain their expertise when there was no genuine warfare in which to employ it. That Robert excelled was proved in later years by the many occasions on which he owed his life to horsemanship and feats of arms.

It was customary for the sons of noblemen to spend their later boyhood and youth in some noble household other than their parental home, to serve some kinsman ally of their father as page and squire, and to acquire the polish of knightly conduct and general good manners. It has to be assumed that Robert served this 'noble apprenticeship', but who was responsible for this phase of his upbringing is not known. It is possible that he might have been sent to his grandfather at Lochmaben, for there could have been no better mentor and exemplar than the old Lord of Annandale, and if Robert spent part of his childhood and youth at Lochmaben the later belief that he had been born there would have been quite reasonably founded.

In 1286 he emerges from his childhood obscurity to the adult role of a witness to a deed of Alexander McDonald of Islay, together with his father the Earl of Carrick, and the Bishop of Argyll and other clerics.[24] This was the fateful year of the death of Alexander III, which was to have so profound an effect upon the fortunes of the Bruces, and upon the whole kingdom.

One of the most tantalizing difficulties for a biographer of Robert the Bruce – and for a reader – is not knowing what he looked like. It is impossible to visualize him, at any period of his life, except imaginatively, for no contemporary described him. On the whole, the medieval world seems to have preferred symbolic images to individual features; the effigy or the true Great Seal of a king provides the image of kingship rather than the portrait of a man. But it is surprising that John Barbour, who included a vivid word picture of his secondary hero, Sir James Douglas, did not do the same for his subject 'The Brus' himself.

The first description of King Robert was written some two centuries after his death, and the only hope for its credibility is that it might be based on carefully treasured memories of the King, but there is no certainty of that. However, according to the Scottish historian John Mair, in his *Historiae Majories Britannicae*:

> His figure was graceful and athletic, with broad shoulders; his features were handsome; he had the yellow hair of the northern race, with blue and sparkling eyes. His intellect was quick, and he had the gift of fluent speech in the vernacular, delightful to listen to.[25]

This might be an idealized memory of a handsome, fair-haired and persuasive man; or it might be a fictitious evocation of the sort of man a hero ought to be. The reader is at liberty either to accept it or reject it.

3

————|✳|✳|✳|————

TO CHOOSE A KING

'When good King Alexander died
That Scotland had as leader and guide,
Six years and more the country lay
In desolation after his day;
Until at last the barons went
To an assembly with intent
To choose a king their land to steer
That needs must be the rightful heir
With clear descent from royalty
And greatest claim to sovereignty . . .'[1]

ALEXANDER III OF SCOTLAND is often described as being the last of Scotland's Celtic kings. He was indeed the last ruler of the ancient Celtic dynasty, the House of Dunkeld,[2] but in him the Celtic blood was very much diluted. He had had a French mother (Marie de Coucy), an Anglo-Norman grandmother (Ermengarde de Beaumont), great-grand-mother (Ada de Warener) and great-great-grandmother (Matilda of Huntingdon). His great-great-great-grandmother was St Margaret of Scotland, a daughter of the old Anglo-Saxon royal dynasty, the House of Wessex, and the wife of King Malcolm III Canmore (Ceann-Mor – Great Head or Good Chief), the last King of Scots to have been wholly Celtic in blood. Thus the Scottish royal house had been assimilated into the royalty and aristocracy of western Europe, and it had become customary for the Kings of Scots to seek their brides in the neighbouring kingdoms of England and France. An unnoticed consequence of these foreign marriages, or internationalization of the Royal House, was that the successors of Alexander III, John Balliol and Robert the Bruce, both had a higher proportion of Celtic ancestry than he.

When Alexander III died there was no impression of the end of an era, no sense that Scotland faced a period of desolation. Though it would seem so in retrospect, at the time attention was fixed upon the Maid of Norway, with some courtesy still paid to the fading hope of Queen Yolande's pregnancy.

The funeral of Alexander III took place at Dunfermline on 29 March 1286, and Parliament assembled at Scone on 2 April. The Lord of Annandale appeared before it to protest against the right of any female to inherit the kingdom (i.e. either the Maid of Norway or a posthumous daughter of Alexander III), and to press his own claim as descendant of King David I and a former heir-designate of Alexander II. Parliament then adjourned until John Balliol should have chance to appear and state his own claim. There was 'bitter pleading' between the two claimants, until a sensible decision was reached that all magnates should swear to keep the peace, and should take an oath of fealty to 'the nearest by blood who by right must inherit'.[3] This was skilfully worded, for the heir might be the hypothetical child of Queen Yolande, or the Maid of Norway, or, if female succession were rejected, then either Bruce or Balliol.

An interim government was appointed, to hold office in the name of the 'Community of the Realm', i.e. the 'bishops, abbots, priors, earls, barons and free tenants of Scotland and the Community of the same supporting them'.[4] The body of Guardians consisted of six: two earls, two bishops and two barons; these were Duncan, Earl of Fife, the premier earl of Scotland, and Alexander Comyn, Earl of Buchan; William Fraser, Bishop of St Andrews, regarded as the premier bishop though Scotland had no primatial see, and Robert Wishart, Bishop of Glasgow; James Stewart, High Steward of Scotland, and John Comyn, Lord of Badenoch.

In the interests of keeping the peace neither Bruce nor Balliol had been appointed a Guardian, but the sympathies of the Guardians were evenly divided, Fife, Stewart and Wishart being friendly to Bruce, while Fraser favoured Balliol, and Balliol was related to the Comyns by marriage. The territorial influence of the Guardians, as their titles indicate, was broadly spread over Scotland – the lands of the Stewarts being in the south-west. A feudal kingdom without a king might be compared to a ship without the helmsman,[5] but the rule of the Guardians indicated that the Scots had not lost their sense of direction without a king.

The legacy of Alexander III was their certainty that they had to defend the integrity of the kingdom. In the absence of a king the Guardians commissioned a Great Seal of the Kingdom which bore the motto ANDREA SCOTIS DUX ESTO COMPATRIOTIS ('Saint Andrew be the leader of the compatriot Scots'),[6] making the patron saint a representative of the king.

The peace of the kingdom was disturbed early in the Guardianship when the Lord of Annandale and the Earl of Carrick seized the royal castles of Dumfries and Wigtown and the Castle of Buittle belonging to the lordship of Galloway, which can only have been intended to strengthen their own position against John Balliol. Control of Dumfries in particular improved communication between the power centres of Carrick and Annandale, and impeded access from the lordship of Galloway to the centre of the kingdom. Later in the year, on 20 September 1286, the Bruces and a group of allies including James Stewart and Alexander MacDonald of Islay signed an agreement known as the 'Turnberry Bond', since it was signed at that castle, in which they pledged their support to Richard de Burgh, Earl of Ulster, reserving their fealty to the King of England (owed by the Earl of Ulster) and to the person who would inherit the kingdom of Scotland 'by reason of the blood of the Lord Alexander . . . King of Scotland who last died' (owed by Annandale, Carrick and the other Scots). Whatever the pretext of the bond, it suggests a power build-up by the Bruces, and a lingering reluctance to admit fealty to the Maid of Norway. But not long after this the hope of any other heir of Alexander's blood was finally extinguished.

Immediately after the funeral of Alexander III, two Scottish Dominicans were sent to inform Edward I of the King's death. However the King responded to the news – presumably with personal expressions of sorrow – he did not see it as a pretext for interfering in Scottish affairs. His current interests took him in another direction. In the spring of 1286 he left for France, and was entirely preoccupied with the affairs of Gascony until 1289. In September 1286 he was at Saintes when he was visited by a Scottish embassy led by the Bishop of Brechin, who somewhat belatedly informed him of the appointment of the Guardians. He expressed his goodwill towards them, and demonstrated it by agreeing to their request to hold in abeyance a border dispute, which in his absence was causing trouble between the two kingdoms.[7]

The Guardians would have been grateful for this example of his 'good neighbourhood' (i.e. neighbourliness),[8] for although the factions within Scotland had not broken into civil war, the country was in a restless condition. In 1289 one of the Guardians, the elderly Earl of Buchan, died a natural death; but later in the year his colleague the Earl of Fife was ambushed and murdered by a group of his own kinsmen. The deceased Guardians were not replaced, and the government continued in the hands of the surviving four. Curiously, between 1286 and 1289, nothing was done to establish the succession of the Maid of Norway; it almost seems as though there was a reluctance to accept her. Perhaps Bruce of Annandale's show of force had been made in expectation that a preference for him would be revealed, but instead it had revealed a prejudice against the assertion of claims by force of arms.

The stalemate was broken in 1289, apparently by the Norwegians. On 1 April 1289, at Bergen, Eric II appointed an embassy to visit Edward I, to discuss the status and the marriage of the Maid of Norway.[9] King Eric may have known that Alexander had favoured an English marriage for her, and he may have sensed that it would require English interest in the match to focus the attention of the Scots upon her status. On his return from Gascony, Edward responded to the Norwegian initiative. At his request, on 3 October 1289, the Guardians designated three of themselves, the Bishops of St Andrews and Glasgow and John Comyn of Badenoch, and the Lord of Annandale, to meet the Norwegian embassy in King Edward's presence, at Salisbury. Here Edward acted as an arbitrator between the Norwegians and the Scots. The Norwegians requested that the Maid be accepted as 'Lady, Queen and heiress' by the people of Scotland. This was agreed, and by the 'Treaty of Salisbury' of 6 November 1289 it was ruled that the Maid was to arrive in Scotland or England by 1 November 1290 'free and quit of all contract of marriage or betrothal' and that if 'the foresaid lady' should arrive in Edward's keeping he would deliver her to Scotland 'when the kingdom shall have been well settled and in peace'. The Scots promised not to arrange her marriage except with the 'ordinance, will and counsel' of King Edward, and the assent of the King of Norway.[10]

Without asserting any claim to feudal superiority, Edward I had taken a giant stride into the arena of Scottish politics: in the marriage of the 'Lady, Queen and heiress' of Scotland, his was to be the 'ordinance', her father's role only that of giving assent, and that of the Guardians nothing.

However, on 14 March the lay and ecclesiastical magnates of Scotland met at Birgham, and ratified the Treaty of Salisbury. Before they separated, they received the first rumour that Edward had sought a papal dispensation for the marriage of his heir, Edward of Caernarvon and the Maid of Norway, who were related within the forbidden degrees of kindred and affinity. The rumour was welcomed, and on 17 March a letter was sent to Edward consenting to the proposed marriage, on condition that the King of England met certain terms — these being intended to safeguard the status of Scotland.

When Alexander III wrote to Edward I on 20 April 1284 'much good may come to pass yet through . . . the daughter . . . of our beloved, the late Queen of Norway', Edward I's heir was his eldest surviving son Alfonso, who died in August of the same year. In the meantime, Edward of Caernarvon had been born on 25 April 1284. When Alexander wrote he would have had the elder prince in mind; but within a short time the message would have been applicable to the younger. Such was the uncertainty of the succession and the Procrustean nature of the royal marriage bed.

In July 1290 the Scottish magnates met again at Birgham, to negotiate the treaty that would unite the Maid of Norway and Edward of Caernarvon, while maintaining the separate identities of the two kingdoms; for Edward would become King of Scots *ius uxoris*, and Margaret of Norway would become Queen of England as her husband's consort. The treaty was preoccupied with maintaining the status of Scotland, since it would be the Consort's kingdom. No doubt the Guardians would have been happier if the proposed marriages had conformed to the pattern of earlier Anglo-Scottish marriage, with an English princess marrying a King of Scots. However, with all the safeguards that they could imagine as being necessary, the Scots protected the status of the kingdom. 'No-one holding-in-chief [i.e. no tenant-in-chief] of the foresaid King of Scotland shall be compelled to pass outwith the kingdom to do homage and fealty . . . No parliament shall be held outwith the kingdom . . . on matters touching the kingdom . . .' Unnoticed among the 'small print' (as we should call it), or neat clerkly hand of the period, were the phrases 'saving the right of our said lord [the future king] and of any other whom soever, which has pertained to him . . . before the time of the present agreement, or which in any right way ought to pertain in the future . . .'[11] Thus did a vague form of words render all the safeguards nugatory; it was with such cloudy provisions that Edward I was accustomed to justify himself when he reneged on agreements with his own magnates. However, all was goodwill when Edward I ratified the Treaty of Birgham at Northampton on 28 August 1290. If he was looking forward to a time when Scotland would become subordinate to England under the rule of his son, just as a wife was supposed to become subordinate to her husband in marriage, he was showing the patience of a dynast. There were, however, just a few preliminary indications that he was beginning to be tempted by the more impatient ambitions of a conqueror.

On 4 June he sent Walter de Huntercombe to occupy the Isle of Man. Since it was a recently conquered territory of the Scottish Crown, and may have been restive, it could appear that he had helpfully sent a peace-keeping force. But the Isle of Man was strategically valuable to England as well as Scotland, and it effectively changed hands in a move which was tantamount to picking Scotland's pocket. Then, at Northampton on 28 August, when he ratified the Treaty of Northampton, Edward also appointed Anthony Bek, Bishop of Durham, to act as Lieutenant of Scotland on behalf of Edward of Caernarvon and Margaret of Norway, though they had not yet been married and were neither of them within the kingdom (where, in any case, Edward had no rights before his marriage to its Queen). Anthony Bek was a prelate of secular and political character, multi-beneficed, rich, extravagant and haughty in manner. He travelled with a retinue of knights whom he was ready to lead into battle. His only concession to a clerical way of life was a chastity so exaggerated that he was said never to look a woman in the face. The Guardians were requested by Edward to receive him 'kindly and courteously' and to 'put yourselves at his bidding in all matters needful for the foremost and peaceful state of the kingdom'.[12] In this letter for the first time the fabric of the King's velvet glove began to show thin. Everything, however, was done in the name of keeping the peace in preparation for the arrival of the Maid of Norway.

Edward had also sent a ship to fetch her. It sailed from Yarmouth on 20 May 1290, exotically provisioned with sweetmeats, dried fruits, gingerbread, rice, sturgeon and whalemeat.[13] Edward may have expected the King of Norway to sail with his daughter and provisioned the ship for the King's entertainment. But Eric did not intend either to leave his kingdom or entrust his daughter to the English for her voyage. The ship returned to England the following month, and made landfall near the mouth of the Humber, with several dead sailors and others sick on board, the sturgeon and whalemeat, perhaps, being to blame.

The Maid of Norway sailed from her own country in September, in one of her father's ships, accompanied by Narne, Bishop of Bergen, and her Norwegian attendants Ban Thorir Haaknson and Fan Ingebirorg Erlingsdottir.[14] Departing at a notoriously stormy time of year, the ship may have been wrecked in Orkney, or driven to take shelter there. In Orkney the Maid of Norway died 'between the hands of Bishop Narne, and in the presence of the best men who followed her from Norway'.[15] The body of the Maid was taken back to Bergen, where the coffin was opened, and the body identified by King Eric 'and himself acknowledged that it was his daughter's corpse'.[16]

With the death of the Maid of Norway the direct line of the House of Dunkeld was extinguished, and the restless ambitions of the claimants to the throne of Scotland were reignited.

While the ambition of King Edward I changed its perspective, the Guardians of Scotland, in the well-chosen words of a modern historian, had 'conditioned themselves to see only his Janus face of peace'.[17] If there was any uneasiness at Edward's role in preparing the way for the marriage of the 'Lady, Queen and heir' of Scotland and the heir of England, there were reassurances to be found in past events. The Earl of Carrick could have offered recollections of Edward's courtesy towards Alexander III, when he himself had acted as the King's proxy in 1278. After all, the old question of the Kings of Scots paying homage for their kingdom had been raised by the Bishop of Norwich, not by the King of England, who had accepted King Alexander's reply without demur. If the King of England deployed some forces to keep the peace, it was all 'good neighbourhood', and no cause for anxiety . . .

So they may have persuaded themselves, quite forgetting how Edward had already dealt with Wales. According to the Chronicle of Waverley Abbey, even in 1291 Edward I informed his magnates and councillors that he intended to subjugate Scotland, just as he had already subjugated Wales.[18] If he had made such a statement to his closest advisers, he might not have surprised them. A contemporary who viewed him without illusions described the obverse and reverse of his character: his valour and his deviousness:

> He is valiant as a lion, quick to attack the strongest and fearing the onslaught of none. But if a lion in pride and fierceness, he is a panther in fickleness and inconstancy, changing his word and promise, cloaking himself by pleasant speech . . . The treachery and falsehood by which he is advanced he calls prudence . . . and whatever he likes he says is lawful.[19]

He was soon to have opportunity to indulge his judicial tastes, with little pleasure to those who found themselves subject to his specious arrangements.

In September 1290 the magnates of Scotland began to forgather at Perth, presumably in expectation of the imminent arrival of the Maid of Norway, and in preparation for her inauguration as Queen of Scots, at Scone. But soon there came the first disturbing rumours that she had died in Orkney. The Lord of Annandale advanced on Perth with a great following in arms. John Balliol, Lord of Galloway (whose mother, the Lady Dervorguilla, had, most conveniently for him, died at the beginning of the year), proclaimed himself 'heir of Scotland'.[20] Bishop Fraser of St Andrews, foreseeing civil war, wrote to Edward I, who had already shown his concern to maintain peace, and at the same time indicated his personal support for John Balliol.

> . . . There is a fear of a general war and a great slaughter of men, unless the Highest [i.e. God], by means of your industry and good service apply a speedy remedy . . . We have agreed amongst ourselves to remain about Perth, until we have certain news, by the knights who are sent to Orkney, what is the condition of our Lady – would that it may be prosperous and happy . . . If Sir John de Balliol comes to your presence we advise you to take care so to treat with him that in any

event your honour and advantage may be preserved. If it turn out that our forsaid Lady has departed this life . . . let your excellency deign if you please to approach towards the March [i.e. the Borders], for the consolation of the Scottish people, and for saving the shedding of blood . . . and set over them for King him who of right ought to have the succession, if so he that be will follow your counsel . . .[21]

It is an often repeated statement that Edward I was invited to arbitrate in the succession dispute. But he received no invitation from the Guardians, or any body of magnates purporting to speak for the Community of the Realm. Bishop Fraser's plea for intervention was a personal one.

However, Edward also received an appeal of a different kind. This was the 'Appeal of the Seven Earls', in which it was claimed that the 'seven Earls of Scotland' alone had the right of 'making a king' and inaugurating him. They protested that two serving Guardians, Bishop Fraser and John Comyn of Badenoch, were planning to make John Balliol king, and they appealed to Edward to support them in asserting their ancient right. Their candidate for the kingship was Robert Bruce of Annandale.[22] These 'seven Earls' remain a slightly mysterious body. On the death of King William the Lion in 1214, his son had been escorted from Stirling to Scone by seven earls (Fife, Strathern, Atholl, Angus, Menteith, Buchan and Dunbar) and there inaugurated as King Alexander II.[23] This provided a relatively recent precedent for the claim. There were thirteen earls of Scotland, and the seven who sent the appeal (of which the seals have not survived) obviously were not the same seven. Duncan, Earl of Fife, had been murdered in 1289, but the appeal declared that of the seven earls 'the son of Duncan late Earl of Fife, of worthy memory is one' (though he was a small child),[24] so it appears that the idea of seven earls as a notional group, representing the thirteen, is what they had in mind.[25] Edward I had no intention of admitting their right, but the appeal provided further encouragement to interference.

However, Edward I did not require an official invitation to intervene; he arrogated to himself the power to settle the dispute, not by arbitration, but by adjudication.[26]

Edward moved north, but his progress was checked when news reached him that his Queen, Eleanor of Castile, who was following him, had fallen ill at Harby, near Lincoln. Seldom had they been separated in thirty-six years of marriage, for on all his travels, even the Crusade, she had accompanied him or followed him, not even permitting sixteen pregnancies to keep her at home. They were parted by her sudden death, and Edward revealed a gentle facet of his character with the words 'I loved her dearly during her lifetime; I shall not cease to love her now that she is dead'. He demonstrated his grief by providing three tombs for her remains: one at Lincoln for her entrails; one at Blackfriars for her heart; the main one in Westminster Abbey for her body. The twelve Eleanor Crosses marked the places where the cortège bearing the body paused on the way to Westminster.[27]

It has been suggested that Edward's character deteriorated with the removal of her emollient influence; but there is no indication that she had softened his severity towards the Welsh. But as he grew older he grew more wrathful and sombre, his temper exacerbated by every indication of opposition, and by his disappointment with Edward of Caernarvon, his only surviving son.

In the spring of 1291 Edward moved north again, to Norham on Tweed, the castle of Anthony Bek, Bishop of Durham. There he requested the claimants to the Scottish throne (now known as the 'Competitors'), to meet him on 30 May, assuring them that attending him on English soil would not create a precedent.[28]

A great gathering of magnates, lay and ecclesiastical, Scots and English, assembled at Norham. It has been suggested that the assembly comprised the parliaments of both kingdoms (or, on the Scots side, an 'assembly of the Estates, since there was no Scottish sovereign, whose presence was necessary to make a complete parliament').[29] At Norham, Edward demanded of the Scots, as a preliminary to the decision of the succession dispute, that he should be recognized as the suzerain of Scotland. And he presented his demand in a manner particularly difficult to rebut: 'Can you produce any evidence to show that I am not the rightful suzerain?'[30]

The Scots were dumbfounded. No one, unless possessed of prophetic powers, would have expected such a demand to be made. For if Edward had in truth regarded himself as possessing the rights of suzerainty, the moment to have asserted them would have been after the death of the late King, when the right of the suzerain would have been to administer the kingdom on behalf of the infant heir. He could argue that his rights had been 'reserved' at the Treaty of Birgham, and were now being revived. But the Treaty had been generally understood as securing the status of Scotland, and the Scots were utterly nonplussed by Edward's demand.

The Scots were granted twenty-four hours in which to reply, and when they protested, were permitted three weeks. Edward, however, had ordered the levies of the Northern Shires of England to join him at Norham on 3 June; the delay would give him the additional advantage of having his demand supported by armed force.

The reply of the Scots, on behalf of the Community of the Realm, has been attributed to Bishop Wishart of Glasgow, who was to prove an indomitable defender of Scottish Independence:

Sir,

To this statement [of overlordship] the good people who have sent us here make answer that they do not in the least believe that you would ask so great a thing if you were not convinced of your sound right to it. But they have no knowledge of your right, nor did they ever see it claimed or used by you or your ancestors; therefore they answer . . . that they have no power to reply to your statement, in default of a lord [a king] to whom the demand ought to be addressed, and who will have power to make answer about it. *For if it should happen that they agreed to your demand, no right or profit would accrue to you, nor be lost to their liege lord.* But the good people of the realm earnestly demand that he who shall be king in the aforesaid kingdom shall do to you whatsoever reason and justice may demand, for he, and no other, will have power to reply and to act in the matter.[31]

It was a courteous and subtle reply, for the Bishop (or whoever else composed it) may have foreseen that Edward would enforce acceptance of his demand, for the italicized passage is a proviso as subtle as any that Edward himself could have devised for his own uses. Edward no doubt perceived this, for although the letter was an official reply to his demand, he dismissed it as 'nothing to the purpose' (*nihil tamen efficax*), a dismissal described by a modern historian as 'the first thoroughly discreditable action in his dealings with the Scottish nation'[32] – if the assertion of suzerainty itself was not indeed the first.

Edward increased his pressure by informing the Competitors that there would be no award of the kingship unless his suzerainty were admitted. It would have been difficult for Bruce of Annandale or Balliol of Galloway to have refused this demand, for both desired to be king, and both were vassals of Edward I already, in respect of their English lands (both were English landholders on a large scale, Balliol with manors in seventeen English counties). It must have been obvious to them that in accepting the kingship of Scotland from the hand of Edward I, the status of the successful Competitor would not be as independent as that of Alexander III had been, but Edward had manipulated them so skilfully that there appeared to be no alternative. Their anxieties were probably increased by the fact that the decision was not to be between them alone: claims from other men of royal descent had increased the Competitors by seven. On 5 June 1291 they set their seals to a 'submission' acknowledging Edward not only as their overlord but as 'sovereign lord' of the land.[33] The total nine were Robert de Bruce of Annandale, John Balliol, Lord of Galloway, John de Hastings, Lord of Abergavenny, John Comyn, Lord of Badenoch, Patrick de Dunbar, Earl of March, William de Vesci, Nicholas de Soules, William de Ross, and Florent V, Count of Holland. (For their relationships to the Royal House of Scotland, see Genealogical Table.)

The submission of the Guardians followed, on or by 11 June, in return for three concessions by Edward. He had already announced the first, on 6 June: that until the award was made he would maintain the customary laws, liberties and usages of Scotland, saving only the homage of whoever should become king. The two other concessions were announced on 12 June: the first that the award of the throne would be made within the realm of Scotland; the second that the realm and its royal castles (which Edward had insisted should be handed over to him, encountering some resistance) would be handed over to the successful Competitor within two months of the award, on condition of homage being rendered by the new king for the kingdom, Edward's claim to being 'sovereign lord' being maintained. The Competitors were assured that trial of their claims would be heard without any delay, and Edward further promised that in future on the death of a King of Scots who left an undisputed heir, nothing but homage and acknowledgement of the English King's sovereign lordship would be required.[34]

The Guardians resigned their authority to Edward, and were

immediately reappointed, with an English baron named Brian Fitzalan of Bedale added to their number and appointed as a fifth Guardian.

On 13 June, on the green of the village of Upsettlington, on the Scottish bank of the Tweed opposite Norham, the Guardians, the Competitors, some ecclesiastics and many magnates, barons and knights of Scotland, swore fealty to Edward I. Edward then made a progress through the more accessible areas of the kingdom, which took him to Edinburgh, Stirling, Dunfermline, St Andrews and Perth. He received many offers of fealty, and made arrangements that fealty could be sworn to his representatives in places throughout the realm which he had not reached. His progress occupied the latter half of June and the month of July; but at the beginning of August he was ready to hear the pleas of the Competitors before the Court of Claims – a court without precedents, of his own invention.

The demolition of Scottish independence had, in effect, been achieved between 30 May and 13 June; the progress merely served to confirm it. It had been achieved with a minimal show of force, but no doubt with a great deployment of the force of personality, and skilful diplomacy. The proceedings of the Court of Claims would be more prolonged.

When the Court of Claims assembled before Edward I in Berwick Castle, on 3 August 1291, three more Competitors appeared, three barons of royal descent named Patrick Galithley, Roger de Mandeville, and Robert de Pinkney (for their relationship to the Royal House of Scotland, see Genealogical Table). They, and other Competitors either remotely or illegitimately connected with the Royal House, were not expecting to be awarded the throne on some outside chance like winning the lottery; they were registering their claims, so that these were duly recorded, if future events should project them into prominence. A series of untimely deaths had led to a disputed succession; a similar sequence of events could do so again. These claims were presented to the Court in the form of petitions, which were sewn into a leather sack, and retained at the castle for safe-keeping.

The Court then held a preliminary hearing of the claims that were most seriously regarded. These were the claims of the original Competitors, Robert de Bruce and John Balliol, with John de Hastings and Florent, Count of Holland. Bruce, Balliol and Hastings were all descended from David, Earl of Huntingdon, the third grandson of King David I. Earl David had three daughters, Margaret, Isabella and Ada. John Balliol was the grandson of Margaret, Robert the Bruce was the son of Isabella, and John de Hastings was the grandson of Ada. To modern eyes Balliol's claim looks the best, as descendant of the eldest daughter. The essence of Bruce's claim was that he was one generation nearer the Royal House. Hastings claimed that the kingdom ought to be divided, like an ordinary fief, between the descendants of the daughters, who should be regarded as co-heiresses (as had happened with the co-heiresses of the English Bruces; *vide supra* Chapter 2, p. 24). Florent, Count of Holland, had a claim that would have disposed of Bruce, Balliol and Hastings, could it have been proved. He descended from Earl Henry, the son of David I, who had predeceased his own sons Malcolm IV, William the Lion and David of Huntingdon. Count Florent claimed that David of Huntingdon had abrogated his right of succession in return for a grant of lands in Scotland – the district of Garioch – and that King William the Lion had accordingly designated the descendants of their sister Ada as successors to the throne. Count Florent claimed that a document proving this was lodged in the Scottish Treasury in Edinburgh Castle, and if not there, elsewhere in Scotland, and asked to be allowed time for a search.[35] His request was granted, and Edward I adjourned the Court to 2 June 1292. When it reconvened it was adjourned again to 14 October.

When the Court reconvened yet another Competitor had appeared, in the person of King Eric II of Norway, who ingeniously claimed by 'ascent' instead of descent: as the father of the formerly acknowledged 'Lady and Queen', the Maid of Norway, he ought to be accepted as King. This was bold but unconvincing. Yet had his wife lived and been accepted as Queen of Scots, he would have become King, *jure uxoris*.[36]

In spite of the courtesy shown to Count Florent and the distraction provided by King Eric, the Court hearings now proceeded as though the only serious contenders were Bruce and Balliol. Under Edward I (theoretically president, but in fact presiding judge), the Court was composed of 104 Auditors: twenty-four approved by Edward, forty by Bruce, and forty by Balliol.

The claim of Balliol was undoubtedly the best, if the rule of primogeniture were applied, but though it was gaining in popularity as a

means of deciding inheritance, it was by no means universally recognized, and there was no certainty that it applied to the royal succession
of Scotland.[37] Bruce's claim that as a grandson of David, Earl of
Huntingdon, he was a generation nearer royalty than either of the great-
grandsons, Balliol and Hastings, was taken seriously. There were also
the additional arguments that in 1238 he had been designated as heir by
Alexander II (though soon displaced by the birth of the future
Alexander III), and that he had the support of the 'seven Earls'. Some
historians have cast doubt on his claim to have been Alexander II's
'chosen heir', but surely the statement was too readily amenable to
proof for a false claim to be possible. And the date was still within the
living memory of men younger than the Competitor, who was now
eighty-two.

During the long adjournment of the Court Edward had canvassed
the opinion of a wide range of legal experts. The French jurist Bonet
gave his opinion that the succession ought to go to the claimant who
was born first (i.e. Bruce) despite being of a younger line; and the
Master General of the Minorities reached the same conclusion, drawing
a precedent from the Old Testament.[38]

According to the *Scotichronicon* Edward was inclined to favour Bruce
until cautioned by Anthony Bek, who said to him:

> If Robert Bruce becomes King of Scotland, where will Edward King
> of England stand? For this Robert is of the best stock of all England
> and is personally very powerful in the kingdom of Scotland, and in
> times gone by many troubles have been inflicted on the kings of
> England by the kings of Scotland.' To this the same king, shaking his
> head, so to speak, replied in the French tongue saying 'Per le sang de
> Dieu tu as bien chanté' that is to say 'By Christ's blood you have sung
> well! The matter will proceed otherwise than I had previously
> arranged'.[39]

The *Scotichronicon* being a pro-Bruce source, this story could be a late
invention to propagandize the belief that Bruce the Competitor
suffered injustice. But the vivid little sentence in French lends it a certain
credibility.

So does the fact that after the eighty Scottish Auditors had failed to
reach agreement on what system the succession should follow, the

English Auditors proposed that the case should be decided in accordance with the laws of England. As recently as 1290 Edward had defined the English system as that of seniority, which meant that when deciding between the descendants of daughters the progeny of the elder would have to be exhausted before the descendants of the younger would have a valid claim.[40]

In accordance with this judgement, on 6 November 1292 Robert de Bruce of Annandale was informed that he had failed in his claim. At his great age it must have been a devastating blow to his ambition. Time had almost run out for him, but this did not mean that he had abandoned his conviction of the righteousness of his claim, which the next generation of the family could pursue. The following day, 7 November, he delegated his claim to his son, the Earl of Carrick, and his heirs with the words:

> We give and grant of our free will to our son and his heirs, full and free power to sue for the realm, and to promote in his own name the right which pertains to him in the matter, in the way which seems best to him, and to do everything which we would have set afoot before the writing of the charter . . .[41]

His charter, or 'Quitclaim', was witnessed by Gilbert de Clare, Earl of Gloucester, the nephew of his first wife, Isobel de Clare, and his warm supporter. The old Lord of Annandale must have recognized that the Earl of Carrick was not a man of great ambition; indeed, outside his marriage bed he was generally lethargic. But in young Robert de Bruce, his grandson, the Lord of Annandale may have recognized a longing that matched his own and a nascent ambition to fulfil it. Two days later the Earl of Carrick resigned his earldom to his son; he had held it in right of his wife, and the Countess Marjorie had died earlier in the year, so it was fitting that the earldom should pass to her son. Thus Robert de Bruce VII witnessed his grandfather's disappointment, and at the very instant of sensing such injustice found himself emerging into the world as a powerful magnate in his own right.

Two final efforts to block the award of the kingship to John Balliol followed: the pleas of Count Florent and of John de Hastings were yet to be heard. Bruce the Competitor did a deal with each of them in turn. He had already agreed with Count Florent that if either became king he would grant the other one-third of the kingdom as a fief: if Bruce had succeeded his offer could be equalled by the grant of his English lands to Florent. If Florent became king, the grant to Bruce would leave the descendants a great power-base from which, possibly, to win the whole kingdom at some future date. Florent's plea failed, for the document on which he had based it was not to be found. Bruce then gave his support to the plea of John de Hastings, that Scotland should be divided among the descendants of the daughters of David of Huntingdon, as co-heiresses. Had Bruce won a third of the kingdom through this claim he would have indemnified Hastings in the same way as he would have done Count Florent, and would have left his descendants two-thirds of the kingdom, after which they could pursue the claim as they saw fit. This seems to be the sense of the 'Quitclaim' to the Earl of Carrick.

However, the Court rejected the plea of Hastings, and judged that Scotland, as a kingdom, was not divisible in the manner of an ordinary fief. By the elimination of all other pleas, John Balliol emerged as the successful Competitor. On 17 November Edward I's Judgement, and award of the kingdom to John Balliol, was read aloud to the assembly by the English Chief Justice, Roger Brabazon. According to the *Scotichronicon*:

> After the judgement was given, however, the Earl of Gloucester, holding Robert Bruce by the hand in sight of all, spoke thus: 'Take heed, O King, of the kind of judgement you have given today, and remember that you must be judged at the last judgement'. And immediately this Robert withdrew at the same Earl's bidding and never offered homage and fealty to John de Balliol.[42]

Gilbert de Clare, Earl of Gloucester and the King's son-in-law (he had married Edward's daughter Joan of Acre in 1290), evidently felt that he had the right to speak to him more forthrightly than others would dare to do, and in leading his aged kinsman from the room so dramatically he would have emphasized the conviction of the Bruces and their partisans that they had suffered injustice.

The Lord of Annandale returned to his castle of Lochmaben, where he spent his last years, until his death in 1295.

The claim of the Bruces to the throne of Scotland was not regarded

as having been abandoned, but as being in abeyance. It had been transferred from one generation to the next, to be revived in the future. The
son of the Competitor, if he lacked the opportunity and the determination to pursue the claim, was equally resolved not to compromise it by
swearing fealty to John Balliol. Accordingly he left Scotland, and taking
his daughter Isabella, paid a lengthy visit to Norway. The following
summer Isabella de Bruce married Eric II of Norway, who was now
twenty-five, and a widower since the death of Margaret, the daughter
of Alexander III.[43] If the Competitor's son had not seen his father
become a king, at least he had the satisfaction of making his daughter
a queen.

4

'SCOTTORUM MALLEUS'

'Edwardus Primus, Scottorum Malleus, hic est'

('Edward the first, the Hammer of the Scots, is here')[1]

JOHN BALLIOL was inaugurated as King of Scots on the Feast of St Andrew, Scotland's patron saint, 30 November 1292. In most respects the ritual was conformable to the inaugurations of his predecessors. The Kings of Scots were not crowned, but were conducted to Scone by their magnates, to be enthroned on the Sacred Stone. To the Earl of Fife, as premier Earl of Scotland, belonged the right of enthroning the king, by leading him to take his place on the Stone. The role of the Church was to place the royal mantle on the King's shoulders as a symbol of divine protection. The Kings of Scots possessed a crown, sceptre and orb, and probably wore the crown and carried the symbols of royalty at their inauguration, but the significant rituals were the secular enthronement and the ecclesiastical enrobing.

At the inauguration of Alexander III a highland *seannachie* (genealogist) had recited the King's ancestry in Gaelic: *'Benech de re Albane, Alexander Mac Alexander, Mac William, Mac Henry, Mac David . . .'* (God bless the King of Alba, Alexander son of Alexander, son of William, son of Henry, son of David) . . . a line extending beyond Fergus, the first King of the Scots in Albany to Hiber the Scot, the son of Gaythelus . . . by Scota, daughter of the King of Egypt, the Pharaoh Centhres.[2]

Though any of the Competitors could have been linked to this mythic ancestry, the recitation of it did not take place at John Balliol's inauguration, and was not revived on future occasions. However, though the Earl of Fife, as a child, could not lead John Balliol at his enthronement, a proxy was appointed to perform the rite – an English knight, Sir John de St John. Perhaps that an Englishman performed this essentially Scottish role emphasized for all present that the King himself was a vassal of England.

After his inauguration John Balliol travelled south to Newcastle, where King Edward was keeping his Christmas Court, and there on 26 December he paid homage to Edward I for his kingdom.

His return to Scotland and his reception there was described by the Chronicler Rishanger, in words of contempt:

> John hurried to Scotland, fluttering to his crown. But the Scots con-
> senting or not received him with extreme annoyance. They dis-
> missed his attendants, familiar to him and of his own race, and
> deputed strangers to act as his administrators . . . But he, simple and
> stupid, almost mute and speechless, did not open his mouth . . .
> Thus he dwelt among them for a whole year, as a lamb among
> wolves.[3]

The Lanercost Chronicler had a single, dismissive adjective for him: 'brainless' (*acephalus*).[4]

Rishanger's account of John Balliol's reception in Scotland is rather more than a waspish little vignette. It contains a triple condemnation: that he was unwelcome as king; that he was essentially a stranger; that he was utterly incompetent (the last point even more strongly expressed by the chronicler of Lanercost). This view of John Balliol fuelled the myth that he was a puppet king imposed upon the Scots by Edward I, in opposition to a general conviction that Robert de Bruce of Annandale had the better claim; a myth it suited the Bruces to propagate, and which is probably still generally believed. But how true were Rishanger's accusations?

Edward I's judgement in the 'Great Cause' was legally well founded, and absolutely correct once it had been established that it was to be decided in accordance with the legal system based on seniority. Once the principle of primogeniture in the male line, to be followed if that became extinct by seniority in the female line, had been universally accepted, then the correctness of Edward's decision seemed indisput-able. (So much so that most historians unequivocally state the Balliol claim as the better, though in the context of their own times the Bruces were genuinely convinced of the superiority of their own claim, which some distinguished legal opinion upheld.)

Obviously the elevation of Balliol would have been received with 'extreme annoyance' by those who had preferred the Bruce claim. But modern analysis of the Bruce and Balliol supporters has shown that whereas magnatial support was about equally divided between them, the Balliol party contained a larger number of higher-ranking church-men, so Balliol's inauguration as King John would have been welcome to an influential body of his subjects, and once inaugurated he was generally accepted, with whatever gradations of private sentiment, simply because the Scots were intensely thankful to have a king again.

The accusation that he was a stranger to his kingdom is more difficult to answer, because it really rests upon what he seemed like to his con-temporaries. It has already been said that he had more Celtic ancestry than Alexander III, through his mother Dervorguilla. The Balliols themselves had held lands in Scotland since the twelfth century, but were also substantial landholders in England and France. Balliol's English manors were spread throughout seventeen counties, and he retained his paternal estates in Picardy.[5] It is quite possible that a prefer-ence for life in England and France had led him to seem a relative stranger despite his ancestry.

The condemnations of Balliol's mental powers are harsh indeed. As a magnate of Scotland and England he might have managed his estates and contributed to the affairs of both kingdoms well enough in times of peace. But he was fundamentally a weak and indecisive man who could not sustain his role in adversity. If some of the adjectives applied to him – 'simple', 'stupid', 'brainless' – seem too cruel, he had not long been king before he did indeed seem to be 'a lamb among wolves'.

At the outset of the reign he was well advised by the very able Comyns. His sister Eleanor was the wife of John Comyn of Badenoch, the former Guardian, whose own claim to the Scottish throne had been registered in the 'Great Cause', but not pressed. It was one of several claims which had been dismissed because they had not been argued. The implication was that as the Comyn plea was inferior to that of John Balliol, it was to be regarded as subsidiary to it within the same group-ing. In recompense for their solidarity, the Comyns would expect their share of the rewards of power.

Well advised by kinsmen and supporters better versed in Scottish affairs than he, King John in his first parliament, of February 1293, gave indications that he intended to build upon Alexander III's policy of assimilating the west, by the creation of three new sheriffdoms in Skye, Lorne and Kintyre.[6] But even as he began to assert his authority it was undermined by a series of actions through which Edward I raised the claims of overlordship to a level that rendered John Balliol's vassal status unendurable.

By now the happy relations which had existed between Alexander III and Edward I belonged to a past that Edward had deliberately consigned to oblivion. The possibility of a dynastic union of the kingdoms having been disappointed, Edward had revived the old and almost dormant claim of suzerainty, and having raised his claim to that of absolute sovereignty, then fed the growing hunger of his ambition with the more substantial satisfaction of complete annexation. Rather than having been a fully prepared scheme, in existence from the time of Alexander III's death, Edward I's ambition to absorb Scotland seems to have grown gradually, continually expanded by the success of each inflation of his claims.

A sequence of appeals from Scottish to English justice was used by Edward to stress King John's inferior status in the most galling manner. In Scotland the King was regarded as the source of justice 'whose kingly duty it was above all other duties, to punish wrongdoers and judge equitably between subject and subject . . . If King John's capacity as supreme secular judge were diminished, his position was open to challenge . . . He might be regarded as a provincial governor . . . He would certainly not be a King.'[7] Edward's demonstrable intention in accepting appeals from King John's justice was to reduce him to the status of a provincial governor. A Scottish petition on behalf of King John pointed out to Edward that the hearing of appeals 'outwith the kingdom' was contrary to the Treaty of Birgham. Edward's response was to extract from John an acknowledgement that Edward was released from the terms of the Treaty and from any of the promises made by him during the interregnum.[8]

The most famous claims 'outwith the kingdom' were those of John de Mazun and MacDuff of Fife. Mazun was a Bordeaux wine merchant who claimed a debt owing him by King Alexander III. Mazun was difficult and litigious and had refused offers of settlement both from the King and later from the Guardians; also dissatisfied with King John, he appealed to Edward I. MacDuff was the younger brother of the late Earl of Fife (the Guardian, murdered in 1289). MacDuff claimed that he had not been permitted to take possession of the lands willed to him by his father, but had been imprisoned by King John (though clearly not for long).

King John was summoned to appear before the Court of the King's Bench in May 1293, for failure to do justice to Mazun, a summons which he refused to answer. The MacDuff case also came before the King's Bench, and was adjourned to the Michaelmas Parliament in November, which John attended, to be subjected to the most public humiliation in the interval between the first and second summonses. King Edward's council had drawn up a set of rules to govern appeals from Scotland: the King of Scots must always attend appeals in person, and might forfeit his lordship over the fief of the appellant if the judgement went against him.

At the November parliament King John was treated with studied discourtesy, being led to stand at the bar of the house to hear the appeal against him.

John, well primed by his councillors, refused to answer the appeal on the grounds that he 'dared not and could not answer without the advice of the good men of his realm', and he likewise refused to recognize the jurisdiction of the court by asking for an adjournment. The response was crushing. John was immediately judged to be guilty of extreme contempt against the court and his own 'sovereign lord', and was sentenced to the loss of his three chief castles and towns.[9]

King John's attempt at self-reliance crumbled. He submitted a 'humble petition' to King Edward, requesting time to consult his own people, and agreeing to appear before the next parliament. He was granted an adjournment to 14 June 1294. His return to Scotland must have been almost as humiliating as his appearance in England, a 'lamb among wolves' indeed.

Viewing these events in retrospect it looks as though Edward I raised his demands as overlord with the deliberate intention of goading King John into revolt, so that he would have the justification of crushing him as a rebellious vassal. But this may be to credit Edward with preternatural powers of foresight. He could not *know* what John might do under any given set of circumstances, but he continued to increase his pressure on the unfortunate King of Scots and upon his kingdom.

Certainly he did not foresee the situation in which he himself would be cast in the role of contumacious vassal. As Duke of Aquitaine, Edward I was the vassal of Philip IV of France, and at the beginning of the 1290s Anglo-French relations were poisoned by piracy between English and French sailors, especially those of the Cinque Ports and of the Ports of Normandy. King Philip's complaints of English piracy had been unredressed. Philip summoned Edward to appear before the Parlement of Paris to submit to his judgement. When Edward, like King John under similar circumstances, refused to attend, King Philip judged him a contumacious vassal, and on 19 May 1294 took possession of the English lands of Gascony. Edward, with more resources at his back, as he supposed, than King John, did not, like John, react with craven capitulation. He renounced his homage to Philip IV (if a vassal proposed to resist his lord, a formal *défi* – withdrawal of fealty, the sign of true hard defiance – absolved him of the charge of disloyalty). He sent King Philip a declaration of war.

The sight of the King of England in difficulties inspired the Welsh, who had submitted to English rule for ten years and resented Edward's demand that they should fight for him in France, to rebel against him under the leadership of Madog ap Llewelyn. Edward was forced to abandon his intended French expedition, and turn aside to deal with the Welsh rebellion.

In the summer of 1294 King John was again in England, and was prevailed upon to promise Scottish participation in Edward's projected expedition. (The last King of Scots who had gone to war in support of an English king had been Malcolm 'the Maiden', who had accompanied Henry II to the Siege of Toulouse in 1159, to the chagrin of his magnates, who were concerned that his action could be held to imply vassal status.[10]) John's status was not in doubt, but his promise to support Edward evidently seemed to his Councillors unnecessarily abject, after the humiliations he had already undergone. The rebellion of the Welsh probably served to rouse the Scots from the shocked apathy with which they had responded to Edward's bullying tactics. By May 1295 the Welsh revolt had been crushed, but by this time a new mood of resistance had seized King John's Councillors, who determined upon a Franco-Scottish treaty against the English King. John evidently lagged behind the mood of his Councillors, for in July 1295, when envoys were appointed to negotiate the treaty, at the same time a new advisory body was formed in Scotland, consisting of four earls, four bishops and four barons. It was, in effect, a governing body, to implement the newly determined policy, which King John would not have had the courage to initiate or the consistency to pursue. That this new body was intended to have policy-making powers was indicated by its form: it represented the same groups of the community as the original body of Guardians – earls, churchmen and barons – but was double the size.

It has been stated that the Franco-Scottish Treaty of 1295 laid the foundations of what became the 'Auld Alliance' of Scotland and France. This is arguable, for it was not the first Franco-Scottish treaty, and the alliance of the two countries did not continue uninterruptedly thereafter. Later Anglo-Scottish treaties attempted to restore peace and good relations between the neighbouring kingdoms. But, in the long view, it seemed to set a new pattern. Edward I, by his own disproportionate ambition, had destroyed the 'good neighbourhood' with England which had bid fair to become the 'Auld Alliance', well founded on both proximity and intermarriage, and had driven his erstwhile allies to seek a new alliance which would more often prove its value to France than to Scotland in the ensuing centuries. The new alliance did not fix the pattern of future politics, but it introduced a dominant theme.

The Franco-Scottish Treaty drafted in Paris in October 1295, and ratified at Dunfermline in February 1296, was a defensive and offensive alliance against England, in which both parties bound themselves to negotiate a separate peace. It was intended to be confirmed, and its lasting character at least indicated, by a marriage between King John's son Edward Balliol and King Philip's niece Jeanne de Valois, but the marriage was never solemnized.[11] The French King required that the Treaty be ratified not only by King John, but also by the Scottish nobility, higher clergy, knights and 'communities of the towns'.[12] This made it a treaty fully representative of the Community of the Realm, and may also have carried the implication that the King of Scots had the reputation of a man of straw.

France and England, as the original disputants in the quarrel over piracy, each sought to buttress themselves with alliances, which threatened to convert their dispute into a European war. To their alliance with Scotland, France added a Franco-Norwegian alliance. At this juncture relations between Eric II and King John were disputatious, but the Franco-Norwegian Treaty contained guarantees by Eric that he would

not make war on the Scots by reason of any past disputation with them
'nor would devise new motives for such a war but rather seek to avoid
it'.[13] The Norwegians were to put an invasion fleet at the disposal of the
French; the Scots were to invade England by land.

Edward's intention was to encircle France with his European
alliances. He made a treaty with the German King Adolf of Nassau,
and alliances with other lesser rulers including John, Count of Holland
(son of the late Competitor, Count Florent, who was murdered with
the approval if not the connivance of Edward I).[14] But before any
action could be taken against the King of France, Edward was determined to stamp out the little flame of resistance that had been ignited
in Scotland, before it could blaze up and take hold upon the nation. He
summoned the feudal host to meet at Newcastle-on-Tyne, on 1 March
1296, to liaise with a fleet which would sail up the coast from East
Anglia.

Before Edward I had given judgement in the 'Great Cause', according
to the *Scotichronicon*:

> . . . he summoned up the elder Robert de Bruce and asked him if he
> would hold the aforesaid kingdom of him in chief [as a tenant-in-
> chief], in which case he would make and constitute him king thereof.
> Robert answered him frankly and said: 'If I can obtain the aforesaid
> kingdom by way of law and a trustworthy jury, it is well indeed; but
> if not, I shall never in gaining it for myself reduce to servitude the
> aforesaid kingdom which all its kings with great toil and trouble have
> until now preserved and held without servitude in firmly-rooted
> freedom'. When he [Edward] had heard this and cunningly had
> Robert removed, Edward summoned John de Balliol and put to him
> the same question as before. After quickly deliberating with his advis-
> ors (who had been quite corrupted) Balliol agreed to the aforesaid
> King's wish that he should hold the kingdom of him and do homage
> for the same.[15]

The belief that Robert de Bruce of Annandale would not have done
as Balliol did became an article of faith in the Bruce myth. But, in fact,
since before the Court of Claims opened the Competitors had

acknowledged Edward I as their suzerain, it would have been extraordinarily difficult, if not impossible, for Robert de Bruce, had the adjudication been in his favour, to have reasserted the independence of the kingdom. Doubtless he liked to believe that he would have done so, and did his best to propagate the belief that asserting his intention had played its part in turning the adjudication against him. The more deeply King John floundered in the morass into which Edward led him, the more gratifying would the spectacle have been for the old Lord of Annandale, watching affairs from his retirement at Lochmaben.

He died there on Maundy Thursday, 1295, evidently having retained his mental powers to the last, for his final intervention in politics was to secure the election of his own nominee, Master Thomas Dalton of Kirkudbright, to the bishopric of Galloway. Dalton was canonically elected by the prior and canons of Whithorn, the cathedral church of the diocese, but King John protested that the election had been obtained by bribery; possibly it had, but King John was obliged to accept the election of a Bruce nominee to a see which lay within his ancestral lands. Bishop Dalton was consecrated in October 1294. Another humiliation for King John which must have given his defeated rival a glow of pleasure to inflict.

The Competitor's son, Robert de Bruce VI, 'by refusing homage to Balliol . . . kept open his father's claim to the throne',[16] and having gone to Norway with his daughter Isabella in 1292, he remained there after her marriage to King Eric the following year, and did not return to Scotland until after his father's death.

Under these circumstances, the marriage of King Eric to Isabella de Bruce did not improve Scoto-Norwegian relations; it was the very reverse of traditional treaty marriages, being with a Scottish noblewoman whose family was at enmity with the King of Scots. Eric, at this time, was attempting to reclaim the Western Isles, ceded to Scotland under the Treaty of Reith of 1266, claiming that the 'annual' of one hundred marks in perpetuity had fallen into arrears. The modern historian is surely right who comments 'To King John, it must have seemed that Edward, Eric, and the Bruces had banded together to undermine his authority and prestige, perhaps even to dismember his kingdom'.[17]

The young Robert de Bruce, during the last days of his grandfather and the absence of his father, was obliged to assume adult responsibilities sooner than he would have expected. He would have been responsible for the wellbeing of his four younger brothers, Edward, Thomas, Alexander and Neil, and of his sisters Mary, Christian, Matilda and Margaret. In the Scottish parliament held at Stirling in August 1293 he was confirmed as Earl of Carrick, his sponsors being his family's allies, James Stewart, the High Steward of Scotland, and Donald, Earl of Mar.[18] The following month he was probably in England, visiting the English estates of the Bruces, and it was most likely from London that he despatched wedding presents to his sister Isabella. He sent her blue, scarlet and fur-trimmed gowns, bed-linen, green and gold coverlets, and a handsome array of table silver.[19] The likelihood that Edward was wooing the Bruces as part of his policy of undermining John Balliol is suggested by his permitting young Robert to take loans from the Royal Exchequer.[20]

On the death of the old Lord of Annandale in 1295, his son Robert de Bruce VI returned from Norway, and was appointed by King Edward to the governorship of Carlisle, an office formerly held by his father, and it was later reported that King Edward also promised him the throne of Scotland, when the rebellious King John had been deposed.[21]

A short episode in the life of young Robert de Bruce, but one that was to have a decisive effect on Scottish history, was his marriage to the daughter of the Earl of Mar, in 1295. Isabella of Mar bore Robert a daughter, named Marjorie after his mother; the baby was born in 1296, and cost the mother her life. But Marjorie de Bruce would do what the Maid of Norway had failed to do: she would transmit the royal succession from one dynasty to the next, and ensure that there was no repetition of the succession crisis of 1286, which brought the kingdom to desolation in the year of her birth.

In 1296 the surviving Bruces, father and son, united in their refusal to acknowledge the kingship of John Balliol, and secure in the favour of Edward I refused to obey the King of Scots' call to arms.

According to the Lanercost Chronicle:

a wapinschaw [inspection of weapons] was held and account being made of those who were capable of military service, all who had power, wealth, arms and strength were warned to be ready to assemble at Caldenley [Caddonlee, near Selkirk] on the Sunday in Passion Week.[22]

English nobles who held lands in Scotland, but preferred their loyalty to the English King (as they mostly did, simply because their larger estates were in England), where expelled from Scotland, and their lands confiscated and given to Scots; while English clerics and even some English members of Scottish monastic communities were expelled from the kingdom, as possible fifth columnists.[23]

In these circumstances it was inevitable, and from the viewpoint of King John perfectly just, that the disaffected Bruces should lose their lands. Accordingly, Annandale was granted by King John to his father-in-law, John Comyn, Earl of Buchan, thus adding another brand to a feud that was already burning very well.

Among the Scottish magnates who rode to the muster at Caddonlee on Passion Sunday, 18 March 1296, there must have been some men reflective enough to recall that it was exactly ten years since the death of Alexander III, to compare the decline in status of the kingdom and the kingship with its prosperity and independence in his days, and to contrast friendly relations between the two kingdoms within such recent memory with the imminent prospect of going to war.

It would also have been painfully obvious to any man with military sense or knowledge of the two kingdoms that in any forthcoming conflict the odds were heavily stacked against the Scots. In medieval warfare, cavalry was traditionally regarded as the most important force. The charge of a massed body of well-mounted and heavily armed knights was usually what decided a battle: an effective charge simply swept the enemy off the field, after which the fugitives could be pursued and cut down at will. There was usually a massacre of defeated infantry. So far as knights were concerned, slaughter was inhibited by considerations of ransom. It was more advantageous to capture a knight, and even more so a nobleman, than to kill him, for negotiating a ransom or two could convert warfare from a heavy personal expense into a profitable business venture, for a lucky warrior.

Scotland, with a population approximately one-fifth of that of England, and with the feudal system of knight service not extended throughout the whole country, inevitably could field only a very much smaller force of knights, equerries and mounted men-at-arms. Besides, there was the difficulty of breeding and feeding in sufficient numbers the heavy warhorses, or destriers, which carried knights in battle, and in the tournament. They were costly to feed, in a country relatively short of pasture in comparison to England, and they were expensive to train and maintain. With these limitations, the Scots were usually poorly equipped with heavy cavalry, and preferred to field mobile squadrons of light horsemen, known as 'nokelars', who proved their usefulness in the lightning raids into enemy territory which became one of the most successful aspects of Scottish warfare in the years to come.

By far the largest part of any Scottish army was composed of the commonalty who were obliged to perform *Servitum Scoticanum* (Scottish Service, which it would scarcely be anachronistic to call 'National Service'), under which all able-bodied men between sixteen and sixty could be summoned within their sheriffdoms to serve in the defence of the realm. These men would have converged upon Caddonlee armed with swords, spears, or 'Lochaber Axes' (long-shafted battle-axes with a long curved blade ending in a point).[24] The men of Selkirk Forest were armed with short, light bows; they were renowned as skilful archers, but their weapons were no match for the Welsh longbow, which was just being adopted by English archers, in whose hands it would become a devastating weapon by the mid-fourteenth century. The Scots who went to war against Edward I and Edward II were fortunate that the English longbowmen had not yet reached the zenith of their expertise, nor were deployed to full advantage.

Besides the resources of population which enabled the English King to raise a much larger army than the King of Scots, the English army was fundamentally different in two ways from the *communis exercitus* (common army): it was the efficient military machine with which Edward I had conquered the Welsh, and it was paid, for the English King was wealthy enough to pay daily wages to all his troops, from the haughtiest earl to the humblest groom.[25] Both the Scottish and English armies traditionally owed military service for forty days, but pay obviously made the English soldiers willing to serve for longer periods, while the Scots had to be encouraged to keep the field by the prospect of booty. While the Scottish nobility and knighthood doubtless kept their martial skills honed in the tournament, the *communis exercitus*, after the long and largely peaceful reign of Alexander III, was inevitably without military experience. The natural qualities of the Scots as fighting men were demonstrated by the speed with which their inexperienced army became formidable, but defeat came before victory.

Hostilities began unofficially when the English Robert de Ros, Lord of Wark, in Northumberland, who was about to marry a Scotswoman, decided to show solidarity with her countrymen by delivering his castle to the Scots. Ros's brother, who remained loyal to Edward, sent an appeal for help to relieve the castle. Edward sent a force, but Robert de Ros, with a body of Scots from Roxburgh, attacked its encampment. Edward then advanced on the castle himself, relieved it, and remained there to celebrate Easter, 25 March, with religious observance.

Immediately after the festival the war erupted with an orgy of slaughter on both sides. Hitherto the gradual encroachment of English power, the subordination of the Scottish kingship to English suzerainty, had not affected the commonalty of either country. It was the killing in the spring of 1296 which finally destroyed a century of friendly relations, and heralded three centuries of sporadic warfare which created a perpetual legacy of resentment and suspicion. This was the *damnosa haereditas* of Edward I's ambition.

The Scots struck first, which no doubt enabled Edward to maintain his self-righteous view of his own aims: 'the path by which he attains his ends, however crooked, he calls straight . . .'[26] On 26 March John Comyn the younger of Buchan, the son of the former Guardian, led a strong Scottish force from Annandale, which swept to the walls of Carlisle and attempted to take the city by storm. It was strongly fortified, and was successfully defended by its Governor, Robert de Bruce VI, the dispossessed Lord of Annandale, and his son, the young Earl of Carrick. Repulsed before Carlisle, Buchan's force swung southeast, cutting a swathe of destruction through Northumberland. At either Corbridge or Hexham (the chroniclers differ on the place but not the event) they locked two hundred schoolboys into a school, set fire to it and burned them to death, a massacre of innocents that set the tone of a war in which the civilian populace could expect no mercy. What casts some doubt on the story is the scale of the reported massacre. Hexham and Corbridge were both small centres of population, and it seems extremely unlikely that even Hexham, though it had a substantial priory, would have supported a school large enough to have two hundred scholars – though a massacre of twenty would have been no less cruel a deed.

While Buchan's force indulged in aimless slaughter, Edward, unimpeded, advanced upon Berwick. Unlike Carlisle, Berwick was not well fortified. It was surrounded by an earthwork and a timber stockade, which during the years of peace there had been no need to replace with more modern defences. But behind its green banks, Berwick was a prosperous centre of commerce, and Scotland's leading port for trade with northern Europe. It contained a colony of Flemish merchants occupying their own 'Red Hall', and of German merchants in their 'White Hall'; the castle harboured a garrison to protect the town, and the harbour was crowded with Scottish and foreign shipping.

King Edward had brought his navy from Newcastle, and ordered a preliminary attack from the sea. This first foray was defeated when four English ships ran aground and the Scots sallied out and set them afire. In a surge of confidence, the Scots from the top of their banks yelled insults at the besieging army, and sang ribald songs guaranteed to incite their attackers to fury.

Against the assault of the English army neither the old defences nor the resistance of the townsfolk were of any avail. The town fell on 30 March 1296, and the sack continued for two days, with indiscriminate massacre of the inhabitants of both sexes and all ages, and the burning of thirty Flemish merchants in the Red Hall. The castle was held until its Governor, Sir William Douglas, deservedly known as 'Le Hardi', offered himself as a hostage, on condition that the garrison might depart with the honours of war. The sights that they witnessed as they departed attested how circumscribed were notions of honour. The town stank of death, and common pits had to be dug to bury the thousands of corpses.[27] It was said that Edward I had called a halt to the slaughter only when he witnessed the killing of a pregnant woman and unborn child.

> This Kyng Edward saw in that tyde
> A woman slayne, and off hyr syde
> A babe he saw fall owt, sprawland
> Besyde that woman slayne lyand
> 'Lasses, lasses' than cryid he
> 'Leve off, leve off,' that word suld be.

[King Edward saw at this tide
A woman slain and from her side
A babe he saw fall out, sprawling
Beside that woman slain lying
'Laissez, laissez' then cried he –
'Leave off, leave off' that word should be.][28]

The sack of Berwick was probably one of the most savage acts of war ever committed in these islands, but the reporting of the culminating atrocity may have been one of those 'atrocity stories' characteristic of all wars, in which each side attributes to the enemy acts of savagery which it could not imagine that its own more decent soldiery would commit.

On 5 April, while Berwick must still have been stinking and smouldering, two Franciscan friars arrived to deliver to Edward King John's formal '*défi*', or renunciation of fealty. It was a dignified form of words, though utterly ineffective, and far too late, but it is worth quoting as an unexaggerated statement of the wrongs Edward I had committed:

> To the eminent prince Edward, by the Grace of God King of England, John, by the same Grace King of Scotland. You yourself, and others of your realm . . . have . . . inflicted over and over again by naked force grievous and intolerable injuries, slights and wrongs upon us and the inhabitants of our realm . . . for instance by summoning us outside our realm at the mere beck and call of anybody, as your own whim dictated and by harassing us unjustifiably . . . [and] . . . now you have come to the frontiers of our realm in warlike array . . . and brutally committed acts of slaughter and burning . . . we cannot any longer endure these injuries, insults and grievous wrongs . . . nor can we remain in your fealty and homage . . . and we desire to assert ourselves against you, for our own defence and that of our realm . . . and so by the present letter we renounce the fealty and homage which we have done to you . . .[29]

To King John the situation did not seem irredeemable, because although Berwick had fallen, the army of Scotland had not yet been engaged. But Edward's response to the communication was brief and brutal: 'Be it unto the fool according to his folly'.

It appeared that Edward's recent policy had been to provoke John Balliol into revolt, so that he could then, in accordance with feudal notions of legality, crush him as a contumacious vassal.

Beyond Berwick the next stronghold barring the English advance was Dunbar. It had been held by Edward's supporter Patrick, Earl of Dunbar, but during his absence his Countess had handed over the castle to the Scots. Edward sent forward a force commanded by the Earl Warenne, to besiege Dunbar. The defenders, like the citizens of Berwick a few weeks previously, indulged themselves in yelling defiance from the walls. 'Tailed dogs!' they shouted, the standard racist taunt against the English, referring to the general belief, or insulting pretence, that all Englishmen were born with tails. No doubt they felt confident of being relieved by the approach of the main Scottish army, for Warenne divided his forces, leaving his junior officers to contain the garrison of Dunbar, and marching with his veterans to meet the Scottish host at nearby Spottsmuir.[30] The English force had to descend into the valley of the Spott Burn, in which they were temporarily out of sight of the Scots, on the higher ground. The Scottish knights, thinking that the English had turned tail, broke ranks to pursue them, but encountered the English advancing in good order. The English pressed forward steadily, driving the ill-prepared Scots into flight. The battle ended like many another medieval engagement, with a host of valuable prisoners held for ransom, and a massacre of the infantry. The defeat of Dunbar put an end to King John's hope of reasserting his independence.

After Dunbar Edward imposed harsh terms on the Scots: he demanded that King John should resign his kingdom and renounce his treaty with France. Bishop Bek of Durham, who had been King John's ally, attempted to negotiate a face-saving peace for him; but John, wandering indecisively from one place to another, let slip the opportunity for negotiation, until he faced a demand for unconditional surrender. Under remorseless pressure, on 2 July at Kincardine, King John issued an abject document of surrender:

> . . . seeing that we have by evil and false council, and our own folly, grievously offended and angered our lord Edward, by the Grace of God, King of England . . . Therefore we, acting under no constraint, and of our own free will, have surrendered to him the land of Scotland and all its people . . .[31]

This was not the limit of John's humiliation. Five days later, at a gathering in the chuchyard of Stracathro, he renounced the treaty with France, and at a final ceremony of degradation in the burgh of Montrose on 8 July, he resigned his kingdom into the hands of Edward I. On this occasion John appeared as King for the last time, and the royal insignia and armorial bearings were stripped off him. This was the origin of his contemptuous nickname, 'Toom Tabard' ('Empty Surcoat'), because he had been stripped of all the means of identification known to this period. Without the lion rampant of Scotland embroidered on his surcoat, which made him identifiable to any knight in Christendom, who though he might be illiterate could read the symbols of heraldry, John Balliol became a non-person. After his degradation Balliol was sent as a prisoner to the Tower of London, where he remained for three years, after which he was permitted greater liberty.

Edward's victory was not intended to be purely symbolic. The castles of Dunbar, Roxburgh, Jedburgh and Dumbarton were surrendered to him. Edinburgh endured a brief siege, but yielded within a week. Stirling was abandoned by its garrison, leaving only the castle gatekeeper to surrender the keys.[32] Edward himself made a triumphal progress to the North, which took him as far as Elgin, before returning to Berwick on 22 August. In the proud words of a contemporary diarist, Edward had 'conquered and serched the kyngdom of Scotteland . . . in xxi wekis withought anymore'.[33]

After the fall of John Balliol, Edward ordered the Scottish national records, the regalia and other treasures to be sent to England. King John had been inaugurated with the regalia of Alexander III. The crown would have been a Gothic 'lily crown' of the type represented on the Great Seal. Alexander's sceptre was a *Virga Aaron*, a blossoming rod, which appears on the seals of both Alexander and King John. It has been suggested that this beautiful sceptre could have been made from the Golden Rose sent by Pope Lucius III to King William the Lion in 1182: this special mark of papal favour would have been an appropriate symbol of divinely sanctioned authority. The long rose or spray of roses was mounted on a gold wand described as *rosam auream in virga etiam auream erectam*.[34] Probably there was also an orb and a state sword. (These appear on the royal seals of earlier kings, and are likely to have been part of the regalia of King John.) Another national treasure removed by Edward was the deeply venerated 'Black Rood', a crucifix (possibly carved of ebony) which had belonged to St Margaret of Scotland.

The greatest symbolic loss, however, was that of the Stone of Destiny, 'the innermost sacrosanct mystery among the insignia of Scottish monarchy'.[35] When Edward visited Perth in the summer of 1296 he ordered that it should be removed from the Abbey of Scone and sent to Westminster Abbey, where it was set in the base of a chair that was originally intended to be the seat of the priest who celebrated the Mass (who sits at the side of the altar for a period of silence towards the end of the service) and which later became the coronation chair.[36]

The English were well aware that in acquiring this symbol of power they had also acquired something both sacred and legendary. A contemporary song tells one of the many legends concerning its origin:

> Q[e]i est la piere de Escose, vous die pur verite
> Sur que les Roys d'Escose estoint mis en see
> Johan Balliolle drien just, a ceo q'est counte
> Qe sur ceste piere rescent sa dignite . . .

> En Egipte Moise a le peple precha
> Scota la file Fara on bien l'escota,
> Quare il dite en esprite, 'Que ceste piere auera
> De molt estraunge terre conquerour serra'.

> Gaidelons et Scota ceste piere menerount
> Quant de la terre Egypte en Escose passerount
> Ne geres loyns de Scone quaint arriveront
> De la noun de Scota la Escosse terre numount.

> Puis la mort de Scota son baron femme ne prist
> Mais en la terre de Galway sa demore prist.
> De son nonne demoisne le noune de Galway mist
> Issi nest qe par cour nouns Escosse te Galway ist . . .

> [What the stone of Scotland is, you shall understand:
> On it were enthroned the kings of Scotland
> John Balliol was the last, as is now well known
> Who received his dignity seated on the stone . . .

In Egypt to the people Moses came to preach,
Scota, Pharaoh's daughter, heard what he would teach.
He, speaking with the Spirit, said 'Who shall have this stone
A very distant country shall conquer for his own'.

Gaidelon and Scota stole the stone away
From Egypt, toward Scotland, when they made their way
Not so far from Scone was the place they came,
And from the name of Scota, Scotland took its name.

When Scota had died, her lord did not remarry
But in the land of Galloway afterwards did tarry
And it is from his name derives the name of Galloway
So Galloway and Scotland recall them to this day . . .][37]
(English version by CB)

One can imagine the French song sung to a rather melancholy and plan-
gent melody in aristocratic households, while the London citizenry cho-
rused the triumphant doggerel:

> Thair Kinges sette of Scone
> Es driven over done
> To London i-ledde
>
> [Their kings' seat of Scone
> Is driven over down
> To London lead][38]

There was, however, a persistent rumour that a substituted stone was
presented to Edward, while the real Stone of Destiny was reverently
hidden. But, true or false, the Stone that remained in Westminster
Abbey from 1296 to 1996 became a revered symbol because of what it
was believed to be, and because of its hallowing as the 'Coronation
Stone'.[39]

Having despatched Scotland's treasures to London, Edward
remained at Berwick, to organize the administration of the 'land of
Scotland', no longer designated a kingdom.

A reconstructed Berwick, with modern fortifications, was to be the
centre of that administration. King Edward assumed the role that he
had claimed previously, of suzerain or 'sovereign lord' of Scotland, but

he did not assume the title King of Scots or Lord of Scotland. It appeared that the kingdom was not abolished, but was in abeyance.[40] Edward may have intended to suppress the identity of Scotland entirely, and incorporate it into England, or he may have decided to take time to consider his next move. Since Scotland appeared to have been hammered into submission, it seemed that he could entrust it to subordinates, while he turned his attention to outstanding problems in France. He appointed the Earl Warenne as Lieutenant of the Kingdom, an appropriate reward for the victor of Dunbar. Hugh de Cressingham was appointed Treasurer, Walter of Amersham Chancellor, and William Ormesby Chief Justice. They were served by a host of lesser officials who from the English viewpoint ran an efficient administration, and from the Scottish viewpoint were ruthless and grasping.

On his triumphant tour of Scotland, Edward had received the homage of many Scottish landowners. But in August 1296 he held a parliament at Berwick at which every substantial freeholder was obliged to appear either to provide in person or to send signed and sealed evidence of his fealty to Edward I. Those who were included in the demand were 'tenants in chief of the Crown and their heirs, substantial under-tenants and their heirs, officers and burgesses of some leading East Country burghs, heads of religious houses, a high proportion of the beneficed clergy [especially those who were university graduates]'.[41] Some historians have imagined a great gathering of these men to offer their fealty, willing or unwilling, at Berwick. A more recent and more realistic view is that while many may have come to Berwick, there would have been a collection of the names and fealties on the basis of sheriffdoms (which would account for why the names of men who owed fealty in more than one capacity would appear more than once).[42] On 28 August 1296 the fealties were formally registered on the 'Ragman Roll' (a great record with an inexplicable name, which a recent historian has suggested may be simply a corruption of 'the rigmarole').[43]

Earlier than this, when Edward was at Wark, at Easter 1296, Robert de Bruce of Annandale and his son the Earl of Carrick ('*Robert de Brus le veil et Robert de Brus le juvene*') together with Patrick, Earl of Dunbar, and Gilbert de Umfraville, Earl of Angus, had issued letters patent declaring their fidelity to Edward I, and recording his reception of their fealty. They further promised, collectively and separately,

I will be faithful and loyal, and will maintain faith and loyalty to King Edward, King of England, and to his heirs, in matters of life and limb and of earthly honour against all mortal men; and never will I bear arms for anyone against him or his heirs . . . so may God help me and the Saints.[44]

King Edward, in his reception of the fealty quoted in this letter, referred to John Balliol as 'the former King of Scotland' ('*Qi fust Roy d'Escoce*'), which undoubtedly would have encouraged Robert de Bruce 'le veil' to hope that Edward would honour his promise to nominate him as King of Scotland in Balliol's place. After the fall of John Balliol, Robert de Bruce the elder took occasion to remind Edward of his promise, but

That old master of guile with no little indignation answered thus in French 'N'avons nous pas aultres choses a fair qu'a gagner vos roy-aumes?', that is to say 'Have we nothing else to do than win kingdoms for you?'. That noble man [Robert de Bruce] discerning from such a response the treachery of the wily King withdrew to his lands in England and put in no further appearance in Scotland.[45]

Bruce's withdrawal from the political scene, whether it was inspired by dudgeon with Edward or despair at the apparent futility of pursuing his claim, left his son in a position of extreme difficulty. The younger Robert's belief in the validity of the Bruce claim remained unimpaired, but he could not pursue it for himself while his father lived.

PART TWO

THE TRIUMPH OF THE KING

———|✴|✴|✴|———

5

————— |✻|✻|✻| —————

A HERO AND A MAN IN PERPLEXITY

'Wou'd ye hear of William Wallace,
And seek him as he goes
Into the land of Lanark
Amang his mortal foes?'[1]

WHEN EDWARD I left Scotland in early September 1296, he expressed
his contempt for the kingdom that he had crushed and the men whose
resistance had been so ineffective by remarking '*Bon besiogne fait qy de
merde se deliver*' ('He does good business who rids himself of shit').[2] His
lieutenant, Earl Warenne, did not even feel it necessary to remain in
Scotland, but went south to his estates in Yorkshire, leaving Scotland to
be administered by his officials and controlled by English garrisons.
The King's contemptuous words and Warenne's departure both
showed a complete miscalculation of the situation, even though
Scotland appeared to be prostrate beneath the feet of the hated triumvirate of Cressingham, Amersham and Ormesby.

Hugh de Cressingham, of whom it was said '*erat enim pulcher et grossus
nimis*' ('he was certainly good-looking but exceedingly fat'),[3] was the
most unpopular of the three – viewed with the particular hatred
reserved for the aristocratic tax-collector. Ormesby, the Chief Justice,
busied himself searching out and passing sentence of outlawry on all
who had refused or evaded fealty to King Edward.

It was now, if not before, that the reign of Alexander III began to be
remembered as a golden age, when Scotland had been peaceful,
prosperous and independent. A 'golden age' is essentially a retrospective concept. As always occurs in times of trouble, a state of being that
had seemed ordinary enough on an everyday basis begins to seem

intensely desirable once it has disappeared. A song of lament, included in Wyntoun's *Metrical Chronicle*, captures the mood:

> Quhan Aysander our Kyng was dede
> That Scotland led in luve and lé [law],
> Away was gans [abundance], off ale and brede,
> Off wyne and wax [candles], off gamyn and glé
>
> Our gold was changyd in to lede
> Chryst, borne in to Vyrgynyté,
> Succour Scotland and remede
> That stad is in perplexyté.[4]

This frequently quoted song evokes in simple words a picture of the peaceful, prosperous, law-abiding Scotland of Alexander's reign, which even if it were in part a utopian vision acted very powerfully upon the imaginations of a people now restless and resentful under the heavy-handed regime of a conqueror. To no one was the vision more inspiring than to William Wallace, second son of Sir Malcolm Wallace of Elderslie, a vassal of James Stewart, High Steward of Scotland. William Wallace's name was not on the 'Ragman Roll', and he was determined never to offer fealty to King Edward, preferring outlawry, and the refuge of Selkirk Forest, where a vast tract of woodland could conceal many wanted men. It might have interested Ormesby more that Sir Malcolm Wallace's eldest son and namesake, the heir of Elderslie, had also withheld his fealty; but in 1297 William Wallace 'raised his head'[5] and immediately dominated the rebellion against English rule.

According to a description written long after his death – one of those tantalizing descriptions that may or may not be based on genuine memories:

> He was a tall man with the body of a giant, cheerful in appearance with agreeable features, broad shouldered and big boned, with belly in proportion and lengthy flank, pleasing in appearance but with a wild look . . . he was most liberal in his gifts, very fair in his judgements, most compassionate in comforting the sad, a most skilful counsellor, very patient when suffering . . .[6]

This is a description of an ideal hero: larger than life in physical and mental qualities, Wallace became a hero to his countrymen because, whether or not he was of giant stature, he fulfilled the definition of a hero: 'Almost anyone can act heroically . . . but the hero embodies something more. He possesses a consistent capacity for action that surpasses the norm of man or woman.'[7]

The source for many of Wallace's heroic exploits, and also many apocryphal anecdotes, is the long verse epic *The Arts and Deeds of the Illustrious and Valiant Champion, Sir William Wallace*, composed by Harry the Minstrel, or 'Blind Harry', in the late fifteenth century. By that period enough time had passed for the addition of legendary accretions to Wallace's story, perhaps the most surprising being episodes in which the large and muscular hero is disguised in female dress. These episodes seem beyond the possible, until one remembers how frequently cross-dressing for purposes of concealment and escape occurs in hero tales, from the mythic disguise of Hercules among the slave women of Queen Omphale to the historic disguise of Prince Charles Edward Stewart as Flora MacDonald's maidservant 'Betty Burke'.

Based on one of Blind Harry's episodes is a popular ballad on this theme, in which Wallace visits his mistress, an unnamed 'ladye', who in return for the promise of a noble marriage has betrayed him to the English. But, on seeing him, she confesses her treachery and cries in an agony of remorse, 'Let me burn upon a hill!' Wallace makes a splendid reply:

> 'Now God forfend', says brave Wallace
> 'I should be so unkind;
> Whatever I am to Scotland's foes
> I'm aye a woman's friend'

He then borrows clothes from her, and walks out of the house, past the English soldiers lying in wait for him. The soldiers unwisely follow 'yon lusty dame', and Wallace draws his sword from beneath his skirts and slays them 'pair by pair'.[8]

This belongs to Wallace folklore, but there is no reason to doubt Blind Harry's story that Wallace married a young woman named Marion Braidfoot, who lived in Lanark, well provided enough to have a house and servants, though Wallace as an outlaw could visit her only in secret.

Presumably he imagined his secret was safe when he used the house as an escape route from the town to the Cartland crags where he could disappear. Marion's attempt to deflect the pursuit fastened suspicion upon her, and the pursuers torched the house, slew the servants, and in Blind Harry's dreadful words 'Put her to death, I cannot tell you how . . .'[9]

According to Blind Harry, it was in revenge for his wife's death that Wallace returned to slay the English Sheriff of Lanark, Sir William Hazelrigg, and, beside himself with grief and rage, hacked the man's body to pieces. Blind Harry mirrors the anguish that causes Wallace to turn his back on personal happiness and dedicate himself to the destruction of his country's enemies, apostrophizing the hero with the words:

> Now leave thy youth and follow thy hard choice,
> Now leave thy lust, now leave thy marriage,
> Now leave thy love and thou shall lose a gage
> Which never in earth shall be redeemed again.
> Follow fortune and all her fierce outrage,
> Go live in war, go live in cruel pain . . .[10]

There is no need to dismiss the death of Wallace's wife as fiction; such tragedies are commonplaces of war in all centuries. But it would be simplistic to suppose that it was the cause of Wallace's rebellion, or even to see him as a leader who acted alone. Wallace dominated the early years of Scotland's struggle for independence for three reasons: because he was a charismatic leader who captured the public imagination; because later his death gave the patriotic cause a martyr; and because his exploits crossed the borders of history to enter popular literature and folk memory. These causes combined to make him a national hero, but he also belongs in a definable historical context.

Wallace's killing of Sir William Hazelrigg sparked the rebellion of 1297, but it had been well planned. According to the Lanercost Chronicle:

> . . . the bishop of the church in Glasgow, whose personal name was Robert Wishart, ever foremost in treason, conspired with the Steward of the realm named James . . . Not daring openly to break their pledged faith to the king, they caused a certain bloody man,

William Wallace, who had formerly been a chief of brigands in Scotland, to revolt against the king and assemble the people in his support.[11]

Both Bishop Wishart and James Stewart had sworn fealty to Edward and their names were on the 'Ragman Roll'; but both had submitted out of expediency, merely serving time.

Robert Wishart was of Norman descent, his surname being a Scottish form of the Norman 'Guiscard'.[12] He had been Bishop of Glasgow since 1273, and had infiltrated a number of his kinsmen into benefices in the diocese. As one of the leading churchmen of Scotland he had a stake in the independence of the kingdom. The Archbishops of York claimed to be metropolitans of Scotland, and the Scottish Church had extended its independent status by placing itself under the direct protection and authority of Rome, and was recognized by the papacy as the 'special daughter' of the Holy See. A means of maintaining the separate status of the Scottish Church had been by securing the appointment of Scots to Scottish benefices. Edward I had recently made his first move to extend the conquest of Scotland to the Scottish Church. On 1 October 1296 he had ordered that only English priests should be appointed to vacant benefices in Galloway, and the following year this order was extended to all Scotland.[13] Nothing could have been more certain to concentrate the sentiments of the Scottish clergy against him. The Church is always said to have been the most consistent supporter of the patriotic cause, and on the whole it was, for reasons well salted with self-interest. But like all generalizations, this must be qualified by exceptions. Edward I always had his supporters among Scottish churchmen – for example, Bishop Henry Cheyne of Aberdeen.

Wishart's ally, James Stewart, was one of the greatest magnates of Scotland, with the hereditary office of High Steward, the lordships of Renfrew, Bute and Kyle Stewart, and of the lands in Teviotdale, Lauderdale and Lothian, all vulnerable to reprisals if his loyalty to Edward faltered. He was a cautious man, who would require to be well assured of success before rebelling. He was the overlord of the Wallaces of Elderslie, and would have recognized in William the fiery quality required of a rebel leader.

There was further encouragement when the rebellion was joined by

Sir William Douglas 'Le Hardi', the erstwhile Governor of Berwick, who had bargained for the safe departure of his garrison and witnessed the horrors of the sack. He was an aristocratic freebooter, with a contempt for authority. His first wife had been the Stewart's sister; his second wife was an Englishwoman, Eleanor Ferrers, whom he had abducted and married by force. Perhaps, like the bride of 'Young Lochinvar', she had not objected; for she was loyal to her husband and the patriotic cause when presented with a moment of choice.

Wallace and Douglas joined forces for an attack on Scone, with the hope of capturing or slaying William Ormesby, who was holding courts of justice there. Ormesby escaped with his life, but with an undignified haste that dented the image of English authority.

Robert de Bruce, Earl of Carrick, was at Carlisle when the rebellion began (his father still held office as Governor of Carlisle), and he was deeply disturbed by it. He and his father, together with Patrick, Earl of Dunbar, and Gilbert de Umfraville, Earl of Angus, had sworn a heavy oath of loyalty to Edward I at Wark, and his name was on the 'Ragman Roll'. He had little cause to lament the fall of John Balliol, but the humiliation heaped on Balliol was also the symbolic humiliation of Scotland. The contempt with which King Edward had addressed his father was, in addition, the humiliation of the Bruce clan. Everything that he had lately witnessed troubled the young man's mind. If Scotland, as the lament for King Alexander expressed it, was 'in perplexity', then so was he.

When King Edward was informed that Sir William Douglas had joined the rebellion, he sent orders to Robert de Bruce to take a force to Douglasdale and seize Sir William's castle, which in his absence was held by his wife. Before setting out, Robert was required to renew his oath of fealty to King Edward. This may have been because he had revealed some sympathy with the rebels, or because he had displayed anger at Edward's rejection of his father's claim. For either reason, Edward would have desired to be sure of him.

The additional oath would have added to his mental turmoil, for Robert de Bruce was not a man to take or break an oath lightly, though it was generally accepted that an oath given under duress was not binding. But there had been no duress when he swore fealty to Edward at Wark. It was a question of which demand on his loyalty had the highest claim: loyalty to his much-abused country, loyalty to his family's claim to the kingship, or loyalty to his oath to the English King.

Robert de Bruce left Carlisle and rode through Annandale, summoning his father's vassals to arms. By the time he reached his destination he had made up his mind. Assembling the knights, he made the first patriotic utterance attributed to him:

> No man holds his own flesh and blood in hatred, and I am no exception. I must join my own people and the nation in which I was born . . . Choose then whether you go with me or return to your homes.[14]

This speech must have been a great shock to the men, who had just obeyed the call to arms issued on behalf of King Edward. Many of them, as vassals of the Lord of Annandale, who had not abjured his fealty to King Edward, preferred to return to their homes, and leave the Earl of Carrick to his new-found loyalty. They departed, leaving him with much depleted forces.

His next move would have been to parley with the châtelaine of Douglas Castle, to whom his change of allegiance was a wonderful stroke of good fortune. It would have been obvious to her that if the Earl of Carrick was not going to besiege her, King Edward would send another, whose loyalty was not in doubt. She decided to accompany the Earl of Carrick to Irvine, where the Scots were encamped, and rejoin her husband. The route took them through the country of Carrick, where Robert de Bruce was able to call his own vassals to arms, and bring a large force to the patriot camp.

The patriots were in disarray, which the Earl of Carrick's arrival did nothing to resolve. James Stewart and Bishop Wishart had supported the claim of Robert de Bruce 'the Competitor' in the Great Cause. William Wallace acknowledged King John as the lawful King of Scotland, and had taken arms in his name. Sir William Douglas had held the castle of Berwick for King John. The arrival of Robert de Bruce, who had been steadfastly loyal to Edward, and had never acknowledged King John, suggested that he had espoused the patriot cause from motives of self-interest. No doubt, taking the long view, he hoped to be king in the end, but in the short view the lawful claim belonged to his father.

While the Scots disputed for whom they were fighting, an English army was approaching. Bishop Anthony Bek, who had been chased out of Glasgow by Wallace, had warned King Edward of the speed with which rebellion was spreading. Edward had ordered two of his northern barons, Henry de Percy and Robert de Clifford, to deal with the rising. They reached Ayr, a few miles south of Irvine, with a body of knights and the shire levies of Cumberland, Westmorland and Lancashire.

The Scots were not prepared to meet such a strong force in the field, and after a prolonged parley they surrendered to King Edward on 7 July 1297, and promised to produce hostages for their good faith. Robert de Bruce was required to surrender his daughter Marjorie as his hostage, and when he refused, three sureties were accepted on his behalf; Bishop Wishart, the Stewart and Sir Alexander Lindsay. It was significant of the importance of his defection that such a hard bargain was driven to bring him into the King's peace. Robert de Bruce the elder was dismissed from his post as Governor of Carlisle, and retired to his estates in southern England. He showed no further interest in his claim to the Scottish throne, though he continued, by his existence, to obstruct the claim of his son. The Stewart and the Earl of Carrick at least remained free, but Bishop Wishart was held prisoner; so was Sir William Douglas, who failed to produce any hostages or sureties. He was imprisoned in Berwick Castle, where he was described as being 'very savage and very abusive', before being transferred to the Tower of London, where he died in 1299.

William Wallace did not surrender, and after the capitulation at Irvine, he was on his own in the west. He did not suffer from confused loyalties. He fought for the independence of Scotland in the name of King John with the same unquestioning loyalty that, centuries later, Jacobite loyalists would show for 'the King over the water'.

Though Wallace had begun his career as an outlaw, he was by now the commander of a large force that represented the old *communis exercitus* – the 'common army' of Scotland, composed of the able-bodied men of sixteen to sixty, summoned to serve within their sheriffdoms. In August he led his army to the east, to lay siege to the English-held castle of Dundee, and to join forces with the leader of the northern rising, who had prospered far better than the quarrelsome commanders of the west.

The leader of the patriot cause in the north was Andrew de Moray, who with his father and uncle had fought at Dunbar and been captured and imprisoned at Chester, whence he had escaped and made for the north. Andrew de Moray was heir to his uncle's lordship of Bothwell and Lanarkshire, and his father's lands in Moray and Cromarty. In May 1297, he called to arms his father's vassals at the Castle of Aroch in the Black Isle, where he was also joined by Alexander Pilche, a burger of Inverness, at the head of a body of citizens.[15]

Their first success was to capture Urquhart Castle on the northern shore of Loch Ness. They went on to capture other English-held castles in north-eastern Scotland, including Inverness, Elgin and Banff. The English Sheriff of Aberdeenshire threw in his lot with them, which gave them control of Aberdeen. The rebellion was extended in the east when Macduff of Fife (whose appeal to English justice had contributed to King John's humiliation), together with his two sons, joined William Wallace. In the late summer of 1297 Andrew de Moray and William Wallace joined forces. King Edward was informed in anguished terms by Hugh de Cressingham that many of the occupying officials had been killed, besieged or imprisoned, and in some shires the Scots had replaced them with officials of their own. The English occupation was still functioning only in Berwickshire and Roxburghshire. For the Scots, it was a time of hope that their kingdom might be reclaimed. The weakness of their position lay in the doubt concerning for whose interest they were fighting.

The Scots owed their success in part to the determination of William Wallace and Andrew de Moray, and in part to the simultaneous difficulties of Edward I. The much higher level of baronial opposition to Edward II tends to deflect attention from the opposition encountered by Edward I. His military adventures were not always popular with subjects who were expected either to join them or contribute to them.

In 1297, when Edward was attempting to mount his much-delayed French expedition, the Earl of Norfolk, Earl Marshal of England, and the Earl of Hereford, Constable of England, both refused to serve overseas. In a famous and dramatic example of defiance, when Edward, exploding with wrath, said to the Marshal, 'By God, my lord, you shall either go or hang!', Norfolk answered, 'By the same oath, lord King, I will neither go nor hang!'[16]

At the same time, Robert Winchelsey, Archbishop of Canterbury, who as a defender of the privileges of the Church was regarded as a worthy successor to St Thomas Becket, forbade the English clergy to contribute to the taxation demanded by King Edward to finance his war. (He was supported by the authority of the papal bull *Clericis Laicos*, which forbade the clergy to pay taxes to secular authority.) In support of Winchelsey, the clergy effectively repudiated their fealty to Edward I, and Edward retaliated by passing sentence of outlawry on the clergy.

In addition to these public and humiliating clashes, Edward experienced defiance in his own family. Attempting to build up his continental alliances, Edward offered the Count of Savoy the hand of his daughter Joan of Acre, recently widowed by the death of her husband Gilbert de Clare, Earl of Gloucester. Joan was forced to reveal that she had made a secret marriage to Raoul de Monthemer, one of her late husband's squires. As a real-life prototype of a favourite figure of medieval romance, the 'Squire of Low Degree' who wins the high-born lady, Monthemer was made to pay for his temerity with a term of imprisonment. Joan was temporarily deprived of her lands, but as Edward I was far more lenient to his daughters than to his troublesome son, Joan was soon forgiven and reunited with Monthemer, who was so far taken into the King's favour that he was granted the title of Earl of Gloucester during the minority of his stepson Gilbert de Clare, Joan's son by her first marriage.

Edward eventually circumvented his difficulties, by means of diplomatic compromises, and departed to France, entrusting the defeat of the Scots' revolt, the strength of which he continued to underestimate, to Earl Warenne.

William Wallace and Andrew de Moray moved south to Stirling, where the crossing of the Forth lay on Warenne's direct route to the north, if he proposed to attempt to recover the strongholds that had fallen to the Scots.

Influenced by the ease of the victory at Dunbar, Warenne was overconfident. In command of a large force of cavalry, he was certain of defeating the foot-soldiers of Scotland's 'common army'. In his past experience, the Scots had been deficient in cavalry, and now they would be more so, because most of the nobility and knighthood captured at

Dunbar remained in Edward's hands. Some of these men were still imprisoned; others had won their liberty by consenting to serve in France. And the nobles and knights who had joined the patriot cause had capitulated at Irvine. In Warenne's view, Wallace and Moray were merely waiting to be crushed.

They, however, had chosen a strong position to defend the crossing of the Forth, and were encamped on the high ground of the Abbey Craig, overlooking Stirling Bridge. The river flows past Stirling, winding a sinuous course through the flat countryside. Warenne encamped in a bend of the river opposite the wooden bridge, whence a causeway led across the soft meadowland towards Stirling. He had no doubt that when he led the army across the bridge the Scots would break ranks as they had done at Dunbar, and that there would be an easy massacre.

Warenne lay encamped for the nights of 9 and 10 September, and on the intervening day two parleys took place. The Stewart and the Earl of Lennox had brought a force of cavalry, but joined neither side. They offered Warenne to negotiate with the Scots for the avoidance of bloodshed, but Wallace and Moray refused to negotiate. This manoeuvre has been seen by some historians as a delaying action, to assist the Scots to strengthen their position further, for the sympathies of both the Stewart and Lennox were not in doubt. Two Dominicans then invited the patriot leaders to surrender with assurance of generous terms, and this time returned with a bellicose answer: 'Tell your Commander that we are not here to make peace but to do battle to defend ourselves and liberate our kingdom. Let them come and we shall prove this in their very beards.'[17]

It appears that Warenne's confidence had been ebbing since his first sight of the Scots' strong position. On the morning of 11 September there was confusion in the English camp at the outset. Someone ordered a party of English infantry to advance across the bridge, and then recalled them when it was discovered that Earl Warenne was still asleep: the battle could not be allowed to begin without the commander-in-chief. When Warenne was ready, he ordered Hugh de Cressingham to lead the cavalry across the bridge, which was only wide enough for the English to ride across two by two.

A Scottish knight named Sir Richard Lundie, who had changed sides at Irvine, disillusioned by the dissension among the Scots, urged Warenne not to send the cavalry across the bridge, but to let him take a force upriver to the Fords of Drip, where there was a broad and unguarded crossing, and take the unsuspecting Scots in the flank. Once they were distracted by this engagement, the cavalry could cross the bridge unimpeded. But Cressingham impatiently overruled his counsels, and Warenne gave the latter the order to advance.

Cressingham led the English knights two by two across the narrow bridge and on to the causeway. For a long time the advance of the cavalry continued without any response from the Scots on the Abbey Craig. Further and further the long line of knights was strung out, and still the Scots did not break ranks. At last Wallace and Moray judged that the English forces were sufficiently exposed for them to attack, and sent their foot-soldiers rushing down from the heights across the meadows, to hit the long column of knights on their extended flank. The destriers plunged off the causeway, and were unable to manoeuvre in the soft ground of the meadows. Fetlock deep in the soft ground, the horses were spitted by spears and gashed by Lochaber axes, and knights spilled helpless on the ground to be slain or captured at will. Meanwhile the further advance of the English was stayed by a second Scottish attack, covering a small detachment of axemen, to hew the timbers of the bridge and send it crashing into the river, to leave the remainder of the English army unable to support the helpless cavalry. Earl Warenne, who had not crossed the bridge, was left to watch the unprecedented spectacle of knights being massacred by infantry. An English knight named Sir Marmaduke de Tweng (who was a cousin of the English branch of the Bruces) was considered to have performed a great feat of arms when he hacked his way free of the massacre and rode hard for the refuge of Stirling Castle, which was still in English hands.

Earl Warenne, having viewed the defeat of his magnificent army with disbelieving horror, then turned tail and rode for Berwick, where it was said that his horse, which had not been fed or watered on the way, foundered on arrival. The Stewart and Lennox threw off the mask of neutrality, and attacked the demoralized remnant of the English army. Hugh de Cressingham had been killed in the mêlée beyond the bridge, and English chroniclers reported that the Scots had flayed his body and sent small pieces of his skin throughout the country as souvenirs of victory.[18] This story has been reported frequently, and without question; but it may be an example of the escalating tales of atrocity that the

Scots and English attributed to each other. Thenceforward the two nations, both of which had believed their neighbours to be civilized people, began to believe that the other was a nation of savages.

The priority of the victorious Scots was to proclaim their kingdom's recovered independence and set it on the road to recovery from the English occupation. The month after Stirling Bridge, on 11 October 1297, Andrew de Moray and William Wallace addressed a joint letter to the mayors and communes of Lübeck and Hamburg, informing them that Scotland had been reclaimed from the power of the English, and the ports of Scotland were once more open to German merchants.[19] Though Berwick had been lost, the recovery of Inverness and Aberdeen facilitated trade with the German ports. The story of Scotland's struggle for independence is frequently told in terms of heroic military actions; yet not only the success but the very possibility of these depended upon Scotland's trade with continental arms manufacturers through merchants who were the international arms dealers of the period.

Before the end of October, Andrew de Moray died, presumably from wounds received at the battle of Stirling Bridge. A wound did not need to be severe to prove fatal, for if even a small wound became septic or gangrenous the wounded man was beyond the help of medical skill. This was probably the fate of Moray.

During October and November, Wallace carried war into England, invading Northumberland and Durham, spreading devastation and terror, and driving the population into headlong flight. In the course of this reign of terror the hero of the Scots became a figure of nightmare to the English, an illustration of the truism that one nation's freedom fighter is another nation's terrorist. The heroic image of such a warrior cannot be shared until the conflict in which he fought has been cleansed of passion, and consigned to a past as free of partisanship as the wars of the Greeks and the Trojans.

An invasion, which gave England the message that Scotland had ceased to be a victim and had become capable of aggression, was accompanied by a diplomatic initiative of more profound value. Bishop Fraser of St Andrews, who years previously had written to King Edward I encouraging him to support John Balliol's claim to the kingship, had recently died in France, never having returned to Scotland after the general capitulation of the kingdom at Berwick in 1296. On 3 November 1297, while William Wallace was in England, the cathedral chapter of St Andrews, at Wallace's instigation, elected as their new Archbishop Master William Lamberton, Chancellor of the Cathedral of Glasgow, a friend of Bishop Wishart who would prove a subtle and determined upholder of the cause of Scottish independence. Lamberton departed to Rome, to be consecrated by Pope Boniface VIII on 1 June 1298.

The successes of Wallace brought the disputatious magnates of Scotland together. In March 1298 the earls, barons and churchmen who supported the patriotic cause met in the Forest of Selkirk. The great southern forest was not unbroken woodland; it contained open areas where Wallace's soldiers could encamp and large forest clearings where gatherings could be held, concealed by the surrounding woods. At the so-called 'Forest Parliament' William Wallace was elected Guardian of Scotland. Unlike the earlier Guardians, he held office alone: the appointment demonstrated confidence in his military prowess and political capability, but may also imply that disagreement among the magnates prevented them from entrusting the office to one of themselves. One of the earls knighted Wallace, thus giving him the status that would enable him to deal with the greater nobility and foreign powers in the theoretical equality of the chivalric order.[20]

There were four earls present at the Forest Parliament: Buchan, Strathearn, Lennox and Carrick. Legend has it that Sir William Wallace was knighted by Robert de Bruce, Earl of Carrick, symbolically linking the legendary heroes, but there is no evidence as to which of the earls performed the ceremony.[21] Wallace continued to act in the name of John Balliol, and documents issued under his Guardianship appeared in the name of 'William Wallace, Knight, Guardian of the Kingdom of Scotland and Commander of its armies in the name of the famous Prince, Lord John, by God's grace illustrious King of Scotland, by consent of the community of that realm'.

Edward I returned to England on 14 March 1298, probably at about the same time that Wallace became Guardian of Scotland. Edward had agreed an armistice with the King of France, which was to last until 6 January 1299. This gave him time to direct his attention to the conquest of Scotland, and he demonstrated his determination by moving his seat of government to York, on 25 May. Thenceforward the conquest of Scotland became his overriding obsession: the challenge which initially seemed to be that of defeating one rebel leader was to multiply itself and outlast his lifetime.

Edward's new invasion of Scotland was elaborately prepared; he composed his quarrel with the Earl Marshal and the Constable of England, who led their own contingents of knights to Scotland. Edward's 'Commissioners of Array' recruited more cavalry from those who owed knight service, and these were paid wages by the King. A formidable force of 2,500 cavalry was amassed; Welsh longbowmen and Gascon crossbowmen were conscripted and waged by the King, together with a large force of Welsh infantry. Unmounted troops totalled some 12,000. A fleet of supply ships sailed up the coast to liaise with the land army at Leith. The English army entered Scotland on 1 July, and by 15 July was encamped at Kirkliston, near Edinburgh, on lands belonging to Bishop Lamberton, which it afforded the English King particular pleasure to despoil. But the most enthusiastic plunder could not provide enough supplies for so vast a host, and the English invasion faced mass starvation, as stormy weather had prevented the arrival of the supply ships. The first ships to arrive carried more wine than food, and much of the liquor and little of the food reached the Welsh, who when drunk brawled with the English, and men of both nations were killed. The Welsh threatened to desert and join the Scots, and might have done had anyone known their whereabouts.

Unfortunately for the Scots, King Edward's prayers to St John of Beverley, whose shrine he had visited on the march north, appeared to find favour with the saint. The supply ships arrived, the army was provisioned, and the pro-English Earl of Dunbar sent King Edward news that the Scots army was encamped near Falkirk. Edward ordered the advance, and moved his army as far as Linlithgow, where it bivouacked, with the knights sleeping on the ground beside their horses. Edward gave an example of hardihood by sharing their discomfort, and in the night he was trampled by his destrier and sustained two broken ribs. In the morning, despite this painful injury, he insisted on mounting and riding at the head of his troops.

Wallace had selected a strong position: he had drawn up his men on a hillside, with a loch and surrounding marsh at the foot of it. A palisade of stakes, roped together, stretched across the slope of the hill.

Behind this defensive line the Scottish infantry was drawn up in four 'schiltroms' (circular formations of spearmen, ringed with shields, between which the spears projected, the classic formation of the Scottish army). Between the schiltroms were drawn up companies of archers from Selkirk Forest. In the rear was a small force of cavalry.[22] Wallace knew that he was occupying less favourable ground than at Stirling Bridge, and that he faced a better general than Earl Warenne. His battlefield oration was short and to the point: 'I have brought you to the ring: dance the best you can.'[23]

The English cavalry charged and, divided by the loch and surrounding marsh, swerved apart to attack the Scots simultaneously on both flanks. The Scottish cavalry fled, the lightly armed archers were mown down, and their commander, the Stewart's brother, was killed. The spearmen of the schiltroms were decimated by a deadly rain of arrows from the Welsh longbows and bolts from the Gascon crossbows. A final cavalry charge broke the formation of the schiltroms, and the battle ended as a massacre. Among the dead were Macduff of Fife and his two sons. Wallace and other survivors fled into the Torwood, a great expanse of woodland between Falkirk and Stirling which, like Selkirk Forest, performed the friendly function of concealment.

The victory of Stirling Bridge had conferred on Wallace an aura of legend; he had achieved the impossible – with an army of infantry he had defeated the chivalry of England. The defeat of Falkirk destroyed his magic; the accepted truth had reasserted itself, that footmen were unable to withstand the charge of armed knights. Unless he could lead the 'common army' to victory, there was no justification for a simple knight to hold office as Guardian of Scotland.

Wallace resigned his Guardianship and was replaced by a pair of Guardians: Robert de Bruce, Earl of Carrick, and John Comyn, 'The Red Comyn' of Badenoch, son of the Comyn of Badenoch who had been one of the original Guardians, and nephew of John Balliol. The new Guardianship may have been intended to create a balance of power between the dominant interests in the kingdom, but it was an impossible partnership, for the interests of Bruce and Comyn were fundamentally opposed, and the two men were incompatible.

The Red Comyn was hot-tempered, fiercely patriotic and utterly committed to the Balliol cause. Robert de Bruce maintained the stance of Bruce the Competitor, who had absolutely refused to acknowledge Balliol as king:

> But off Robert the Brews he
> Gat nowthir homage, na fenté
>
> [But of Robert the Bruce he
> Got neither homage nor fealty][24]

This refusal had continued unbroken through three generations. The Earl of Carrick, the Competitor's grandson, accepted office as Guardian in a regime that took over from a Guardian who had acknowledged John Balliol as the rightful King of Scots. Comyn had every reason for viewing Robert de Bruce with the deepest suspicion; if Bruce, for a brief period, appeared to have set aside his own ambition, certainly he had not abandoned it.

Early in 1299 William Lamberton, the newly consecrated Bishop of St Andrews, returned from Rome accompanied by David de Moray (a kinsman of Andrew de Moray), who had also gone to Rome and been consecrated as Bishop of Moray by Pope Boniface VIII. The two bishops had succeeded in persuading the Pope to intervene with Edward I on behalf of John Balliol, as a result of which Edward had agreed to release John into papal custody. Edward I presumably regarded John as a spent force, but Bishop Lamberton wanted his restoration as King of Scots. His release would have been good news to the Red Comyn, and a threat to the ambitions of Robert de Bruce.

In August 1299 the Scottish patriots, more than usually quarrelsome following the failure of their attempt to recapture Roxburgh Castle, met in Selkirk Forest. An English spy, who had infiltrated their counsels, reported a stormy meeting:

> At the council, Sir David Graham demanded the lands and goods of Sir William Wallace because he was leaving the kingdom without the leave or approval of the Guardians [on a self-appointed diplomatic mission to win support for Scotland abroad]. And Sir Malcolm, Sir William's brother, answered that neither his lands nor his goods should be given away, for they were protected by the peace in which Wallace had left the kingdom. At this the two knights gave the lie to

each other and drew their daggers . . . and John Comyn leapt at the Earl of Carrick and seized him by the throat and the Earl of Buchan turned on the Bishop of St Andrews declaring that treason and *lèse majesté* were being plotted. [Is the implication that the Earl of Carrick was believed to be plotting against Balliol?] Eventually the Stewart and others came between them and quieted them . . .[25]

As a means of keeping the peace between Bruce and Comyn, Bishop Lamberton joined them as senior Guardian, with control of all the castles in Scottish lands, thus removing an obvious source of discord between them. In November 1299 the three Guardians, with their forces based in the Torwood, emerged to lay siege to Stirling Castle. King Edward attempted to mount an expedition for the relief of Stirling, but there was strong resistance to facing the rigours of a winter campaign; the relief was abortive, and the castle fell to the Scots.

However, Edward determined on a new campaign in the spring, and on 30 December 1299 he commanded a full feudal levy to muster at Carlisle on 24 June 1300.[26] Thus the Scots had ample warning that he intended invasion in the west. The Comyns proposed to support the men of Galloway, Balliol's vassals, in resisting the English; Bruce was more concerned to defend his own power-base, in Carrick. To the existing discord between Bruce and Comyn was added a revival of the old enmity between Galloway and Carrick.

In the spring of 1300 Robert de Bruce was edged out of the Guardianship, and his place was taken by Sir Ingram de Umfraville, who was a partisan of the Comyns and a kinsman of Balliol. It seemed that political power was slipping through Bruce's fingers, and when the kingdom faced the threat of new invasion, all that he could do was prepare to defend his own portion of it.

At midsummer King Edward came to Carlisle, accompanied by his son and his new wife, Margaret of France, sister of King Philip IV, whom he had married the previous year as part of a peace process with the French King. In age she would have been a more suitable bride for the King's son, as many people must have murmured at the time, but contrary to appearances, she was probably more fortunate to have the old king for her husband, for the prince was already entwined in the relationship with Piers Gaveston that would doom his own marriage from the outset.

The King intended that the invasion of Galloway should be his son's military debut, and a poem that celebrated the expedition described Edward of Caernarvon in flattering terms:

> He was of a well-proportioned handsome person,
> Of a courteous disposition, and well-bred,
> And desirous of finding an occasion
> To make proof of his strength.
> He managed his steed wonderfully well.[27]

The poet admiringly described the colourful splendours of the English army, the medley of heraldic blazons on shields, surcoats, horse-trappings, pennons, banners and tents. The English advance into Galloway was very different from the disorderly preliminaries to the Falkirk campaign. There was no plundering; wheat for the army's bread ration was imported from Cumbria, and the provender was paid for on the spot. Probably the display of well-ordered power was intended to overawe the Gallovidians, and to suggest the advantage of making submission to such a powerful king. The English army laid siege to the castle of Caerlaverock, near Dumfries, and the poet of the expedition represented its capture after five days as a great feat of arms; but perhaps it was more remarkable that a small garrison had attempted any resistance at all.

King Edward advanced into Galloway, through the low-lying country beside the Solway Firth, with an impenetrable land of high hills and forests on his right hand. He advanced as far as Wigtown without meeting opposition or gaining adherents. There seemed little point in taking a parade of power further and further from its base without a military objective. Edward turned back. At Kirkcudbright he was met by the Earl of Buchan and the Red Comyn, who proposed peace, their terms being the restoration of King John and the opportunity for dispossessed Scottish magnates to repurchase their estates. Edward might have been in retreat through an empty countryside, but he was not in retreat from the Scots. He refused to consider these terms, and the Comyns left him. Shortly afterwards a Scots force appeared to contest the English crossing of the River Cree, but an English cavalry charge routed them, and Edward continued his return march.

On 24 August, King Edward was at Smeetham Abbey (the foundation of King John's mother Lady Devorguilla). Here Archbishop Winchelsey arrived to deliver the papal bull addressed to him by Pope Boniface VIII, *Scimus Fili*.[28] The Pope, who held a high view of his office as the spiritual superior of Christian kings, counselled Edward to cease his attempts to conquer Scotland, since it was a fief of the Holy See. The courageous Winchelsey followed a reading of the bull with an admonition of his own to 'obey for the love of Mount Zion and Jerusalem' (i.e. for the sake of the crusading ideal, to which all Christian kings were theoretically committed). Edward answered violently, 'By God's blood I will not keep my peace for Mount Zion nor silence for Jerusalem but while there is breath to my nostrils I will defend my right, which all the world knows, with all my power.'

His vehement response probably mirrored his anger at the failure of his expedition, which external interference threatened to exacerbate. His vassals were refusing to serve beyond the time limit of their feudal obligations; and the levies from the northern counties were deserting. The campaign of 1300 was effectively a failure. In the autumn Edward accepted the diplomacy of the French King, who contracted a truce between Scotland and England, to extend until 21 May 1301.

The period of the truce was occupied by a war of words. The Pope was informed that England's claim to superiority over Scotland dated from the time when the three sons of the Trojan fugitive Brutus ruled over Albion: Locrinus over England, Albanactus over Scotland and Camber over Wales, and Locrinus as the eldest son was the superior.[29] The reply of the Scots was composed by a learned cleric, Master Baldred Bisset, who asserted, 'The whole of Scotland is named after the woman Scota [the daughter of Pharaoh] . . . Therefore the Scots and Scotland are no concern of the King of England: and the English could have claimed no more of a right to the Kingdom of Scotland than the Egyptians.'[30] In marshalling evidence from national mythology, Baldred deployed his arguments with elegant irony.

> Agoyne all resownys that he could set
> Maystyre Baldred the Beset
> A wys clerk and accumenand
> Ane off the messyngyrs off Scotland
> Answeryd to their resownys welle
> And dystroyed thane ilka dele

[Against all arguments he set
Master Baldred the Bisset
A wise clerk and intelligent
A message from Scotland sent
Rebutting every point well-polished
Every one of them demolished][31]

Before the expiry of the Anglo-Scottish truce a new Guardian of Scotland was appointed to replace the Lamberton-Comyn-Umfraville triumvirate. Once again there was a single Guardian, Sir John de Soules, who was probably the nominee of John Balliol.[32] There was a new seal of government with the name and title of King John on the obverse and the name and style of the Guardian on the reverse. Henceforward documents under the seal were issued in the name of King John, or of Edward Balliol as heir of the kingdom, with the Guardian as witness.[33] Though King John's restoration was far from being a reality, these measures showed the intentions of the Scots patriots.

Edward I was determined to prevent the restoration, and long before the end of the truce he was preparing for a new invasion.

On 7 February 1301 King Edward created his son Prince of Wales, and on the eve of the campaign gave him nominal command of half the English army, under the guidance of an experienced soldier, Henry de Lacy, Earl of Lincoln. On the campaign Edward of Caernarvon was accompanied by the two men whose fates would be closely involved with his own, one in hatred and the other in love: his first cousin and later his bitterest enemy, Thomas of Lancaster, and his alter ego, Piers Gaveston. Already the chief actors of the next reign were moving towards the centre of the stage.

King Edward's new plan was a double invasion; the Prince was to invade the south-west from Carlisle, as his father had done the previous year, but to press onward through Galloway, and up the west coast towards Ayr. In breaking the resistance in the south-west, his father intended he should 'gain the chief honour of taming the pride of the Scots'. The King himself would invade Scotland by way of Berwick, and advance across country, through Tweedale and thence down Clydesdale to capture the castle of Bothwell. The English were still in control of Lothian, so that if Edward and his son could seal off Scotland from the Forth to the Clyde, the resistance in the south-west would be isolated, and could be crushed at leisure. Like many military plans, it looked better on the map than on the ground. King Edward captured Bothwell Castle, on or about 24 September, and the Prince, with the assistance of a force brought over from Ireland, captured Turnberry from Robert de Bruce. But Robert, who since he ceased to be Guardian had been operating on his own in the south-west, remained in control of 'the army of Carrick', his own vassals. Though he had been forced to abandon the castle, the new English garrison was soon beleaguered and isolated, and a series of lightning attacks on the Prince's force drove him to retreat to Carlisle. The steel trap to contain the south-west never closed. King Edward retired from Bothwell to winter at Linlithgow, where the Prince joined him. Father and son could congratulate each other on the capture of two castles, but the main purpose of the expedition had not been achieved.

In the autumn of 1301 John Balliol was released by the Pope from his agreeable custody at Gevrey-Chambertin, and sent by the King of France to his own castle of Bailleul-en-Vimeu, in Picardy, a free man.[34] King Edward was informed that 'some people believe that the King of France will send him with a great force to Scotland as soon as possible'.[35] And the rumour swept Scotland that the restoration of King John was imminent.

King Edward endeavoured to counter the threat by negotiating a new Anglo-French truce (the peace, which his marriage to Margaret of France was supposed to cement, had never been finalized). In the new truce, formalized on 26 January 1302, the Scots were included, but Edward had to agree that the lands, towns and castles recently captured in Scotland would be placed in French custody, awaiting the negotiations for a general peace.[36]

To Robert de Bruce, the increasing perplexity of his position in recent years was compounded by these developments. If Balliol returned, it was the Comyns who would be the powers behind the throne – and he could foresee that his patrimony of Annandale, which Balliol had formerly given to the Earl of Buchan, would be given to him again. Now, pending a general peace, the recently captured castle of Turnberry, his maternal inheritance, would be placed in French hands, and whether it would be returned to him or to the King was not foreseeable.

Only one thing was certain: there was no future for him in Scotland if John Balliol regained the throne. His grandfather, his father and himself had consistently refused to recognize the kingship of Balliol, and he was not about to do so. If he aspired to be king hereafter, his position had never been weaker, and he could not assert his claim so long as his father lived. Whether or not they were estranged, it was a long time since they had met. It was at least consistent with the former policy of his family that he preferred to make peace with King Edward than with John Balliol. Probably at about the time of the conclusion of the Anglo-Franco-Scottish truce, in January 1302, he emerged from the wild country of Carrick and surrendered to Sir John de St John.[37]

6

—————|✳|✳|✳|—————

'HE WOULD BE CROWN'D'

'. . . He would be crown'd;
How that might change his nature, there's the
question.'[1]

WHEN ADMIRERS OF William Wallace and Robert de Bruce discuss
which hero was the greater man, the surrender of Bruce to Edward I
in 1302 seems to leave his supporters at a disadvantage. As a patriot
Wallace was absolutely consistent; he had never acknowledged Edward
I as his overlord. In another sense, Bruce was also consistent; he never
acknowledged John Balliol as King of Scots. Thus, when he himself
became king, he was able to claim that he was the true successor of
Alexander III (the legitimacy of their claim being the credo of the
Bruce family), and the kingship of John Balliol was ignored as an
English intervention.

The years following his surrender to King Edward were probably the
most difficult years of Robert's life, in terms of mental conflict. Later,
after he had made his bid for the throne, he suffered almost unendurable hardships and dangers – such sufferings, he is reputed to have said,
that without the inspiration of regaining Scotland's freedom, he would
not have undergone them to rule the world. But by that time his mind
was clear, and his path was straight, even if almost insuperably difficult
to follow. In the meantime, every decision had to be an *ad hoc* decision,
based on his determination to stay alive and to stay free, to salvage
whatever could be salvaged from an intractable situation, awaiting the
time and chance when his ambition might be realized.

His adherence to Edward was so valuable that his surrender initially
carried no threat to his life; indeed, in the face of a French threat to

restore John Balliol, he was able to exact guarantees of Edward's future favour. The agreement that they reached was formally recorded in a document in French issued under King Edward's privy seal:

Note that because Robert Bruce the younger who was in the homage and allegiance of the King of England for the Earldom of Carrick, but, because of evil advice arose up in war against the King his lord, has surrendered himself to the peace and the will of the King, in hope of receiving his mercy; the King, because of the good service done to the King and his ancestors by the ancestors and kin of Robert, and because of the good service that Robert has promised to do in time to come, has declared [that] . . . Robert, and his vassals and his tenants in Carrick, shall be unharmed in life and limb, and in lands and tenements, and free from imprisonment.

If it should happen that by a papal ordinance or a truce or a peace declared in the war with Scotland or with France, the aforesaid Robert were so hindered that he could not enjoy his own estates, of which he is now seised in Scotland, the King promises to take his loss into acount, so that he may have a reasonable income, as is appropriate to him. The King, so far as in him lies, grants to Robert that he be not disinherited of any land which may come to him by right of his father, in England or in Scotland. The King grants to Robert the wardship and marriage of the son and heir of the Earl of Mar. [Donald, Earl of Mar, the minor, was Robert's nephew, the son of his sister Christian de Bruce by her first husband Gartnait, Earl of Mar, who had died recently. Her second husband was an English knight, Sir Christopher Seton, who became Robert's devoted adherent.]

Because [Robert fears that] the realm of Scotland might be removed from the hands of the King, which God forbid, and delivered to John Balliol or to his son, or that the right might be put in question, or reversed and repealed to a new judgement, the King . . . grants to Robert that he may pursue his right and he will give him a fair hearing and treat him justly in his court, and if by any chance it happen that the right ought to be tried elsewhere than in the King's court, in that case the King promises help and advice to Robert, so far as he can properly give it. If, after the realm of Scotland is at peace in the hands of the King, any persons wish to vex Robert by [words missing] the King will support him in his right and defend him, so far as a lord should do his vassal. As evidence of all these things, the King has caused this letter patent to be written, and sealed with his privy seal.[2]

What exactly 'the right' (*le droit*) in which King Edward promised Robert his 'help and support' (*aide e consail*) was has been much debated.[3] The most sensible conclusion seems to be that of the historian who suggests that King Edward had 'decided to answer a possible papal recognition of Balliol's right by a promise to re-examine the Bruce right', and that in the face of the ominous Franco-papal support for Balliol, Bruce made his peace with Edward I 'on conditions which offered him some chance of the Scottish throne'.[4]

With the recollection of Edward's judgement against his grandfather in the Great Cause, and contemptuous treatment of his father, Robert de Bruce probably had little faith in Edward's undertakings, but while it suited Edward to favour him, he seized the advantage, both for himself and his family. From 1302 his wardship of the young Earl of Mar gave him profitable control of the Mar estates in north-east Scotland, including the strong castle of Kildrummy, and in 1305 he asked for and was granted the forfeited estates of Sir Ingram de Umfraville, when the erstwhile Guardian was exiled.[5] His younger brother Edward de Bruce entered the household of Edward of Caernarvon, which may have been advantageous but is unlikely to have been congenial to him. In knightly accomplishments Edward de Bruce was little inferior to his brother, and in war would prove himself an able if impetuous commander, whereas Edward of Caernarvon, although a good horseman and not devoid of courage, astonished his contemporaries by his lack of interest in martial arts, and his preference for rowing, swimming and rural crafts. For these tastes Edward de Bruce would probably have despised him. Yet not all his knightly companions did so; Donald, Earl of Mar, was a close friend who remained loyal to him in his later misfortune. Robert's third brother, Alexander, also received the King's favour, after a brilliant career at Cambridge where 'No-one who read arts at Cambridge before or since his time ever made such progress. He was master of arts before his brother was King of Scotland.'[6] King Edward provided him with the living of Kirkinner, near Wigtown, and he became Dean of Glasgow in 1306, possibly after his brother became King.[7] This was a typical example of royal or aristocratic nepotism, which frequently led to unsuitable appointments, but perhaps was justified in this instance by the young man's learning.

In 1302 Robert married his second wife, Elizabeth de Burgh, daughter of Richard de Burgh, Earl of Ulster. As the marriage took place after Robert's submission to King Edward, it can be assumed to have had Edward's blessing, for the Earl of Ulster was his ally, albeit a turbulent and independent one. But the marriage had other advantages, too, for it strengthened the Bruce connection with Northern Ireland, which Robert always valued, and it created a new link to the Stewarts, since Egidia de Burgh, Elizabeth's aunt, was the wife of James the High Steward. The marriage, which would soon make the Earl of Ulster's daughter a queen, would also demand all her qualities of fortitude and endurance.

The tripartite truce expired on 30 November 1302, by which time Edward was already preparing for war with Scotland again. The international situation had changed in his favour, for the threats with which the year had opened were removed.

Philip IV of France became involved in a power struggle with Pope Boniface VIII, initiated by the Pope's high claim to authority over temporal rulers. Despite his claim Boniface needed allies, so he abandoned the moral high ground from which he had addressed Edward in *Scimus Fili*, and sought Edward's alliance by turning against the Scots and exhorting them to show obedience to Edward as their overlord. Bishop Wishart he chided for being 'a stone of offence' (a stumbling-block) to this obedience.

While the Pope sought King Edward's friendship, the King of France also needed to make peace with him. He had lost his grip on his recently annexed territories when the citizens of Flanders rose in revolt, slaughtered or expelled the French garrisons in their towns, and then went on to inflict a crushing and humiliating defeat on the army of France at Courtrai, on 11 July 1302. Like Stirling Bridge, but on a grander scale, Courtrai was the defeat of a host of knights by massed spearmen on foot. Once again the unthinkable had happened, and among imaginative commanders it would lead to a great deal of reconsideration of the art of war. For Philip of France one humiliation led to another. Inspired by the Flemings, the citizens of Bordeaux, formerly in Edward's domains, and lately annexed by Philip, also drove the French garrison from the city. Philip decided that the time had come to convert his truce with Edward into a formal peace, even at the cost of a restitution of the annexed territory.

The Scots were desperate not to lose the support of the French, as they had that of the Pope. The Guardian, Sir John de Soules, led a Scots delegation to France to plead their cause with the King. He was accompanied by Bishop Lamberton, the Stewart, the Earl of Buchan, and Sir Ingram de Umfraville. The Red Comyn remained in Scotland as acting Guardian.[8]

Despite their best endeavours, King Philip abandoned them.[9] On 30 May 1303 he sealed an offensive and defensive alliance with King Edward, from which the Scots were excluded. It was to be confirmed by the marriage of Edward of Caernarvon with Philip's daughter, Isabella of France. The marriage, which did not take place until 1307, would be one of the most famously disastrous royal marriages of history.

King Edward was not ready to go to war with the Scots at the beginning of 1303, but he ordered a reconnaissance in strength to be led by Sir John Segrave and Ralph Manton, the 'Officer of the Wardrobe' – 'the royal wardrobe being a department of the household which was used by English Kings in preference to the exchequer to fund their wars'.[10] Manton's role would have been to assess the costs of the projected campaign. On the evening of 24 February they had reached Roslin, south of Edinburgh, and encamped, when they were attacked by a mounted force led by Comyn and Sir Simon Fraser. Manton was killed, and Segrave wounded and taken prisoner, though he was subsequently rescued by a relieving force led by Robert Neville of Raby. Jubilantly, the Scots claimed a major victory; but in reality Roslin was a small affair which did not deflect King Edward from the invasion that he planned for the spring.

It was the most elaborately planned of all his Scottish campaigns, and not unexpectedly, since the Scots had been left naked to their enemies, the most successful. As in 1301, he planned a double invasion: one force, nominally commanded by Edward of Caernarvon, would enter Scotland by the western route; King Edward himself would take the eastern route, and since Robert de Bruce was now his ally, and there was no necessity to attempt to encircle Carrick, he would take the route for the north-east, and attempt to subdue the still-independent north.

Edward of Caernarvon made thorough preparations, gathering supplies of weapons, tents and armour, and ordering three banners bearing his own arms and the emblems of St Edward the Confessor, St Edmund and St George. The Prince left London on 13 March, and reached Scotland in mid-May. He was accompanied by Robert de Bruce, who at the end of the expedition remained in command of the castle of Ayr. In support of them Robert's father-in-law, the Earl of Ulster, brought a force from Ireland, and captured the castles of Rothesay on Bute and Inverkip on the mainland. At the end of the summer Ulster's unpaid soldiery, having maintained themselves by plunder, left for home, though the Earl himself, together with other Anglo-Irish magnates and their retinues, remained to support the English King.

King Edward determined that his invasion of north-eastern Scotland should not be held back by laying siege to Stirling, where the great fortress guarded the ill-fated crossing of the Forth. To circumvent it, he had three floating bridges constructed at King's Lynn, and towed up the coast and into the Firth of Forth. On this occasion the weather favoured his enterprise. By the end of July he had reached Brechin, where his advance was halted by a valiant defence of Brechin Castle by Sir Thomas Maule. The castle surrendered when its commander was killed on the battlements on 9 August, and Edward continued his march, which brought him to his northernmost point, Kinloss Abbey, in September. King Edward then turned south again, travelling by way of Lochindorb, and made Dunfermline Abbey his winter quarters, where he remained from October 1303 to February 1304.

Although Edward had received submissions from many Scots in the course of his northward thrust and return journey, the patriot leaders had continued to resist. From France Bishop Lamberton had written to William Wallace, now back in Scotland again, and exhorted him to renew the struggle against Edward, and had also ordered his officials to provide Wallace with part of the revenue of the diocese.[11] Wallace and Simon Fraser harassed the English occupying forces from their base in Selkirk Forest.

Despite the continuance of unofficial resistance, on 9 February 1304

John Comyn, in his capacity as Guardian, acknowledged defeat, and submitted to King Edward at Staithord, near Perth. Edward's position was not so strong that he could demand an unconditional surrender, and Comyn, negotiating on behalf of the 'Community of Scotland', demanded that the Scots should be 'protected in all their laws, usages, customs, and liberties in every particular as they existed in the time of Alexander III, unless there are laws to be amended, in which case it shall be done with the advice of King Edward and the advice and assent of the responsible men of the land'.[12] The concluding sentence rendered Comyn's demands nugatory, but saved his face. Sentences of exile were passed on some resistance leaders, notably Bishop Wishart, who had already suffered for his patriotism but was to suffer much more. The patriotism of Wishart has received the respect of posterity, but that of Sir John de Soules has been less honoured. But the former Guardian, though he was not personally victimized, preferred perpetual exile to submission to King Edward.

The submission of Comyn and the absence of Soules emphasized the resistance of the patriot who remained at large and unreconciled – Sir William Wallace. Edward's special venom against Wallace must be explained by the fact that Wallace alone had inflicted a major defeat on English arms and had never compromised his independence by even a formal act of homage, like so many of the magnates whose oaths Edward had accepted with cynicism. Edward declared that: 'No words of peace are to be held out to William Wallace in any circumstances.'[13]

The Stewart, Sir Ingram de Umfraville and Sir John de Soules (who did not come) were not to have safe conducts to come to Edward's presence until Wallace had been given up, and Sir John Comyn, Sir Simon Fraser and others were ordered to seek him for twenty days after Christmas, and to watch one another's efforts, so that the man who most exerted himself would be most rewarded, or should be regarded as having expiated past misdeeds.

In February 1304 Robert de Bruce was ordered to leave Ayr and join Sir John Segrave on a *chevauchée* (mounted commando raid) into Selkirk Forest, to capture Wallace and Simon Fraser (who evidently had not complied with the King's recent request to hunt down his ally). There was fighting in the Forest, and the followers of Wallace and Fraser were scattered, but the two leaders escaped. King Edward seems to have believed that Bruce had given them prior warning, for he gave the famous caution 'as the cloak is well made, also make the hood'.[14] (This arcane and menacing utterance presumably meant 'If you wish to cloak your deception you must do better than that'.)

In March 1304 the situation of Robert de Bruce decisively changed. His father died, and at last the Bruce claim to the throne of Scotland devolved upon him. There was no action that he could take immediately, but it concentrated his ambition.

He hurried south to take possession of his English lands. At the same time King Edward decided to lay siege to Stirling Castle, which he had bypassed on his northward march. He sent word to Robert in England, to supply troops for the siege from his patrimony, and on 4 April 1304 Robert replied that he had been endeavouring in every possible way to procure horses and armour for himself and his people, but had had no success whatsoever in attempting to raise loans for the purpose, and so far had not obtained a penny of his rents.[15] Similarly, when Edward asked him to supply siege engines, he complied, but sent them without an essential component part.[16]

These sound like two quite obvious ploys to sabotage Edward's war effort, but probably they were less obvious than they seem. The first might have been a valid excuse, the second a genuine mishap. And in so vast an organizational effort as the siege of one of Scotland's strongest fortresses, Edward had more to think about than the actions of one magnate among the many who were called upon for men and supplies. Robert de Bruce, important though he was, was not always at the centre of the King's attention.

Bruce arrived at Stirling in May, to pay homage to Edward for his English lands, and to watch the castle being pounded by Edward's thirteen great siege machines, now in working order. They had prosaic nicknames: the Vicar, the Parson, the Belfry – examples of the curious military psychology, demonstrated throughout the ages, of giving harmless-sounding names to engines of destruction (e.g. 'Mons Meg', 'Dulle Griet', 'Big Bertha', 'Little Boy', 'Fat Man'). The exception was Edward's newest and most formidable machine, called the 'War Wolf'.

These machines were not the ineffective toys imagined from the perspective of a century that possesses so much more sophisticated weaponry. The siege of Stirling in 1304 witnessed the first known use of gunpowder in Britain.[17] Edward employed a Burgundian military engineer, Jean de Lombardy, who produced 'Greek Fire', a mixture of sulphur and saltpetre packed into earthenware pots and probably also mixed with pitch, to explode and spread fire on impact. These early 'bombs', hurled over the castle walls by the siege machines, could set the timber buildings within the stone curtain walls in a blaze far beyond the resources of the castle well to extinguish.

King Edward's attention to the siege gave Robert de Bruce the opportunity to slip away and meet Bishop Lamberton in the Abbey of Cambuskenneth, in a bend of the Forth, on the low-lying land below the castle. There, with the sounds of war audible in the distance, they spoke of Scotland's future, Robert's claim, Lamberton's commitment to it, and most probably also of the prospects of Edward's death. When he died, Robert's best chance to assert his claim would come. Edward was old by the standards of medieval kingship, and his undiminished courage almost cost him his life before the walls of Stirling, when his horse, frighted by the crash of a stone projectile from the walls, reared and fell on him. In all the chances of war he had seemed to lead a charmed life, but he could not be immortal. The Bishop's talk with Robert essentially marked the end of Balliol's kingship; the support of the papal members of the Church was henceforth transferred to Bruce. On 11 June 1304 Bruce and Lamberton signed a bond at the Abbey which said nothing of these things, but formalized their secret agreement which would be revealed by its fruits. The terms of the agreement were:

> That they should mutually help each other in all their several businesses and affairs at all times and against all other persons whatever without any deceit and that neither of them should undertake any important business without the other of them. They will mutually warn each other against any impending danger and do the best to avert the same from each other and for the full performance of the agreement they bound themselves by oath and under the penalty of the sum of £10,000 to be applied for the recovery of the Holy Land.[18]

Neither signatory was in doubt that this bond, however studiously vague, placed both of them in great danger, should King Edward come to hear of it. But he did not do so, for all his attention was upon the siege.

Stirling Castle was defended by Sir William Oliphant, who had been appointed by Sir John de Soules to hold the castle in the name of King John. At the beginning of the siege, Oliphant requested leave to send a message to Soules, to know whether he should surrender the castle or attempt to hold it. King Edward denied Oliphant this courtesy with the words 'If he thinks it will be better for him to defend the castle than to yield it, he will see'.[19] Oliphant chose to defend it, and recognizing that the king on whose behalf he had been entrusted with it would never return, he proclaimed that he was defending it on behalf of 'the Lion', the symbol of Scottish monarchy represented on the royal standard on the castle keep.[20] He was not fighting 'for an abstraction, which was alien to the age',[21] but for a heraldic symbol, which was entirely in accordance with it.

Edward I ended the siege as unchivalrously as he had begun it. Having refused Oliphant permission to communicate with Sir John de Soules at the beginning, he refused to let him surrender with military honours at the end. He insisted on unconditional surrender, and then threatened the commander and garrison with the penalties of a traitor's death, until the respect of his entourage for Oliphant's courage made him think better of it. Even so, he refused to accept the surrender until he had taken the opportunity to observe the effects of the lately arrived 'War Wolf' on the castle walls. Queen Margaret and her ladies were given the opportunity to watch this exciting spectacle, before the commander and garrison were permitted to leave, and required to sue for their lives, as a prelude to being imprisoned.

To be magnanimous to a brave enemy was a tenet of the chivalric code quite frequently observed, but King Edward, in the increasingly savage temper of his last years, often ignored it. Appropriately magnanimous treatment of Oliphant would have been to let him depart to France. Imprisonment was ungenerous, but at least it gave him his life.

When William Wallace fell into English hands the following year, he could not expect even the most grudging show of mercy. Though he was a knight, and an erstwhile Guardian of Scotland, and should at least have been regarded as a prisoner of war, Edward persisted in regarding him as an outlaw and felon, and yet more unjustly as a traitor.

None of the magnates or knights who had been required to hunt for him was responsible for his capture; probably none had attempted it, despite Edward's minatory instructions that they should watch one another's efforts. After all, it is not difficult to look zealous and do nothing.

In response to Lamberton's plea, Wallace had taken up arms again, and throughout the summer of 1304 he attacked the English occupying forces as opportunity offered, until he was defeated in an engagement on the banks of the River Earn, after which he remained at large as a fugitive for almost another year. On 3 August 1305 Wallace was taken in or near Glasgow, by servants of Sir John de Menteith (otherwise Sir John Stewart of Menteith), keeper of Dumbarton Castle for Edward I. According to some accounts he was betrayed to Menteith's servants by a man named Robert Rae, to others by a disaffected servant named Jack Short, whose brother he had killed.[22]

Menteith, as a member of Edward's administration, had little choice but to send Wallace to London, and though he later joined the patriot cause and served it well, posterity has never ceased to regard him as Wallace's Judas, although to the more obscure Rae or Short belongs the greater blame.

Wallace was led to London with his feet tied beneath his horse's belly, a degrading mark of captivity. He was brought into the capital on 22 August, and lodged at the house of an alderman named William de Leyre. The following morning he was led on horseback to Westminster Hall, crowned with laurel leaves, because, it was said, of his alleged boast that one day he would wear a crown at Westminster. This often-repeated statement has never been examined, but obviously it was alien to Wallace's aspirations, to the whole purpose of his life, that he should ever have aspired to be 'crowned at Westminster' as a king. What is the probable meaning of his repeated 'boast' is that in a moment of pessimism he had said that one day he would be crowned at Westminster as a traitor, for a crown of green leaves was the crown of mockery placed on the head of a traitor before his execution. The following year, when the equally unfortunate Sir Simon Fraser was led to execution in London, a song of jubilation related that he had:

> A galand of leves on hys hed y dyht of green
> For he shuld be y-now

Both of heze and of lowe
for traytour, y wene

[A garland of leaves on his head set of green
So all should him know
Both high and low
for traitor, I ween][23]

The garland signified that Wallace had been prejudged a traitor before
the trial began. It was, in fact, a show trial at which a long indictment was
read out, followed by the preordained sentence. In the indictment it was
stated that Wallace, 'oblivious of your fealty and allegiance', was accused
of the murder of Sir William Hazelrigg, Sheriff of Lanark, and of a long
list of acts of war, atrocities and destruction. In conclusion, he was sentenced to a traitor's death, the details of which, resonantly read out,
would have struck terror to the heart of any man. In answer, Wallace
denied the charge of treason, since he had never sworn fealty to King
Edward, and admitted all the other charges which 'were no more than
proof that he had carried out his avowed aims with great success'.[24]

The sentence was carried out on the same day. Wallace was bound to
a hurdle, and dragged by a circuitous route from Westminster to the
Tower of London, and thence to Aldgate and finally to Smithfield, for
the gratification of the maximum number of citizens. At Smithfield he
was hanged, cut down still living, castrated, disembowelled and decapitated, a death devised to inflict the extremity of degradation and agony.
The body was quartered, the parts to be exposed in Newcastle-on-Tyne,
Berwick, Stirling and Perth, and the head was displayed on London
Bridge.[25] The mutilated remains were publicly burnt.

The London populace felt no pity for a pitiless enemy. The end of
Wallace was greeted with public exultation:

Sir Edward oure Kyng, that full ys of pieté
The Waleis quertes sende to is oune contré
On four half to hong, heure myrour to be
Theropon to thencke, that monie myhte se
     ant drede
     Why wolden he be war
     Of the bataile of Dunbar
     How ende hem on spede?

[Sir Edward our king, who is full of piety
The Wallace's quarters sent to his own country
In four parts to hang, their mirror to be
Thereupon to think, that many might see
  And dread.
  Why would they beware
  Of the battle of Dunbar
  How evilly they sped?][26]

But King Edward, however much his harsh sentence gratified his own subjects, had made an immense error of judgement in regard to the Scots. He had executed as a traitor a man who was no traitor, and whose devotion to his own cause was easy to admire because it was so exceptionally unmixed with self-interest. In the eyes of the patriot Scots, Wallace had given everything he had, and gained nothing in return except a vile death. If Edward had sent Wallace to the Tower and forgotten him, then the majority of his compatriots might have done the same. As it was, they decided 'Rycht suth it is, a martyr was Wallace'.[27]

The immediate reaction of Robert de Bruce to the execution of William Wallace is not known. Thoughts are not the material of official records, and keeping a personal record of one's thoughts was not then one of the uses of literacy. If an opinion was not expressed formally in a letter, or included in reported speech by a chronicler, it was lost. The secret thoughts of medieval men can only be deduced from their public actions.

The value that Robert de Bruce put upon Scotland's freedom the world would learn thereafter; so the value that he would have set upon a man who had fought and died for it can be deduced from his own actions. But when Wallace was captured and sent to his death, Robert de Bruce was participating in Edward I's new plans for the government of Scotland. That he would have felt anger and revulsion at Wallace's sentence is certain; that he would have felt shame and frustration at his own compromised position may be guessed. And in that situation, he could not have risked uttering an opinion, unless to a man whose discretion he trusted utterly – perhaps to Lamberton or Wishart, the men who were ready to encourage and assist his own ambition.

At first sight it seems strange that Edward should have conducted a particularly ruthless siege and treated his conquered foes with extreme harshness and simultaneously should have consulted with the leaders of the Community of Scotland on a form of administration that would grant them a limited share in the government of the country (defined as the 'land', not the 'realm' of Scotland).[28] Perhaps it was a classic 'stick and carrot' technique, in which the Scots were invited to see the advantages of collaboration contrasted with the penalties of resistance.

In the spring of 1305 Edward appointed Robert de Bruce, Bishop Wishart and Sir John Mowbray (one earl, one bishop, one baron, to represent the community) to offer their recommendations on the future government of Scotland. They recommended that the Community should be empowered to elect ten persons to attend the next English parliament to advise on a new constitution. In the case of Robert de Bruce and Bishop Wishart, this certainly did not represent their ideal blueprint for the future of their country, so it can only have been a temporizing policy intended to relieve the lot of their countrymen in the short term.

King Edward accepted their recommendation. A Scottish parliament met at Perth in May 1305, and the ten constitutional advisers were duly elected.[29] Neither Robert de Bruce nor Bishop Wishart was among the ten, and they remained in Scotland when the ten went south to attend the English parliament on 15 September, and promulgated the 'Ordinance for Government of the land of Scotland'.[30]

As Viceroy of Scotland, King Edward appointed his nephew, John of Brittany, Earl of Richmond. (He was the younger son of the king's sister Beatrice, and her husband Duke John II of Brittany, who died in 1305. Their elder son, who became Duke Arthur II of Brittany, married Queen Yolande, widow of King Alexander III of Scotland.) The Chancellor of Scotland, William of Benercotes, and the Chamberlain, John of Sandal, were both Englishmen. But there was to be a Scottish Council of twenty-two members, to advise the Viceroy. It included Bishop Lamberton, Robert de Bruce and John Comyn, three former Guardians. The two latter, who had formerly found it impossible to co-operate, now faced the opportunity or the threat of being colleagues again. To administer the law, joint pairs of justices were appointed, each pair to comprise an Englishman and a Scotsman, to hold authority in four areas: Lothian, Galloway (or south-west Scotland as a whole) the country south of the mountains (i.e. the Cairngorms), and the country to the north of that mountain range. It appeared that the Scots were to have a substantial consultative influence in the new regime. But real power would be in the hands of the Viceroy, the Chancellor and the Chamberlain, who could remove or replace lesser officials at their own discretion. 'There was no escaping the fact that Scotland was once more . . . a conquered country . . . governed by the foreign officials of a foreign king.'[31]

It may seem surprising that King Edward appointed his nephew rather than his son as Viceroy of Scotland, for Edward of Caernarvon had acquitted himself well enough on the earlier Scottish campaigns, when it must have seemed that he was being trained for the succession. But since the early summer of 1305 the Prince had been out of favour and forbidden his father's presence, so his disfavour was further underlined by the honour bestowed on the King's nephew.[32] The occasion of the Prince's disgrace was apparently quite trivial. According to one account the Prince had insulted Walter Langton, Bishop of Coventry and Lichfield, a treasurer of the exchequer and highly regarded adviser to the King. According to another, the Prince with Piers Gaveston and other companions had broken into a park belonging to the Bishop, and poached some of the Bishop's deer.[33] Such an irresponsible exploit might have been expiated by an apology and a suitable act of restitution, but apparently the King thought it absolutely unpardonable in the heir to the throne, who was probably expected to maintain an unnaturally high standard of conduct. Edward I had conveniently forgotten that when he was young he had once ordered his companions to cut off a young man's ear and gouge out one of his eyes, in a motiveless attack that caused the chronicler Matthew Paris to remark, 'If he does these things when the wood is green, what can be hoped for when it is seasoned?'[34] In his old age, though his subjects might regard him as 'full of piety', his streak of unpredictable cruelty remained. In an explosion of wrath, the King banished his son from the court, and forbade the exchequer to give him any financial support. The Prince was humiliatingly obliged to live on the generosity of his friends, some of whom no doubt saw helping him as investing in the favour of the future king. One who did so success-fully was Sir Hugh Despenser the elder, who rose to high favour later in the reign of Edward II; another was the treasurer of his household, Walter Reynolds, for whom he secured the archbishopric of Canterbury.

Edward of Caernarvon was reconciled with his father in the autumn, and the occasion was celebrated by a great feast in Westminster Hall on 12 October 1305, at which the Prince presided. But if their guests imagined that the feasting would restore the King and his son to their former good relations, they were wrong. On the Prince's side, the injustice of such a long humiliation would fester; on the King's side, the amount of support the Prince had received would feed his suspicions that men were beginning to turn to the rising sun.

To Robert de Bruce, strife between the King and his son could only have been good news, since it might help to deflect the King's increasingly suspicious mind from himself. Even better news was the illness that confined the King to bed during the autumn, when it seemed probable that he had not much longer to live. Cautiously Robert began to plan for the future. Exactly what he intended cannot be known, because whatever it was went spectacularly awry; but the likelihood is that he planned a coup in the event of the King's death.

According to Sir Thomas Grey, the author of the *Scalachronica*, Robert de Bruce 'retained a strong following through kinsmanship and alliance, always hoping for the establishment of his claim of succession to the realm of Scotland'.[35] Sir Thomas Grey is a good source, informed of the events of this period by his father, who fought with distinction in the wars of Edward I. The chronicler himself was the Warden of Norham Castle, under Edward III. Captured by the Scots in 1355, he was imprisoned in Edinburgh Castle, where he was allowed the use of the library. There, 'as he had hardly anything else to do', he employed his enforced leisure in writing his chronicle.[36] As a *miles literatus* he has a secular viewpoint and a military perspective inevitably lacking in ecclesiastical chroniclers.

If Robert de Bruce had his eyes on establishing his claim to the succession on Edward's death, his greatest need was for allies, whom he collected as Grey reports. But even more important than the armed following that every magnate could call upon was the support of powerful political allies. Robert could already count upon the Bishops Lamberton and Wishart, but he also needed secular support; above all, he needed to make an ally of his erstwhile enemy, the Red Comyn.

John Comyn, since the death of his father, the former Guardian (*c.* 1302), was regarded as the head of his kindred. Among the magnates of Scotland, his power equalled that of Robert de Bruce, and his reputation as a defender of the patriotic cause stood higher. He was the nephew of John Balliol, whose right he had always upheld. The Earl of Buchan was his cousin; his brother-in-law was Aymer de Valance, the future Earl of Pembroke. With his descent, reputation and connections, he seemed an impassable barrier to Bruce's ambitions, unless he could be commuted into an ally.

The story of Robert de Bruce's bargain with Comyn, and its fatal outcome, is told in slightly differing versions by the chroniclers. The chances are that no version is true, because no one knew exactly what passed between the two men; but the stories contain an element of truth, elaborated and dramatized perhaps, but all leading to the same conclusion.

According to the *Scotichronicon*, one day when Bruce and Comyn were riding out of the town of Stirling together, Bruce made his proposition:

> . . . although by right and by the customs and laws of the country the honour of the royal dignity and the succession to it . . . were recognized as belonging to him [Bruce] in preference to any others, yet . . . he made an offer to the said John to choose one of two alternatives – either to reign and assume to himself the entire government of the kingdom . . . while granting to the same Robert all his lands and possessions, or to assume perpetual rights over all the lands and possessions of the said Robert for himself . . . leaving to the same Robert the kingdom and kingly honour . . .[37]

John Comyn accepted the second proposition, and the agreement that Robert should be king and Comyn receive his lands was formalized by sealed indentures, and confirmed by oaths of good faith. But Comyn broke his faith:

> By his messages and private letters to the King of England he shamelessly gave away Robert's own secrets . . . thinking that with Robert de Bruce out of the way, he himself might without difficulty gain control of all Scotland with the assent of the King of England.[38]

Robert de Bruce was summoned to London during the winter, and the King, now recovered from his illness, questioned him about the conspiracy of which Comyn accused him, but he 'moderated the King's rage with light hearted quips and clever words . . . He was held in much suspicion by the same King, who was endowed with much shrewdness, and astuteness and well knew how best to simulate a feigned friendship.'[39] The explanation given for Edward's surprising restraint was that he was keeping Robert at court until he was joined by his brothers, when they would all be seized and put to death together.

However, Edward's patience ran out, and one night 'while the wine sparkled in the cup' and the King was on his way to bed, attended by his intimates, he announced his intention of having Robert de Bruce put to death. Among those with the King was his son-in-law Raoul de Monthemer, Earl of Gloucester, a friend of Bruce, who quickly sent out the keeper of the wardrobe, telling him to take Bruce twelve silver pence and a pair of spurs (a symbolic warning, as the man could not be let into the secret. The coins bore the King's head, the coinage implied being 'sold', i.e. betrayed, the spurs indicated the need for haste: 'Flee, you have been betrayed to the King'). Robert understood the message, gave the money to the keeper of the wardrobe and told him to return to Gloucester with his greetings and thanks. He then summoned his master of the household, and told him to dispense wine to everyone, while he himself retired to his room to work with his secretary. He then slipped out secretly, accompanied only by the secretary and a groom, and rode by day and night without resting, until he reached Scotland. In the Borders they met a Scot riding south. They stopped and searched him, and found he carried letters from the Red Comyn to King Edward, urging the imprisonment and execution of Robert de Bruce. They took possession of the letters and left the messenger dead. They reached Lochmaben the seventh day after leaving London, an astonishingly fast journey on the winter roads.

The author of the *Scotichronicon* added that he had heard another version of the story, in which it was Comyn who initiated the plan, and offered the quid pro quo of estates for one and kingship for the other. Robert accepted to be king, saying that justice was on his side, and justice frequently made the weak strong. The indentures were signed and sealed, and Comyn then betrayed the plot to the English King. Edward called a parliament to which Bruce was summoned with other magnates. When Bruce appeared the King handed him the indenture and then challenged him to produce the other half. Bruce asked for a

respite until the next day, pledging his lands to return with the indenture. The King accepted the pledge, and Bruce fled.

Essentially, John Barbour and Andrew of Wyntoun tell the same
story, with minor differences, but most of the same circumstantial
detail. Both make Comyn initiate the secret agreement on the road from
Stirling, and both stress that Bruce felt great pity for the oppressed
people of Scotland, but had kept silent, until Comyn's proposal inspired
him to take action:

> And sura trowblyt ye folk saw he
> Yat he yeroff had get pitte . . .[41]
> (Barbour)
>
> Gret pyté off the folk he had . . .[42]
> (Wyntoun)

No doubt his pity for the people existed and was genuine enough
already, but deepened and developed after he had identified himself
with them as King and suffered among them as a fugitive. At this date,
his own ambition surely occupied a greater place in his thoughts, and
the retrospective influence of pity is inserted by these authors to add a
praiseworthy grace to this period of his life.

As they were chronicling the life of a hero king, their purpose was to
portray him as favourably as possible, even at this disadvantageous
moment, and correspondingly to vilify Comyn. His role as a betrayer
was rendered more nefarious by making him initiator of the plan to
crown Bruce King, with the intention at the outset of betraying him.
Both Barbour and Wyntoun mention the indenture, and the use made
of it to entrap Bruce. Both mention that he was summoned to attend
Parliament (though there was no Parliament in the winter of 1305); both
describe how King Edward confronted him with the document, and
Bruce requested a delay and then fled. Wyntoun includes the intervention of the Earl of Gloucester,[43] but Barbour omits it.

The story must contain some elements of truth, but in all its versions
it has some unlikely ingredients. It is improbable that the initiative came
from Comyn, for the Comyn claim was subsidiary to that of Balliol,
whose faithful adherent John Comyn had always been. Even if King
John had abandoned all desire to occupy the throne of Scotland, his son
Edward Balliol was his heir, and John Comyn's cousin, and there is no

reason to suppose that Comyn intended to usurp his claim. It is very much more likely, in these circumstances, that Bruce proposed the quid pro quo to Comyn, and that it was a one-sided bargain in which Bruce offered his lands in return for Comyn's support. It was a huge bribe, which might have been big enough to tempt Comyn to abandon his allegiance to Balliol, especially if he could argue that abandoning him involved not the same degree of guilt as attempting to take his place. If the offer was made and Comyn accepted, Bruce would have purchased an ally at the cost of augmenting his already great power. It would have been a dangerous partnership even if Comyn had held to it.

The idea that the agreement was made in the form of an indenture stating the terms seems almost incredible. It would have been incriminating to both sides equally, and would have put Comyn in as much danger denouncing Bruce as Bruce ran in being denounced. If there was a written agreement at all, it seems far more likely that it would have been couched in vague terms, like Bruce's earlier agreement with Lamberton. A verbal agreement between Bruce and Comyn seems far more likely, followed by a verbal denunciation. King Edward was already suspicious of Robert de Bruce, and if Comyn had told the King that Bruce had offered him all his lands in return for support in asserting his claim to the throne of Scotland (Comyn, of course, virtuously asserting that he had refused), Edward would have listened.

King Edward's suspicion of Robert de Bruce seems to date from September 1305, when the King's 'Ordinance for the Government of the Land of Scotland' contained the clause 'It is agreed that the Earl of Carrick be ordered to put the castle of Kildrummy in the keeping of a man for whom he himself is willing to answer'.[44] This order gains additional force from being sandwiched between two punitive clauses against offending Scots. Edward also withdrew the gift of the lands of Sir Ingram de Umfraville, which he had earlier granted to Bruce, and restored them to Umfraville, who thenceforward became a partisan of England.

However, while Edward's attitude to Robert de Bruce had evidently cooled, the King was prepared to bide his time and see if a chill wind of warning would make Bruce see the good sense of remaining loyal to him. In these circumstances, the story Comyn could tell, even without documentary proof, could have changed King Edward's attitude completely. Although there was no Parliament at the time indicated by the

chroniclers, King Edward could have had other reasons for requiring
the presence of Robert de Bruce in England: Bruce was still a member
of the advisory council for Scotland, and John of Brittany still had not
gone to take up his appointment. The King could have sent for Bruce
ostensibly to consult him, and then confronted him with Comyn's
accusation.

From that confrontation, the rest would follow, with or without the
warning sent by the Earl of Gloucester. But, many years later, Raoul de
Monthemer received proof of Robert's gratitude, so even if the story
of the silver pence and the spurs was a fable, Gloucester may have
helped him escape.

Robert de Bruce had left his wife and two brothers at Lochmaben, and
when he returned there after his flight from England, he told them the
whole story of Comyn's betrayal, and consequently the dangerous position in which it placed them. Uppermost in Bruce's mind was his anger
against Comyn, and his determination 'to pay him back in a way that
was fitting for his offence'.[45]

Lochmaben lies some nine miles north-east of Dumfries, and John
Comyn was at his castle of Dalswinton, some six miles to the north-
west of it. Robert sent his brothers to Comyn, to arrange a rendezvous
convenient to both of them, in the Church of the Grey Friars in
Dumfries, on 10 February 1306.[46] A church seems an improbable rendezvous for a premeditated murder; rather two enemies might choose
to meet on sacred ground as a mutual assurance against violence. But
Bruce went there in anger, and found Comyn impenitent:

> Robert came upon John in the choir of the Friars of Dumfries in
> front of the high altar. After an animated greeting . . . the missive
> letters of the same John were produced [the letters taken from the
> messenger in the Borders] and the same John was attacked for his
> betrayal and breach of faith. But soon the reply was given 'You lie!'
> A fatal blow was dealt in the same church on this slanderer . . .[47]

Comyn fell to the ground, and Robert ran from the church 'like a man
beyond endurance and beside himself'. He was stopped by two of his
companions, who had waited outside – Sir James de Lindsay and Sir

Roger de Kirkpatrick. They asked him how things had gone in the church. 'Badly,' he said, 'for I think I have killed John the Red Comyn.'[48] Lindsay declared that something so important should not be left in doubt, and the two knights rushed into the church to find that the friars had carried the wounded man behind the altar. The knights finished him off. The coup de grâce was theirs, but the blood guilt was borne by Robert de Bruce, who attributed his later misfortunes to his double misdeed: the sin of sacrilege and the crime of murder.

John Barbour, Bruce's greatest admirer, told the tale more briefly and without any attempt at extenuation:

> Yidder he raid but langer let
> And with schyr hone ye Cumyn met
> In ye Freris at ye hye awter
> And schawyt him with lauchand cher
> Ye endentur, syne with a knyff
> Rycht in yat sted hym reft ye lyff . . .
> He mysdyd yar gretly but wer
> Yat gave na gyrth to ye awter
> Yar for sa hard myschieff him fell
> Yat ik herd never in romanys tell
> Off man sa hard frayit as wes he
> Yat efterwart com to sic bounte
>
> [He lost no time and hurrying on
> At Greyfriars he found Sir John
> Beside the altar; lightly spoke
> And showed him as it were a joke
> The signed indenture; then with a knife
> Right on the spot he reft his life; . . .
> Doubt not it was a foul misdeed
> Of the holy altar to take no heed
> Thereby such hardship Bruce befell
> That ne'er in story heard I tell
> Of any man had such distress
> Before he came to his success.][49]

The *Scotichronicon* is surely right that Bruce confronted Comyn with the letters taken from the messenger on the road, the damning evidence of betrayal, not with his half of the dubious indenture, which would have proved nothing.

Whatever the terms of the deal Bruce and Comyn had discussed, Bruce's moment of murderous rage had done more than abort it: by killing Comyn he had rid himself of one enemy and made himself a multitude. The whole of the Comyn kindred would now be bound by the obligations of blood-feud to seek his life. The denunciations of Bruce which Comyn had uttered to the King of England were clearly confirmed by the murder: Comyn had died in the King's peace, Bruce had put himself beyond the possibility of reconciliation with Edward.

The indications are that Bruce's plans, from the time of his secret bond with Bishop Lamberton, had hinged upon Edward's death. The King had recovered, and though infirm he was still formidable; as soon as he heard of the murder, the whole weight of English arms would be launched against Bruce. The last chance to salvage his own ambition and with it Scotland's freedom turned on his decision that winter morning when his knights emerged from the Grey Friars church and told him that Comyn was beyond question dead.

If Bruce's courage had failed him he might have fled to the Court of Norway, where his sister Isabella, now the Dowager Queen, could have protected him, but she could not have furnished him with arms to fight for his claim. Instead of implementing well-laid plans to take the throne of Scotland, he had to take it, if at all, with a desperate gamble.

On the morning of 10 February 1306, Robert and his companions thought on their feet. With Comyn dead behind the altar of the Grey Friars kirk, left to the attention of the friars, Bruce and his retinue rode to the castle of Dumfries and demanded its surrender. Sir Richard Girard, the commander, yielded himself prisoner, but the King's justices, who were holding sessions in the great hall, attempted to defend themselves behind barricaded doors. Threatened with fire, they came out, and were permitted to take the road for the border unharmed.

Robert now acted with speed and strategic skill, which suggest that he used the contingency plans prepared in readiness for King Edward's death. His own castles of Lochmaben and Loch Doon were provisioned, the Comyn castles of Dalswinton and Tibbers were seized, and he also secured those of Ayr, Dunaverty and Rothesay, which would enable him to maintain contact with and receive supplies from Ireland and the Western Isles. An attempt to persuade Sir John de Menteith to yield his impregnable Dunbarton, commanding the Clyde, was unsuccessful; but already his resources were overstretched, and he was unable to retain control of these fortresses, although in the short term he had gained a power-base from which to make his attempt for the throne.

First, however, he must make his peace with the Church, for sacrilegious murder incurred the penalty of excommunication, which endangered the body as much as the soul, since the excommunicate, like the outlaw, forfeited the protection of both Church and State.

Robert de Bruce rode to Glasgow, made his confession to Bishop Wishart, and received absolution for his sin. It would be cynical to suppose that the Bishop's absolution of his ally was merely a political gesture. Both must be seen as men of their times, for whom religion was at the centre of their lives, implying a sincere belief that serious sin demanded penance and required absolution. Robert, trained in arms, did not hesitate to take life on the battlefield, but showed unusual reluctance to take it elsewhere. As a knight who attempted to live the chivalric code, he was merciful to the defeated. As a Christian he revered the Church and abhorred sacrilege. His horror at his own act would have been genuine, and his repentance sincere. The penance the Bishop imposed belonged to the secrecy of the confessional. But publicly he required Robert to swear an oath that as king he would be at the obedience of the clergy of Scotland (*'Qu'il esteroit a l'ordenaunce de la clergie de Escoce'*).[50] The patriot bishop prudently wished to be assured that the king he supported would be a faithful son of the Church and defender of its independence from England, together with that of the kingdom, as he proved to be.

The Bishop then brought from his cathedral treasury the royal standard of Scotland, with the *lion rampant gules*, hidden since the reign of King Alexander III, and rich robes for the new King to wear at his inauguration. Despite the danger of his situation, and the immense risk of supporting him, Robert received many oaths of fealty. He rode towards Scone, the traditional place of inauguration, with a growing retinue.

There was nothing furtive in his bid for the throne. He wrote to King Edward, boldly demanding recognition as King of Scots. Edward's only response was to demand the return of the castles that Robert had seized, on hearing which Robert remarked, with the cool irony that came to characterize him, that he would continue to capture castles until the King had granted his demand, and if he would not grant it, would defend himself with the longest stick he had ['*et si il ne lui vont granter – il se defendroit de plus long bastoun q'il eust*'].[51]

On the road to Scone, near the Hill of Ericstane, the royal retinue was met by a lone horseman, a dark youth mounted on a splendid palfery. He halted, sprung from his horse, and knelt to hail Robert as King of Scots, and offer his allegiance. He was James Douglas, son of Sir William Douglas 'le Hardi', disinherited since his father's death as an English prisoner. The horse was Bishop Lamberton's, and James had lately been a member of his household. Already the aura of adventurous daring surrounded him. Robert de Bruce looked at him with approval, received him courteously, for his father's sake and his own, and assigned a body of men-at-arms to attend him.

> And thus began their friendship true
> That no mischance could e'er undo
> Nor lessen while they were alive.
> Their friendship more and more would thrive.[52]

It was still Lent when Bruce and his following reached Scone, but it was too great a risk to await the end of the penitential season before holding the ceremony of inauguration. However, there was an intervening festal day, the Feast of the Annunciation, on 25 March. A message was sent to Bishop Lamberton, at Berwick whence James Douglas had come, to apprise him of it.

Everything possible was done to recreate the splendours and solemnity of the ancient inauguration ritual. Even without the Stone of Destiny, stolen or vanished from knowledge as it was, Scone was a sacred place. Seated on some other throne, perhaps the chair of the Abbot of Scone, who was present, with the royal standard unfurled behind him, and robed in the finery brought out by Bishop Wishart, Robert was attended by three bishops: Wishart of Glasgow, Lamberton of St Andrews and David de Moray of Moray; three earls were present: Lennox, Atholl and Menteith. At an ancient inauguration the Earl of Fife would have been present, to lead the King of Scots to be enthroned upon the sacred stone. The present Earl of Fife, sixteen years old, was still a ward of the English king. Since he could not be there, Isabel of

Fife, Countess of Buchan, came to take his place. She was the young Earl's aunt, and the wife of the murdered Comyn's cousin.[53] But she chose to claim her familial right to enthrone the King over her husband's blood-feud against him. Her husband was in England, she at her home of Balmullo, whence she rode to Scone on one of her husband's destriers, arriving to lead Robert de Bruce to his throne, and set a gold circlet on his head.[54] Since the ancient crown had gone with the other treasure to England, Robert had evidently decided to vary the old ritual with this simple rite of coronation, to add to the solemnity of an essentially makeshift occasion.

Isabel of Fife had done more than crown the King; she had abandoned her position to do so, for she could not return to her alienated husband thereafter. This no doubt led to the rumour that she was the mistress of Robert de Bruce, probably an assumption made by those who had no inkling of the importance of the relationship between the house of Fife and the royal house of Scotland. She had conveyed the mystique of that link upon the new king, and she would pay a terrible price for it.

Two days later, on Palm Sunday, 27 March, Bishop Lamberton celebrated pontifical High Mass for the new King, and paid homage to him for the temporalities of the See of St Andrews.[55] Perhaps the homage of the universally respected premier Bishop of Scotland, more than the ceremony itself, served to proclaim that the new King was not an adventurer, but the elected and acknowledged leader of a resurgent kingdom.

At the same time, the inauguration at Scone seems to mark a change of character from the ambitious, devious, self-serving Robert de Bruce, Earl of Carrick, to the dedicated and single-minded Robert the Bruce, the archetypical patriot-king. Certainly the course of events that had made him king did not admit of second thoughts; but in fighting for the independence of his kingdom he displayed a patience and endurance that seem to belong to an entirely different man from the hot-headed slayer of the Red Comyn.

Traumatic experience can transform, and it may be that the shock and shame of the sacrilegious murder, the penance and absolution, and the dedication implicit in the ceremony at Scone, wrought that transformation. Or it may be that the transformation was not as immediate as it appears in the foreshortening perspective of history. The patience, endurance and indomitable will that are the defining characteristics of Robert the Bruce may have been the graces received by a penitent man resolved on self-renewal, or they may been the hard-earned qualities of a man who developed them in adversity.

7

—————|✳|✳|✳|—————

THE FUGITIVE

Ni me Scotorum libertas prisca moneret
Tot mala non porteriet orbis ob imperium

(If the old freedom of the Scots had not spurred me on
I'd not have borne these ills for the World's dominion)

Words attributed to Robert the Bruce[1]

NEWS OF EVENTS in Scotland reached Edward I in fragmentary form. At first he knew only that 'certain Scots have in malice slain John Comyn'. When he knew the truth, which caused him great rage though perhaps little surprise, he informed the Pope in the third person that

> Robert de Brus . . . s'en feust levez par traison contre soen Seignor lige le dit Roi d'Engletere en qui homage et foiaut il fust, et avoir murdrez Mons Johan Comyn Seignor de Badenagn en leglise des Freres Mencours de la ville de Dunfres, pres del haute autiel por ce que le dit Mons Johan ne voleit assentyr a la traison que le dit Robert pensa de faire contre le dit Roi d'Engleterre, cest a savoir de relever contre li de guerre et de soi faire Roi d'Escoce.

> [Robert de Bruce has loosed treason against his liege lord the King of England, to whom he owed homage and fealty, and has murdered John Comyn Lord of Badenoch in the church of the Friars minor in the town of Dumfries, beside the high altars, because the said John would not give assent to the treason which the said Robert planned to commit against the said King of England, that being to revive the war against him and make himself King of Scotland.][2]

King Edward's own summing up is the earliest version of the event, which validates the basic truth of the more dramatic versions of the chroniclers.

The Pope to whom Edward wrote was Clement V (elected 1305), formerly Bertrand de Gor, Archbishop of Bordeaux, a Gascon, and therefore by birth a subject of the English Crown. His antecedents and his pliant character both disposed him to oblige King Edward, but he probably required little persuasion to authorize the excommunication of the new King of Scots, which was pronounced by the Archbishop of Canterbury and the Bishop of Carlisle on 5 June 1306.[3] The Scots were well aware that the papacy was amenable to political pressure, for they too had attempted to exert it in the past, and would do so in the future. But though King Robert's excommunication was obviously politically motivated, there was little argument that it was also justified, and might influence the pious and the superstitious among the Scots, as Edward intended that it should. It initiated a new dimension of spiritual conflict between clergy who accepted Bishop Wishart's absolution of the King, and those who accepted his excommunication by the English bishops.

King Edward was by now extremely infirm, but his willpower was unimpaired. His determination to conquer Scotland was refuelled by his desire to conquer Robert the Bruce, who, from his viewpoint, was guilty not only of treason and murder, but also of abominable ingratitude.

As a preliminary for war he held a great festivity surely intended to prepare his son for the succession; and to demonstrate that Edward of Caernarvon would succeed to his father's Scottish ambitions as well as to his throne. The King issued a general proclamation that on the feast of Pentecost, 22 May 1306, his son would be knighted, and he required all esquires eligible for the order of knighthood to present themselves, and receive it, at the same time.[4]

Two hundred and ninety-seven young men responded to the summons, and were lodged in tents in the gardens of the Knights Templar on the banks of the Thames, between Westminster and the City of London. The night of fasting, prayer and vigil enjoined upon candidates for knighthood degenerated into a night of drunken uproar. But in the morning the great ceremony took place with seemly splendour. In Westminster Abbey the Prince was knighted by his father, and invested as Duke of Aquitaine. With this addition to his appanage he became Prince of Wales, Duke of Aquitaine, Earl of Chester, Count of Ponthieu and Montreuil, Lord of Oleron and the Agenais, a lord of great lands with wide responsibilities, fittingly preparing him to take up his greater responsibility as King of England.

Having received this honour, the Prince in turn bestowed the order of knighthood on all 297 candidates. Then they processed to Westminster Hall, to a great banquet at which eighty minstrels entertained an audience that may have totalled a thousand knights.[5]

The culmination of the feast was the bearing-in of a dish on which two swans lay imprisoned beneath a mesh of gold chains. First the King rose and swore 'before God and the Swans to avenge the death of Comyn, and thereafter never to bear arms against fellow Christians, but once again to go on Crusade'.[6] Edward of Caernarvon, more realistically, swore that he would never sleep two nights in the same place until he had reached Scotland. Other oath-takers followed, pledging themselves in various ways to the avenging of Comyn and the destruction of Bruce.

An English chronicler declared that it was the most splendid festivity England had witnessed since the coronation of King Arthur. Edward I was frequently compared with Arthur, which he encouraged for purposes of propaganda, since the mythic king was believed to have been the ruler of all Britain. The ritual of oath-taking may have been intended to revive the tradition of Arthurian knights 'to pledge themselves to high and perilous enterprises',[7] but if swearing oaths upon birds was an innovation, it became a chivalric fashion throughout the later Middle Ages.[8]

The pageantry of the oath-taking was supported by serious military preparations. The garrisons of Carlisle and Berwick were reinforced, Henry Percy was apointed to command the royal forces in the west, and Aymer de Valance, Earl of Pembroke, in the east. Supply ships from the Cinque Ports were directed to Skinburness, the port of Carlisle. On 8 June Edward of Caernarvon left London in command of the King's army, while King Edward followed by easy stages; by 8 July he had travelled only as far as Nottingham.[9]

King Robert, in the meantime, was in north-eastern Scotland, recruiting supporters, and where he found men unwilling to join him, extorting contributions. The floodtide of fortune that had carried him to triumph at Scone had undeniably begun to ebb. Dumfries was recaptured, and soon after Tibbers and Dalswinton, and the recruiting drive was numerically disappointing. The murder of Comyn had alienated many potential supporters. Most of the knights who joined King Robert came from his own northern estates in the Garrioch, from the lands of his ward, the Earl of Mar, and those of his allies, the Earls of Atholl and Lennox. Some supporters may have joined Robert at the urging of James the Stewart (whose sympathies were with Robert, though he was offically in King Edward's peace), and of Sir John de Soules, who remained in France. Few or none of Robert's supporters at this period came from north of Inverness, though surprisingly he had some English supporters, including Sir Christopher Seton, the husband of his sister Christian, and Sir William 'the Barondoun' (of Burradon, Northumberland). Already with King Robert were the inseparable companions of his impending misfortunes and his later triumphs: Sir Neil Campbell of Lochawe, husband of his sister Mary, Sir Gilbert de Cattay, and young James Douglas.[10] The King's brothers were also with him, and temporarily his young kinsman Thomas Randolph (usually called his nephew, though the exact relationship is uncertain, but Randolph is generally thought to have been the son of an elder half-sister of King Robert, married to Sir Thomas Randolph of Nithsdale).[11]

As midsummer approached, King Robert had collected the support of some 135 knights, and an unknown number of men-at-arms and foot-soldiers. The Earl of Pembroke had mustered 300 knights and some 1,300 infantrymen.[12] While Robert was in the north-east, Pembroke advanced to Perth, meeting little opposition, and occupied the town. On the way north he captured Bishop Wishart at Cupar Castle, Fife, which the gallant bishop attempted to defend '*comme homme de guerre*'. At Scotlandwell, Kinross-shire, Bishop Lamberton surrendered to Pembroke, but not before he had directed his tenants to go and join King Robert. The style of their response to Pembroke's advance indicates the characters of the two bishops; Wishart was utterly uncompromising; Lamberton, supple and devious, would yield to English force when he must, but never surrender his ultimate goal of Scottish independence, ecclesiastical and national. The bishops were sent south and imprisoned separately in the castles of Winchester and Porchester, in chains. They were fortunate that their holy orders preserved their lives.

The capture of the two bishops was a great loss to King Robert, though public knowledge that two powerful ecclesiastics were suffering for his cause may have been of some moral value. His remaining episcopal supporter, David de Moray, Bishop of Moray, preached throughout his diocese that those who fought for King Robert were 'not less deserving of merit . . . than if they should fight in the Holy Land against pagans or Saracens'.[13]

The Earl of Pembroke, in the meantime, was publicizing a different message. He had been commanded by King Edward to 'byrn and slay and rais dragoun'.[14] To 'raise dragon' meant that Pembroke would unfurl the dragon standard which informed the enemy that the normal conventions of war were in abeyance: knights could not expect to claim the customary privilege of ransoming themselves, and if captured they would be regarded as outlaws, and could expect execution.[15]

When King Robert moved south to meet Pembroke he left his Queen at Kildrummy Castle, in the care of his youngest brother Sir Neil de Bruce. She had a little court of ladies, composed of her step-daughter, the Lady Marjorie de Bruce, King Robert's daughter by his first wife Isabella of Mar, the King's sisters Christian and Mary, and the Countess of Buchan. They shared the common danger of loyalty to him. An English chronicler reported that the Queen told Robert that though he might be king for the summer, he could not hope to resist beyond the turn of the year:

> I think you may be King of Summer
> King of Winter you will not be.[16]

In this Cassandra-like utterance she was probably quoting the opinion of her father, the Earl of Ulster, and not necessarily showing the lack of sympathy with her husband's ambitions sometimes attributed to her on the strength of it. She was soon to share his misfortunes as a fugitive, to be separated from him as a prisoner, and finally to be reunited with him in victory. It seems reasonable to suppose that she identified her fortunes with his, even if she suffered a well-expressed wave of doubt at the beginning.

On the late afternoon of 18 June 1306 King Robert's army appeared before the walls of Perth. He had no siege engines, and the forces inside the town outnumbered those without. But he made a bold chivalric gesture, rode forward to the town gate and issued a personal challenge to Pembroke either to come out and fight, or else to surrender the town. Robert knew Aymer de Valance, whose reputation for courage and honour might lead him to respond to such a challenge; but he may not have grasped the full savagery of King Edward's latest ordinances, or the influence wielded by Comyn's supporters. According to Barbour it was Sir Ingram de Umfraville, the erstwhile Guardian and partisan of Comyn, who advised Pembroke to accept the challenge to battle for the following day, and attack the unsuspecting Scots during the night.

Pembroke accepted this dishonourable suggestion, and promised battle the next morning. Robert drew off his forces, and encamped six miles away in the wood of Methven. Pembroke's word having been accepted, it was not thought necessary to set a watch. While 'ye third part' went foraging, the rest of Bruce's men unarmed themselves and chose their bivouacs.

The English waited until dusk before they struck – not full dark for it was necessary to be able to recognize the enemy individually, the whole purpose being to capture the King. The fighting in the wood was savage. Robert called his men to arms, the knights mounted, and the ensuing struggle centred round the person of the King. In Barbour's words:

> Men mycht haiff seyn into yat thrang
> Knychtis yat wycht and hardy war
> Wyndyr hors feyt defoulyt yar
> Sum woundyt and sum all ded
> Ye gles woux off ye blud. . .
> And ye King himselff alsna
> Wes set intill ful hard assay
> Throw Schyr Philip ye Mowbray
> Yat raid till him full hardyly
> And hynt hys rengze and syne gan cry
> Help help I have ye new maid king

> [One might have seen among that throng
> Knights that were brave and of renown
> Beneath the horses trampled down.
> There some were wounded, some murdered

The Great Seal of Robert the Bruce

Robert the Bruce slays Henry de Bohun on the Eve of the Battle of Bannockburn

Signet of Robert I

Silver penny of Robert I of Scotland

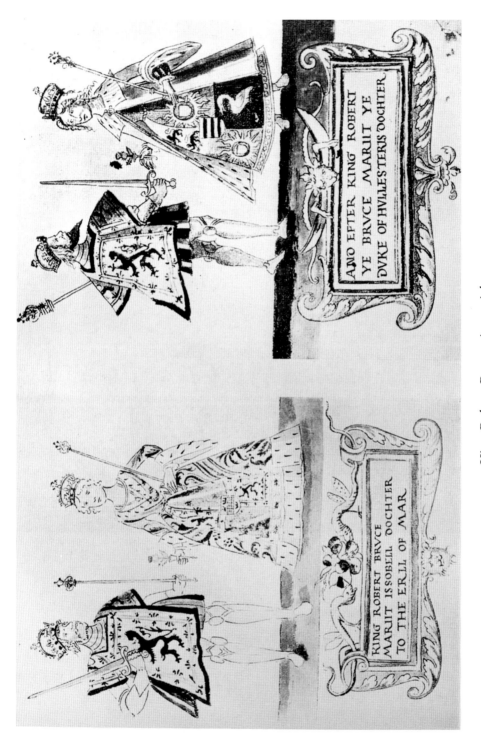

King Robert Bruce, Armorial

ANO EFTER KING ROBERT
YE BRVCE MARIIT YE
DVKE OF HVLLESTERIS DOCHTER

KING ROBERT BRVCE
MARIIT ISSOBELL DOCHTER
TO THE ERLL OF MAR

Declaration of Arbroath

The Stone of Scone

Bruce's Stone at Moss Raploch

With blood the grass became all red . . .
The King that still so bravely bore
The brunt of fight was brought to bay
By stout Sir Philip the Mowbray,
That charged until he came close by
And seized his rein and cried high
'Help, help I have the new-made King!']¹⁷
(trans. A.A.H. Douglas)

Sir Christopher Seton attacked Mowbray so fiercely that the King was able to break away and rally his men again, but the initial surprise and the superior numbers broke their resistance; they scattered through the wood and fled, some escaping as darkness fell, others left in enemy hands. The King escaped, accompanied by the Earl of Atholl, Sir William the Barondoun, Sir Neil Campbell, Sir Gilbert de la Haye, his brother Edward de Bruce, and James Douglas. Less than four months after his coronation, King Robert was a fugitive.

The King and his company retreated into the foothills of the Mounth to await the fugitives from Methven. As the stragglers came they brought no good news. Hope faded for the Earl of Lennox, who had vanished, and with the passage of time was presumed dead. But many of the King's knights were captured at Methven, including Sir Alexander Fraser, Sir David Inchmartin, Sir Hugh de la Hay, Sir John Somerville, Alexander Scrymgeour, the royal standard-bearer, and the King's nephew, Thomas Randolph. Sir Simon Fraser and Sir Christopher Seton were captured later.¹⁸

Pembroke's intervention saved some of the prisoners, including Thomas Randolph, on condition that they transferred their loyalty and henceforth fought for England. But other prisoners were executed with varying degrees of savagery, and in different towns, so that their deaths should provide as widespread an example as possible of the futility of resistance. Sir Christopher Seton was captured at Loch Doon and executed in Dumfries. Sir Simon Fraser was sent to London, where his arrival caused almost as much excitement as that of Wallace. The Londoners were treated to a similar spectacle of butchery, and Fraser's head joined that of Wallace on London Bridge. Once again the citizens

rejoiced at Scotland's defeat, and sang jeeringly of its fugitive King:
'King Hobbe to the moors is gone.'[19]

King Robert's band of fugitives, once regrouped, numbered about
five hundred, according to Barbour; but recruitment was difficult, for
the commons dared not support him when he lacked the strength to
protect them. They yielded to English rule despite their sympathy for
King Robert.

> Yet for the bondage they were in
> they could but wish that he might win.[20]

However, such intimidated sympathy was little consolation for the
bitterness of defeat, and for the loss of friends and loyal supporters, on
the field of battle and by ignominious death. The King was stricken not
only by his defeat but by the inescapable conclusions to be drawn from
it.

> In yis maner rebutyt was
> Ye Bruys yat mekill murnyn mais
> For his men yat war slayne and tane
> And he wes alsa sa will off wane
> Yat he trowit in nane sekyrly
> Owtane yaim off his cumpany . . .[21]

> [Thus was the Bruce defeated; he
> Mourned deeply for the company
> Of men that had been killed or taken
> And in his heart was greatly shaken
> In none he trusted certainly
> Except his own small company . . .[22]

What would have shaken his confidence more than the defeat itself was
the recognition that he alone was to blame. He had blindly assumed that
he was fighting a conventional war in which battles were fought when
and where the commanders agreed, and captured knights were ransomed. And he, who had offered battle like a king, had been out-
manoeuvred through his own arrogant folly. He had been treated like
an outlaw, and his followers were dying like outlaws. From the shame
and self-reproach of such a defeat would follow the question, was it the

consequence of his sacrilege? Was it the punishment of God on the excommunicate? Such would have been the crisis of confidence of a pious and guilt-stricken man, who would begin to doubt that anyone except his closest friends would dare to be loyal to him.

Amidst these anxieties, the outstanding problem was how to provide for the safety of the Queen and the ladies. Following the battle of Methven King Edward had issued a proclamation that the armies of those who had fought for Robert the Bruce were also outlaw, which signified that anyone who robbed, abducted, raped or murdered them would go unpunished. As a result, many women left their homes, and took to the hills with the fugitive patriots.[23]

The King had decided to look westward, and seek new support in the Western Isles, where the MacDonalds of Islay, allies of his family, and foes of the MacDougalls, who were kindred and supporters of the Comyns, could be relied upon for help. In these circumstances he could not leave the Queen and the ladies of his family in the north-east. Accordingly, he sent word to his brother Neil to escort his charges from Kildrummy to Aberdeen, where Robert himself ventured out of the mountains to meet them. After some three weeks of living on a diet of meat and water, and shod only with the buskins of new deerskin that they made from the hides of the harts they had slaughtered for food, the King and his company would have presented a sorry contrast to the splendour of the company that had seen the King crowned at Scone. But, said Barbour, the queen and the other ladies for love and loyalty went willingly with the King and his companions, and readily shared their hardships.[24]

They were soon facing unimagined privations, and Barbour's narrative includes a charming vignette of the care that James Douglas took to provide for them.

> Then to the hills they made their way
> Where grievous lack of food had they
> But James of Douglas busily
> (For always at some ploy was he)
> Sought to provide the ladies food
> With all devices that he could.
> Venison sometimes he brought
> And sometimes with his hands he wrought

> Good snares for salmon and small fishes,
> Trout and eels and other dishes . . .[25]

James Douglas is the secondary hero of Barbour's epic, and if Barbour's first theme is that 'Freedom is a noble thing', his second theme is the heroic friendship between the King who fought for freedom and the younger hero who fought with him. For Douglas, Barbour very unusually provides a physical description; perhaps because Douglas was remembered as being oddly different from the accepted image of the fair and handsome hero:

> But he was not so fair that we
> Should praise his looks in high degree.
> In visage he was rather grey;
> His hair was black, so I heard say,
> His limbs were finely made and long,
> His bones were large, his shoulders strong,
> His body was well-knit and slim
> As those say that set eyes on him.
> When happy, lovable was he,
> And meek and sweet in company,
> But those with him in battle saw
> Another countenance he wore![26]

The following year the chivalrous young man would reveal his other countenance as a ruthless terrorist.

Barbour described how the King and his companions lived, foraging and moving furtively across country, but not the route they followed, saying only that thus they lived until they came to 'the head of Tay'. They approached the Shrine of St Fillan of Glenlochart, a Celtic saint for whom the King had a special veneration. The saint had been an Irish missionary to Scotland, believed to have died in AD 777. The pastoral staff of St Fillan in a silver-gilt reliquary was in the keeping of a 'dewar' or hereditary keeper of sacred relics, appointed by the 'courbs', the descendants or successors of St Fillan, who had been hereditary abbots in the days of the Celtic Church, and were now lords of Glenlochart.[27] With this powerful relic Robert desired to be blessed, and in preparation made his confession and received absolution from Abbot Maurice of Inchaffray. He then received the blessing before his assembled followers.[28] This new cleansing of his sin may have been undertaken to counteract the papal excommunication laid on him after the absolution by Bishop Wishart, and the public blessing of the Celtic saint may have been sought not only for reasons of piety but to reassure any of his followers intimidated by the papal anathema. Unfortunately it did not immediately appear that heaven blessed Robert's enterprise, though perhaps he attributed the fact that he survived the next disaster to St Fillan's protection.

The King was now in the lands of the MacDougalls of Lorn, and in great danger, for John MacDougall, or 'John of Lorn', was the son-in-law of the murdered Comyn, and intent upon avenging him. Near Tyndrum at a place named Dalrigh (Dail-Righ – Field of the King) he ambushed the King's company in a narrow defile.

Lorn's highland warriors, numbering a thousand according to Barbour, which, if true, composed a force outnumbering the King's company by two to one, charged down the steep hillside armed with Lochaber axes, and crashed into the small force advancing into the defile, killing and wounding men and horses with great sweeping axe-strokes. The losses were heavy, with Gilbert de la Haye and James Douglas among the wounded.

When the impetus of the first charge had spent itself, the King rallied his men and ordered a retreat. His first thought was to protect the Queen and the ladies from capture. As the survivors of the small force retreated along the defile, he defended them with a rearguard action. Barbour described the King's superb feat of arms when he was attacked by two brothers named MacIndrosser, and a third unnamed warrior, a 'stout ill feloune'. One grabbed the King's bridle, and had his arm and shoulder sliced from his body with a single stroke of the King's sword. The second man grabbed his stirrup on the other side, but the King shifted his foot and stamped on the man's hand, pinning it to the stirrup and dragging him along as the King's horse plunged forward. The third man leapt up behind, to attempt to pull the King from his horse. But with a convulsive heave, the King threw his weight forward, casting the man half over his shoulder, and split his head with a sword-cut, before turning to despatch the man at his stirrup with another blow.

At the sight of three mortal strokes delivered with such precision, the enemy drew back, and Robert was able to bring the survivors out of the defile without further loss.[29]

To this episode the romantic story of the 'Brooch of Lorn', not mentioned by Barbour, was later attached. Sir Walter Scott told the story twice, in Tales of a Grandfather, his volume of stories from Scottish history for children, and in the narrative poem 'The Lord of the Isles'.

In the prose version the King's three assailants are described as a father and two sons named McAndrosser. The sons seize the King's bridle and stirrup as described by Barbour:

> The father, seeing his two sons thus slain, flew at Robert Bruce, and grasped him by the mantle so close to his body that he would not have room to wield his long sword. But with the heavy pommel . . . the King struck his third assailant so dreadful a blow that he dashed out his brains. Still, however, the Highlander kept his dying grasp on the King's mantle, so that . . . Bruce was obliged to undo the brooch or clasp, by which it was fastened, and leave that and the mantle itself behind him. The brooch, which thus fell into the possession of the MacDougalls of Lorn, is still preserved in that ancient family as a memorial that the celebrated Robert Bruce once narrowly escaped falling into the hands of their ancestor.[30]

In 'The Lord of the Isles', the minstrel of John of Lorn vaunts his lord's possession of the brooch:

> Whence the brooch of burning gold
> That clasps the Chieftain's mantle-fold
> Wrought and chased with rare device
> Studded fair with gems of price . . .
> Moulded thou for monarch's use
> By the overweening Bruce
> When the royal robe he tied
> O'er a heart of wrath and pride;
> Thence in triumph wert thou torn
> By the victor Lord of Lorn!

The song, sung in the hall of Ardlornish Castle, is heard by a stranger-knight who declares that not John of Lorn himself but his 'three vassals loyal and true' were responsible for the capture of the brooch, and died to save Lorn from the King. The knight then hands the minstrel a gold chain and desires him in future to 'speak more nobly of the Bruce' – and thus reveals that he himself is the fugitive king.[31]

The episode in Ardlornish is fictitious, but in the Appendix to 'The Lord of the Isles' Scott gives another version of the engagement at Dalry.

> There is a tradition in the family of the MacDougals of Lorn that their chieftain engaged in personal combat with Bruce himself . . . that Mac-Dougal was struck down by the King . . . and would have been slain on the spot, had not two of Lorn's vassals, a father and son, whom tradition terms McKeork, rescued him by seizing the mantle of the monarch. Bruce . . . was forced to abandon the mantle, and the brooch which fastened it. A studded brooch, said to have been that which King Robert lost upon this occasion, was long treasured by the family of MacDougal, and was lost in a fire . . .[32]

Scott boldly affirmed that 'the metrical history of Barbour throws an air of credibility upon the tradition', but honestly admitted that Barbour 'makes no mention of the personal danger to Lorn, or of the loss of Bruce's mantle'.[33] And, he should have added, no mention of the brooch at all.

A later examination of the legend confirmed that the MacDougalls possessed a brooch believed to have been seized from Robert the Bruce, until the year 1647. It was then kept in Gylen Castle on the Isle of Kerrera, which was captured and burnt in that year, in the Civil War. The brooch was the spoil of Campbell of Braglin, and thereafter remained in the possession of the Campbells for almost two centuries, almost forgotten. A large brooch found at the bottom of the Campbell of Bragins' muniment chest in 1819 was assumed to be the Brooch of Lorn, and in 1824 General Campbell of Lochnell gave it to his friend and neighbour, Sir John MacDougall.[34]

This brooch, not of 'burning gold' but of silver, is a reliquary brooch four inches in diameter, with a large central crystal covering fragments of human bone. Surrounding the central reliquary are eight little silver turrets, each topped with a pearl. It belongs to a group of reliquary brooches including the 'Lochbury Brooch' and the 'Ilqudale Brooch' now dated to c. 1500.[35]

Since the story of the Brooch of Lorn originates in the notoriously nebulous area of family tradition, and in its detailed versions derives from the writings of Scott, whose role as a creator of tradition is well known,[36] and since the so-called 'Brooch of Lorn' emerged from a long disappearance, and was dated to a later century, the story must be classified as legend, not history.[37]

Before the battle of Methven the supporters of Robert the Bruce had constituted an army. After this first defeat they had become a fugitive war band; after the losses of Dalry they were merely a bunch of fugitives.

Though they had escaped, and even briefly discomfited the forces of John of Lorn, their situation was desperate. They would be obliged to move quickly, for the enemy would return. But one thing was certain – they no longer possessed the strength to guarantee the safety of the Queen and the ladies.

On the day after Dalry, Robert took what must have been an agonizing decision, and later a cause of much heart-searching. He decided the fugitives should separate; the ladies should have all the horses, and an escort to return to Kildrummy.[38] If they reached the castle in safety they could rest there, and then make for the far north-east. If they could reach Orkney they would join the Bishop of Moray, who was there already, and thence they could sail to Norway, and claim the protection of the Dowager Queen, Isabella de Bruce.

It was a dangerous plan, for Pembroke was still in the north-east. On 3 August he occupied Aberdeen, but it is unlikely that news of this would have reached Robert whether the fall of Aberdeen had occurred before the battle of Dalry or after it, the date of the battle being uncertain.[39]

The King chose an escort of the most reliable mounted men-at-arms, commanded by Sir Neil de Bruce. The Earl of Atholl, who admitted that he had reached the limits of his endurance, asked leave to join it, to which the King gave his blessing.[40] The Queen and her party mounted, and farewells were said.

> One might have seen, had one been there
> At leave-taking, the ladies weep,

> And salt tears down their faces sweep;
> And brave knights, for their dear ones' sake,
> Would sigh and weep and mourning make
> And kiss their loved ones on their way . . .[41]

The Queen and her little company rode out of sight, and out of knowledge for many months. It was not until the following year that Robert learnt what had befallen them. Many times in the course of the winter he must have feared when no word reached him from Orkney or Norway; for had they reached their destination, surely they would have sent word. On the other hand, he too was a fugitive, and a messenger might not find him . . .

After another hazardous and hungry journey the Queen and her companions reached Kildrummy in safety, a fleeting return to a civilized world of comfort and plenty. But, said Barbour, no comfort would turn her thoughts from the danger of the King, who now had no more than two hundred men.[42]

The respite was brief, for soon word came that Edward of Caernarvon and the Earl of Pembroke were advancing to besiege Kildrummy. Sir Neil de Bruce remained to defend the castle, while the Queen and the ladies fled for the north escorted by the Earl of Atholl. Kildrummy fell early in September. It had been well provisioned and should have withstood a siege for some time, but a traitor within the walls set fire to the grain store, and with the resultant conflagration out of control, the garrison was forced to surrender.[43]

In the meantime the Queen and her company had reached Tain on the southern shore of the Dornoch Firth, where they lodged in the Garth of St Duthac's shrine, which should have provided sanctuary. But the Earl of Ross, a Comyn supporter, broke sanctuary, seized the Queen and all her companions, and sent them as prisoners to King Edward.[44]

The old King, in his latest attempt to conquer Scotland, had left the invasion to his son and Pembroke and their subordinates, while he himself remained at Lanercost Priory.[45] He had arrived there in a litter, and was obviously a dying man, but neither his own sufferings nor the approach of death inspired him to mercy. Indeed, his treatment of the prisoners suggests an element of dementia. Sir Neil de Bruce had surrendered on terms, but these were ignored, and he was drawn, hanged and beheaded at Berwick. Edward's Queen Margaret of France and several English magnates interceded for the Earl of Atholl.[46] They pleaded that as the king's kinsman he deserved preferential treatment (his father was an illegitimate descendant of King John).[47] The King's response was to order that he should be hanged on a gibbet higher than that of any other felon, and afterwards beheaded and burnt. His head joined those of Wallace and Fraser on London Bridge.

No doubt King Edward persuaded himself that in sparing the lives of the women prisoners he was obeying the laws of chivalry, but his severity was contrary to its spirit and to normal practice. Isabel of Fife, Countess of Buchan, no doubt to punish her grave offence of crowning King Robert, was imprisoned in a cage on a tower of the castle of Berwick. Sir Thomas Grey, in the *Scalachronica*, states clearly that it had 'sparred sides, that all might look in from curiosity'.[48] Mary de Bruce, whose husband Neil Campbell was in arms with the King, was consigned to a similar cage on the walls of Roxburgh. The only escape from the weather or the public gaze was to retire into the privy. Initially King Edward ordered that twelve-year-old Marjorie de Bruce should be imprisoned in a cage on the Tower of London, but fortunately for her either the King was persuaded otherwise, or a glimmer of mercy prevailed, for she was sent to the Gilbertine convent at Walton, Yorkshire. Christian de Bruce, perhaps because her husband Sir Christopher Seton had been recently executed, was also more leniently treated, being sent to another Gilbertine house, at Sixhills, Lincolnshire. The Queen was imprisoned in a royal manor at Burstwick-in-Holderness, where she was attended by two waiting women, selected as being elderly and grim. Her status as Queen was not acknowledged, and her conditions were harsh, for she complained that she had 'neither attire for her person or head, nor a bed, nor furniture of her chamber'.[49] But at least the power of her father, the Earl of Ulster, acted as an invisible mantle of protection, and kept her out of a cage.

Isabel of Fife was not released from her cage until 1310, when she was permitted to leave it for confinement in the Carmelite convent of Berwick. Mary de Bruce left Roxburgh Castle in 1310, for imprisonment under easier conditions in Newcastle. They owed their removal from the cages not to any sudden pity, but to a shift in the balance of power. By 1310 King Robert's cause had prospered so much that the ill-used women became valuable state prisoners; it would have been foolish to let them die of exposure when they might be useful for negotiations, as hostages.

If King Edward's ferocity towards his prisoners hinted at dementia, so did his extraordinary treatment of his son in the winter of 1306. With the Bruce rebellion seemingly crushed, principally by Pembroke, but with substantial support by Edward of Caernarvon,[50] the Prince naturally felt that his father might be disposed to grant him a favour. But, knowing the old King's unpredictable temper, he sent a very reluctant Bishop Langton to make his petition. According to the Guisborough chronicler, Langton said, 'My lord King, I am sent on behalf of the Prince your son, though as God lives, unwillingly, to seek in his name your license to promote his knight Piers Gaveston to the rank of Count of Ponthieu.' The King turned on the hapless Langton in immediate fury: 'Who are you who dares to ask such things? As God lives, if not for fear of the Lord and because you said at the outset you undertook this business unwillingly, you would not escape my grasp. Now, however, I shall see what he who sent you has to say in your presence.' The Prince was sent for, and the King demanded, 'On what business did you send this man?' The Prince replied, 'That with your consent I might give the county of Ponthieu to Lord Piers Gaveston.' The King shouted at him, 'You wretched bastard, do you want to give lands away now? You who never gained any? As God lives, if not for a fear of breaking up the kingdom you should never enjoy your inheritance!' Clutching at his son's hair, he tore out handfuls, before ordering him from the room.[51]

He was still a terrifying wreck of a man, and when his rage had spent itself, he acted upon it in cold decision, ordering Gaveston into exile, and making the Prince and Gaveston swear on the Holy Sacrament to obey him, and Gaveston not to return until sent for. Gaveston evidently was not blamed for the Prince's presumption. He was told to go to Germany and generously provided for, assurance being held out that he would be allowed to return in due course.[52] The Prince escorted Gaveston to Dover, and told him to go to Ponthieu, treating his father's command with contempt behind his back.

This strife between father and son, and preliminary indications of Edward of Caernarvon's determination to exalt Gaveston above his rank or deserts, set the scene for a troubled beginning to a new reign,

which everyone could see would not be long deferred. To the fugitive
King of Scots, strife in England would provide a welcome slackening
of hostility when it was most needed.

One of the most attractive qualities of Robert the Bruce was his
resilience of spirit. One that must have endeared him to his followers
was his apparent optimism, his capacity to give encouragement, even
when circumstances seemed to offer none. After the rout of Dalry he
was able to assure the tattered remnant of his followers:

> . . . Despondency
> Is far the worst thing that may be.
> Too much despondency and care
> May quickly lead to sheer despair . . .
> If heart be in a sorry plight
> Then body is not worth a mite . . .[53]

He produced a fund of encouraging stories, in which the vanquished
were victorious at the end. And it was later remembered that he had
endured all his reverses of fortune 'with a cheerful and indomitable
spirit'.[54]

When the Queen and her party had departed on their luckless
journey, the King and his small band prepared to move south-west-
wards, heading for the MacDonald castle of Dunaverty, near the
southern tip of the Kintyre peninsula. One of the King's biographers
cites a local tradition that before leaving the vicinity of Dalry the King
and his knights abandoned their armour in readiness to travel on
foot.[55] This is surely true, for the accoutrements of a knight would be
impossibly cumbersome for a fugitive in the heather. In addition to his
knee-length and long-sleeved hauberk or shirt of mail, pliable but
heavy, the knight would have a *coif de maille*, a mail hood and neck-cov-
ering, a helmet – either a flat-topped pot helm or a pointed-topped
bascinet, and mail leggings. He also might have small pieces of plate
armour such as jointed *genouillières* to protect his knees, *jambasts* his
shins, *rambraces* for his forearms. All this would have to be jettisoned if
he became a fugitive, as would his heraldic shield and surcoat, so

necessary for identification in battle and now so hugely undesirable. Under his armour the knight wore an *abeton* or canvas tunic padded with horsehair, which protected him from chafing and bruising, but this was also the normal battledress of the dismounted man-at-arms and the highland warrior. In this costume, and armed with their swords, axes and daggers, and some with bows, and now looking like a band of highland fighting men, the King and his companions began their journey through hostile country.

Discomfort was added to danger as the weather changed, and they endured 'hunger cold and drenching rain',[56] as they subsisted on the poacher's diet of fish and small game, enlivened perhaps by the occasional handful of blackberries. By devious paths they reached the eastern shore of Loch Lomond, near the foot of Ben Lomond, where the loch is narrow. Rather than risk a long detour through enemy country round the south of the loch, they looked for boats in which to row across. There was no craft to be seen, until at last James Douglas found a half-sunken rowing boat.[57] It was emptied, and proved to be capable of carrying three men at a time. King Robert and James Douglas were rowed across first, followed by others two by two in the boat, and by some who swam.

The King read aloud to those who joined him from the *chanson de geste* of *Fierabras*,[58] which tells of a minor adventure of Charlemagne's paladins, Roland and Oliver. It was intended to be amusing rather than highly heroic. Oliver fights a long and comic duel with the Saracen warrior Fierabras, Oliver is captured by the Saracens, with other Frankish knights, but Fierabras' sister Floripas determines to rescue them. Meanwhile Charlemagne has sent a rescue party led by Roland. Captured also, they are led before Fierabras' father, the Emir. Floripas saves them too, and demands the hand of the knight Guy de Boulogne as her reward. His feeling that his bride ought to be the gift of his liege lord Charlemagne almost causes disaster:

> 'Sir' said Floripas 'This man give me'
> 'By my head' said Roland 'so shall it be
> Come forward Sir Guy, and this lady take ye'
> 'Sir', replied Guy 'May God punish me
> If any but Charlemagne give her to me'.
> When Floripas heard to rage was she stung

'By Mehemet' she swore 'you shall all be hung!'
'Sir Guy' said Roland 'Do what we desire'
'Sir' answered Sir Guy 'just as you require'[59]

This light-hearted treatment of danger and romance was no doubt
exactly the right entertainment for a tense hour. One wonders why
Robert had with him this book in particular. Was it a favourite he habit-
ually carried with him? Was it given him at parting by the Queen or one
of the other ladies? The comparative rarity of books and the prestige
of literacy made this small episode and even the name of the book
memorable enough for someone to tell it to Barbour.

When all the King's men had been ferried across the loch there was
a sense of relief. On the western shore of Loch Lomond they were in
the lands of the Earl of Lennox, and, whatever had befallen him after
Methven, they should be among friends. They risked a full-scale hunt
in the Highland manner, and divided into two parties, under the King
and James Douglas, one to drive the game, the other to kill. Before they
had met with much success, a third hunting party appeared, and as
though summoned by magic it was headed by the Earl of Lennox, who
said he had recognized the sound of the King's horn. Lennox and
Robert embraced each other and wept, the tears acknowledging each
man's unspoken fear that the other had been killed at Methven.[60]

Lennox's situation was similar to that of Robert himself a few years
previously, as a leader of resistance in his own lands. He brought the
King and his companions to his own encampment and feasted them,
and then prepared to go with them to Dunaverty. In the meantime, Neil
Campbell had gone on alone to gather ships for the voyage.

When they reached the coast, Campbell had assembled a flotilla of
galleys, well provisioned. They put to sea, and everyone took a turn to
row, and, says Barbour with painfully vivid detail, hands more accustomed to holding the spear gripped the oars so tightly that one could
often see the skin left on the wood.[61] They rowed past the Isle of Bute,
where many people ran along the shore to watch them. They passed
down the Firth of Clyde, rounded Arran and crossed the open water to
the Mull of Kintyre.

Lennox was the last to leave the mainland, and was pursued by
unnamed enemies, whom he later described as men who should have
been loyal to him. He escaped by the traditional ruse of lightening his

ship by jettisoning supplies which the pursuers wasted time in hauling aboard, and so he got away and rejoined the King.

In Kintyre the King had stronger support than a band of fugitives. Neil Campbell had lands in Kintyre, and so did Angus Og ('the Young') MacDonald of Islay, who currently held Dunaverty for the King. The MacDonalds had been allies of England at the same period as Robert, but Angus Og and his brother Donald had supported Robert when he claimed the throne. Their attachment to his cause was reinforced by mutual enmity to the MacDougalls of Lorn, allied with Edward since the murder of Comyn.

Though welcomed to Dunaverty by Angus Og, whatever the king's plans had been, he could not remain there. Advance warning came of the approach of an English fleet, which had sailed from Skinburness by Carlisle, by way of the Solway Firth and the coast of Carrick to cross to Kintyre. It carried a force led by Sir John de Menteith and Sir John de Botetourt, who laid siege to Dunaverty on 22 September, evidently informed that King Robert had taken refuge there, and intending to capture him.[62]

After only three days at Dunaverty, Robert and his companions put to sea again, probably making for Northern Ireland. But mountainous seas forced them to land on the island of Rathlin, a few miles off the coast of Antrim.

The direction of their voyage from Kintyre suggests that Ireland was their destination, for Rathlin itself had little to offer as a refuge. If Robert had wanted to avoid being besieged in a strong castle, he would not have found being attacked on a small island any more attractive. A narrow island some six miles long would be impossible to defend, and not large enough to feed a force of armed men for long. It was suitable as a brief refuge, but not as a base.

The Lord of Rathlin was Hugh Bisset of the Glens of Antrim, a politically ambiguous figure; a supporter of King Edward, but at the same time an enemy of the MacDougalls. The following spring Bisset was instructed to take a fleet to sea, to attempt to capture Robert himself, or to prevent reinforcements reaching him if he gained the Scottish mainland.[63] But like the magnates instructed to hunt for Wallace in earlier years, Bisset may have obeyed King Edward's directions with deliberate inefficiency. Though he opposed the Bruce intervention in Ireland in 1315, he came out as a supporter of King Robert in 1319.[64] In 1306 he was not a man whose lands offered the fugitive King an ideal refuge.

Having landed at Rathlin, Robert secured his position as best he could by having the whole population rounded up and brought to him to swear fealty. According to Barbour, in this operation no one was slain; the islanders acknowledged Robert as king and promised to provide food for his war band, now grown to three hundred men, for as long as he should remain on the island.[65] Robert in turn confirmed the islanders in their tenures, asserting by implication that he, not King Edward, was Bisset's overlord.

Perhaps the promise of the islanders to provide sustenance gave rise to the belief that the King wintered on Rathlin, and thence returned to Scotland the following spring, as Barbour reported.[66] But the island was too small to feed so many men for so long a period, and too dangerous a place for a fugitive to remain for so long. Besides which, if Robert intended to reassert his claim to his kingdom the following year, it behoved him to do so with a stronger force. He needed to spend the winter gathering supporters, money and arms; but if his contemporaries lost track of where he went, so did posterity.

8

————— |✳|✳|✳| —————

THE RENEWAL OF THE WAR

'On foot should be all Scottish weir [war]
By hill and moss themselves to bear
Let woods for walls be bow and spear
That enemies do them no deir [harm]
In safe places to keep all store
And burn the plainland them before
Then shall they pass away in haste
When they shall find the land lie waste
With wiles and wakings of the night
And muckle noises made on height
Then shall ye turn with great affray
As they were chased with sword away
This is the council and intent
Of Good King Robert's Testament'

'Good King Robert's Testament'[1]

THE NARROW ESCAPE of Lennox and the siege of Dunaverty had shown that the pursuit of the King and his adherents was not far behind. Robert may have designated Rathlin as a rendezvous at the end of the winter (thus confirming the impression that he had remained there throughout) before planning a tour of promising areas to collect new supporters.

Ireland was an infinitely promising recruiting ground. As *Dominus Hibernius* (Lord of Ireland), Edward I claimed the allegiance of the Irish, but the loyalties of the Irish were older and more localized, and often decided by immediate considerations of advantage. Edward may have expected that Ireland would support him against Robert the Bruce. 'But Ireland is a country where the expected often does not

149

happen.'[2] Robert himself was lord of lands in Antrim and Derry, including the port of Olderfleet (now Larne), Glenarn and lands near Coleraine and Port Stewart.[3] His old friend and ally James the Stewart also held lands in Northern Ireland, through his marriage to Egudie de Burgh, at the Roe on Loch Foyle. Richard de Burgh, Earl of Ulster, Robert's father-in-law, remained overtly loyal to Edward I, but there were rumours that he was in league with Robert.[4] Beyond the network of kindred and alliance there was the opportunity to recruit Irish mercenaries, either for pay or with the prospect of self-collected pay in the form of plunder.

Robert probably sent his brothers Thomas and Alexander to Ireland, bearing a letter addressed to 'All the Kings of Ireland [Irish chiefs were kings in their own estimation], to the Prelates and Clergy, and to the Inhabitants of all Ireland, his friends', exhorting them, on the grounds of common ancestry, language (Gaelic) and customs to negotiate with his envoys on the means of recovering their ancient liberty. He bound himself to abide by whatever the envoys might negotiate.[5] Though the dating of the letter is uncertain, the embassage is indicated by the return of Thomas and Alexander de Bruce to Scotland early in 1307, with Irish support.

Robert's escape from his pursuers and subsequent disappearance gave rise to the rumour that he had gone to Norway. But there are several arguments against this. If he had appeared at a foreign court, it would have been international news, but there was no report of him in Norway. From Rathlin he would have voyaged by way of the north-west coast and through the Pentland Firth to Orkney, where he would have met the Bishop of Moray, who had taken refuge there. He would have learnt that the Queen and her companions had never arrived there, and probably would have discovered about their capture at Tain, but he remained ignorant of this until the spring. Besides, to seek foreign help, the only pretext for a visit to Norway, was far less important than to win the Scottish support on which his claim to the throne ultimately must depend. The means of winning support closest to hand was to capitalize on the local enmity to the MacDougalls in the Western Isles.

According to the *Scotichronicon* it was 'by the assistance and power' of a noblewoman named 'Christiana of the Isles' that 'after many and various roundabout journeys and innumerable toils pains and afflictions' Robert was enabled to return to the mainland and invade his own earldom of Carrick.[6] 'Christiana of the Isles' was Christian MacRuarie, only daughter and heir of Alan MacRuarie of Garmoran, descendant of Gomerled, Prince of the Isles. She was a woman of immense power as Lady of Knoydart, Moidart, Arisaig, Rum, Eigg, Uist, Barra and Gigha.[7] And Robert could claim kinship with her, for she was the widow of Donald of Mar, younger brother of Gartnait, Earl of Mar, first husband of Robert's sister Christian de Bruce, and brother of his first wife Isabella of Mar. She was willing to help him, and the 'roundabout journeys' to which the *Scotichronicon* refers were probably an unremitting tour through her lands on the mainland and in the isles. With a force drawn from the lands of the MacDonalds and of Christiana of the Isles, Robert probably returned to Rathlin to rendezvous with his brothers.[8] Before the end of the year he sent agents secretly to Carrick to collect his Martinmas rents, in readiness to pay his new recruits.[9]

By the beginning of February 1307 Robert and his brothers were ready for the invasion. It was not a good moment, for three fleets had been ordered to sea to intercept Robert's ships. As early as 4 January 1307, Hugh Bisset had been ordered to equip his fleet urgently, though he did not put to sea until 2 May.[10] However, another fleet under Simon de Montacute cruised between the Western Isles and Ireland, while the Earl of Pembroke and Sir John de Menteith waited at Ayr to oppose the expected invasion, and also had a fleet of fifteen ships patrolling the Firth of Clyde.[11]

In spite of these hazards the King's expedition went ahead, possibly because of the difficulty of holding a force of armed men inactive, or possibly because of a false rumour of the death of Edward I, who lay bedridden at Lanercost.[12] Edward, far from being dead, issued an endless stream of orders for Robert's capture. The King of Scots escaped the vigilance of the English patrols, but his brothers were less lucky.

The King divided his forces. His brothers sailed first, with a fleet of eighteen ships. They were accompanied by Sir Reginald de Crawford, the 'Lord of Cantyre' (Malcolm MacQuillan, a chieftain of Kintyre), and 'a certain kinglet of Ireland' (unnamed), with a large following.[13] They sailed into Loch Ryan on 10 February 1307, and on landing were immediately attacked by a strong force of Gallovidians commanded by

Dougal MacDouall, a Comyn supporter, and defeated with great slaughter. Malcolm MacQuillan and the Irish chieftain were beheaded on the shore, and their heads were sent to King Edward at Lancercost.[14] Thomas and Alexander de Bruce and Reginald de Crawford were sent to Edward of Caernarvon at Wetheral Priory on 19 February.[15] The prisoners were sent to Carlisle, where Thomas de Bruce, though badly wounded in the engagement at Loch Ryan, was drawn through the streets by horses before his execution. Crawford and Alexander de Bruce, whose holy orders should have protected his life, were both hanged and then beheaded.[16]

This disastrous expedition, at such heavy cost, deflected attention from the King's own crossing; at about the same time as his brothers entered Loch Ryan, King Robert landed undetected on Arran. James Douglas had already reached Arran with a small advance party, and had captured a useful consignment of arms and provisions destined for the English garrison at Brodick Castle. In a fortified camp he awaited the arrival of the King. According to Barbour, when the King landed and enquired for recently arrived strangers a local woman reported the landing of 'strong men' who had seized the governor's stores, and promised to show him their encampment in a wild glen, demonstrating her good faith by offering to go with him. Courteously addressing her as 'my syster fayr', the King accepted, and was led within signal of the camp where he blew his horn for identification. James Douglas and Sir Robert Boyd came out of the encampment to welcome him. They embraced one another in a joyful meeting unalloyed by any news of what had happened to the other expedition.[17] Sir Robert Boyd had been captured at Kildrummy with Sir Neil de Bruce, but had escaped to rejoin the King. His news that the Queen and her companions had left Kildrummy before the siege began was the last news of the ladies, and good news as far as it went. At one of the rare moments of joy in a period of deadly peril, the capture of Neil was ominous news, but still his fate remained uncertain.

The King laid careful plans for the invasion of Carrick. He chose a man of Carrick named Cuthbert and sent him to reconnoitre, and in partic-ular to discover whether the people of Carrick were ready to revolt against the English occupying forces. It was arranged that if Cuthbert judged the circumstances propitious for invasion, on an agreed day he should light a fire near Turnberry headland.

In the early afternoon of that day, a tiny point of light appeared on the mainland coast. The King's companions were eager for action, and he announced that they would depart at dusk, so as to land on the coast of Carrick under cover of darkness.

The galleys were launched and, as the King was pacing the shore overseeing the final preparations, he was approached by the woman with whom he had been staying (his 'ost' – hostess), who claimed to have second sight. She drew him aside and said:

> Here there is none can prophesy
> The things to come as well as I . . .
> Ere long you shall be King, good sire,
> And rule the land to your desire.[18]

She did not conceal that he would encounter great difficulties, but promised that he should overcome them all. With this encouragement he went on board. The fleet of galleys put to sea, with the fire blazing encouragingly from the opposite shore as darkness fell.

Sir Walter Scott in his notes to 'The Lord of the Isles' recorded a local belief that the fire had appeared 'unassisted by the hand of any mortal being', and that the headland that was supposed to be the site of it had been known for time out of mind as 'the Bogles' Brae'.[19] This provided him with the pretext to describe a splendid supernatural blaze which dyed sea and sky an eerie crimson, but the local legend has probably succumbed to the obvious truth that the fire was either accidental or fortuitously lit by someone unconnected with the King's plan.

When the galleys beached in the firelight, an anxious Cuthbert emerged from the shadows to the rocks and poured out an unhappy tale of the condition of Carrick, with its people completely cowed by the English occupation and locally terrorized by Sir Henry Percy, who held Turnberry Castle with a garrison of a hundred men, and double that number quartered in nearby cottages and farms. No one would dare to rebel for fear of savage reprisals.

The King's temper, under iron control since the death of Comyn, flared up.

> Then said the king, in full great ire
> 'Thou traitor! Why hast made the fire?'[20]

But there was no drawn dagger, and he listened to the words of Cuthbert's explanation. Cuthbert had not lit it, but had found it already burning when darkness fell, and could only lurk in hiding nearby to warn the King when he landed.

Having heard him out, the King turned to consult his companions. His brother, Edward de Bruce, spoke for them all when he declared that nothing would make him put to sea again. Having arrived they should take their fortune good or bad. The King sensed the mood, and, perhaps encouraged by the words of the seer of Arran earlier in the day, decided that their best plan was a bold attack on the soldiers billeted outside the castle walls.

Supremely confident in their hold upon the countryside, the soldiers who were not on castle duty slept soundly without having posted a watch. King Robert's men set upon them and indulged in an orgy of slaughter, gratifying themselves with the pleasure of paying back years of wrongs. There was no counter-attack from the castle. The clash of arms, the cries and screams and neighing of horses, were clearly audible to Sir Henry Percy and his garrison, but from the castle walls the turmoil was invisible in the darkness. It was impossible to guess the size of the attacking force. Percy left the victims to their fate and waited to confront the aftermath of the massacre until the Scots had withdrawn, loaded with an immense haul of plunder, including much-needed supplies of arms and armour. They remained for three days in the vicinity of Turnberry, while the King organized a share-out of the booty, before disappearing into the wild hinterland of Carrick.

The success of the attack may have created the impression that the King's force was much larger than a few hundred men. There was a brief respite while a massive retaliation was prepared. During the next few weeks in the mountains of Carrick, the King discovered the accuracy of Cuthbert's report. Even in his own earldom, where people were naturally inclined to support him, they were too terrified of the English to make any show of friendship.

Then, one day, 'a lady of that country' appeared with an escort of forty men-at-arms whom she had brought as a contribution to his little army.[21] She was his kinswoman, Christian of Carrick, who may have been his mistress, probably when he had led the resistance in Carrick, after he was ousted from the Guardianship. (This is surmised, because he had two illegitimate children named Nigel of Carrick and Christian of Carrick.[22])

Christian was 'wonder blyth off his arywyng' (wonderfully glad of his arriving), but she had terrible news to bring him. She told him of the capture and imprisonment of his wife, daughter and sisters and the Countess of Buchan, of their incarceration in cages and solitary confinement; of the execution of Sir Neil de Bruce, the Earl of Atholl and Christopher Seton; of the defeat of the Loch Ryan expedition, and the executions of Thomas and Alexander de Bruce and their allies. It was a tale of unremitting disaster, told with tears and heard with outrage.

Barbour gives Robert the Bruce a dignified speech of grief, with a special word of sorrow for Christopher Seton, whose sacrifice seemed all the greater because he was not one of the King's own blood. And Robert is made to vow vengeance for them all, and determination to recover the kingdom from King Edward's hands. But it is natural to imagine that the deaths and sufferings of his family, his well-loved brother-in-law and many allies induced a deeper despair, a longer period of anguish and self-doubt, before his natural hue of resolution returned.

It is to this darkest moment of his career that the legend of the spider has attached itself. According to the traditional version of the story, the King returned to the cave in which he had lately slept, and threw himself down in despair, gazing blankly at the roof, as he contemplated abandoning his ambition, which had lost so many valuable lives, and might cost more. The temptation of taking his sword abroad as Crusader, mercenary captain or knight errant seemed more desirable than spilling the blood of his friends in a vain attempt to win the throne of Scotland. But as his ambition wavered, his attention was caught by a spider spinning its web in the roof of the cave. It was attempting to attach one of the main threads from one point of rock to another. Six times it made the effort, and failed to make the connection. But at the seventh attempt it attached its thread in its chosen place, and went on to complete the web. The King, comparing its efforts to his own, resolved that if so small a creature could persevere until it succeeded, a king could do no less.

This most famous anecdote of Robert the Bruce is probably known to thousands of people who know none of the historical facts of his life, and to many who know them it is an article of faith. Despite its lack of a contemporary source, it has probably commanded belief as the essential anecdote of Robert the Bruce because it fits convincingly into the historic sequence of events and because it illumines a defining aspect of his character, his resilient determination to succeed. It has made him the exemplar of perseverance.

But it also belongs, and probably should be defined as belonging, within the context of folklore. The intervention of a spider in the life of a hero, especially a fugitive hero, is common to many cultures. In an ancient Hebrew story, when David was being pursued by Saul he took refuge in a cave, and 'God sent a spider to weave its web across the opening and Saul called his men away saying it was useless to search within, since the web showed that no-one could have entered'.[23] The same story was told of Mohammed when pursued by the Coreishites, and of the twelfth-century Japanese hero Yoritomo, who was saved from his enemies by a spider's web spun across the opening of a hollow tree in which he had hidden.[24] A similar story was told of the hermit St Ronan of Brittany (a saint being a hero as a practitioner of heroic virtue and a warrior against evil). St Ronan was visited by the saintly Bishop Corentin, who wished to resign the bishopric of Quimper in his favour; but Corentin found the door of St Ronan's hermitage closed by a spider's web, which, when he tried to enter, proved an indestructible barrier, from which he understood that his errand was in vain.[25]

An example of the hero-spider encounter from more recent times tells how a spider dropped from the ceiling of a room of Sans Souci into a cup of hot chocolate about to be drunk by Frederick the Great. Frederick ordered the cup to be removed and another brought, and the cook, who had poisoned the first cup, supposing his crime to have been discovered, shot himself, and thus Frederick owed his life to the spider.[26]

The spider became a creature of folklore in many cultures because it seemed to be magical in its capacity to spin its web from its own body, and because it seemed to be uncannily cunning in weaving its web and snaring and slaying its prey. Perhaps in its triple activity of spinning, weaving and slaying it appears to have an affinity with the Fates. If the probability that the story of Robert the Bruce and the spider is unhistoric is disappointing to its many believers, the likelihood that it is folkloric does not lessen its significance, for the encounter of the hero and the spider is a signifier of his mythic status within his culture.

Though Barbour did not recount the spider story, he contributed to King Robert's heroic status with a sequence of exploits that also belong within the historic context but possess a folkloric character. These stories belong to the spring of 1307, when a cordon of enemies surrounded Carrick, confining King Robert and his small force within the mountainous tract of country, hunting him with armed bands and using bloodhounds to track him.

The English forces were under the supreme command of the Earl of Pembroke, who led an army of two thousand men based at Carlisle. Sir Ingram de Umfraville and Sir John de Menteith held Ayr with an English garrison, where they were joined by John of Lorn with the force that had defeated the King at Dalry. Sir Dougal MacDouall, lately knighted by Edward I to reward him for the victory at Loch Ryan, advanced to the south-western border of Carrick, while Sir Robert Clifford and his forces kept watch at the fords of the River Cree, and Sir John de Botetourt patrolled Nithsdale. King Robert had also gained a new Scottish enemy in the young Earl of Atholl, David de Strathbogie, son of the earl who had been executed in his cause.[27]

Surrounded by so many formidable enemies, Robert owed his life many times over to last-minute warnings, to his sharply attuned judgement of character, and to his prowess in arms. If Barbour's stories of his amazing escapes are the least historical part of his narrative, in that they cannot be checked against documented events, they illustrate the sort of story that was being told of the King when Barbour gathered his material. They were believed to be true, or judged sufficiently characteristic of him to be accepted as true. The growth of a 'Bruce legend' by this period is suggested by the number of times the King overcomes a group of three enemies, a proof of heroic prowess being the victory of one over the sacred or magical combination of three.

On one of these occasions an unnamed kinsman of the King was suborned by the English with an offer of a substantial grant of land for him and his heirs to kill the King.[28] However, Robert received a warning that the man would play him false. This man knew the King's habits well enough to be aware that every morning he would go into the woods by himself or with one attendant to stand guard 'For to do yar his prevete' (to do his private business there). When the treacherous kinsman and his two sons found him, Robert had his sword slung round his neck, and his attendant page stood by with a bow and arrow, but the would-be assassins were more heavily armed, the father with a sword, the elder son with a sword and an axe, the younger with a sword and a spear. The King took the page's bow and arrows, and told him to stand back, and to run away if he were killed. The King then ordered the three to approach no nearer, and when they continued to advance with reassuring words he transfixed the father with an arrow through the eye. The axe-wielding son he despatched with a single blow of his sword. He felt a moment of fear ('him dried sum thing') at the attack of the spearman, but with one blow of the sword he hacked off the point of the spear, and with a second stroke split the man's head and neck in two. As the page came running back to him, he wiped the sword blade and remarked sombrely that all three had been good men before they were tempted to treason.

On another occasion the King was alone with his foster-brother (whose existence testifies to a Celtic aspect of his upbringing). They had spent the day avoiding pursuit by John of Lorn and his men. They had fought and killed five pursuers, specially picked for their fleetness of foot. The King had despatched the three who attacked him and assisted his foster-brother in dealing with the other two. Then they had waded along the bed of a burn to confuse the bloodhound that was on the King's trail. It had once belonged to him, and had perhaps been caught by his enemies after Dalry, and unless he had managed to shake it off, its devotion would have proved fatal.[29] Wearily heading back into the hills, Robert and his foster-brother met three men, one of them carrying a trussed-up sheep on his shoulders. They said they were looking for Robert the Bruce and wished to join him. Robert, cautious of the unknown, merely said that he would guide them to him. But his speech and demeanour made them guess his identity, and he 'yat wes witty' (who was quick-thinking), sensing treachery behind a sudden show of obsequiousness, told them to walk on in front until they knew one another better. One of them said that he had no reason to think ill of them. Robert replied that he did not, but still insisted they should walk ahead.

Soon they came to an empty farmhouse, which they entered. The sheep was slaughtered, and the three men invited the King and his foster-brother to share it. But the King maintained his caution and still insisted that the two parties kept apart. Two fires were built, the sheep was cut in half, and the two portions were roasted and eaten at opposite ends of the room. But then, weary, warm and well fed, Robert found it impossible to keep awake. He asked his foster-brother to keep watch for a while, who promised to do his best; but soon he too slept and snored loudly.

The three traitors then rose up and moved stealthily down the room, with swords and axes in their hands. Fortunately the King was a light sleeper. He sprang up, treading upon his foster-brother as he did so. He too woke, but 'rais disily' (rose dizzily), not alert enough to avoid the first blow. He fell dead, and the King faced his adversaries alone. But 'throw Goddis grace and his manheid' (through God's grace and his own manhood), he killed all three. He went on his way alone, angrily grieving for yet another loyal companion who had died in his service.[30]

On the third occasion on which Robert overcame three adversaries, he seemed to be enjoying a respite from war or flight. He had been hunting, and was sitting on the grass at the edge of a wood, with two hounds stretched out beside him. But even in this sylvan scene 'he his swerd ay with him bar'[31] (he always carried his sword with him). Suddenly three men emerged from the wood and surrounded him, with bows and arrows aimed at him. They were cousins of John Comyn, come to avenge his death upon the King. Robert, recognizing them as members of the ruling class, not common murderers, immediately struck the right note by taunting them with cowardice.

> For shame now! Have you lost your pride!
> Brave men you are tis plain to see
> When I am one and you are three
> Safely to shoot at me from there!
> If ye have courage to come near
> And bravely with your swords to fight
> And overcome you by your might
> Then much more honoured will ye be![32]

The taunt had its effect. They threw down their bows and came at him with their swords. Robert slew the first assailant. Then one of his hounds leapt at the throat of the second and knocked him down, and the King dealt him his death blow. The third man turned to flee into the wood, but again the hound leapt at him, and the King finished him off. When Robert's companions, hearing sounds of combat, came running to protect him, he gave honour where it was due:

> Said he 'One man no more I slew
> God and my hound account for two'.[33]

In this hero-tale, besides overcoming the folkloric triad of enemies, the King has also acquired a traditional heroic adjunct of a faithful hound.

Whenever possible Barbour anchored his stories to reality with circumstantial details. He named even the most obscure participants when he knew the names (e.g. Cuthbert, whose plans for the signal fire went awry, and many others later in the narrative who will be mentioned in their context). Thus, when he frankly admitted not knowing a character's identity (e.g. that of the King's treacherous kinsman who was suborned by the offer of a land grant), the admission of ignorance has the paradoxical effect of confirming his bona fides.

He recounted that Robert was warned against this treacherous kinsman, probably by a woman, though he could not be sure of this:

> But such luck did he always have
> That when men planned a treacherous crime
> He always heard of it in time;
> And many times, as I heard say
> From women that with him would play.[34]

A statement that implies that he made use of casual love affairs for the purposes of espionage. He was successful with women, inspiring both love and loyalty from them at all levels of society. Isabel of Fife, at great cost to herself, gave him the mystique of her family's role in the ancient rite of inauguration; Christiana of the Isles gave him valuable military support; Christian of Carrick risked great danger to bring him her forty men-at-arms, and returned many times with gifts of money and food.[35] And Barbour's narrative is full of fleeting encounters with anonymous women who offer help, encouragement and information: the woman who brought him to James Douglas's camp in Arran, the prophetess who assured him of ultimate triumph, the mistresses who warned him of treachery. That some of his love affairs were more serious is implied by the record of six illegitimate children whom he acknowledged and provided for, though the names of their mothers are not known (but the territorial designation 'of Carrick' suggests that Christian of Carrick was the mother of two of them).[36]

Barbour's purpose, in introducing these episodes, often insignificant in themselves, is to display the King's courtesy towards women, and the loyalty which he inspired. Both are shown in a meeting that occurs immediately after the fight which has resulted in the death of the King's foster-brother. Weary and heart-sick, the King comes to a cottage in which he hopes to find a temporary refuge, and within is a woman sitting alone from whom he asks shelter, describing himself simply as 'a travelling man'. She replies that all travellers are welcome for the sake of one. And who might that be, he asks. She answers, for the sake of Robert the Bruce, the rightful King, who though now beset by his enemies will surely triumph in the end. Evidently deeply moved, but still cautious, 'Dame, luffis you him sa weil?' (lovest thou him so well?), he asks, and she replies that she does 'sa God me see' (as God sees me). He then tells her that he himself is Robert the Bruce, and she, shocked that the King should be alone, asks him where all his men are. He replies simply, 'At yis tyme, dame, ik haiff no man' (At this time, dame, I have no men). And she says, 'It may na wys be swa' (It may no wise be so), and immediately fetches her two sons, who become 'his sworn men'.[37]

A local tradition makes the woman an old widow with three sons by different husbands, named Murdoch, McKie and MacLurg. The three demonstrated their worth to the King by displaying their prowess with bow and arrow; Murdoch aimed at a pair of ravens perching on a crag and transfixed both birds with one arrow; McKie brought down a raven on the wing; but MacLurg missed his mark. Years later it is said King Robert asked the widow to claim a reward of him for her encouragement and help in his great need. She asked for a 'wee bit passel o' land atween Palnure and Penkiln', and in response the King granted her the whole stretch of land between the two places, a holding some five miles long. At her death it was divided between her three sons, who founded the families of Murdoch of Cumloden, McKie of Larg and MacLurg of Kirroughtie. The crag on which Murdoch shot the two ravens became known as Craigencaillie – 'the crag of the old woman'.[38]

In Barbour's version of the story the King sits down to eat with the woman and her sons, and while they are at table 'gret stamping' is heard outside the house.[39] The King's new followers prepare to defend him, but soon the King recognizes the voices of James Douglas and his brother Edward de Bruce, come to seek him with a company of 150 men. After a joyful reunion and thanks given for the King's numerous escapes from danger, Douglas tells him of a nearby English encampment, which they are strong enough to attack if they can take it by surprise. In Barbour's narrative this is the turning point at which King Robert ceases to be the fugitive hero and becomes the aggressor.[40]

This raid on an English encampment may have been the one commemorated by a monument on the low-lying eastern side of Clatteringshaws Loch, which can be approached by the course of the Palnure Burn. Near the loch, beside a large boulder named 'Bruce's Stone', is an inscription that reads 'Here on Moss Raploch King Robert the Bruce defeated an English army in 1307. It is said that Bruce rested against the stone after the battle.' It was not an army that he defeated, but a small force, carelessly encamped. However, the incident must have caused disproportionate shock waves amongst Robert's English and Scottish enemies, as their prey turned predator.

The failure of the concerted efforts of his enemies to capture Robert the Bruce, and doubtless the spreading stories of his heroic exploits, made local sympathizers less timid. New recruits joined him, and in the words of a recent historian of his campaigns, 'as so often is the case with outlaws and terrorists, an air of expectation and romance began to cling to the Bruce cause'.[41]

Having been treated like an outlaw, Robert the Bruce retaliated by acting like an outlaw. It was an immense leap of imagination for a magnate raised in the conventions of chivalric warfare to abandon them and to adopt and bring to perfection a system of guerrilla tactics, which he employed in the service of a grand strategy to recapture the kingdom.

His methods are summed up in the well-known rhyme entitled 'Good King Robert's Testament' (quoted as the epigraph to this chapter), which is a translation of a Latin verse in the *Scotichronicon*.[42] As described in the rhyme, these methods were a) abandonment of the use of cavalry, b) concealment of men and supplies in inaccessible terrain, c) ruses to exaggerate the numbers of the forces concealed, d) traditional 'scorched earth policy' forcing the enemy to retreat from the 'sword of hunger'. Guerrilla tactics had been used by the hard-pressed Scots at various times since the beginning of their struggle against Edward I, but it was King Robert's particular genius to elevate what had been merely a means of harrying superior forces into an effective method of defeating them.

As his position strengthened, the King was able to fund his war by extorting 'blackmail' from enemy communities, who if not willingly at least thankfully paid for immunity from destruction. If they were not willing, one taste of 'herschip' (harrying) was usually enough. When Robert began to capture strongholds, he systematically destroyed them, to prevent their being any use to the enemy should the site be recaptured. He may have developed this policy as a result of having witnessed Edward I's siege of Stirling in 1304, and seen the futility of attempting to defend a castle against the advanced siege machines Edward could deploy.[43]

In April 1307 Robert was encamped at the head of Glen Trool, which, if the earlier raid is correctly identified, he would have reached by way of the Black Water of Dee, past the south of Loch Dee and along the course of the Glenherd Burn to camp at the eastern end of Loch Trool.[44]

The Earl of Pembroke, informed of his whereabouts, decided 'with his chevalry to come upon hi sodanly' (to send a *chevauchée* to attack him). First he despatched a poorly dressed woman to enter the King's camp to beg for food, and to report on the size and position of his forces. The King, unarmed and at leisure, saw the woman wandering around the camp and immediately suspected her of being a spy. He had her arrested. In terror of her life, she told him that Pembroke and Clifford, with 'the flour off Northumberland' (the flower – i.e. the best men of that county), were planning to attack him.[45]

The King armed without delay and prepared a pre-emptive attack. The long, slender loch almost fills Glen Trool, except for the narrow lochside track, and at the eastern end the sides of the glen rise steeply to the neighbouring mountains; Muldonoch to the south and to the north Buchan Hill and the dark heights of the Merrick beyond. Into this natural ambush the English raiding party unhesitatingly rode (perhaps the spy, whom Barbour does not mention again, had returned with mendacious encouragement), to be repulsed with small loss but considerable humiliation.[46] Pembroke himself may not have taken part in the raid. It was probably jointly led by Sir Henry Clifford and Sir John de Vaux, who afterwards blamed each other for the débâcle, and came to blows.[47] It was a very small-scale engagement, but as future events were to show, a valuable propaganda victory for King Robert.

Early in May Robert had moved northwards from Glen Trool and was encamped at Galston, where he received a formal challenge from Pembroke. As early as February Pembroke had been quite unfairly accused by King Edward of making little attempt to crush the Scottish rebels, of acting over-cautiously, and of attempting to conceal the fact by sending no reports.[48] Pembroke, who was both courageous and energetic, would have been galled by these accusations, and after the failure of the Glen Trool raid, doubly eager to justify himself. Robert accepted Pembroke's challenge and agreed to battle on 10 March, naming nearby Loudon Hill as his chosen ground. He selected a strong position on the slope of the hill, under the sharp crag which rises like a jagged tooth from the surrounding countryside. Stretches of swamp lay on either side of the hill, making an encircling attack impossible. Robert further improved the position by having three lines of trenches dug. His forces now numbered six hundred fugitive men, who were drawn up in two divisions behind the defensive ditches.

According to Barbour, Pembroke had three thousand men. He described the advance of the magnificently accoutred knights, with the brilliant colours of their shields, banners and pennons spread out across the fields, the sunlight flaming on their hauberks and bascinets, making them glitter like angels from heaven.[49] Then the trumpets sounded, and they charged 'with heid stouped and speris staught' (with heads low and spears levelled),[50] thundering towards the immobile ranks of spearmen, apparently bringing inevitable annihilation. King Robert himself, with Edward de Bruce and James Douglas, stood shoulder to shoulder with the anonymous spearmen, beyond the unseen barrier of the first trench.

Suddenly the charging knights became a chaotic mass of fallen men and horses, floundering in the trench and impaled on the spears. In the confusion there was easy and enthusiastic slaughter. Within a short time a hundred or more knights lay dead.[51]

This might have been a small loss to demoralize so completely a force of three thousand, and probably Barbour's estimate of Pembroke's numbers was greatly exaggerated. However few or many they were, they had been divided into rearguard and vanguard, and when the rear saw what had befallen the van 'Yai fled for-awter mar respyte' (without delay they took to flight).[52] Pembroke, unable to rally them, retreated to Bothwell Castle, leaving prisoners in the hands of the Scots.

It seems extraordinary that King Robert, who consistently preferred raid and surprise to pitched battle, should have accepted Pembroke's challenge. Possibly, confident in his choice of the terrain and his capacity to convert it into a large-scale ambush, he saw the opportunity to raise the morale of his newly formed fighting force, eager to shed the blood of the oppressor. Not the least of his military skills was ability to sense the mood of his men. Possibly he also had to avenge the humiliation that Pembroke had inflicted on him at Methven, and he could feel gratified to have done so.

The victory caused a surge of rejoicing and hope, and more supporters joined the King.

On 15 May, five days after the engagement at Loudon Hill, a pro-English Scot wrote to an English official, from Forfar.

I hear that Bruce never had the good will of his own followers or the people generally so much with him as now. It appears that God is with him, for he has destroyed King Edward's power both among English and Scots. The people believe that Bruce will carry all before him. . . . exhorted by false preachers from Bruce's army. If Bruce can get away in this direction or towards the parts of Ross he will find the people all ready at his will . . . May it please God to prolong King Edward's life, for men say openly that when he is gone victory will go to Bruce. For these preachers have told the people that they have found a prophecy of Merlin, that after the death of 'Le Roy Coveytous' the people of Scotland and Wales shall band together and have full lordship and live in peace together to the end of the world.[53]

King Robert was far from having destroyed King Edward's power, but the letter shows the powerful effect that two repulses had had upon English morale, and the speed with which the news of them had trav-

elled. It also hints at the existence of a surprisingly sophisticated propaganda machine, with the use of 'false priests' to spread rumours of a
prophecy of Merlin well calculated to arouse public excitement.
Whether or not the conquered Welsh would respond to his appeal to
pan-Celticism, the Scots could be expected to feel a surge of enthusiasm at the death of 'Le Roy Coveytous' and join a new attempt to throw
off their chains.

It seemed safe to prophesy the imminent death of Edward I, but the
old king, with a final flowering of his incredible will-power, dragged
himself from his bed at Lanercost and summoned his army to assemble at Carlisle. Having been stimulated with a cordial made of amber,
jacinth, musk, pearls, gold and silver, and other medicines fetched from
York by Peter the Surgeon,[54] he was able to review his army at Carlisle,
at Pentecost (14 May).

News of the repulse in Glen Trool, the defeat of Pembroke at
Loudon Hill, and, ten days later, the pursuit of another English force
right up to the walls of Ayr, probably decided Edward I to take the field
himself. He was unable to move throughout June, but on 3 July he left
Carlisle at the head of his army, on horseback. He was so frail that over
the next three days the army moved only six miles. On 6 July it was
encamped at Burgh-by-Sands near the southern shore of the Solway
Estuary. The following morning, when the King's servants came to lift
him from his bed and help him to eat, he sank back dead in their arms
as they tried to raise him.[55] It was a quiet death for a King whose mind
was still bent on conquest.

Froissart told the story that the dying Edward I made his son
promise that his body should be boiled until the flesh parted from the
bones, that the flesh should be buried, and that every time the Scots
rebelled, the bones should be carried with the expedition that marched
against them.[56]

If Edward I had made this demand it would not have been regarded
as macabre. It was a method of preparing dead bodies for easy trans-
portation devised in thirteenth-century Germany, and used to bring
home the remains of St Louis and other crusaders.[57] To attribute to
Edward I the desire that his bones should be carried into battle against
the Scots was a picturesque way of illustrating his undying obsession
with the conquest of Scotland.

However, Edward of Caernarvon was not at his father's deathbed to make the reported promise. Summoned by messengers, he arrived some days later.[58]

Though reproached by many historians for disregarding a promise that he had not had the opportunity to make, he accorded the corpse of his father traditional honours. It was embalmed in the normal manner, and the entrails and brain were buried at the Abbey of Holm Cultram, Cumberland (which, incongruously, was also the burial place of King Robert's father).[59]

Edward II, accompanied by Anthony Bek, Bishop of Durham, attended his father's corpse for several days on its southward journey, before returning to Carlisle to receive the homage of his father's vassals, and then moving on to Scotland to receive that of pro-English Scots at Dumfries.[60] The body of Edward I was carried to Waltham Abbey, where it lay in state until the autumn; the funeral took place on 27 October 1307, in Westminster Abbey. The tomb was closed with an unadorned slab of polished Purbeck marble, to which the famous inscription proclaiming the king '*Scottorum Malleus*' was added in a later century.[61]

At Dumfries, Edward II was joined by Piers Gaveston, whom he had immediately recalled from exile. There, on 6 August, he created Gaveston Earl of Cornwall, conferring on him a royal earldom, previously held by the late King's cousin, Edmund of Cornwall.[62]

Edward then made some show of taking up his father's campaign by marching his army as far as Cannock on the border of Ayrshire, but before the end of August provisions ran short. The enemy was not to be found, so Edward willingly withdrew to England, for he had pleasanter priorities than campaigning.

If Edward II succeeded with the goodwill of his father's magnates and officials, he very quickly dissipated it, and for this his devotion to Gaveston was the dominant if not the only cause. In September Gaveston went to Cornwall to take possession of his lands, and at the beginning of October he returned to London and participated in the ruin of Bishop Walter Langton, the late King's treasurer, against whom he and the new King bore an old grudge, and who conveniently could be blamed for the empty state of the royal treasury. If Gaveston bore the blame for Langton's fall, Edward bore the blame for favouring Gaveston, for whom no honour was too high. On 1 November he was married to Margaret de Clare, daughter of the King's eldest sister Joan of Acre, by her first husband Gilbert de Clare, Earl of Gloucester, thus drawing him into the inner circle of the royal family. On 20 December he was appointed *Custos Regni* (Keeper of the Realm) in readiness for the King's departure to France, to pay homage for his French lands and solemnize his marriage to King Philip IV's daughter, Isabella of France. It seems that the famous opening lines of Marlowe's *Edward II*, 'My father is deceased, come Gaveston, and share the kingdom with thy greatest friend', accurately sum up his intentions for his favourite.

The opinions of Gaveston's scholarly modern biographers on his relations with the King are absolutely opposed. According to one, 'there is no question that the King and his favourite were lovers'.[63] According to the other, Gaveston was intolerable to the magnates because Edward adopted him as his brother, thus conferring upon him an unacceptable status.[64] It is possible to quote many contemporary sources in support of either argument, and both authors marshal an impressive array of sources. Many will lend themselves to either argument; the Lanercost chronicler, for example, wrote that Edward I had exiled Gaveston 'because of the improper familiarity which my lord Edward the younger entertained with him, speaking of him openly as his brother'.[65] The author of the contemporary *Vita Edwardi Secondi* wrote the much-quoted words: 'I do not remember to have heard that one man so loved another.'[66] But he also quoted the King speaking of 'my brother Piers'.[67]

The two interpretations are not necessarily mutually exclusive. It seems obvious that Edward loved Gaveston not as a favourite but as an alter ego, and there was no way in which he could confer on his beloved the equality that such love required except by giving him the pseudo-royalty of an adoptive brother. Unhappily, it was a solution that rendered Gaveston more obnoxious than before. As Piers Gaveston became an object of universal detestation, 'that accursed individual', and 'accounted a sorcerer', his real personality vanished beneath the vituperation heaped upon him. A glimpse of the real man is captured in the *Scalachronica*, whose author's father, Sir Thomas Grey the elder, would have remembered him. '[He was] very magnificent, liberal and well-bred in manner, but somewhat haughty and super-cilious.'[68]

He was also, through no desire of his own, a valuable ally to Robert the Bruce, for while Edward II defended his other self against the rising tide of magnatial enmity, King Robert had a respite from war with England, and a chance to strike a decisive blow against his home-grown enemies.

9

————|✻|✻|✻|————

THE WAR IN THE NORTH

'When [Robert] was told by someone that the tyrant
Edward had died, he broke into loud laughter. Seeing
this the few who stood round him were amazed, for
they had not seen him laugh during the whole year past.
"Rejoice," he said to his men, "and laugh with me, for
the Lord is my helper and I shall fear no more what
men can do to me. The Lord is my helper, and I shall
see the downfall of my enemies . . . But know, fellow
soldiers, that I do not laugh at the death of an enemy,
but for the liberation of our people and country.'[1]

THOUGH EDWARD I had been dying for many months, his death
brought his enemies a sense of release, such had been the power of his
reputation, and the remorseless pressure of his will. But while King
Robert and his partisans laughed out loud for sheer joy and relief at the
happier outlook for their country, the magnates of England were filled
with gloom at the altered prospects for theirs, with Edward II soon
compared to Rehoboam, the son of Solomon, 'who neglected the
counsel of the elders and followed the advice of the young'.[2] And so
long as 'the young' principally meant Gaveston, there was little chance
that the King would earn the better opinion of his magnates.

However well informed King Robert may have been of events in
England, he could not have foreseen the years of strife provoked by the
King's devotion to Gaveston, or the struggle between Edward and the
group of magnates headed by his cousin Thomas of Lancaster to
control the King's ambitious and insouciant rule by means of the
'Ordinances'. But King Robert could at least foresee that Edward II's
attention would be deflected from Scotland for some months by the

obligations to attend his father's funeral, meet his first Parliament, travel to France for his marriage, pay homage for his French lands, and return to solemnize his coronation. It was an additional piece of good fortune that Edward II replaced the Earl of Pembroke as Viceroy of Scotland with John of Brittany, Earl of Richmond, who had been appointed by Edward I in 1305, but superseded by Pembroke, who, with his French military experience, had been promoted to crush the rebellion of Robert the Bruce.[3] Though Pembroke had suffered two reverses, he was still acknowledged to be a formidable enemy, whereas his replacement was a notoriously indecisive commander. Pembroke left Scotland at the end of September or beginning of October 1307.

Apart from the English occupying forces, King Robert's main groups of opponents in Scotland were the MacDoualls of Galloway in the south-west, the MacDougalls of Lorn in the western Highlands, the Comyns led by the Earl of Buchan in the north-east, and the Earl of Ross, whose authority extended into the far north, since he was also the Guardian of the young Earl of Sutherland. In the climate of uncertainty following the withdrawal of Edward II from Scotland and the removal of Pembroke, there was probably little aggressive action to be anticipated from the English, who would content themselves with holding the castles and towns they occupied, feeling secure in the knowledge of Robert's lack of siege engines.

Robert knew that his ultimate success as King of Scots depended upon breaking or reconciling the opposition to him within the kingdom. The manner in which he dealt with his enemies suggests the mind of a statesman and a strategist. His grand design was to prevent the unification of his enemies, whose combined forces would outnumber his own, and instead to defeat them piecemeal by eliminating each group in turn, a plan which demanded speed, ruthlessness, and flexibility in action.

He struck first at the nearest group of enemies, the MacDoualls of Galloway, Comyn kindred and Balliol supporters, upon whom he also wished to avenge the death of his brothers Thomas and Alexander, handed over to the English for execution by Dougal MacDouall. In September King Robert's forces, greatly augmented since Loudon Hill, surged through Galloway, setting the whole lordship ablaze from end to end and sending a stream of refugees over the border into England, driving their cattle before them, to take shelter in the Cumbrian forest

of Inglewood.[4] The Gallovidians who had not fled were forced to pay
heavily for a truce, which helped to finance the next phase of the King's
campaign. No doubt the harrying of Galloway also provided a substantial haul of armour, weapons and provisions.

The King now divided his forces. He left a contingent under James
Douglas, to defend and extend the patriotic cause in the south-west. He
himself, accompanied by his brother Edward, and his constant
companions the Earl of Lennox, Sir Neil Campbell, Sir Gilbert de
Cattaye and Sir Robert Boyd, led his army, continuously augmented by
new supporters, towards the north-east.

So long as Robert's forces were contained in the south-west he would
remain a freedom fighter or a terrorist, according to the viewpoint of
his friends or enemies. His decision to assert his claim in the north-east
was his crossing of the Rubicon.

Robert marched his army northward through the western Highlands,
supported by a fleet of galleys under the command of Angus Og, which
flanked his progress up the Firth of Lorne and through Loch Linnhe.
Their combined forces overawed the MacDougalls of Lorn without a
fight. Fortuitously John of Lorn had fallen ill, and it was probably he
who asked for a truce, though he later claimed it was Robert who had
done so. Early the following year John of Lorn wrote his own account
of events to Edward II with an appeal for help. Writing in March 1308,
he told King Edward that he had been confined to bed for the past six
months.

> Robert Bruce approached these parts by land and sea with 10,000
> men they say, or 15,000 . . . The barons of Argyll gave me no aid. Yet
> Bruce asked for a truce . . . I have heard, my lord, that when Bruce
> came he was boasting and claiming that I had come to his peace, in
> order to inflate his own reputation, so that others would rise more
> readily to his support . . . if you hear this from others you are not to
> believe it; for I shall always be ready to carry out your orders with all
> my power . . . I am not sure of my neighbours in any direction. As
> soon as you and your army come, then, if my health permits, I shall
> not be found wanting, but will come to your service . . .[5]

John of Lorn probably exaggerated the numbers of his enemies, to
excuse his negotiation of a truce. The combined forces of King Robert

and Angus Og might have been more realistically numbered at 1,500 than 15,000.

With the MacDougalls temporarily out of action, King Robert led his army through the Great Glen. When he reached the north-east he could be confident of finding support in his own lands of Garioch, and in Moray, where Bishop David de Moray, now returned from his refuge in Orkney, had been preaching the patriot cause. Also, according to the anonymous newsletter of the previous spring, King Robert could expect to find supporters when he reached 'the ports of Ross'.[6]

At the foot of the Great Glen, Robert captured the Comyn stronghold of Inverlochy, followed by Castle Urquhart on the northern shore of Loch Ness. At the head of the glen he linked up with the Bishop of Moray and his supporters, who included Sir William Wiseman and Sir David de Barclay, and other knights of Moray. Their combined forces captured and burned Inverness and Nairn. All the captured castles were razed to the ground, in accordance with King Robert's policy of rendering them useless to the enemy.[7]

The King was now ready for a reckoning with the Earl of Ross, and might have required a bloody one, for Ross had violated the sanctuary at Tain, seized the Queen and her companions and delivered them to Edward I. But the King found Ross ready to make a truce, and he accepted it. In view of the vast area of the Earl's influence, it would be better to win him as an ally than batter him into submission as a crushed and resentful subject. It was a statesmanlike decision to forgo the temptation of vengeance, and it was well repaid the following year when Ross gave his allegiance willingly. In the meantime the truce was concluded, to last until 2 June 1308.

The Earl of Ross somewhat tardily wrote to Edward II, in January 1308, with his excuses for having negotiated a truce.

We heard of the coming of Sir Robert Bruce towards the parts of Ross with great power, so that we had no power against him but nevertheless we caused our men to be called up and we were stationed for a fortnight with three thousand men, at our own expense, on the borders of our earldom and in two other earldoms, Sutherland and Caithness, and Bruce would have destroyed them utterly if we had not made a truce with him at the entreaty of good men, both clergy and others, until next June . . .[8]

Ross went on to explain that he still would not have made a truce but for the absence of the English Warden of Moray, Sir Reginald Cheyne, whose men would not obey him without the warden's authority, and he appealed to King Edward to send help. The letter probably reached London when the King had gone to France for his marriage, for it was inscribed with a memorandum '*Ad istem petitionem non potest responderi sine Rege*' (It is not possible to answer this petition without the King).[9] The letter remained unanswered, and help was not forthcoming, which no doubt played its part in Ross's later decision to go over to Robert the Bruce.

Robert could not expect to reach an accommodation with the Comyns. The feud resulting from his murder of the Red Comyn precluded the possibility of a peaceful settlement. In November he swung east, to confront John Comyn, Earl of Buchan, in his own earldom. On his way, he attacked the English-held town and castle of Elgin, but was repulsed. When surprise failed he had neither the time nor the means for a long siege. He marched through his own estate of the Garioch, which bordered on Buchan. Here local support ensured him of a strong base from which to launch his attack.

He had reached Inverurie, the chief town of the Garioch, when he was struck by a mysterious illness.

> That put him to such great distress
> That soon he neither drank nor ate
> No medicine could his company get
> For his distress, that might avail,
> And all his strength began to fail.
> On horse nor foot he could not go.[10]

He seemed likely to die, and his companions were utterly demoralized and terrified 'for all yar confort in him wes' (for all their comfort in him was).[11]

According to Barbour, it was Sir Edward de Bruce who took the decision to withdraw from Inverurie, with the King carried on a litter. The King's forces found a refuge inaccessible to their enemies, in a wooded marsh called the Slioch, near Huntly.[12]

In the meantime the Earl of Buchan had mustered his forces, and joined by David de Strathbogie, Earl of Atholl, and the pro-English Sir

John de Mowbray, prepared to engage the King's forces. His sudden sickness, and the retreat from Inverurie, made it seem that Robert's good fortune had deserted him, and he was once more reduced to the condition of a fugitive.

It was Christmas Day, and there had been a heavy fall of snow, when Buchan and his forces reached the Slioch. There was a skirmish between archers from both armies on the edge of the wood. The King's men had the best of the encounter, and Buchan withdrew to seek reinforcements.

King Robert's forces remained at the Slioch for another week, but their position was growing untenable; the King was still helpless, and provisions were running out. On 31 December Buchan returned with a larger force of infantry. Again Edward de Bruce took the initiative, and marched the King's forces out of the Slioch in close formation, surrounding the King on his litter. Their appearance was so formidable that Buchan drew off without a fight, and the King's forces reached Strathbogie, and there they stayed for some time, until the King began to recover.[13] But once again, bitter weather and shortage of provisions forced them to move on. It was probably at the end of January that the King decided to return to Inverurie.

During that month the Earl of Buchan had attempted to win the support of the Earl of Ross, but Ross refused to break his truce with the King.[14] However, Buchan, reinforced by the pro-English Sir David de Brechin from Angus, and with an English force contributed by Sir John de Mowbray, gathered his army at Old Meldrum, and sent a small force to reconnoitre the King's position at Inverurie. Buchan's force surprised the King's outposts; some men were killed and the rest fled into the town.

According to the *Scotichronicon*, when the King heard this he

ordered his men to arm themselves and place him on his horse. When this was done, although because of the severity of his illness he could not sit erect on his horse without relying on the help of two of his men, he nevertheless hurried with the appearance of eagerness at the head of his troops against his enemies right to the place of battle. And when the other side saw him ready along with his men for battle, they were terrified by the mere sight of him. They all turned to flee, and were pursued for twelve leagues as far as Fyrie [a castle in English control]. When this rout was over and the enemy had been overwhelmed and scattered he destroyed the earldom of Buchan with fire. He killed those of his enemies whom he chose and exempted those whom he wanted to live, especially Scots who had come over to his side, graciously allowing them to live in peace.[15]

After the rout of Inverurie the Earl of Buchan fled to England, where he died before the end of the year. Sir David de Brechin fled to his own castle of Brechin, and a few months later made his peace with King Robert. The devastation of the Earl of Buchan's lands, remembered with terror for fifty years as the 'Herschip of Buchan', marked the extinction of the Comyns' power in Scotland.

All the time that Robert the Bruce lay sick at the Slioch and in Strathbogie, his greatest fear must have been that the precious time granted him by the death of Edward I, and the necessary preoccupations of the new King, would run out before he could make any further use of it.

In opening his campaign in the autumn and pursuing it through the winter, he was operating outside the normal campaigning season, which gave him the added advantage of knowing that the sending of reinforcements north by land or revictualling English-held ports by sea would be difficult and might be impossible. But when the spring came the appeals for help sent by Edward II's deputies and supporters remained unanswered until late May, when King Edward sent letters which thanked them for their faithful service, and desired them to remain at their posts.[16] He was unable to send support, and grateful though King Robert must have been for this inexplicable inactivity, it was probably a long time before he knew the cause.

The English magnates had been understandably indignant when King Edward appointed Gaveston as *Custos Regni* (Keeper of the Realm) during his visit to France. In the King's absence Gaveston's administration was perfectly prudent and efficient, but his arrogant manners aroused increasing resentment. It was even reported that 'the Earls coming before him to discuss business were forced to kneel in order to bring their reasons before him'.[17]

On 7 February 1308 King Edward landed at Dover with his French bride, and immediately, seeing Gaveston among the magnates assembled to meet him, Edward ran to him and 'giving him kisses and repeated embraces, he was adored with a singular familiarity'.[18]

The coronation took place on 25 February, having been rescheduled from the intended date of 18 February, following a demand by a group of English magnates and members of the French royal family that Piers Gaveston be banished from the realm. King Edward only delayed the demand by promising 'in good faith to undertake whatever they sought in the next Parliament'; so the coronation was celebrated, with little rejoicing, on the later date.

The commons, unaware of the tensions among their rulers, assembled in the greatest crowds that had been seen since Edward of Caernarvon was knighted in 1306. They were no doubt disappointed that he entered Westminster Abbey by a door from the Palace of Westminster 'to avoid the crush of the populace', and in consequence they missed the culminating outrage offered to the magnates of England that day, which was the sight of Piers Gaveston, dressed in royal purple sewn with pearls (unlike the other magnates, who wore cloth of gold), and bearing the Crown of St Edward in the state procession before the King.

The young Queen Isabella, her brother Charles (later King Charles IV of France) and her uncles Charles de Valois and Louis d'Evreux, were probably far more enraged that at the coronation banquet the King ignored Isabella and concentrated his attention entirely upon Gaveston. The Queen's kinsmen left the banquet in protest, and an English earl (unnamed) who expressed a wish to kill Gaveston then and there was dissuaded with the words '*Non in die festo . . .*' (Not on a feast day),[19] which did not augur well for Gaveston's future fate.

When Parliament assembled on 28 April (having been postponed from 28 February) Edward II was faced with a strong opposition headed by Henry de Lacy, Earl of Lincoln, which demanded the exile of Gaveston. Edward, determined not to be parted from him, initially resisted, and since the opposition refused to yield, England lurched towards civil war. On 18 May Edward submitted to the inevitable, and agreed that Gaveston should leave the country by 25 June, and that the estates of the earldom of Cornwall should revert to the Crown, though Gaveston might keep the title. Edward compensated Gaveston by endowing him with estates in other parts of England and in Gascony, and nullified the disgrace of exile by appointing Gaveston Lieutenant of Ireland. Then, to demonstrate the honourable nature of his departure, the King accompanied him to Bristol, whence he sailed.

While this political and emotional drama was played out, King Robert had recovered his health and resumed his campaign in northeastern Scotland. In the course of the spring he captured and destroyed the remaining strongholds of the Comyns and most of the castles held by King Edward's deputies. He took Tarradale, which belonged to Buchan's brother Alexander Comyn, and Buchan's castles of Slains, Kinedar, Rattray, Dundarg and Kelly. He took Balvenie, which may have been held by either Buchan or Sir Reginald Cheynie, and the latter lost Duffus. King Robert also captured the castles of Fyvie, Kintore and Aboyne.[20] Sir William Wiseman captured the castle of Skelbo in Sutherland on his behalf.

In April 1308 the King attacked Elgin for the second time, but was repulsed by the timely arrival of Sir John de Mowbray with a relieving force; Mowbray had fled from the rout of Inverurie, but had not yet given up the fight against Robert the Bruce. It was indeed remarkable how determined was the resistance of the supporters of Edward II, considering his failure to send them reinforcements. But Elgin capitulated to King Robert's third attack, in May 1308, which probably suggests that English morale had finally crumbled. In July the citizens of Aberdeen rose in revolt against their English garrison, and delivered the town to Robert the Bruce. The castle surrendered shortly afterwards.[21] Between the Tay and the Moray Firth the English occupation was now confined to four towns: Perth, Dundee, Forfar and, isolated far to the north of the others, the small port of Banff. Before the end of the year Forfar was captured by Philip the Forrester, keeper of the nearby royal forest of Platar, who with a small company scaled the walls by night and massacred the garrison.[22]

Of all the places that fell to Robert the Bruce in 1308 the most valuable was Aberdeen, a major seaport through which he could trade with the Continent. Since the assertion of his claim to the Scottish throne, one of Robert's greatest problems had been acquiring supplies of arms and armour for his growing numbers of men. So far, arms acquired from captured castles and prisoners, and the booty of local raids, had been his sources of supply. Henceforward, the possession of Aberdeen opened the possibility of arms trade with Flanders, Germany, Scandinavia and, surprisingly, England.

Trade between Flanders and Aberdeen was long established, and a colony of Flemish merchants in the city helped to maintain close relations. The Flemish cloth industry relied upon supplies of wool from both Scotland and England, and before the end of the thirteenth century competition from Italian merchants for English wool had raised the value of supplies for Scotland.[23]

The war of battles and sieges was underscored by a trade war, in which Edward II, once the conflict had re-engaged his attention, endeavoured to prevent Continental merchants and his own subjects from trading with the Scots. In October 1309 he complained to the Count of Flanders that the Scots and their German allies were buying arms in Flanders, and demanded that they should be forbidden to enter the country. But the trade continued as before.[24]

Edward II was equally unsuccessful in preventing the merchants of England's east coast ports – Hull, King's Lynn, Harwich and Norwich – from trading with the enemy. Even less likely was any chance of preventing Berwick, so recently wrested from Scotland, from doing so. By 1314 merchants from the East Anglian ports were reported to be travelling the inland counties of England, accompanied by Scots, and purchasing supplies ostensibly for King Edward's forthcoming Scottish campaign, but which were forwarded to the army of Robert the Bruce.[25] Edward II was also unsuccessful in preventing the arms trade between Scotland and Ireland, which, since Ireland had no weapons manufacture, was based upon the re-export to Scotland of English arms. The arms dealers of the fourteenth century were as profit-oriented as their modern counterparts. The acquisition of Aberdeen marked the beginning of a trade which for King Robert was probably as decisive as any military action in securing his ultimate victory.

By July 1308 King Robert was preparing to move against the MacDougalls of Lorn. The truce with John of Lorn, once renewed in the interim, was now about to expire, and the King had sent for James Douglas to join forces with him in the forthcoming campaign.

Since they had parted company the previous year, Douglas's success had paralleled the King's. Though his movements were more localized, his success was supremely important to the patriot cause. In the period of approximately eleven months he had won control of Douglasdale, upper Clydesdale and of the forest as far as Jedburgh.[26]

The most dramatic and individually remembered of his exploits was his first attack on his own castle of Douglas, which, since he lacked resources to hold it, he subjected to ruinous and bloody sack. In Barbour's narrative, the episode is set in the context of 1307, and dated with circumstantial detail to Palm Sunday (March 19). This seems too early, given the fugitive condition of the King's small force in the opening months of that year; later historians have suggested Palm Sunday, 17 April 1308.[27]

James made contact with a Douglasdale farmer named Tom Dickson, who had been a loyal vassal of his father, and a friend to him in childhood. Dickson concealed him and his small company until the morning of Palm Sunday, when the garrison of the castle attended the local church, bearing palms. Douglas with his companions and some local supporters entered the church, and others waited outside. Suddenly, within the church, someone shouted the war-cry 'Douglas! Douglas!' Fighting began and many of the garrison were killed and others taken prisoner. Dickson was killed in the church, which made Douglas's mood the more pitiless. Taking the prisoners, he led his men to the castle, which they found occupied only by the porter and the cook, such had been the easy confidence of the occupiers. Cook and porter were killed, and Douglas and his men sat down to the dinner which had been prepared for others. They then collected everything they could bring away.

> And namly wapnys and armyng,
> Siluer and tresour and clethyng
>
> [And many weapons and armour
> Silver, treasure and clothes][28]

They then gathered the castle's stores of wheat, flour, meal and malt and piled them together in the cellar. They stove in the wine casks, and piled on the casks for fuel. They decapitated the prisoners and heaped the bodies on top, and set the pyre alight. Their final act before leaving the castle was to foul the well with salt and the bodies of dead horses. The people of Douglasdale, highly gratified at this blow against the occupying forces, jocularly called this scene at the castle 'the Douglas Larder', and the name was immortalized by Barbour.[29]

The story has been retold so many times, and its ironically anodyne title so frequently repeated, that it has become an adventurous exploit from which the intrinsic horror has been almost expunged. But the late-twentieth-century reader, to whom visual images of the horrors of war have become distressingly familiar, should have no difficulty in imagining the reality of the scene, and the impression created upon the next English force that arrived to occupy Douglas Castle by the sight of the charred bodies of their compatriots, and the rancid stench of their pyre. Those who saw it saw the 'other countenance' of the chivalrous young man who caught fish and game for the fugitive Queen and ladies in the summer of 1306.

Douglas Castle was no sooner reoccupied, cleansed and provisioned than James Douglas struck again. He concealed a large body of men in an ambush near the castle, and sent a small party to drive off the cattle which were grazing outside the castle walls. The new captain of the castle, whose name, says Barbour, was Thirlwall, led a sortie to attack the raiders. He had ridden out so impetuously that he went bareheaded. The raiders fled in the direction of the ambush, hotly pursued by Thirlwall and his men. Then Douglas and his company broke from their hiding place and counter-attacked so fiercely that the English force turned and fled, and most were cut down before they could regain the castle. The few survivors slammed the gates in the face of their pursuers and prepared to defend the castle. But Douglas had not come to besiege it, and he and his company disappeared into the countryside again. The survivors of the garrison were left to collect their dead, amongst whom was the unfortunate Thirlwall.

When James Douglas finally captured his ancestral castle, he again employed a ruse to tempt the garrison to make a sortie. This time a line of pack-horses loaded with hay invited the easy acquisition of provender, which was running short for the garrison's own horses. In the distance the figures leading the horses had looked like gowned country-women taking their hay to market. Great was the attackers' surprise when these figures threw aside their deceptive long cloaks, dropped their bundles of hay, leapt on their horses and turned to fight. The larger force which again had waited in ambush now emerged to support them, and as on the previous occasion the party from the castle was overwhelmed with great loss, and its captain killed. But this time Douglas's force was much larger, and he was able to storm the castle.

Barbour tells that the captain of the castle had been a knight named Sir John of Webton, and that among his possessions was found a letter from a lady who had promised that if he could defend 'ye adventuris castell off Douglas' (the perilous Castle Douglas) for a year, she would marry him.[30] James Douglas, perhaps inspired to a chivalrous mood by this touching discovery, permitted all the prisoners taken in the castle to depart unharmed.

Then, in accordance with the King's policy, he razed the castle to the ground, an act that demonstrates his loyalty to the King, and which must have caused him great regret, for it was his own chief stronghold even though he could not enjoy possession of it, and the symbol of his family's authority in the area for generations.

James Douglas's three attacks on the castle of Douglas, whether they were spread over 1307–8 or crowded into the first half of 1308, greatly enhanced his reputation among the English as a figure of terror, who seemed to possess an uncanny power to appear out of nowhere, wreak destruction, and vanish without a trace. He won legendary fame as the diabolical 'Black Douglas' to his enemies, and the heroic 'Good Lord James' to his friends, and to generations of admiring Scots. As Barbour's vignettes honestly show, he was capable on a whim of cold-blooded terrorism and of gestures of chivalrous generosity.

After the destruction of Douglas Castle James Douglas moved into Selkirk Forest, extending his control over it. In a forest skirmish he captured King Robert's nephew, Thomas Randolph, who had been fighting with the English ever since he had been spared by the Earl of Pembroke after the battle of Methven, on this condition. James Douglas carried Randolph with him when he marched to join forces with the King.

The meeting of the King and his nephew, as represented by Barbour, shows Randolph as having been temporarily indoctrinated with the English view of the King, and also conveys the blend of good humour and natural authority with which King Robert won and held the devotion of his followers. The King was delighted by the arrival of James Douglas, and the news of success that he brought:

> To see him come the King rejoiced
> And many times his thanks he voiced

And said to his nephew with a smile
'Thou hast denied thy faith a while
Now be thou reconciled to me'
But to the King thus answered he
'Ye chide me but say I tis ye
That should be chidden rightfully!
For since ye war against the king
Of England ye had better bring
Your claims to test of open fight
Instead of cowardice and sleight'.
The king replied 'Things well may move
Ere very long to such a proof.
But since thou speakst disdainfully
Tis well that I should punish thee
For insolence, till mayhap thou
Shalt know the right and to it bow!'[31]

Randolph remained in custody for a short while, probably a prisoner of James Douglas, for a warm friendship grew between the two men, though it contained an element of competitiveness on which the King kept a watchful eye. And Randolph soon saw that the King's method of waging war was not 'cowardice and sleight' but skilful use of limited resources, and that he did not always shun 'open fight', as an impressive victory would shortly prove. Repenting of his arrogant discourtesy, Randolph offered his loyalty to King Robert, gave him distinguished service, and in return received both affection and rewards. Perhaps the King valued his young kinsman all the more since the war had claimed the lives of three loyal brothers.

A medieval king was expected to honour and advance his kinsmen, and to reward men who served him well. He would be criticized for lack of generosity had he failed to do so as much as for immoderate generosity if his rewards were excessive. King Robert committed neither error. He was certainly generous to his kinsmen and those who married into his family, but he was even-handed in rewarding his adherents, especially the members of that small band who had supported him from the beginning. Among these it was generally acknowledged that James Douglas was closest to him, and partly through the infleunce of Barbour's portrayal this relationship has been represented as a legendary heroic friendship, like that of Roland and Oliver. But though there was evidently deep affection and mutual regard between them, Douglas was in no sense a royal favourite. He did not monopolize the King's attention, he did not receive disproportionate favours, he did not arouse the jealousy of his peers. Indeed, the skill with which King Robert balanced the claims of kinship and friendship and distributed rewards and honours was a model of kingly conduct, as the loyalty offered to him bore witness.

In early August 1308 the combined forces of Robert the Bruce and James Douglas moved westward to open the campaign against the MacDougalls of Lorn.

A probable place for their rendezvous would have been Tyndrum, near the sight of their previous encounter with John of Lorn at Dalry, which they were now to avenge. From Tyndrum their march to Lorn would take them by way of Glen Lochy and Strath Orchy to the head of Loch Awe, across the head of the Y-shaped loch, and along the north shore of its western arm. This part of the route forms the pass of Brander, where the narrow track clung to the precipitous side of Ben Cruachan (which Barbour erroneously believed to be the highest mountain in Britain).[32] Below the track was a steep drop into the waters of Loch Awe.

This was an ideal spot for an ambush, and John of Lorn, who had collected a force of some two thousand men, prepared to repeat the tactics he had used successfully at Dalry. John ranged his men high on the mountainside along the pass, ready to roll down boulders upon the King's forces as they marched along the narrow track, and then to charge down and complete the destruction by driving them into the loch. John himself, still not fully recovered from his long illness, waited to watch the destruction of his enemies from a galley on the loch.

But King Robert 'persawyt rycht weill yar satette' (saw through their ploy), and before his army entered the pass he sent James Douglas with a force of archers to occupy the higher shores of the mountainside. They gained the heights above John of Lorn's men, and two sets of eyes watched for the King's advance.

Far below, the small, foreshortened figures of the King's advance guard of lightly armed infantry appeared in the pass, loosely strung out and moving swiftly. The men of Lorn precipitated their avalanche of boulders, but these came thundering down the mountainside towards a column forewarned of the danger, and for the most part they passed harmlessly through the gaps in the lines and crashed into the loch.

The King's men turned and charged uphill towards the enemy, who would still have the advantage of the ground. But from the heights above a deadly shower of arrows struck them in the back, and then Douglas's force charged down upon them with drawn swords. Assailed from above and below, the men of Lorn put up a stalwart fight, before they broke and fled towards the western extremity of the loch. Here a single bridge carried the road over the River Awe. The men of Lorn were intent upon destroying the bridge to impede the King's advance. But they were pursued so closely that the bridge was captured intact.[33]

John of Lorn, having witnessed the defeat of his army, fled southward down the loch in his galley, and probably took refuge in the castle of Inchconnell.[34] King Robert, having broken the resistance in the pass, pursued the enemy over the bridge, and advanced to besiege the MacDougall stronghold of Dunstaffnage. The castle was vigorously attacked, and was surrendered to King Robert by John of Lorn's father, Alexander MacDougall of Argyll, who acknowledged Robert's kingship and yielded himself as hostage for the good behaviour of his followers.[35] He remained in the King's peace for about a year, before rejoining his son, who in the meantime had fled to England.[36] The power of the MacDougalls was effectively broken, but there was no 'herschip' of Lorn like that of Buchan. Contrary to his usual practice of destroying captured castles, as a precautionary measure against local insurgence, King Robert garrisoned and provisioned Dunstaffnage and left an occupying force to maintain his authority in the area.

While the King and James Douglas had undertaken the campaign against the MacDougalls of Lorn, Edward de Bruce had led an expedition into Galloway, where the truce forced upon the Gallovidians the previous year had also expired. He was opposed by Dougal MacDouall supported by an English contingent under Sir Ingram de Umfraville and Sir Aymer de St John. Edward de Bruce defeated them at a crossing of the River Dee, near the castle of Buittle.[37] Thereafter savage harrying of the countryside sent a new stream of refugees fleeing to England, among them the family of Dougal MacDouall. Dougal himself remained, and was given command of the garrison of

Dumfries, from which he was able to continue his resistance to Edward de Bruce at the same time.[38] In the autumn Edward moved into Lanarkshire to join forces with James Douglas, returning from the campaign against John of Lorn, and together they besieged and captured the castle of Rutherglen.

Early the next year King Robert created Edward de Bruce Lord of Galloway, but though he had overrun the country he could not claim secure possession of it so long as several strongholds of the south-west remained in English hands. Besides Buittle and Dumfries these were Lochmaben, Caerlaverock, Tibbers and Dalswinton, and further west Loch Doon and the port and castle of Ayr. The last of these isolated remnants of English occupation was not reclaimed until 1313.[39]

In the early autumn of 1308 King Robert returned to the north-east. He did not return there directly, by his former route up the Great Glen, but went first to Inchmahome Priory on the islet in the Lake of Menteith, to Dunkeld, and thence to the neighbourhood of Perth, which was still in enemy hands.[40] These movements are known because the King dated his first surviving instruments of government from these three places, thus proving that he now had the opportunity to turn his attention to the administration of his kingdom.[41] It was fortunate for Scotland that he showed equal ability in fighting and governing. This dual capacity was expected of medieval kings, though the expectation was fulfilled by relatively few.

King Robert's purpose in returning to the north-east was to reach a settlement with the last of his domestic enemies, the Earl of Ross. The King's successes over the last year, and the failure of Edward II to support his Scottish allies, might have been sufficient to convince the Earl that his wisest course was to come to terms with Robert the Bruce. But perhaps the shrewdest assessment of Ross's character is that 'His natural inclination [was] for the independence of Scotland, provided it could be indulged in without unpleasant consequences for his security ...'.[42] Ross confessed to 'Sir Robert by the Grace of God King of Scots . . . all transgressions or offences against him and his', and in return received the King's forgiveness. Having submitted himself unconditionally to the King, he had his own lands restored to him, and received additional grants of the 'Lands of Dingwall and Ferincrosky in the sheriffdom of Sutherland'. In return for this 'benign liberality' he promised the King faithful service, and he lived up to his word.[43] The

Earl's submission and reception into the King's grace took place in a ceremony at Auldearn near Nairn, on 31 October 1308. The sureties for his good behaviour were the patriotic Bishop David de Mowbray, and Thomas of Ross, Bishop of Dundee. The King's friendship with the Earl of Ross was later confirmed by the marriage of his heir Hugh of Ross and the third of the King's younger sisters, Matilda de Bruce, who had not shared in the flight from Kildrummy and consequently had not been captured by Hugh's father. It was an appropriate union to symbolize a new relationship between Bruce and Ross.

The strength of King Robert's position at the beginning of 1309, and the corresponding weakness of Edward II's, was demonstrated by the arrival in Scotland of English envoys, supported by emissaries from the Pope, to negotiate for peace. A truce between the two kingdoms was concluded, to last until 1 November 1309. This marked a significant change in Anglo-Scottish relations, the point at which Robert the Bruce ceased to be treated as an outlaw, and was tacitly acknowledged as the leader of the Scots. But for years to come every peace process would be foredoomed by Edward II's refusal to acknowledge Robert as King of Scots, and Robert's refusal to conclude a peace upon any other terms than the full acceptance of his title and the independence of his kingdom. Until those conditions should be fulfilled, nothing more binding than a temporary truce would be accepted.

In March 1309 the cessation of hostilities enabled King Robert to hold his first Parliament, which met at St Andrews. Its chief purpose was to give a public demonstration of the reality of Robert's kingship, and confirmation of his right to the throne.

The occasion enabled King Robert to give the maximum publicity to the first communication he had received from a foreign power in which he was addressed as King of Scots. This was a letter from King Philip IV of France, in which he expressed his affection for Robert, reminded him of the old alliance between their kingdoms, and invited him to join in a forthcoming Crusade. The idea that a Crusade could deflect the Scots from war with England lacked reality, but a letter from one king to another should have public debate and official reply. Thus the best use was made of it. The reply of the Scottish Parliament blended courtesy with irony. Parliament thanked King Philip for his affection for their king, reminded him of the destruction which England had inflicted upon Scotland, but assured him that when the Scots had negotiated their 'pristine liberty' the King and his subjects would readily join in his Crusade.[44]

Robert's first Parliament was well attended by both lay magnates and clergy. Among the former were the three Earls of Lennox, Ross and Sutherland. The heirs of five earldoms, Fife, Menteith, Mar, Buchan and Caithness, were in wardship, but the 'communities' of their earldoms sent representatives to Parliament. (To account for the remaining Scottish earldoms, the Earls of Angus, Dunbar and Strathearn were pro-English and the Earl of Carrick was the King himself.) Three of the great hereditary office-holders were present. Sir Gilbert de la Haye, who had been with the King as a fugitive, now assumed his status as Constable of Scotland; James the Stewart, who had held office as High Steward of Scotland under Alexander III, whose sympathies had been with the cause of independence throughout a devious and cautious career, and who had declared openly for King Robert; and Sir Robert Keith the Marischal, who had recently joined the King. Sir Edward de Bruce was present as Lord of Galloway, Thomas Randolph as Lord of Nithsdale, James Douglas as Lord of Douglas, Angus MacDonald of the Isles attended, with many other highland and island lords, including Alexander MacDougall of Argyll, who came either unwillingly or under duress. Also present were Sir Neil Campbell, Sir Robert Boyd, Sir Alexander Lindsay, Sir David de Barclay and Sir William Wiseman. Recent adherents were Hugh of Ross, the Earl's son, Alexander Stewart of Bonhil, the Stewart's nephew, Sir John de Menteith, and Sir William de Vipont from Berwickshire, an area of the country which King Robert's campaigns had not yet touched.

The attendance of the clergy was equally impressive. There were five bishops: Moray, Ross, Brechin, Dunkeld and Dunblane. The last was Nicholas Balmyle, who had been Chancellor of Scotland under the Guardian Sir John de Soules, and who had been elected to the bishopric of Dunblane the previous year, probably with the influence of King Robert.[45] The new Chancellor, whom the King had probably appointed at his coronation, was Dom Bernard, soon to become Abbot of Arbroath, a great figure among the patriotic clergymen who supported the King.[46] Two of these remained prisoners of the English: Bishop Wishart of Glasgow and Bishop Lamberton of St Andrews, though it is possible that Lamberton attended the Parliament, released on parole by Edward II to act as an intermediary in Anglo-Scottish relations. Wishart was represented by a delegate from his diocese.[47]

On 17 March all the clergy assembled in Parliament, describing themselves as 'The Bishops, Abbots, Priors and others of the clergy duly constituted in the realm of Scotland', and issued a 'Declaration of the Clergy' in which they pronounced that Robert de Bruce, Lord of Annandale, the 'Competitor', had had the superior title to the throne of Scotland, and ought, by the laws and customs of the realm and the wishes of the people, to have become King; that as a result of the elevation of John Balliol to the throne, of his deposition and of the English invasions, great evils had befallen the kingdom; that the people of Scotland, wishing no longer to endure the calamities, had by the working of divine providence taken for their king Robert de Bruce, grandson of the Competitor, and raised him to the throne, and having been made King of Scots, through Christ's mercy, Robert had recovered and restored the kingdom, following the example of many former kings of Scotland, by whom it had been won and held. In an attempt to deal with any pro-Balliol counter-claims which might rest upon the Scots' past acceptance of Balliol's kingship, the Declaration of the Clergy stated that

if anyone in opposition [to King Robert] should claim right to the Scottish Kingdom by means of documents sealed in the past and containing the consent of the people, be it known that this was effected by irresistible force and violence, by numberless fears, bodily torture, and other terrors which could well pervert the opinions and minds of righteous men and strike dread into the stoutest hearts.[48]

The Declaration of the Clergy was reissued by the annual convocation of the Scottish clergy in February 1310 for the purpose of proclaiming the kingship of Robert the Bruce to the General Council of the Church assembled at Vienne.[49]

In the Parliament of 1309 the lay magnates also made a similar, possibly identical, declaration to that of the clergy, affirming that King Robert was the true and nearest heir of King Alexander last deceased.[50]

These documents based the kingship of Robert the Bruce on firm foundations: legitimacy, divine approval, the choice of the people, and military success, and the strongest of these was the last. For it was victory which implied divine approval, justified the choosing of a king, and enabled the assertion of Robert's superior claim to the throne to be promulgated.

These documents made official history of the Bruce myth that Robert de Bruce 'the Competitor' had the better claim to the Scottish throne, and had the general support of the Scottish people, and that John Balliol had been a puppet of England, imposed upon them against their desires. The victory of this narrative over the much more complex realities of the 'Great Cause' was easy, because Balliol's humiliation at the hands of Edward I and Robert's recovery of the kingdom made the Scots desire it to be true.

The progress of that recovery, from Robert's desperate days as a fugitive to his triumphant assertion of his kingship at St Andrews, would have been beyond anyone's power to prophesy in 1306. By 1309 he had been acknowledged by a major foreign power as King of Scots. But he was in possession only of two-thirds of the kingdom. The English occupation of Lothian remained unshaken, and beyond it England still held the major city of Perth, Dundee and the ports of Banff in the north-east and Ayr in the west, besides Dumfries and the south-western castles. There was hard fighting in prospect to reclaim the remainder of the kingdom.

10

———— |✳|✳|✳| ————

WAR WITH KING EDWARD

'Robert Bruce knowing himself unequal to the King of
England in strength or fortune, decided that it would be
better to resist our king by secret warfare rather than to
dispute his right in open battle.'[1]

ROBERT THE BRUCE spent the summer and autumn of 1309 making a
royal progress down the west coast of Scotland, from Loch Broom to
Dunstaffnage.[2] It seems likely that he would have been transported by
Angus MacDonald of Islay, whose fleet of galleys had contributed to
his victory the previous year. This progress enabled him to display the
power and authority of his kingship to supporters who had last seen
him as a fugitive, among them Christiana of the Isles, whose contribution to his little army had enabled him to reopen the war in Carrick in
1307. His return to the western Highlands demonstrated the magnitude
of his achievement in the ensuing two years. Also, in visiting these
remote parts of the country and maintaining contact with his Gaelic-
speaking subjects, he was seeking to draw together in loyalty to him
those areas of the realm that now acknowledged his authority. This was
a prudent preparation for campaigns to reclaim the remainder.

In the course of the progress King Robert received a mission from
Ireland, headed by his father-in-law, Richard de Burgh, Earl of Ulster.
The earl brought a large company of Irish magnates and their followers, with light horsemen and foot-soldiers. Piers Gaveston, as Deputy
of Ireland, had covenanted two thousand pounds of the costs of this
expedition.[3] The impetus may have come from Alexander of Argyll,
who had lately left King Robert and joined his son; now he and John of
Lorn were asserting their loyalty to Edward II, and agitating for a

resumption of the war against Robert. Though the Earl of Ulster came in a time of truce, his following would have been large enough for use as a fighting force if conditions in the west had favoured military action; but there was no disaffection among the populace of Argyll to tempt such a change of plan, and whatever the Earl of Ulster had been expected to achieve, diplomatic or military, he departed again without any recorded result. He had disapproved of Robert's bid to make himself King of Scots, but having seen how far he had succeeded, there was little incentive to take arms against him on behalf of so inactive a king as Edward II. A few years later Ulster, who remained officially King Edward's ally, was reputed to have concluded a truce with King Robert.[4]

Edward II intended to renew the war with Scotland, but during 1309, while the King of Scots continued to strengthen his position, Edward's chief preoccupation was to obtain the return of Gaveston from Ireland, for which he required the approval of the Pope, the King of France, and the English magnates whom Gaveston had so recklessly alienated.

Archbishop Winchelsey of Canterbury had pronounced a conditional excommunication on Gaveston should he return to England, and refused to rescind it, but the Pope could override his decision, and Edward was able to persuade Pope Celement V to do so, with the encouragement of gifts and grants in Gascony to two of the Gascon Pope's nephews.[5] The King of France had been displeased by Edward's publicly displayed devotion to Gaveston which had so insulted Isabella of France at the coronation, and by Edward's continuing preference for Gaveston's company; he had approved the exile of the favourite, but was persuaded to look more leniently on him when Edward granted Ponthieu and Montreuil to Isabella. Edward also sought his father-in-law's approval by agreeing that the suppression of the Order of the Knights Templars, initiated by the King of France, should proceed in England.[6]

Persuasive letters and well-calculated bribes conciliated Gaveston's foreign enemies; but the return of Gaveston would remain impossible if the English magnates refused to countenance it. According to the well-informed author of the contemporary *Vita Edwardi Secundi*, the King 'bent one after another to his will, with gifts, promises and blandishments'.[7] He had no difficulty in persuading his cousin John of

Brittany, Earl of Richmond, who was consistently loyal to him, or his nephew Gilbert de Clare, Earl of Gloucester. (Gilbert had inherited the title in 1307 on the death of his mother, Joan of Acre, whose second husband, Raoul de Monthemer, had held it during her lifetime.) The King also persuaded the Earl of Lincoln to agree to the return of Gaveston, though most of the magnates remained reluctant.

However, obsession with Gaveston was not their only complaint against the King. They had amassed a long list of grievances, including various forms of extortion to supply the royal household, devaluation of the coinage, sale of writs of pardon to criminals, and many injustices of royal officials exceeding their authority.[8]

When the English Parliament met at Westminster on 27 April 1309 it presented a dramatic contrast to the harmony between King and magnates which had characterized the Scottish Parliament the previous month. Edward asked his Parliament for a grant of taxation to pursue the war in Scotland, and for agreement to the return of Gaveston. In response, he received a long petition of grievances demanding redress, conditional upon which the taxation would be granted. The return of Gaveston was refused. The King, showing some bargaining skill, promised consideration of the grievances and adjourned the Parliament to 27 July, to reconvene at Stamford.

In the interim Edward continued his campaign of persuasion, and with the help of the old Earl of Lincoln, who was respected by everyone, he induced the earls, whatever their private misgivings, to yield their consent to the return of Gaveston. The only exception among them was the King's cousin, Thomas, Earl of Lancaster, who, in contrast to his other cousin, the loyal Earl of Richmond, henceforward became more and more inimical towards him. But, having won sufficient acquiescence, Edward summoned Gaveston from Ireland, rode to Chester to meet him, and brought him to Stamford, to appear before Parliament and enjoy the triumph of reinstatement in his former possessions as Earl of Cornwall.[9] As quid pro quo for Gaveston's recall and the grant of taxation, Edward promised the redress of grievances, and the Statute of Stamford recorded that he 'granted them fully'.[10] The fact that he did nothing to implement his promise speedily lost him the goodwill he had gained.

Gaveston had acquitted himself well in Ireland, but back in England he soon made himself more obnoxious than ever. The most serious complaint about him was that he seemed to have complete control of royal patronage; he received many generous gifts from the King, and directed a steady stream of grants to his own nominees.[11] But more personally irksome was the streak of malicious frivolity which led him to amuse the King by inventing *turpia cognomina* (insulting nicknames) for the magnates.[12] 'Burst belly' was no doubt cruelly apt for the fat old Earl of Lincoln; 'Joseph the Jew' highly insulting to the dark, sallow-faced Pembroke in a period of universal anti-Semitism; 'Cuckold's bird' or 'Bastard' for Gloucester implied that he was the son of Monthemer and not of his official father;[13] the significance of 'the Black Dog of Arden' for Warwick is not obvious, but it provoked Warwick's riposte 'If he call me a dog, be sure that I will bite him so soon as I shall perceive my opportunity.'[14]

In October Edward summoned his magnates to meet at York to plan a Scottish campaign, but five earls including Lancaster, Lincoln and Warwick refused to attend, and the planning of the campaign had to be deferred to the following year. Edward and Gaveston spent Christmas at the King's favourite manor of Langley, 'fully making up for former absence by their long wished-for sessions of daily and intimate conversation'.[15]

Over the winter there was disorder throughout the country, especially in the north, and the Parliament which Edward had summoned to meet at York in February was relocated to Westminster. On 8 February, the magnates had assembled, in arms, but refused to enter Parliament if Gaveston were present. After the King had sent him to an unnamed 'very safe place',[16] Parliament opened on 27 February. The King was presented with a list of grievances which formed a comprehensive accusation of misgovernment: he was influenced by evil counsellors (a veiled reference to Gaveston); he maintained his household by extortion (this meant *prises*, or seizures of goods to supply the royal household, without immediate repayment); whereas his father had kept the realm intact, he had lost Scotland (an exaggeration, but well on the way to being true); he had demanded taxation and used it neither to prosecute the war with Scotland, nor to finance his household.[17]

In the face of such a damning picture of incompetence presented to him by an armed Parliament, Edward had no choice but to admit the need for reform, and yield to measures which in effect would take the government out of his hands. On 16 March he reluctantly accepted that a self-selected body of twenty-one 'Lords Ordainers', composed of bishops, earls, and barons, should by Michaelmas (11 November) 1311 present their 'Ordinances' for complete overhaul of the government.[18]

Robert the Bruce might have felt tempted to give thanks to God for the existence of Gaveston, as the prime cause of the King of England's troubles. Without the conflicts arising over Gaveston, the war with Scotland would have been resumed far sooner, and it seemed that the longer the conflict continued the longer the war would be deferred. The detailed reporting of events in England may have been slow to reach Scotland, but the general picture was clear: it was obvious that Edward II was in serious difficulties when in November 1309 he gave the commanders of his garrisons permission to negotiate truces with the enemy, and the commanders of Berwick and Carlisle concluded truces to last until 14 January 1310.[19] In December, as his difficulty intensified, he ordered the garrison commanders of Banff, Dundee, Perth and Ayr to conclude truces until Whitsun (7 June) 1310.[20] A general truce, to be observed until the same date, followed, 'for the English do not willingly enter Scotland to wage war before summer, chiefly because earlier in the year they find no food for their horses'.[21]

By early summer a new campaign had become a matter of urgency. Edward had been warned by a deputation of pro-English Scots that if he did not bring an army to Scotland the remainder of the kingdom would be lost. Since his recent Parliament had accused him of having 'lost Scotland' already, a successful campaign would be an obvious way to redeem his reputation. It would have the additional advantages of protecting Gaveston, who would accompany the King to Scotland, and of providing an escape from the Ordainers. Edward added to their difficulties and demonstrated the seriousness of his war effort by transferring the exchequer and justices to York, as his father had done years earlier.

Only three earls responded to the King's summons to the feudal host: Gloucester, Warenne and Gaveston as Earl of Cornwall. The other eight were either serving as Ordainers or were in sympathy with them. Nonetheless, the King gathered a formidable army from the lesser magnates and their retinues. He was joined by veterans of his father's Scottish wars: Sir John de Segrave, Sir John de St John, Sir

Robert de Clifford, Sir Henry de Percy. The royal household itself raised
a force of fifty knights and knights banneret, and two hundred squires.
The city of London contributed a force of a hundred crossbowmen for
the defence of Berwick, which would release soldiers of the garrison to
serve in the field. The King's army had some three thousand infantry,
of whom four hundred were English, the rest Welsh. Dover and forty-
one of the English ports provided a fleet of provision ships.[22]

The King's army assembled at Berwick, but following the example of
his father's Scottish invasions, Edward also planned an attack on the
west. He granted Knapdale to the pro-English John MacSween, on
condition that he could wrest it from Sir John de Menteith, to whom it
had been granted by Robert the Bruce. From Ireland John of Lorn was
to invade Argyll, and the Earl of Ulster to land in force at Ayr.[23]

Preparations for such a large-scale invasion had consumed the best
part of the campaigning season, and it was already September when
Edward's army left Berwick.

Robert the Bruce acknowledged that his own forces were unequal to
the challenge of meeting the English army in the field. Deciding to rely
on the tactics of 'Good King Robert's Testament', he withdrew his
army beyond the Forth, while King Edward made a tour of the
English-held castles of southern Scotland, and reprovisioned them.

Frustrating as it was to watch his projected task of capturing these
castles rendered more difficult, King Robert allowed Edward's army to
advance, impeded only by stealthy attackers from the forest snapping at
his flanks and disappearing as swiftly as they had come.

King Edward reached Biggar at about the end of September, and
there encamped, expecting the main army of the Scots to arrive and do
battle, but he remained unchallenged. He broke camp and moved
north-west to the major stronghold of Bothwell, which was not a royal
castle but was held by Walter FitzGilbert for the Earl of Hereford.[24]
Thence he marched down the valley of the Clyde to Renfrew. Here, at
the westernmost extremity of his expedition, it appeared that his plans
were crumbling. He learned that MacSween had been defeated by Sir
John de Menteith, and that neither expedition from Ireland had sailed.[25]
Without their support he could not risk advancing further west.
Retreating eastward by a different route, he probably visited
Kirkintilloch and Falkirk, before pausing at Linlithgow towards the end
of October. By 31 November he was back at Berwick.[26]

The retreating army was subjected to increasingly aggressive attacks by King Robert, whose forces were now based in the forest. The author of the *Vita Edwardi Secundi*, who was probably a chancery clerk named John Walwyn, wrote what sounds like an eye-witness account of one of these attacks:

At that time Robert Bruce, who lurked continually in hiding, did them all the injury that he could. One day, when some English and Welsh, always ready for plunder, had gone out on a raid, accompanied for protection by many horsemen from the army, Robert Bruce's men, who had been concealed in caves and in the woodlands, made a serious attack on our men. Our horsemen, seeing that they could not help the infantry, returned to the main force with a frightful uproar, all immediately leapt to arms and hastened with one accord to the help of those who had been left amongst the enemy; but assistance came too late to prevent the slaughter of our men . . . Before our knights arrived, up to three hundred Welsh and English had been slaughtered, and the enemy returned to their caves. From such ambushes our men often suffered heavy losses. For Robert Bruce, knowing himself unequal to the King of England in strength or fortune, decided that it would be better to resist our King by secret warfare rather than to dispute his right in open battle. Indeed I might be tempted to sound the praises of Sir Robert Bruce did not the guilt of homicide and the dark stain of treachery bid me keep silent . . .[27]

The author evidently understood King Robert's tactics, and could only restrain his instinctive admiration for a resourceful enemy of reminding himself of Robert's guilt for the murder of the Red Comyn.

As soon as King Edward had returned to Berwick, according to the Lanercost Chronicle 'Robert and his people invaded Lothian and inflicted much damage upon those who were in the King of England's peace. The King, therefore, pursued them with a small force, but the Earl of Cornwall remained at Roxburgh to guard that district.'[28]

But once again, as Edward advanced Robert retreated, and 'always as the army approached he kept to the trackless boggy mountain places . . .'[29] Unable to bring him to battle, Edward returned to Berwick a second time.

As the end of the year approached any further campaigning was out

of the question. There would be no fodder available for the horses of
Edward's cavalry, and his infantry had gone home, having rendered
their forty days of feudal service.[30] Edward was determined not to
return to England and face the Ordainers. He intended to renew his
campaign the following year; in the meantime he made overtures to
King Robert for a truce. On 17 December Sir Robert de Clifford and
Sir Robert FitzPain met King Robert at Selkirk, and it was reported that
Gloucester and Gaveston were to have met him shortly afterwards at 'a
place near Melrose, but it was said he [Robert] had been warned by
some he would be taken, and therefore departed, so they have had no
parley'.[31] This suggests that Edward may have sanctioned a dishonourable plot to seize Robert the Bruce at the parley, and his escape may
explain the comment of the author of the *Vita* that although the King
of England 'were to lay siege to Scotland for seven years, he would
never consign Robert Bruce to his prison'.[32]

At the end of December a rumour reached King Edward that a fleet
of galleys had been collected in the Western Isles, in preparation for a
Scottish attack on the Isle of Man. This was presumably a false rumour,
for though Robert intended the recapture of Man, he was unlikely to
undertake it while Edward remained in Scotland. However, other
rumours followed, that King Robert was with his army in Galloway, and
that he was seeking recruits from the north-east. King Edward sent
Gaveston with two hundred men-at-arms to Perth, in the hope that he
could cut communications between Galloway and the north-east.[33]
Gaveston remained at Perth until Easter (11 April).

During Lent 1311 Henry de Lacy, Earl of Lincoln, died. He had been
acting as *Custos Regni* (Keeper of the Realm) in the King's absence, and
had been a moderating influence on the Ordainers. But Edward II had
an additional reason to regret his death. Thomas of Lancaster was
married to Lincoln's daughter and sole heiress, Alice de Lacy, and in
right of his wife he inherited her father's two earldoms of Lincoln and
Salisbury. These additions to his own three earldoms of Lancaster,
Leicester and Derby made him the most powerful of the English magnates. His enmity for Gaveston and enthusiasm for the Ordinances had
already made him a critic if not an enemy of the King.

Shortly after Easter, Lancaster rode north with a retinue of a
hundred knights and a large following of men-at-arms, to pay homage
to King Edward for his new lands. But he refused to pay homage in

Berwick, which though under English control was 'outside the realm'. Edward refused to come to England to receive his homage, until Lancaster threatened to take possession of his lands without having offered it. Edward thereupon yielded, and crossed the border to Haggerston, where Lancaster offered his homage, and the King and his cousin kissed each other with apparent amity. But Gaveston was beside the King, and 'the Earl would neither kiss him, nor even salute him, whereat Piers was offended beyond measure'.[34] Edward, no doubt, recognized a warning of trouble to come. He sent the Earl of Gloucester to England, to take office as *Custos Regni*, while he himself remained in Scotland, and made a final effort to breathe life into his moribund campaign.

In mid-May he paid for the levying of six hundred infantrymen from Northumberland, and on 20 May he took the unprecedented step of attempting a general feudal levy without parliamentary sanction. The response was extremely poor, and on 5 July the illegal levy was cancelled.[35] His attempts to reactivate the previous year's plans for invasion from Ireland were equally unsuccessful. Edward accepted that he would have to abandon his campaign, and return to England to meet the demands of the Ordainers. On 16 June he issued a summons to Parliament, which would meet on 16 August.[36] The King left Scotland at the end of July, and shortly afterwards Gaveston took refuge in the castle of Bamburgh, on the Northumbrian coast.[37]

The author of the *Vita Edwardi Secundi* shrewdly remarked that the defeat of a formidable invasion had come about because

> ... the King was really occupied with two projects: one was with the defeat of Robert Bruce, in which he was very remiss, because the greater part of the English baronage brought him no help in this business; the other was with the retention at his side of Piers Gaveston, on whose expulsion and exile almost all the barons of England were determined. In these two matters the king, worried and sorely tried, could not attain one on account of the other.[38]

Robert the Bruce, well aware of the causes of King Edward's troubles since his arrival in Scotland, and of the pressures that had forced his return to England, recognized that for the first time the initiative in the war with England had passed to him.

11

———— |✳|✳|✳| ————

SCOTLAND RECLAIMED

'His was the patriot's burning thought
Of freedom's battle bravely fought.
Of castles stormed and cities freed,
Of deep design and daring deed,
Of England's roses reft and torn
And Scotland's cross in triumph worn,
Of rout and rally, war and truce –
As heroes think, so thought the Bruce.'[1]

IN THE AUTUMN of 1311 King Robert demonstrated his new ascendancy with two large-scale raids into the north of England. The English border country had endured occasional destruction and loss from whirlwind cattle raids by the Scots since 1307. But the invasions of 1311 marked a change in Anglo-Scottish relations. They showed, as Robert intended, that for the first time the north of England was at his mercy, and the King of England was powerless to protect his subjects. The invasions also had a practical purpose, based on a simple concept of poetic justice: the English, who for so many years had inflicted suffering and privation upon the Scots, should be forced to finance the reclamation of Scotland from their domination.

According to the Lanercost Chronicler:

The said Robert then taking note that the King and all the nobles of the realm were . . . in such discord about the said accursed individual [Gaveston], having collected a large army invaded England by the Solway on Thursday before the feast of the Assumption of the Glorious Virgin [12 August, the feast being 15 August], and burnt all the land of the lord of Gilsland and the town of Haltwhistle and a great part of Tyndale, and after eight days returned into Scotland taking with him a very large booty in cattle. But he had killed few men besides those who offered resistance.[2]

This raid was merely a foretaste of the more destructive invasion that followed.

About the feast of the Nativity of the Blessed Virgin [8 September] Robert returned with an army into England, directing his march towards Northumberland, and, passing by Harbottle and Holystone and Redesdale, he burnt the district about Corbridge, destroying everything; also he caused more men to be killed than on the former occasion. And so he turned into the valleys of North and South Tyne, laying waste those parts which he had previously spared, and returned to Scotland after fifteen days; nor could the wardens whom the King of England had stationed on the marches oppose so great a force of Scots as he brought with him.[3]

The Northumbrians, who had incurred heavier losses on the second raid, as a result of offering resistance, now sent envoys to the King of Scots, and purchased 'an exceedingly short truce' until 2 February 1312 for the then very large sum of two thousand pounds.[4]

Later in September Robert either raided or threatened to raid the lands of the pro-English Earl of Dunbar, and 'all those [of the inhabitants] who were still in the King of England's peace' paid very heavily for a truce to last till the same date.[5]

By the time these truces expired, England was on the brink of civil war. In the autumn of 1311 Edward II had been forced to accept the Ordinances, which have been described as 'a complete programme of limited monarchy',[6] to which he gave his reluctant assent on 11 October. But the clause that rendered the whole scheme unworkable was the twentieth, which demanded the perpetual exile of Gaveston. Edward abjectly endeavoured to bargain his acceptance of the Ordinance as a whole against the exclusion of this one clause:

'Whatever has been ordained or decided upon' he said, 'how much soever they may redound to my private disadvantage, shall be established . . . and remain in force forever. But you shall stop persecuting my brother Piers, and allow him to have the Earldom of Cornwall.'[7]

His pleas were brushed aside by the Ordainers, and Gaveston was forced to leave the realm on 3 November. But evidently Edward found life without him unendurable. At the beginning of 1312 Gaveston was back in England, and on 20 January, in defiance of the Ordainers, the King restored him to his title and estates. Archbishop Winchelsey responded by renewing Gaveston's excommunication, and the Ordainers prepared for civil war.[8]

The King and Gaveston were at York from 18 January to 8 April, whence they moved to Newcastle. Their move towards Scotland had no bellicose intention; their hope was to negotiate a refuge there for Gaveston. The author of the *Vita Edwardi Secundi* condemned this as a 'fatuous scheme' which had no possibility of success:

> For when Robert Bruce was sounded about keeping faith with Piers and the terms of peace, when, too, many offers were made to him, and at length that the kingdom of Scotland itself should be allowed to Sir Robert freely and forever, he is said to have replied to the King's message in this manner 'How shall the King of England keep faith with me, since he does not observe the sworn promise made to his liegemen, whose homage and fealty he has received, and with whom he is bound in reciprocity to bear faith? No trust can be put in such a fickle man, his promises will not deceive me'.[9]

Though Robert the Bruce appreciated Gaveston's usefulness as the source of Edward's trouble with his magnates, he had no reason to show friendliness to the man himself. Besides, Gaveston was far more useful as a trouble-maker in England than he would have been as a refugee in Scotland, so Robert's refusal to receive him was not surprising. Neither was his refusal of Edward's desperate offer to recognize him as King of Scots: it was not on such terms that Robert would accept English recognition. An abject offer by an isolated King would be rejected unanimously by the Ordainers, who at this point seemed likely to have the power to speak for England. Robert was resolved that when the enemy was forced to acknowledge his kingship, that acknowledgement should be unequivocal and should contain no pretext for subsequent repudiation. From Edward's viewpoint, the fact that he had once made the offer and Robert had spurned it may have fuelled his determination that under no circumstances would he ever make it again.

Now threatened by the approach of an army under Thomas of Lancaster, Edward and Gaveston fled from Newcastle to Tynemouth and sailed down the coast to Scarborough. Gaveston took refuge in Scarborough Castle, while the King moved inland to seek reinforcements. Lancaster's army cut communications between them, while Pembroke, Warenne and Percy besieged the castle. It was poorly provisioned, and on 19 May Gaveston surrendered to Pembroke, who, with the other besiegers, guaranteed his safety with an oath on the holy sacrament.[10] Gaveston was escorted south by Pembroke, and it was agreed that he should appear before Parliament which would decide his future. In the interim he was to be lodged in his own castle of Wallingford. The party had reached Deddington in Oxfordshire, where Pembroke left his prisoner for a night, to visit his wife who was lodged at a nearby manor. On the morning of 10 June, before Pembroke's return, the Earl of Warwick (keeping his promise to 'bite' Gaveston at the first opportunity) arrived and carried him off as a prisoner to Warwick Castle. Over the next few days Warwick was joined by Lancaster, Hereford and Arundel, who had decided that rough justice for Gaveston was preferable to a parliamentary decision, and Lancaster took responsibility for his fate. On the morning of 19 June Gaveston was taken from Warwick Castle to Blacklow Hill near the village of Leek Wotton, on land belonging to Lancaster, and there beheaded.[11]

The murder of the most detested man in England solved no problems. The King's grief and fury centred upon a determination to be revenged on Thomas of Lancaster. Pembroke and Warenne, incensed that their oaths to Gaveston had been dishonoured, and Pembroke the more chagrined that his own negligence had permitted the capture of Gaveston, joined the King. Lancaster, Warwick, Hereford and Arundel aligned themselves against him, and civil war appeared inevitable.

It seemed that Gaveston dead was as useful to Robert the Bruce as Gaveston living. Robert took advantage of the chaos in the south to launch a bigger invasion on northern England than those of the previous year.

> Robert de Brus, King of Scotland came with a great army in the
> month of August to the monastery of Lanercost, and remained there
> three days, making many of the canons prisoners and doing an
> infinity of injury, but at last the canons were set at liberty by
> himself.[12]

This was the first time that the Lanercost Chronicler gave Robert the
style of King of Scotland, perhaps an unconscious response to what
was now a self-evident truth. From Lanercost Robert led his army east,
'burnt the towns of Hexham and Corbridge . . . and took booty and
much spoil and prisoners, nor was there anyone who dared resist'.[13]

Robert encamped near Corbridge, and sent part of his army under
Edward de Bruce and James Douglas to attack Durham, which had
confidently imagined itself to be well beyond the range of marauding
Scots. But the invaders

> arriving there suddenly on market day, carried off all that was found
> in the town, and gave a great part of it to the flames . . . The people
> of Durham, fearing more mischief from them, and despairing of
> help from the King, compounded with them, giving two thousand
> pounds to obtain truce for that bishopric until the nativity of John
> the Baptist [24 June 1313].[14]

The offer was accepted only on condition that the Scots should have
free passage through the bishopric if they wished to raid further south
into England. A new truce with Northumberland followed, to cover the
same period, at the cost of another two thousand pounds to the
Northumbrians;

> and the people of Westmorland, Copland and Cumberland
> redeemed themselves in a similar way; and as they had not so much
> money in hand . . . they paid a part, and gave as hostages for the rest
> the sons of the chief lords of the country.[15]

After this extremely profitable expedition, Robert returned to Scotland.

The raids were not only effective in terrorizing the north of England
and efficient in extracting payment, they were also highly organized and
disciplined, for it had to be ensured that the immunities once purchased

were guaranteed. There could be no random looting and destruction, but at the same time it had to be equally certain that failure to render the promised payments could not be risked. When the expiry of the truces approached at midsummer 1313, Robert sent word to the northern counties that if new truces were not purchased they would be raided; a threat which immediately brought new promises of payment.[16] But the ability of local communities to find the money was beginning to fail. In April 1314 Cumberland's arrears of payment were punished by an invasion under Edward de Bruce, who occupied Rose Castle, a property of the Bishop of Carlisle. The Scots remained there several days:

> They burnt many towns and two churches, taking men and women prisoners, and collected a great number of cattle in Inglewood Forest . . . they killed few men except those who made determined resistance.[17]

As on the previous raids, there was no casual slaughter, and the hostages taken by Robert the previous year were not injured. The Bishop of Carlisle bought off Edward de Bruce by promising to release two Scottish prisoners, Reginald and Alexander Lindsay, but they did not return to Scotland until the general exchange of prisoners after the battle of Bannockburn.[18]

By the early summer of 1314 the impoverished men and women of northern England were fixing their hopes on the renewed war effort of their own King.

Against the background of the raids the purpose for which they were undertaken continued: the recovery of towns, ports and castles from English occupation.

England's most northerly outpost of Banff had surrendered during the winter of 1310–11, before Edward II left Scotland. Nine English castle garrisons are not mentioned after Edward's retreat from Scotland, which suggests that they must have surrendered then or shortly afterwards; these were Cavers, Dalswinton, Dirleton, Kirkintilloch, Loch Doon, Luffness, Muchkart, Selkirk and Yester.[19] Ayr surrendered at the end of 1311.

In April 1312 Dundee fell, after a three-month siege, financed by the truces taken for the earldom of Dunbar and from Northumberland the previous autumn.[20] When a siege outlasted the forty days' free service of a feudal obligation, continuing service thereafter had to be paid for. But Robert could not afford either the time or the money for a sequence of expensive sieges: the English-held strongholds must be captured while England was embroiled in civil stife, and even the money paid over by the communities of northern England would not fund the construction of a train of expensive siege machines or the expertise to work them.

An alternative system of siege warfare was a combination of surprise tactics with a simpler form of military technology. The Lanercost Chronicler described with laborious wonderment the new type of siege ladder designed by the Scots. This was a rope ladder with wooden steps held in place by knots, and with fenders fixed at the level of each third step to prevent the ladder from lying flat against the wall. Each rope ladder was attached to an iron hook 'measuring at least one foot along one limb, and this was to lie over the wall; but the other limb being of the same length hung downwards towards the ground, having at its end a round hole wherein the point of a lance could be inserted'. By this means the ladder could be lifted into position on the wall, 'and the greater the weight of the climber, the more firmly the iron hook clung over the wall'.[21]

These ladders were probably being manufactured in large numbers during the summer of 1312, while King Robert held a Parliament at Ayr in July, and the following month led the invasion of northern England. In October he held another Parliament at Inverness, to which he was accompanied by David de Strathbogie, Earl of Atholl, who had lately offered his allegiance, and by Thomas Randolph. At this Parliament, Atholl, who had been actively pro-English until the beginning of the year, was confirmed in possession of his earldom, and Thomas Randolph was created Earl of Moray, giving him a title that had laid dormant in the possession of the Crown since 1130.[22] It was an appropriate title for the King's nephew and gave him wide powers over one of the ancient provinces of the kingdom. Possibly it was conferred on him to counterbalance the powers of the Earl of Atholl, whose territories marched with his own, and whose loyalty was as yet unproved.

At Inverness King Robert met the envoys of King Haakon V of

Norway, and on 29 October 1312 ratified the new treaty with Norway, which had been negotiated by the Chancellor, Bernard Abbot of Abroath, and Farquhar Bellejambe, Bishop of Caithness, a churchman who had been appointed Archdean of Caithness by Edward I in 1297, and whose recent adherence to King Robert emphasized the growing support he received from the Scottish Church.[23]

The new treaty with Norway re-enacted the Treaty of Perth of 1266, which had conceded Scottish possession of the Western Isles in return for an annual payment in perpetuity. It showed a genuine spirit of friendship in that Scottish failure to pay the 'annual' in recent years was overlooked and sensible arrangements were made for the settlement of incidents of piracy by Scottish and Norwegian subjects.[24] The Scoto-Norwegian treaty was the first international treaty which acknowledged Robert as 'by the Grace of God King of Scots', an indisputable enhancement of his prestige.[25]

In November the King moved south again, to try out his new method of siege warfare on the remaining English strongholds. It was a bold choice to begin with Berwick, the most strongly garrisoned of the English-held towns, and the closest to the border. But Berwick was desirable to reclaim as once Scotland's most prosperous port, and since as the headquarters for English invasions.

On the dark night of 6 December, King Robert directed the attack. Two ladders were successfully fixed to the walls of Berwick Castle, the attackers began to scale them, 'and had not a dog betrayed the approach of the Scots by loud barking, it is believed that he [Robert] would quickly have taken the castle and in consequence the town . . . thus a dog saved the town on that occasion, just as of old geese saved Rome . . .'[26] The Scots fled, leaving their ladders, which were hauled up by the defenders, and the following day displayed on a pillory in the town.

Having lost the advantage of surprise at Berwick, the King moved northward to besiege Perth, which was more vulnerable since the fall of Dundee, as it could no longer be provisioned by sea. However, Perth had strong fortifications; it was girdled by stone walls and towers built by Edward I, the River Tay provided a natural moat on one side of the town, and an artificial moat, fed by the river, curved round the remainder of the walls. King Robert's army surrounded the town and encamped as though preparing to starve it into submission.

They maintained the siege for perhaps a couple of weeks, before appearing to lose heart. They broke camp, packed up armour, weapons and supplies in full view of the walls, and marched away, to the triumphant jeers and yells of the garrison.[27]

The King's forces marched a few miles and disappeared into concealing woodlands. Days passed, and the defenders of Perth assumed that they had gone to fight elsewhere. On 6 January they returned under cover of darkness. One night during the siege soundings had been taken of the moat, and a place found where men could wade across. The task force, led by the King, returned to this spot:

> He took his ladder in his hand
> To make example to his band
> And then, arrayed in all his gear,
> He plunged and tested with his spear
> Till he was right across the moat.
> The water mounted to his throat![28]

Robert was followed by a 'bold and warlike knight of France' who had joined him for adventure and was filled with admiration that a king should risk himself in such a daring enterprise. But King Robert knew the temper of his countrymen, and understood that personal leadership inspired them to feats of arms that a non-fighting commander could never have demanded of them.

They lifted the ladders on their spears, attached them to the wall, and climbed over the parapet, the eager Frenchman first, then the King, followed by a silent multitude of Scots. When the whole force had gathered, unchallenged, they poured into the town. The surprise was total, and the resistance slight. In the morning the town was in the hands of the Scots. The commander of the garrison was Sir William Oliphant, who had defended Stirling against Edward I in 1304. After four years as an English prisoner he had regained his liberty by agreeing to fight against the Scots. Robert sent him as a prisoner to the Western Isles. Also captured at Perth was the hitherto pro-English Malise, Earl of Strathearn. His son and namesake, who had been fighting with the King, brought his father before Robert, and Strathearn offered his allegiance, which was accepted. The English garrison was permitted to depart and the fortifications were demolished. A generous share-out of booty rewarded Robert's soldiers.

With the fall of Perth, the only east coast castle remaining in English hands was Dunbar, and with possession of all the ports north of Berwick, Scottish opportunities for North Sea trade were greatly expanded. There was also an increase in the activities of Scottish privateers who preyed on English shipping.

King Robert then moved to the west, where the country was under the control of Edward de Bruce, but three English garrisons, Dumfries, Buittle and Caerlaverock, still held out. Robert besieged Dumfries, which was surrendered on 7 February 1313 by Sir Douglas MacDouall, who six years before had sent Thomas and Alexander de Bruce to their deaths. MacDouall probably expected no mercy, but Robert, always preferring reconciliation to revenge, gave him his life and freedom. But MacDouall spurned the olive branch and went immediately to the English-held Isle of Man. Robert remained to the south-west and received the surrender of Buittle and Caerlaverock before the end of March.[29]

His next objective was the Isle of Man. His intention to reclaim it had been rumoured before, but this was his first opportunity to risk leaving the Scottish mainland. The south-west of Scotland was entirely under his control, and he need fear no intervention from England. Though civil war had been averted there by the diplomacy of the Pope and the King of France, no agreement had yet been reached between Edward II and the Ordainers. The King decided to turn his back on his troubles and take Queen Isabella to France to attend the festivities in honour of the knighting of her three brothers.[30] This was a period of harmony in the troubled marriage of Edward and Isabella, for in November 1312 Isabella had performed her dynastic duty and borne an heir to the throne (the future Edward III), a cause of general rejoicing.

On 17 May, Robert the Bruce, his army transported by a fleet of galleys, landed at Ramsey on the Isle of Man, marched the length of the island, pausing to stay a night at the nunnery of Douglas, and the following day laid siege to the castle of Rushen.[31] English control of the Isle of Man was probably very uncertain, for there had been no continuity of rule in recent years. Edward II had granted it to Piers Gaveston in 1307, and on his first exile, to Anthony Bek, Bishop of Durham, who had died in 1311. It had then passed to Henry de Beaumont, whose friendship with the King won him the enmity of the Ordainers. A Simon de Montacute attempted to seize the island from

Beaumont, but was pardoned by the King for his previous good service. In March 1313 Dougal MacDouall was appointed commander of the garrison of Rushen. According to an Irish source:

> On the last days of May Robert de Brus sent certain galleys to parts of Ulster with his pirates to despoil them. The Ulstermen resisted them and manfully drove them off. It was said nevertheless that Robert landed by licence of the Earl [of Ulster] who had taken a truce.[32]

This probably means that the Earl had agreed to pay for a truce, and that the raid was to collect payment, to pay for the siege of Rushen. Whether or not the raid was successful, Rushen fell on 21 June after a siege of five weeks, and control of the Isle of Man passed to the Scots. It proved hard to hold. In 1315 it was invaded by John of Lorn, who in 1317 was expelled after hard fighting by Thomas Randolph, to whom King Robert had granted it. Man remained part of the Scottish realm until 1333, when it was retaken by the English.[33] It has not changed hands since, and retains a limited autonomy to the present day.

At Rushen, Dougal MacDouall surrendered to Robert the Bruce for the second time, and again he was allowed to go free. Having granted him his life and liberty once, the King would not go back on his word. MacDouall sailed to Ireland, and for the rest of his life remained faithful to his chosen cause; he died in the English service in 1327.

King Robert was not invariably lenient to his enemies. He showed a calculated ruthlessness in his raids on northern England, and was aware that he must not be seen to be too lenient by his enemies, or his powers of intimidation would diminish. But he was naturally inclined to mercy. Always he attempted reconciliation with Scots who had previously fought for the enemy. He frequently showed magnanimity towards captured foes. He never indulged in aimless slaughter or permitted atrocities. It would be true to say that Robert the Bruce rose above the normal standards of his times as frequently as Edward I had fallen below them.

While King Robert was reclaiming the Isle of Man, Edward de Bruce was besieging Stirling Castle. He had been encamped before it from

Lent to midsummer, apparently with little effect, until he received an offer from its commander, Sir Philip de Mowbray: if no English army arrived within three leagues (nine miles) of Stirling to do battle for it by the following Midsummer's Day (24 June), Mowbray would surrender.

Edward's well-known preference for the excitement of the battlefield to the tedium of siege warfare may have made him amenable to Mowbray's offer, or he may have assumed that Edward II's troubles made the arrival of a relieving army improbable. Without reflecting that in a year the whole situation might change, he accepted Mowbray's terms.

Shortly after midsummer Robert returned from the Isle of Man to learn of his brother's reckless bargain. He was justifiably angered, for it endangered his entire strategy by inviting the English to invade and do battle. John Barbour gives the King a speech in which he sternly rebukes his brother, and points out all the dangers which Edward had failed to consider.

> The King said, when the day he knew
> 'That was a foolish thing to do!
> I never heard of such a long
> Forewarning to a king so strong
> As is the monarch of that land
> For now he has to help his hand
> Both Wales and Ireland in his train
> And added to these, Aquitaine.
> And still a part of this country
> Acknowledges his sovereignty.
> For overflowing wealth is his
> And he can pay for mercenaries
> Against so many we are few
> And justice to us God may do
> But there is jeopardy therein
> By one short fight to lose or win!'[34]

Characteristically, King Robert, with far more political acumen than his brother, immediately thought of King Edward's vast resources rather than his immediate troubles, and recognized that the threat to Stirling and the chivalric bargain offered a challenge to English prestige which would unite the King and his disaffected magnates.

The prospect of an English invasion within the year made it all the more imperative to recapture the remaining English strongholds. Lothian and adjacent areas of south-east Scotland, held in subjection by strongly garrisoned castles, still acknowledged King Edward's rule: to capture the castles would be to deprive him of his power-base when he entered Scotland.

The people of the south-east under English occupation showed a typical mosaic of resistance and collaboration. According to a frequently quoted passage of the Lanercost Chronicle:

> The Scots were so divided among themselves that sometimes the father was on the Scottish side and the son on the English or *vice versa*; also one brother might be with the Scots and another with the English; yea, even the same individual be first with one party and then with the other. But all those who were with the English were merely feigning, either because it was the stronger party, or in order to save the lands they possessed in England; for their hearts were always with their own people, although their persons might not be so.[35]

The hold of the English upon the south-east had begun to crumble, as landowners from the area offered their allegiance to King Robert. The most prominent were Sir Robert Keith the Marischal and Sir William de Vieuxpont, who had attended the Parliament of 1309, and other knights had followed their example.[36] The sympathies of the commons are indicated by the exploits of the folk heroes, named by Barbour, who played leading parts in the capture of the English-held castles.

In September 1313 Linlithgow was captured by a local farmer. It was not the great castle whose ruins dominate Linlithgow Loch to the present day; it was a sturdy peel tower, strategically important as it lay on the road between Edinburgh and Stirling.

The farmer, William Bannock, was accustomed to sell his hay to the Linlithgow garrison. He sent word that he had a particularly good load available, and was contracted to deliver it. In his ox cart, eight armed men were concealed under the hay. A few more lay in ambush near the castle walls, when Bannock arrived to deliver his hay, himself walking beside his oxen, another man driving the cart. The unsuspecting porter opened the gates to admit them, and Bannock stopped the cart in the gateway, so that the gates could not be closed. The driver cut the traces, and the armed men emerged from the hay. Bannock felled the porter with a blow, and shouted 'Call all! Call all!' to summon the additional men from their ambush. His small force quickly overpowered and killed the garrison, and Linlithgow was theirs. Bannock delivered the peel tower to King Robert, and was generously rewarded.[37]

Early the following year James Douglas captured the great castle of Roxburgh, combining the type of ruse he had used to capture his own castle of Douglas with the use of scaling ladders of the new type. The folk hero on this occasion was Sim of the Leadhouse, 'a skilled and clever craftsman',[38] who manufactured the ladders.

On the night of Shrove Tuesday, 19 February 1314, a herd of small black cattle was seen straying near the walls of Roxburgh Castle. One of the sentinels remarked to another that their owner must have gone merry-making and left them out. The other replied with unconscious irony that the Douglas would probably come and drive them off. It was a traditional night of merry-making, before the long hardship of the Lenten fast, and most of the castle garrison was feasting and singing in the great hall. The cattle, which might not have looked more convincing than pantomime horses by daylight, or to sober eyes, were Douglas's men creeping towards the castle walls draped in black cloaks.

The first to stand upright and lift his ladder on to the wall was Sim of the Leadhouse. Unfortunately the iron grappling-hook clinked against the stone, and the sentry hurried to investigate the sound, and encountered Sim as he climbed over the parapet. But, before he summoned help, Sim 'stabbed him upward with a knife',[39] then fought and finally killed the second sentry while Douglas and his companions fixed their ladders and scaled the wall. Once they were in, the partying garrison were easy prey, and the castle was soon in their hands, except for one tower, in which the governor, a Gascon knight called Sir Guillemin de Fiennes, barricaded himself with a few companions. He continued to defend it the next day, until he was wounded in the face by an arrow. He then surrendered, and Douglas gave him and the survivors of the garrison safe conduct to England, where Fiennes died of his wound shortly afterwards.[40]

Sim of the Leadhouse took the news of the capture of Roxburgh to the King, and was well rewarded, and Edward de Bruce was sent to oversee the demolition of the castle.

Thomas Randolph, Earl of Moray, was in the meantime besieging
Edinburgh, with little success; but not to be outdone by Douglas he
decided to attempt a surprise attack. Crowning its great rock,
Edinburgh looked as impregnable as Stirling. But was it also inaccessible? Gazing up at the crag, Thomas Randolph questioned it.

Enquiries produced a man named William Francis, the third of
Barbour's folk heroes, who told Randolph that as a youth he had lived
in the castle with his father, who had charge of one of the castle buildings. He had 'loved a wench here in the town' and had climbed down
the rock to visit her by night and returned before daybreak so many
times that he could find the way again 'however murky be the night'.[41]

On the night of 14 March William Francis led Thomas Randolph
himself, with a picked force of thirty men, up the precipitous north face
of the castle rock. Their stealthy approach was to be covered by a diversionary attack on the main gate of the castle. Barbour added an extra
touch of drama to his account, describing how the assault party rested
on a large rock to get their second wind, and the sentries walking the
castle wall paused directly above them. One man, to tease his fellows,
threw a stone over the wall into the darkness, calling out 'Away, I see you
well!'[42] The stone flew over the heads of the men crouching below, and
the watch moved on.

The attackers completed their ascent, fixed the scaling ladders to the
wall, and were swiftly over the parapet, Francis first, Randolph second,
followed by Sir Andrew Grey and the rest. They clashed first with the
watch, where shouts of 'Treason! Treason!' roused the garrison.
Randolph's second party, hearing sounds of fighting, attacked the East
Port, dividing the forces of the defenders. After hard fighting within the
castle, the assault party reached the gates to admit their comrades, and
the defenders were swiftly overcome. Many of the garrison were killed,
some in attempting to escape over the walls. The rest surrendered, with
the Governor of the castle, a Gascon named Sir Piers Liband. He
offered his allegiance to King Robert, but shortly afterwards reneged on
his oath and was executed as a traitor; he had committed the one crime
for which a man put himself beyond the scope of the King's mercy.
William Francis was rewarded with a grant of lands in Roxburghshire.[43]
King Robert ordered the demolition of all the buildings on the castle
rock, with the exception of the little Chapel of St Margaret of Scotland.

By the spring of 1314 the reclamation of Scotland was almost complete. Much had been achieved in the last twelve months. In the southeast the English now held only Berwick, Dunbar and Jedburgh. To the west of Stirling the Earl of Hereford's castle of Bothwell was still held by Sir Walter FitzGilbert, who was left undisturbed, possibly in the expectation that he would surrender the castle of his own volition.

As a result of King Robert's programme of demolition, the English hold upon Scotland had not only been broken, but rendered impossible to restore; for even if Edward II were to invade and be victorious, the strongholds upon which his occupation had relied no longer existed. King Robert had pointed out to Edward de Bruce that the English King possessed great resources to raise an army, but they were not great enough to rebuild the strongholds of an occupying power.

12

————|✳|✳|✳|————

THE YEAR OF VICTORY 1314

'After the aforesaid victory Robert de Brus was
commonly called
King of Scotland by all men, because he had acquired
Scotland by force of arms.'[1]

EDWARD II RETURNED from France in July 1313 to learn that he had lost the Isle of Man to Robert the Bruce. Then came Sir Philip de Mowbray, under safe conduct from the King of Scots, to report to King Edward the bargain he had struck for the relief of Stirling. The bargain that King Robert had seen as setting his whole achievement in jeopardy was good news indeed to the King of England. As a challenge England could not ignore, it was a perfect *causus belli*. A victory in Scotland would vindicate his reputation; he could even envisage reclaiming all his father's conquests. Best of all, Mowbray's agreed date of Midsummer's Day 1314 gave ample time for military preparations.

Before these could begin, it was essential to reach an accommodation with Thomas of Lancaster and his allies. Edward could blame the failure of his Scottish campaign of 1310/11 on its lack of support by the magnates, and he was determined that this situation should not be repeated.

Through the good offices of the French King's brother, Louis, Count of Evreux, a compromise between the King and the magnates was reached by October 1313. It was a triumph of diplomacy. On 13 October the Earls of Lancaster, Hereford and Warwick confessed their guilt for the death of Gaveston, and offered humble apology to the King; in return, Edward granted pardons to them and five hundred of their adherents. No mention was made of the Ordinances.[2] Two ban-

quets were given, one by the King and the other by Lancaster, to celebrate an accord that future events would prove to have been insincere.
The conflicts and resentments involved were too profound to be
handled in such a facile manner. But the reconciliation provided a
sufficient degree of unity to enable Edward to begin preparations for
his Scottish campaign.

In November he received a letter purporting to come from the
people of Scotland imploring his aid against Robert the Bruce. In fact,
it was addressed to him by the Earl of Dunbar and by Sir Adam
Gordon, the Justiciar of Lothian, and spoke only for the community of
the earldom of Dunbar, which as a supposedly pro-English community
had been treated like those of the northern English counties, and
forced to pay heavily for truces. King Edward replied with the assurance that his army would be at Berwick before the following midsummer.[3]

In December the first writs of summons for military service were
issued, ordering attendance at Berwick on 10 June 1314, 'to put down
and suppress the wicked rebellion of Robert Bruce and his accomplices
in the King's land of Scotland',[4] language which shows that while the
pretext for the campaign was the relief of Stirling, the intention was the
reconquest of Scotland. Edward II had inherited his father's attitude to
Scotland and the Scots without question; the 'land of Scotland' (not
acknowledged to be a kingdom) was part of his realm, King Robert and
his adherents 'wicked rebels'. In his determination to crush them and
reconquer Scotland, if nothing else, Edward II would have had the
whole-hearted approval of his father. He could hope that his call to
arms would ignite the enthusiasm of the magnates and knights who had
fought for Edward I. For the first time, Edward II might feel that the
burden of being the son of an admired father could be turned to advantage.

In the opening months of 1314 the continuing attrition of English
power in Scotland, with the fall of Roxburgh and Edinburgh, added
urgency and force to Edward's summons to war. Yet the response
of the magnates was not unanimous. Thomas of Lancaster, imitated
by the Earls of Warwick, Arundel and Warenne, refused to accompany the King on campaign, thus demonstrating the hollowness of
the recent reconciliation. Their excuse was that the King had not
sought the approval of Parliament for making war, but they con-

tributed their obligatory quotas of knights and men-at-arms to the campaign.

However, King Edward was fully supported, and accompanied, by Humphrey de Bohun, Earl of Hereford and Constable of England, Aymer de Valance, Earl of Pembroke, and Gilbert de Clare, Earl of Gloucester. One Scottish earl still adhered to him, Robert de Umfraville, Earl of Angus.[5] John of Brittany, Earl of Richmond, always loyal to Edward II, was on embassy in France.[6]

There was an impressive turn-out of lesser magnates and distinguished knights, many of whom had fought in Edward I's campaigns, among them Gloucester's stepfather, Sir Raoul de Monthemer, Angus's brother, Sir Ingram de Umfraville, the erstwhile Guardian of Scotland, Sir Marmaduke de Tweng, the gallant survivor of the Battle of Stirling Bridge, Sir John Comyn, the son of the Red Comyn, and Sir Giles d'Argentan, who was accounted by his contemporaries the 'third best knight of his day' (the first and second being the Emperor Henry of Luxembourg and Robert the Bruce).[7] Edward had shown his desire to have Sir Giles at his side by ransoming him from the Greek Emperor, after Sir Giles had fallen into the hands of inimical fellow Christians on his way to Rhodes, and had been imprisoned at Salonika.[8] Edward also issued a general invitation to knights from abroad to join his campaign. Barbour says they came from France, Gascony, Germany, Flanders, Brittany and Aquitaine. The *Scotichronicon* speaks of their coming also from Guelders, Bohemia, Holland, Zealand and Brabant, and a contemporary poem specifically mentions four Teutonic knights.[9]

At the end of May King Edward was at Berwick, awaiting the arrival of his forces. As magnates and knights gathered round him, and contingents of infantry arrived from all over England and Wales, Edward became exalted with the certainty of impending victory:

> Right joyful in his heart was he
> And thought that there could never be
> A king on earth that might withstand.
> He reckoned all was in his hand!
> And liberally among his men
> He dealt the land of Scotland then.
> He showed great generosity
> With other people's property.[10]

Another indication that his ambition was a complete reconquest was his attempt to co-ordinate a simultaneous attack on the west of Scotland, as his father had done in earlier invasions and he himself had unsuccessfully attempted to do in 1310 and 1311. The Earl of Ulster was summoned to bring an army from Ireland including a force of four thousand infantry, and John of Lorn was appointed admiral of the western fleet to transport it. But though troops were raised in Ireland and Barbour mentions an Irish contingent at the Battle of Bannockburn, a modern military historian affirms 'there is scant record of action in the west'.[11] Nor does King Robert, awaiting the English invasion from Berwick, appear to have expected action elsewhere. Presumably he was well informed enough to know that military preparations in Ireland had not kept pace with those of King Edward; it was not until 1315 that John of Lorn invaded the Isle of Man.

The numbers of King Edward's army have been the subject of much scholarly controversy, initiated by the incredibility of Barbour's statement that he had a hundred thousand men and more.[12] Barbour's declared intention of writing nothing but the truth was never forgotten, but he shared the weakness of his contemporaries in estimating numbers. When he wrote, he was relying upon the memories of men who had seen a vast army, and probably exaggerated what they remembered. His 'hundred thousand' was not an estimate, but an impression of immensity.

Modern research has shown that Edward II summoned five thousand infantrymen from north and south Wales, and these would probably have been a mixture of spearmen and archers.[13] The Welsh were already renowned for their archery, but fortunately for the Scots they had not yet developed their lethal expertise with the longbow which Edward III was to deploy with such devastating effect in his campaigns in France later in the century. In addition to the Welsh archers, one hundred archers and crossbowmen were required from Bristol. On 24 March Edward II issued summonses for levying some sixteen thousand infantrymen from thirteen English counties. The total summonses to England and Wales (and excluding those to Ireland) should have brought more than twenty-one thousand foot-soldiers to the infantry rendezvous at Wark-on-Tweed near Berwick, on 10 June 1314. However, the musters were not always fully made up, and desertion was always rife, so a plausible total for Edward's infantry would be some fifteen thousand.[14]

According to the *Vita Edwardi Secundi*, King Edward had two thousand cavalry. This is an unusually low estimate for a chronicler, but the author was very close to the events he chronicled, not reliant on the exaggerations of others. The King's own household contained eighty-nine knights and thirty-two higher-ranking bannerets.[15] The earls had provided their contingents, to the number of some 890 knights, squires and mounted men-at-arms.[16] This number may have been exceeded by additional cavalry paid for by the royal wardobe.[17] With the arrival of the knights from abroad, the number of two thousand was reached or surpassed. This was a formidable force of cavalry, but it lacked organization. All the knights were concerned with their own prestige and prowess, and many of the anecdotes of the ensuing battle concern their wayward behaviour.

The army was probably comparable in size to any with which Edward I had invaded Scotland, and with experiences of privations on past campaigns, Edward II was determined it should be well provisioned. Sixty ships were summoned from the English ports to bring supplies by sea.[18] Following in the wake of the army, 106 four-horse carts and 110 eight-oxen wagons would be loaded with supplies.[19]

On 17 June the English forces left Wark and Berwick:

> So the King of England advanced in pomp with his forces and with an abundance of supplies for them. He arranged for the collection of herds of cattle and flocks of sheep and pigs beyond number, corn and barley with portable mills for supplying the army, and wine in large jars and casks. Gold and silver and golden and silver vessels and every kind of precious furnishings he took from the King's treasury. He himself set out with his attendants, his vehicles and wagons, carts and horsemen, ... archers, crossbowmen, and men at arms ... while trumpets and horns rang out so that every district which they reached became fearful with frightened dread. So like locusts they covered the entire surface of the land until they reached Bannockburn.[20]

Somewhere in this vast concourse, perhaps riding in one of the wagons, was Friar Baston, a Carmelite, renowned as a Latin poet. King Edward, with fatal hubris, had brought him along to witness the battle, and immortalize the victory in verse.[21]

The bargain of Edward de Bruce and Sir Philip de Mowbray had given King Robert one valuable advantage: he knew exactly where the English invasion would arrive. To relieve Stirling, King Edward's army had to take the Roman road from Edinburgh to Stirling, which a few miles north-west of Falkirk passed through a forest called the Torwood or 'les Torres', well described by its old Gaelic name of *coille torr*, 'the wood of rocky outcrops'. Beyond the Torwood the road dipped to ford the Bannock Burn, then mounted again to pass through the edge of the wooded 'New Park', a hunting preserve enclosed by King Alexander III, so called to differentiate it from the older 'King's Park', which the road bypassed further on, before approaching the burgh of Stirling, beyond which rose the castle, dominating the landscape from its vast crag.

To the south-west of the road beyond the New Park lay hilly wooded country, intersected by some narrow tracks, but not by any road suitable to an invading army. North-east of the Roman road the land fell away steeply to the flat, marshy area of the Carse of Stirling, then known as 'The Pows' or 'Les Polles' from the many streams (Gaelic *pols*) that flowed across it in wandering courses to join the River Forth. The most substantial of these was the Bannock Burn, which rose in the hills south-west of the New Park, and beyond the ford on the Roman road flowed between steep banks, past the scattered settlement of Bannock, and wandered away across the wetland of Les Polles, becoming tidal in its lower reaches. To the north of Les Polles the sinuous course of the Forth gleamed in the distance, and beyond it lay Cambuskenneth Abbey.

There were no direct routes across Les Polles, which was too marshy to support a road, though no doubt there were tracks and paths. However, north-east of the road, following a lower contour but above the wetland, there was a track or bridlepath to Stirling. The character of the terrain, as it then was, would have forced the invading army to keep to the Roman road, though change of land use has led to controversy concerning the site of the battle itself. (The ensuing account follows the view that it took place to the north of the settlement of Bannock, and across the burn, on the firm ground then descriptively known as the 'Dryfield of Balquiderock'.[22])

King Robert summoned his army to assemble in the Torwood. From all over Scotland men began began to converge there before the end of April. His army was entirely different in character from King Edward's, being composed wholly of infantry, except for a force of five hundred light horsemen commanded by Sir Robert Keith the Marischal. Since the defeat at Methven, King Robert's forces had had no use for destriers. As a fugitive and guerrilla leader, King Robert and his companions had fought on foot. The tactics of 'Good King Robert's Testament' had no use for horses, and the raids of 1311/12 required mobile bands of light horse, like those now under Keith's command. In readiness for the forthcoming campaign there was neither opportunity to acquire destriers, which had to be imported, nor time to retrain Scottish knights in the forgotten technique of cavalry warfare.

King Robert's knights were accustomed to fighting on foot with their men, and the training that the army amassing in the Torwood received was in ever greater discipline and flexibility as an infantry force. The schiltrom, developed as an essentially defensive formation, designed to stand firm with spears bristling in every direction, was retrained to act as a mobile force, so that it could charge like a phalanx or resume its traditionally defensive position at command. In such an imaginative tactical advance King Robert showed his military genius, and developed a means whereby heavy cavalry, normally regarded as invincible, might be defeated by an army of foot-soldiers.

Sir Thomas Grey, the author of the *Scalachronica*, claimed that King Robert had learnt the lessons of the Battle of Courtrai, at which the burghers of Flanders had astonished Europe by defeating the chivalry of France in 1302.[23] This is likely enough, but King Robert would also have remembered the lesson of Wallace's victory at Stirling Bridge, that the terrain of battle must also put the cavalry at disadvantage. This lesson he would also put to good effect on the field of Bannockburn.

As the fighting men of Scotland assembled, King Robert

> . . . welcomed them with gladsome cheer
> Addressing kind words here and there
> And they, when they beheld their lord
> Welcoming them with homely word

Were greatly pleased, and for his sake
Would any peril undertake
And gladly fight, and gladly die,
To keep his honour proud and high.[24]

In addition to possessing the magic of the common touch which
Barbour evokes in these lines, the King already possessed the aura of a
hero. Indeed, the mythic poetic glory of heroism and victory surrounded both the King and his commanders alike. By deeds of personal
prowess the King, Douglas and Randolph had captured Perth,
Roxburgh and Edinburgh. The names of heroic men of the commons
were linked with theirs in these actions, and everyone who came to fight
with them could feel himself a hero by association. In this mood the
Scots felt themselves invincible.

King Robert created an army of four infantry divisions, one commanded by himself, the others by Thomas Randolph, James Douglas
and Edward de Bruce. The King's division, according to Barbour, was
composed of the men of his own earldom of Carrick, and men from
Bute, Kintyre, Argyll and the Isles. Angus MacDonald of Islay and his
contingent would fight in the King's division.[25] The composition of the
other divisions is not described, but presumably the recruits were
assigned to each commander on a territorial basis, which would give
Thomas Randolph, Earl of Moray, a division composed of men from
Moray and probably contingents from further north, and Edward de
Bruce a division composed of men from the south-west, including
Galloway. Douglas had associated with him in command of his division
Walter, High Steward of Scotland, son of James the Stewart, who had
died in 1309. As the young Stewart was a minor, Douglas had overall
command. Their division was probably composed of men from
Lanark, Renfrew and the Borders.[26]

The size of King Robert's army can only be guessed. Barbour,
though his numerical estimates were wildly large, believed that the
Scottish army was less than one-third the size of the English.[27] If each
of the Scottish divisions comprised between one thousand and fifteen
hundred, this would produce a total of five to six thousand.[28] Added to
these were Sir Robert Keith's light horse, and a corps of archers from
Selkirk Forest. At the most generous estimate the Scottish army would
not have totalled more than seven thousand men. An additional force

under David de Strathbogie, Earl of Atholl, was expected, but did not arrive.

If the Scots numbered seven thousand, the English army was the larger by at least ten thousand men. But on the day of battle the huge force of English infantry saw little or no action, and in the decisive struggle between Scottish foot and English cavalry the numerical advantage lay with the Scots.

King Robert had no intention of giving battle in the Torwood. When he received word that King Edward's army had reached Edinburgh, he retreated closer to Stirling, and occupied a stronger position, in the New Park. For the short march from the Torwood to the New Park, Randolph was appointed to command the vanguard. His division advanced towards the north-east of the park and took up a position overlooking the Kirkton of St Ninian's. Edward de Bruce followed, then James Douglas, their divisions positioned in a chain along the edge of the wood. King Robert brought up the vanguard, and took the most south-westerly position, with a clear view over the open ground between the edge of the park and the ford of the Bannock Burn, which the enemy would be obliged to cross. The King explained his choice of position to his commanders by saying that if the enemy attacked them in the park, their cavalry would be in difficulties among the trees, and if they fought on the marshy ground below the road, the streams would cause them even greater confusion.[29] His preference was for the latter, and to prevent the enemy from having free access to the open ground beyond the ford, he had a wide area on the New Park side of the ford honeycombed with small pits, a foot in length and knee deep. These were camouflaged with a light covering of twigs and grass.

The King sent the non-combatants to the north of the New Park, where they made an encampment in the dip between Coxet Hill and Gillies Hill. They are sometimes described as 'camp followers', which has a disreputable sound. Barbour referred to them as the 'small folk': servants, grooms, baggage train and 'catering corps'. There was also a supply depot, well out of the way of the enemy advance, on the other side of the Forth, beside Cambuskenneth Abbey, guarded by a small detachment under a knight named Sir William of Airth.

The morning after the King had positioned his army in the New Park was Sunday, 23 June, the vigil of St John the Baptist, and a fast day. Early in the morning Mass was celebrated for the army, followed by prayers for victory, and a breakfast of bread and water. Then King Robert had it publicly proclaimed that any man whose heart was not in the fight, or who was not prepared to conquer or die as God willed, had leave to depart. The Scots, fired with religious and patriotic fervour, returned tumultuous shouts that none would go.[30]

Word had been brought that the enemy had reached Falkirk, only fourteen miles from Stirling itself. King Robert sent James Douglas and Sir Robert Keith to reconnoitre. They took a small party of horsemen and rode back into the Torwood.

King Edward had reached Edinburgh on or about 19 June, and halted there while his supply ships put in at the port of Leith and provisioned the army. After this delay, time was running short to reach Stirling by Midsummer's Day. On 22 June, while King Robert was positioning his army in the New Park, King Edward endeavoured to make up for lost time with a forced march of twenty miles to Falkirk. Long hours of daylight made the march possible, but hot and cloudless weather brought the infantry close to exhaustion.

The following day the English cavalry had ridden on far ahead when James Douglas and Sir Robert Keith observed them from a hidden vantage point along the route. They did not underestimate the daunting array of well-mounted knights, who approached with the sunlight flashing on their bascinets and illumining the bright enamels of their shields. To Douglas and Keith the vivid shields and surcoats, the banners and pennons, were not simply a medly of blazons; with instinctive heraldic literacy they would have identified at a glance many champions from England and abroad who had come to fight against them. They returned to King Robert to report what they had seen. He told them to make no mention of the splendour of the enemy, but to report only that the English were advancing in great disarray.[31] There was some truth in this too, for the English army was strung out for many miles behind its advance guard.

King Edward halted in the Torwood, to allow the straggling column to close up. Here Sir Philip de Mowbray visited him, presumably with a safe conduct from the King of Scots.[32] No doubt he would have been directed to take the track for Stirling, to ensure that he did not discover the existence of the camouflaged pits. He was certainly ignorant of their existence, but he was able to tell King Edward that the Scots were occupying an extremely strong position in the New Park, and had blocked all the woodland tracks against a possible advance in that direction. But the main purpose of his visit was to assure King Edward that since he had now arrived within the requisite distance of Stirling Castle by the vigil of St John, which was also Midsummer's Eve, Mowbray 'considered himself relieved'.[33] He was not obliged to surrender, and there was no need for King Edward to bring the Scots to battle.

This was not a message that King Edward wished to hear. He had come to inflict a crushing defeat on the Scots, to regain his father's conquests, and to win the prestige that had so far eluded him.

A stormy discussion ensued, in which Mowbray's view was brushed aside, and the English commanders showed themselves as eager as the King to fight the Scots. King Edward appointed the young Earl of Gloucester, Gilbert de Clare, to command the vanguard, and ordered him to advance along the Roman road and attack the Scots positions in the New Park.[34] Immediately the Earl of Hereford demanded the right, as Constable of England, to command the vanguard.[35] Edward attempted to settle the dispute by giving them joint command which doubtless left both dissatisfied.

A second force, under the joint command of Sir Robert de Clifford and Sir Henry de Beaumont, was ordered to 'make a circuit upon the other side of the wood towards the Castle, keeping the open ground',[36] i.e. to follow the track towards Stirling. Their intention, according to Barbour, was to enter the castle as the official relieving party.[37] King Edward was evidently determined to occupy the castle whether Sir Philip de Mowbray considered it necessary or not.

It was late afternoon when the Scots in the New Park saw the vanguard of the English army approaching the ford. The broad front narrowed to a column which splashed through the burn with Gloucester and Hereford in the lead. As they came up the slope beyond the ford, a knight spurred on ahead of them. It was Hereford's nephew, Sir Henry de Bohun. He had seen in the distance a mail-clad horseman on a grey palfrey (a light saddle horse), riding along the edge of the wood. An axe was in his hand, and over his bascinet he wore a leather cap surmounted by a crown.[38] Sir Henry identified the King of Scots, issuing his final orders to the men drawn up under the trees. Sir Henry saw his opportunity for glory, to win the battle by slaying the King. Couching his lance, he charged towards him. Alerted by the thunder of hooves, King Robert swung round to face the attack. It would have been prudent to have retreated, but retreat was unthinkable before the massed ranks of the Scots. King Robert set spurs to his palfrey, as though he and his opponent were evenly matched champions in the lists.

> Together charged they galloping.
> Sir Henry missed the noble King!
> And he, that in his stirrups stood,
> Lifted his axe, so sharp and good,
> And such a mighty stroke he aimed
> That neither hat nor helmet stemmed
> The force of that tremendous blow.
> Down did the bold Sir Henry go.
> The hand-axe shaft was broke in two.
> His skull was almost cleft right through,
> And there he lay bereft of might.
> So fell the first stroke of the fight.[39]

The King's men, exalted by his triumph, surged forward to attack the English and pushed them back in confusion towards the ford, where many knights had been thrown from their horses as they plunged unsuspectingly into the camouflaged pits. Gloucester was unhorsed, but rescued from capture by his squires. After a fierce engagement the English retreated beyond the ford, and King Robert recalled his men, and ordered them back to their positions in the wood. He was surrounded by his commanders, who reproached him as much as they dared for adventuring himself in single combat with Sir Henry de Bohun, in which his death might have brought ruin to them all. The King made light of their reproaches by speaking regretfully of his broken axe.[40]

From his vantage point at the edge of the wood, the King surveyed the movements of the enemy, and saw the detachment of knights under Sir Robert de Clifford and Sir Henry de Beaumont riding along the track towards Stirling. They would have crossed the Bannock Burn, not at the ford, but near the hamlet of Bannock, to pick up the track, and they were about level with the Kirkton of St Ninian's when the glint of the late sun on their armour caught the King's eye. Thomas Randolph, Earl of Moray, should have been with his division, ready to deal with such an eventuality. The King said to him grimly 'A rose has fallen from your chaplet!' (a chaplet of roses being the crown of the victor in a tournament). Randolph hurried off in shame to gather his men and intercept the enemy.[41]

The English knights numbered three hundred, according to the author of the *Scalachronica*, whose father, Sir Thomas Grey the elder, was one of them. They checked at the sight of the phalanx of spearmen charging towards them out of the New Park. Sir Henry de Beaumont shouted 'Let us halt a little! Let them come on. Give them room!' His meaning was to let them come into the open, where there was freedom of manoeuvre to attack them. The spearmen reformed into a schiltrom, a dense and deadly obstacle barring their route. Sir Thomas Grey said to Beaumont, 'Whatever you give them I doubt not that they will have all soon enough.'

'Very well,' Beaumont replied, 'if you are afraid, be off.'

'Sir,' said Sir Thomas, 'it is not for fear that I shall fly this day!'[42] He pushed his horse between that of Beaumont and Sir William Deyncourt, and together they charged against the Scottish spears. Sir William was killed immediately, Sir Thomas Grey unhorsed and taken prisoner, the first of many English knights to fall into the hands of the Scots.

Again and again Beaumont and Clifford's knights charged the schiltrom, and found themselves unable to break the ring of spears. The knights began to throw axes, maces and even swords at the spearmen, until a heap of weapons lay in the hollow centre of the ring.

James Douglas, who had remained with the King, watched the conflict with mounting anxiety, fearing for Thomas Randolph's life. He begged the King's permission to go to his aid. The King refused. He was still uncertain whether the English force which had retreated beyond the ford would reform and attack again. But they showed no sign of doing so, and when Douglas entreated him a second time, he let him go.

As Douglas brought up his reinforcements, he saw the English attack slacken and falter. He ordered his men to halt, now more concerned for

Randolph's honour than for his life. He said that since Randolph had borne the brunt of the attack, he alone should have the credit for having repulsed it. He approached only when the English knights turned and retreated along the track towards Bannock. Randolph's men sat down on the ground, streaming with sweat, and took off their bascinets. They were surrounded again as Douglas's men surged round to congratulate them. No doubt there were wounded men among them, but only one of their number had been killed. Moray led his men back to the King, who

> ... made good cheer to them that they
> Had borne themselves so well that day.[43]

The Scots could congratulate themselves that they had inflicted two separate defeats on English arms. Neither had been a mere skirmish. The cavalry attack at the ford had been intended as the opening manoeuvre of full-scale battle. Its repulse had been achieved by a combination of the ferocity of the Scots' counter-attack, and the confusion caused by the pits. The death of Sir Henry de Bohun would have been witnessed only by the foremost ranks of the English, but as an almost superhuman feat of arms it would have lost nothing in the telling.

The second action, though the smaller of the two, was scarcely less momentous. The English attempt to reclaim Stirling Castle had been foiled, and the efficacy of the new tactics of the Scottish infantry had been powerfully demonstrated. The morale of the English plummeted as much as that of the Scots was exalted.[44]

Nonetheless, King Robert seems to have suffered a crisis of decision on the wisdom of giving battle to the English on the following day. To do so would be to risk the whole resources of his kingdom in a single engagement, the risk that he had always sought to avoid. Having mauled the English to good effect, the Scots could withdraw and revert to their former strategy, leaving the English to march in pursuit until eventually starvation forced them to retreat. Stirling would be a temporary sacrifice, but hunger could be relied upon to drive the English out again by the end of the year. The King consulted his commanders, saying that whether they desired to withdraw or to stand and fight, he would abide by their decision. With one voice they proclaimed their preference for staying to do battle. Their fervour resolved the King's doubts, and he felt great gladness of heart.[45]

Later in the evening, as though to confirm the rightness of the decision, a defector arrived from the English camp. Sir Alexander Seton, a Scot in the English service, decided to change sides, in anticipation of the English defeat that he foresaw. He sought an audience with King Robert, and said to him, 'Sir, now is the time if ever you intend to win Scotland. The English have lost heart, they are discouraged . . . I swear on my head, and on pain of being hanged and drawn that if you attack them in the morning you will defeat them easily without loss.'[46]

The English infantry had seen nothing of the action on Midsummer's Eve. They were encamped to the south of the Bannock Burn, exhausted by forced marches on two successive hot days, and demoralized by tales of two defeats that the knighthood of England had suffered at the hands of the Scots. In five hundred places among them, said Barbour, men could be heard murmuring that their lords had gone to war unrighteously, God was offended, and defeat would follow.[47] To stem the tide of defeatism heralds were sent throughout the host to proclaim that what happened in small skirmishes was of no significance, that victory in the main battle was certain, and the rewards would be great. This effort at artificial morale-raising was as unsuccessful as such attempts usually are. The infantrymen helped themselves to wine from the supply-wagons and quelled their anxieties by spending the night in drunken revelry.[48]

King Edward held a council of war at which it was decided that the cavalry should cross the Bannock Burn on to the wetland where their horses could be watered. Thence they could move on to firm dry ground, facing the Scots' positions in the New Park across the Roman road, an approach that provided an opportunity for a cavalry charge, avoiding the hazard of the pits near the ford. This choice of battlefield was based on good reconnaissance, and perhaps on knowledge of the terrain contributed by veterans of earlier campaigns.

The English cavalry crossed the Bannock Burn on to the Carse of Balquiderock, which was so marshy and criss-crossed with streams and ditches that they were obliged to tear down huts and houses and use doors and roofing material to stabilize the ground. Barbour reported that the men of the castle garrison arrived after dark (around midnight, in the short summer night), bringing doors and window shutters to help bridge the streams.[49] The carse had evidently proved far more of a morass than had been expected. But before dawn the knights and men at arms had brought their destriers on to the firm ground of the Dryfield of Balquiderock in readiness for battle.[50]

While the English cavalry spent the night floundering around in the carse, King Robert's army, encamped in the woods of the New Park, spent the night in vigilant quiet. At dawn the King made his confession to Maurice, Abbot of Inchaffray, who then celebrated Mass before the army, in a prominent place at the edge of the wood.[51] Abbot Maurice had brought the relics of St Fillan, and Abbot Bernard of Arbroath the reliquary casket of St Columba (the Monymusk reliquary) to confer the saints' blessing on the army. Abbot Bernard set down the King's address to his assembled officers and men, which in the manner of battlefield oratory would have been heard by relatively few, but reported in general terms to the rest:

My lords, my people, who set great store by freedom, for which the Kings of Scotland have suffered many trials, dying for the Lord, think now of the many hardships we have endured, fighting for eight years and more for our right to the kingdom, honour and liberty. We have lost brothers, friends and kinsmen. Your kinsmen and friends are captives. Prelates and churchmen are in prison, and no order of Mother Church is safe. The nobles of the land have died in bloody warfare. These armed magnates who you see before you have already insolently ordered our destruction, and that of our kingdom and people. They do not believe that we can resist. They glory in their horses and baggage train. For us, the name of the Lord must be our hope of victory in war. This is a blessed day, on which St John the Baptist was born. St Andrew and St Thomas the Martyr, together with the Saints of Scotland will fight today for the honour of the people, with Christ the Lord going before them. Under his leadership you will conquer, and end the war. If you heartily repent of your sins, our royal power proclaims that all offences against us are remitted to all who fight well for the kingdom of our fathers.[52]

Barbour reported that the King also promised remission of feudal dues to the heirs of any who should die in battle.[53]

King Robert then conferred the order of knighthood on the men he had chosen for the honour of being knighted on the field of battle. These included Walter Stewart and James Douglas. Some historians have found it hard to believe that so distinguished a commander as Douglas was not already a knight, and have supposed that he was advanced to the rank of knight banneret.[54] But documentary evidence is that previously he had been a baron without being a knight, contemporary references to him using the style 'James, Lord of Douglas'.[55]

This ceremony completed, the Scots advanced from the borders of the wood with their banners displayed, the Abbot of Inchaffray walking before them bearing a crucifix. At a sign from him the whole army knelt as one man, and recited the paternoster.[56] The religious fervour that would characterize the armies of the Covenant in the seventeenth century seems to have been the mood of the Scots on the morning of Bannockburn.

From the far side of the Dryfield of Balquiderock, Edward II, in the front rank of his army, watched the advance of the Scots in amazement and said, 'What! Will you Scotsmen fight?' Sir Ingram de Umfraville, at his side, agreed that it was the most amazing thing he had seen by day or night. They had expected to charge the Scots' positions, not to see footmen come out to challenge cavalry 'on open, smooth and solid ground'.[57] Then they saw the Scots army kneel in prayer, and Edward, misinterpreting their action, exclaimed, 'Yon folk kneel to ask mercy!' Sir Ingram de Umfraville replied, 'You speak the truth. They ask mercy, but not from you. They call on God to forgive their trespasses. I tell you one thing for certain – these men will win all or die'.

'So be it then,' replied King Edward, and signed for the trumpets to sound the onset.[58]

King Robert held his own division in reserve (his standard traditionally set up at the Borestone). The other three divisions of his army, commanded by Edward de Bruce on the right, Thomas Randolph in the centre and James Douglas on the left, advanced on a broad front. The infantrymen, with axes at their sides and their spears in their hands, 'appeared like a thick-set hedge, and such a phalanx could not easily be broken'.[59]

The charge of the English vanguard was led by the Earl of Gloucester. He had told King Edward that he ought to rest his army for a day before giving battle, and Edward had publicly accused him of cowardice. Burning to disprove the insult, he mounted his horse without his surcoat, and led the charge without the means of identification that would have marked him as highly valuable for ransom.

According to an eye-witness, who described the battle to the Lanercost Chronicler,

> when both armies engaged each other, and the great horses of the English charged the pikes of the Scots, as it were into a dense forest, there arose a great and terrible crash of spears broken and of destriers wounded to death.[60]

Gloucester was killed in the charge, together with Sir Edmund de Mauley, the steward of King Edward's household, Sir John Comyn, Sir Pain de Tiptoft and Sir Robert de Clifford.[61] On a field encumbered by the corpses of men and horses, the wounded and the dying, and the riderless destriers, the English vanguard found it impossible to withdraw and reform for a second charge. Nor had the ranks of cavalry drawn up in their rear any freedom to manoeuvre.

Edward de Bruce's division had taken the brunt of the charge, their 'thick-set hedge' of spears unbroken. Now, as they pressed remorselessly forward, the divisions of Thomas Randolph and James Douglas advanced on their left to attack those massed ranks of English cavalry who had no opportunity to charge at all. The Dryfield of Balquiderock was bounded by the Bannock Burn to the south and the Pelstream Burn to the north, which restricted the movements of the cavalry under circumstances that had not been foreseen. Instead of charging from the Dryfield into the New Park, the English were now penned on the Dryfield, and being forced backwards by a wall of spears.

One of the English commanders took the only initiative that might have saved the day, by bringing the Welsh archers into action, probably on the north bank of the Pelstream Burn, whence they discharged flights of arrows that wreaked heavy casualties in the ranks of the Scots.

King Robert, seeing this manoeuvre from his vantage point in the New Park, directed Sir Robert Keith, whose force he had hitherto held in reserve, to attack them. Keith's light horse hit the archers like a whirlwind and scattered them from the field. The Scottish archers then came up to take their place, and though the Welsh archers had been the larger and more formidable force, the bowmen of Selkirk Forest discharged their arrows into the English cavalry and 'dealt them many wounds severe . . . and slew of them a multititude'.[62]

King Robert now brought up his own division, probably advancing on the flank that had suffered heavy casualties from the archers. If they had been shooting across the Pelstream Burn, he would have come up to the support of James Douglas's division.[63] With the weight of another mass of spearmen thrown against them, the English were inexorably pushed back into the Carse of Balquiderock.

'The English columns', wrote Sir Thomas Grey, '. . . were jammed together, and could not operate against them [the Scots], so direfully were their horses impaled on the pikes.'[64] When these were broken, the Scots hacked and hewed the enemy with their axes. Blood formed pools on the ground, and welled into the streams in which men and horses were floundering.

The Scots raised a great cry of 'On them! On them! On them, they fail!'[65] At this cry, or at another given signal, columns of Scots appeared from between the hills of the New Park, and added their cries of 'Slay Slay! Upon them hastily!'[66] The hard-beset English were in no condition to notice that the banners of this new host were made of sheets tied on to poles. The 'small folk' for whom King Robert had found a dramatic if not military use filled the enemy with fear that a second Scottish army was advancing to the attack.

The English were already defeated, though still fighting resolutely, when this prospect struck them with despair, and their resistance broke.

According to the Lanercost Chronicle, the English, having crossed the Bannock Burn the previous night, '. . . now wanted to re-cross it in confusion [and] many nobles and others fell into it with their horses in the crush, while others escaped with much difficulty, and many were never able to extricate themselves from the ditch'.[67] Before its confluence with the Pelstream Burn, the Bannock Burn flowed between steep banks, and it was here that many men and horses were drowned. The burn, said Barbour, became so choked with corpses that later fugitives from the battle crossed it dry-shod on the drowned bodies of earlier ones.[68] But those who crossed came to the more treacherous wetland of 'Les Polles', where the tidal reach of the Bannock Burn claimed more lives, as did the River Forth, across which many fugitives attempted to swim to safety. By now the fugitives were not being pursued by the weary Scottish spearmen, but by the exultant 'small folk' who

> Among them ran and many slew
> That had no strength to fight anew
> Right pitiful it was to see . . .[69]

Thus the battle ended, in muddy massacre by non-combatants.

King Edward II had fought bravely in the battle, and, with an obstinacy worthy of his father, refused to concede defeat until Aymer de Valence, Earl of Pembroke, seized his rein and dragged him from the field. It was essential that he should not fall into the hands of the enemy. None would wish to kill him, but many sought to capture him.

> As the Scottish knights, who were on foot, laid hold on the harnessing of the King's charger in order to stop him, he struck out so vigorously behind him with his mace that there was none whom he touched that he did not fell to the ground.[70]

His bodyguard of five hundred knights closed round him, and with Pembroke on one side and Sir Giles de Argentan on the other, they escorted him from the field. When they had ridden a short distance, Sir Giles de Argentan said, 'Sire, your rein was committed to me; you are now in safety. I am not accustomed to fly, nor am I going to begin now. I commend you to God.' Then, setting spurs to his horse, he returned to the affray, where he was slain.[71]

The King's escort brought him to Stirling Castle, but Sir Philip de Mowbray urged him not to enter, pointing out that he would be besieged immediately and taken prisoner. The castle could not continue to hold out, and since Edward's army had been defeated there would be none to rescue him. Mowbray urged him to keep his bodyguard together and flee around the outside of the New Park. King Edward accepted his advice, and rode with his escort round the foot of the castle rock, by way of the Round Table (the King's Knot) and took the route towards Linlithgow.[72]

Sir Robert Keith's force would have been large enough to pursue

King Edward and his knights, but King Robert dared not risk releasing him to do so. A large force of English fugitives, mostly infantrymen who had played no part in the battle, fled towards Stirling Castle and gathered against the base of the castle rock. If anyone managed to rally them, they might yet put up a fight. King Robert kept his army together until it was clear that no further resistance would be offered. However, he allowed James Douglas to take a detachment of sixty horsemen to shadow the fugitive King, though this was too few to attack his larger bodyguard. In the Torwood, Douglas met Sir Laurence Abernethy, a pro-English Scot, belatedly bringing a contingent to join the English army. When he heard of its defeat, he decided to change sides, and did so with sufficient enthusiasm to persuade Douglas to let him join the chase.[73] They pursued the fugitives to the gates of Dunbar Castle, into which Patrick, Earl of Dunbar, admitted the King and some of his following. 'At Dunbar the King embarked with some of his chosen followers in an open boat for Berwick, leaving all the others to their fate'.[74]

Some were captured or killed, the rest eventually made their way to England. The success of Edward's escape was due entirely to the honourable conduct of Sir Philip de Mowbray and the Earl of Dunbar. Had Mowbray received Edward into Stirling Castle and then handed him over to Robert the Bruce, or had Dunbar betrayed Edward when he had him in his power, the King of Scots could have dictated the terms of peace.[75]

Having sped the fugitive King on his way, both Mowbray and Dunbar surrendered their castles to King Robert, and swore allegiance to him. Temperamentally, he would have respected their chivalrous treatment of King Edward, though politically he may have regretted it.

Not all the fugitives from Bannockburn were as fortunate as King Edward. The Earl of Hereford fled westward towards his own castle of Bothwell, accompanied by Robert de Umfraville, Earl of Angus, Sir Ingram de Umfraville, and other English barons and knights. They were admitted to the castle by Hereford's deputy, Sir Walter FitzGilbert, but when Edward de Bruce, sent in pursuit of them with a large company, arrived before Bothwell, FitzGilbert delivered them to him as prisoners and made his peace with King Robert.[76]

One English magnate salvaged honour from defeat. The Earl of Pembroke, having seen King Edward well away from Stirling, returned to the battlefield and collected the Welsh infantrymen levied from his own lands. On foot, he led them through enemy country, and across the Solway to Carlisle. Though the column was continuously harried along the way, and many stragglers were killed, the majority of the Welshmen were led successfully to safety.[77] One of them, on his return to Wales, may have told the story of the battle to the chronicler of Valle Crucis Abbey, for it is in that chronicle that the earliest mention of the battle occurs.[78]

After the battle the first necessity was the identification and disposal of the dead. The Scottish losses were remarkably light. Two knights were killed in the battle, Sir William de Vieuxpont and Sir Walter of Ross, the younger son of the Earl of Ross. On the eve of the battle the commander of the Scottish supply depot at Cambuskenneth, Sir William of Airth, had been killed in a treacherous attack on the depot by the Earl of Atholl. Many of the guards were also killed, and the supplies carried off. Atholl's treachery was intended to avenge the honour of his sister, who had been seduced by Edward de Bruce, and then abandoned in favour of the daughter of the Earl of Ross.[79] It was because of his love for her that Edward de Bruce shed tears for the death of her brother, Sir Walter, the only occasion on which he was ever seen to weep. Atholl paid for his treachery with the forfeiture of his lands, and banishment to England, where he died in 1327.[80]

The English losses among the noble and knightly class were unusually heavy, for many potentially ransomable men were killed in the early stages of the battle, before the Scots could pause to take prisoners. After the battle, wrote Barbour,

> Two hundred pairs of spurs all red
> Were taken from the knights there dead.[81]

In addition to these casualties there were the knights and the nameless dead who had been drowned in the Bannock Burn and the Forth and the streams of 'Les Polles'. There some of them sank without trace.[82] Otherwise, the bodies of the knights were buried in consecrated ground, and those of the English soldiery in common graves.

The body of Gilbert de Clare, Earl of Gloucester, was carried from the battlefield to a nearby church, where King Robert kept a vigil throughout the night. (Gloucester was his kinsman, since his grandfather's first wife had been a Clare.) Later he sent the body, together with that of Sir Robert de Clifford, to King Edward at Berwick, so that their families could claim them for burial.

When King Robert emerged from his vigil on the morning after the battle he was approached by Sir Marmaduke de Tweng, who was distantly related to him through the Yorkshire branch of the Bruce family. The knight had hidden his arms and armour and lurked unarmed until he could see the King. He approached and knelt at his feet. 'Welcome, Sir Marmaduke,' said Robert, 'to what man are you prisoner?'

'To none,' he replied, 'I yield myself to you here, to be at your will.'

'And I receive you, Sir,' the King replied, and gave instructions for Sir Marmaduke to be entertained courteously. He remained long in Scotland as the King's guest, and eventually returned to England with generous gifts and free of ransom.[83] King Robert showed equal generosity to Gloucester's stepfather, Sir Raoul de Monthemer, who long ago had been his friend at the English court, and whose warning had saved him from the wrath of Edward I. In freely releasing Monthemer, who as King Edward II's brother-in-law would have provided a vast ransom, King Robert handsomely discharged his debt of gratitude. Even hostile English chroniclers wrote admiringly of his magnanimity.

The King's own entourage no doubt appreciated his treatment of Friar Baston, who had been captured with his poem celebrating the English victory written beforehand. King Robert required him to recast it as a celebration of the Scottish victory as the price of his freedom. Baston's text, which survives through incorporation in the *Scotichronicon*, shows extensive rewriting. No doubt he left unchanged his onomatopaeic lines evoking the clash of battle, and his general lamentation for wounds and slaughter, but he incorporated mentions of the drunken revelry of the English on the eve of battle, and of King Robert's battlefield oration. He mentioned the camouflaged pits, and accurately described the battlefield as '*arrida terra Stirelini*' (the dry field of Stirling), and he lamented the deaths of Gloucester, Clifford, Mauley and Argentan. In conclusion he immortalized his own authorship and made no attempt to conceal his true sentiments:

> Baston is my surname, and I'm a Carmelite,
> Alas, I grieve to have survived so terrible a fight.

> If I've omitted anything that ought to have been said
> Let others, more unbiased, tell the story in my stead.[84]

Thus he gained his freedom without sacrificing his dignity, which was a price King Robert never required of any man.

To the humiliated King of England, King Robert returned his shield, which had been lost in his flight from the battlefield, and his privy seal, which had been captured with its bearer, Sir Roger Northburgh.

There remained in the hands of the Scots many distinguished prisoners who provided a rich harvest of ransoms. The most valuable was the Earl of Hereford, who was exchanged for the Queen and King Robert's daughter, the Lady Marjorie, his sister Mary, and Bishop Wishart of Glasgow, who was now old and blind. The negotiations for their exchange took time, and it was autumn before they returned to Scotland.[85] The rejoicing on their return could not have been unalloyed, for all of them would have been changed by their sufferings. Queen Elizabeth had been separated from her husband as a young woman, and returned on the verge of middle age, with all the years in which she might have borne heirs to the kingdom wasted in captivity. The Lady Marjorie had been imprisoned as a child and returned as a young woman whose whole adolescence had been spent shut away from the world, without experience of the royal household which would have been her natural milieu, and without mental contact with her father's adventures and triumphs. She, even more than his wife, must have returned as a stranger to the King. Mary de Bruce no doubt bore the physiological scars of the years of imprisonment in her cage at Roxburgh. (Christian de Bruce, whose imprisonment had been less stringent, was returned to Scotland under a separate negotiation.) Isabel of Fife did not return. After her release from her cage at Berwick in 1310 she had been held in the Carmelite convent in Berwick. In 1313 she had passed into the custody of Sir Henry de Beaumont.[86] King Robert would not have forgotten his debt of gratitude to her, so the inference is that she had died before Bannockburn.

King Robert's nephew, Donald, Earl of Mar, who had spent many years at the English court, was given the opportunity to return to Scotland. But he had formed a close friendship with King Edward, and preferred to remain in England.[87] This disappointment to King Robert received its compensation the following year when the young Earl of

Fife, who had also been brought up in England, decided to offer his allegiance to the King of Scots. It was a great satisfaction to him to regain the premier Earl of Scotland. The Earl surrendered his earldom to the King and was restored to it under a tailzie (entail) which empowered the King to assign the earldom to a new heir if the earl should die childless, for when he left England his wife was forcibly detained there. The tailzie was to assure that always in future there should be an Earl of Fife to enthrone the King of Scots at his inauguration.[88]

In the aftermath of Bannockburn many pro-English Scots decided to transfer their allegiance to King Robert. Most prominent among them were the Earls of Dunbar and Fife, whose loyalty to him never wavered. Neither did that of Sir Philip de Mowbray 'until his very day of death'.[89] Sir Ingram de Umfraville and Sir David de Brechin made a temporary change of allegiance, but for the most part those who offered their loyalty to King Robert kept faith.

Soon after Bannockburn, according to Barbour, the King held council and

> In sundry towns he caused proclaim
> That if a man had any claim
> To hold in Scotland land, or fee,
> Within at most twelve months should he
> Appear and claim it, and then do
> Whatever to the King was due.
> If he came not within the year
> Then, let him heed, none would give ear
> To any claim beyond that date.[90]

The Parliament which met at Cambuskenneth in November enacted that all Scottish landholders who failed to comply with this proclamation should be disinherited.[91] The King was willing to accept the claims of Englishmen who held lands in Scotland, on condition that they ceased to hold lands in England.[92] With recollection of the problems caused by divided loyalties in the past, King Robert was determined to have an integrated kingdom. Only a small group of irreconcilables remained, to become 'the Disinherited', whose claims would cause trouble in the distant future.

At the end of 1314, Robert the Bruce was in full possession of his kingdom, except for the town of Berwick in which England maintained its last toehold. But, as the Lanercost Chronicler admitted, he was 'commonly called King of Scotland by all men, because he had acquired Scotland by force of arms'.[93] It remained to exact acknowledgement of his title from the King of England.

PART THREE
FROM WAR TO PEACE
——|✻|✻|✻|——

13

——————|✳|✳|✳|——————

TERROR AND TRUCE

'Everything that we ourselves and our people . . . can
do, we are now, and shall be, prepared to do sincerely
and honourably for the sake of good peace . . . If it
should be agreeable to your will to hold negotiations
with us upon these matters, let your royal will be
communicated to us . . .'

Robert I to Edward II[1]

IN ENGLAND the defeat of Edward II's great army had been unthinkable, and the resultant humiliation was overwhelming. The author of
the *Vita Edwardi Secundi* captured the public mood:

O famous race unconquested through the ages, why do you, who
used to conquer knights, now flee from mere footmen? . . . O day of
vengeance and disaster, day of utter loss and shame, evil and
accursed day . . . that blemished the reputation of the English,
despoiled them and enriched the Scots, in which our earthly belong-
ings were ravished to the value of £200,000 . . .[2]

This enormous, if inventive, estimate of the English losses represented
not only the arms and armour and valuable destriers captured by the
Scots, but the whole English baggage train which had fallen into their
hands with its provisions, draught animals, and all the rich furnishings,
the gold and silver vessels, which King Edward had brought to
Scotland. These had not merely been comforts for a sybaritic king and
his companions, but provisions for the Scottish castles he had intended
to reoccupy or had prematurely granted to his favoured supporters. He

would have been astonished to discover that most of these castles were heaps of rubble, and was doubtless more chagrined by the knowledge that their intended contents had been shared out among the supporters of Robert the Bruce, whose generosity ensured that even the humblest should have some taste of the English booty.

King Edward's shame after the double humiliation of defeat and flight fuelled his resentment against the Scots and made him impervious to overtures for peace. No doubt King Robert's courtesies in sending the bodies of Gloucester and Clifford to Berwick, in releasing Monthemer and Tweng without ransom, and in returning to Edward his privy seal and his shield, were intended as gestures of reconciliation. But Edward would have none of it.

Accordingly, King Robert determined on a change of policy: he would bring Edward to the negotiating table by demonstrating his inability to defend his own realm.

On 1 August 1314 Edward de Bruce, James Douglas and William de Soules, Lord of Liddesdale, 'with cavalry and a large army' invaded England.[3] They passed close to Berwick and

> Devastated almost all Northumberland with fire, except the castles; and so they passed forward into the Bishopric of Durham; but there they did not burn much, for the people of the bishopric ransomed themselves from burning with a large sum of money. Nevertheless, the Scots carried off a booty of cattle and what men they could capture, and so invaded the county of Richmond beyond. The Scots even went as far as the water of Tees, and some of them beyond the town of Richmond . . . Afterwards, reuniting their forces, they all returned by Swaledale and other valleys by Stanemoor, whence they carried off an immense booty of cattle. Also they burnt the towns of Brough, Appleby and Kirkoswald . . . and so, passing near the priory of Lanercost, they entered Scotland, having many men prisoner for whom they might extort money ransom at will.[4]

At a famous landmark, the Rerecross on Stanemoor, they were intercepted by a force sent and commanded by Sir Andrew de Harclay, Governor of Carlisle, but the English force was thrust aside and lost sixteen horses in the action, while the Scots continued on their way with their prisoners and booty.[5]

Immediately after this successful and lucrative raid, King Robert sent a personal letter to Edward II, expressing his desire for peace.[6] The raid had made the point that the English King was incapable of defending the North of England. He had no forces with which to do so, for the army that he had led to the relief of Stirling had ceased to exist. Of the knights who were not captured during or immediately after the battle, it was said that some, wandering in the countryside, were taken prisoner by women, 'nor did any of them get back to England save in abject confusion'.[7] The infantrymen who had crowded at the foot of Stirling Castle rock after the battle had yielded themselves to the Scots the following day, when Sir Philip de Mowbray surrendered the castle. If, in accordance with the usual custom, they were disarmed and permitted to depart, many would have been killed in the hostile country between Stirling and the Borders; many would have wandered the roads of England for weeks or months before, if ever, they reached their homes.

With the dissolution of his army, Edward II was in no position to resist the demands of the Scots. Neither could he resist the demands of Thomas of Lancaster and the other earls who had refused to join the carnage, who could claim that his defeat resulted from his reliance on evil counsel, and would not have occurred had he accepted the Ordinances.[8] Early in September, King Edward moved from Berwick to York to meet Lancaster and his allies, and 'the King refused nothing to the Earls'.[9] Lancaster insisted upon an immediate implementation of the Ordinances, which involved a purge of the royal household and administration which temporarily deprived Edward of all but the shadow of his kingship.

Peace talks with Scotland followed. They opened at Durham on 20 October, and were scheduled to proceed from negotiation on exchange of prisoners to discussion of a 'perpetual peace'.[10] These talks led to the release of the Queen of Scots and the other Scottish prisoners exchanged for the Earl of Hereford, and the return of English prisoners from Scotland, including Robert de Umfraville, Earl of Angus, Sir John de Segrave and Sir Anthony de Lacy. 'From day to day sundry prisoners were released from the hands of the Scots, but only through very heavy pecuniary ransoms.'[11] But thereafter the talks broke down, presumably on the issue of the recognition of Robert the Bruce as King of Scots, and the acknowledgement of Scotland's independence, both of which Edward II steadfastly refused.[12] On 30 November, the feast of St Andrew, King Robert retaliated by leading an invasion of Northumberland in person. He reclaimed the honour of Tynedale, which had belonged to King Alexander III and earlier Kings of Scots, as part of their English fiefs, and received the homage of the inhabitants. There was pro-Scottish feeling in the area, and the men of Tynedale demonstrated their new fealty by attacking their pro-English neighbours:

> They treated [them] inhumanely, carrying off their goods and taking them away as captive. The women too went riding in warlike manner, stealing the goods which their men did not care about, such as shorn wool and linen and carried them off.[13]

Robert gave a clear message that he intended to keep Tynedale by granting the manor of Wark-on-Tyne to William de Sales and land in North Tynedale to Sir Philip de Mowbray.[14]

This invasion, with its threat to English possession of a large tract of Northumberland, may have brought the English to the negotiating table again, for talks were held at Dumfries towards the end of the year, but they had collapsed by Christmas.[15]

In June 1315 Robert raided England again, accompanied by James Douglas. They invaded the bishopric of Durham, and while Robert remained at Chester-le-Street, Douglas was sent to raid Hartlepool, an erstwhile fief of the Bruce family which had refused to return to its fealty. Some townsfolk fled by putting to sea, but Douglas captured many burgesses and their wives for ransom, before rejoining the King. 'Having collected much booty from the whole countryside they all returned to their own country.'[16] After this raid the bishopric purchased a two-year truce.

Each raid had its individual objective, but all conformed to a common pattern outlined in the account of the first post-Bannockburn raid quoted in the Lanercost Chronicle. The Scots invaded from the east, where the open country of Northumberland permitted speed of movement. They did not delay to attack strong castles and defensible towns. They collected herds of cattle and ransomable prisoners, crossed the Pennines by way of the river valleys and the pass over Stanemoor, and re-entered Scotland on the west. In the absence of any system of credit, when truces were bought by local communities they were paid for in coin which the Scots carried home on pack-horses, or hostages were taken for later payment at an agreed date. The Scots were highly disciplined, for truces had to guarantee immunity from destruction. Unfortunately for communities that had struck reliable bargains with the Scots, they had no guarantee against the depredations of local freebooters known as 'schevaldores', who began to operate with the breakdown of English administration.

Where the Scots were not bought off, their destruction was savage and systematic. Most buildings, other than castles and churches, were of wood and thatch; farms, mills and whole villages responded readily to the flames. Dry, ripe crops could be torched, fields of green corn trampled flat by the stolen cattle. At Bamburgh, where the castle was bypassed, local destruction included digging up a rabbit warren.[17] The most desirable loot was armour and weapons, for supplies of which Scotland depended on international trade which was always hazarded by piracy and attacks by English shipping. But the Scottish raiders had an eye for anything valuable or useful: church plate and vestments, books and bedclothes were carried off. Division of spoils and of a proportion of prisoners' ransoms encouraged their enterprise.

The raids were highly profitable, and were intended to finance the war so long as it should last. But their main purpose was to compel England to make peace. Wars end when one of the combatants is exhausted, or so denuded of manpower and resources as to make further warfare unsustainable. Bannockburn had temporarily shattered English morale, but England's resources were far from exhausted, and the determination of her incompetent but obstinate King to resist the demands of the Scots remained unshaken.

It was unfortunate for Robert the Bruce that England's chief centres of population and prosperity lay in the south-eastern quarter of the country. Since it was beyond either his range or his manpower to strike at them, he was forced to confine his strategy of terror and spoilation to northern England. But he struck ever more deeply into it, extending his range from Northumberland and Durham into the richer county of Yorkshire. If Edward II's very possession of his northern counties were threatened, he might bend his stubborn will to acknowledge the independence of Scotland, and make peace.

At the beginning of 1315, according to John Barbour,

> The Earl of Carrick, Edward de Bruce
> For peaceful living had no use
> Stout [brave] as a leopard ay was he
> Scotland, he thought, too small would be
> For him and for his brother, so
> He thought he would his own way go
> And make himself of Ireland King.[18]

This narrative ascribes the next aspect of King Robert's strategy to put pressure on England solely to his brother's ambition, unsatisfied almost to the point of disloyalty by the constraints of his supporting role. In fact, though Edward may have fretted with ambition, his loyalty was never in doubt, as in April 1315 he received the highest proof of the King's confidence, in being formally recognized as the heir to the throne.

The King had not given up hope of legitimate issue, but his wife had not conceived in the early years of their marriage, and after their long separation there was no certainty that she would do so. The heiress presumptive was Marjorie de Bruce, now aged about twenty, but all that had passed since the accession of the Maid of Norway led Scotland to fear the prospect of another 'Sovereign Lady'.[19] With Marjorie's acquiescence, on 27 April 1315 Parliament, which met at Ayr, enacted a 'tailzie' which provided that if the King died without a heir the Crown should pass to Edward de Bruce 'as a man of great prowess in warlike actions for the defence of the rights and liberties of the Scottish realm'.[20] Only if both Robert and Edward should die without male heirs should Marjorie succeed, and it was also enacted that she should marry with her father's consent. Shortly afterwards she married the husband of his choice, Walter the Stewart, a union which a little over half a century later would bring the House of Stewart to the throne. Finally, the tailzie provided that if a minor should succeed, Thomas Randolph, Earl of Moray, should act as Guardian of the Realm and of the child.

Parliament went on to discuss and approve Edward's proposed Irish venture. It seems unlikely that the enterprise sprang from Edward's ambition alone, as represented by Barbour. King Robert had always been aware of the danger of an English-dominated Ireland. Troops from Ireland had played, or had been intended to play, a role in many English invasions of Scotland. That this danger continued had been demonstrated in February 1315, when England's old ally John of Lorn crossed from Ireland and occupied the Isle of Man. No doubt King Robert saw the advantage in harnessing his brother's ambition to his own strategy. If Edward de Bruce could succeed in making himself King of Ireland, a Hiberno-Scottish Bruce hegemony would be created, which would weaken Edward II's position so much that surely he would be forced to make peace on the Bruce brothers' terms.

Edward de Bruce's preparations included seeking allies among the Gaelic Irish, and these included the powerful Domnal O'Neill, King of Tyrone, who may have been a friend from his boyhood.[21] Accompanied by Thomas Randolph, Sir Philip de Mowbray, Sir John Stewart, who may have been a brother of Walter the Stewart, an otherwise little known Sir Fergus of Ardrossan, and 'knights in plenty',[22] Edward de Bruce embarked a 'very strong' force in a fleet of galleys provided by the MacDoualls and MacRuaries. On 26 May they landed at Larne and, meeting no opposition, sent the fleet back to Scotland.[23]

Within the year Edward de Bruce and his companions were spectacularly successful:

> Receiving some slight aid from the Irish, they captured from the King of England's dominion much land and many towns, and so prevailed as to have my lord Edward made king by the Irish [he was crowned High King of Ireland near Dundalk on 2 May 1316]. Let us leave him reigning there for the present.[24]

In England the invasion of Ireland was seen as being part of an even grander design. According to the *Vita Edwardi Secundi*:

> there was a rumour that if he [Edward de Bruce] achieved his wish there [in Ireland] he would at once cross to Wales, and raise the Welsh likewise against our king. For these two races are easily roused to rebellion; they bear hardly the yoke of slavery, and curse the lordship of the English.[25]

This was a remarkably honest description of England's relations with Ireland and Wales to come from the pen of an Englishman. The rumour of Edward de Bruce's intentions seemed to be justified by a manifesto which he addressed to the Welsh, which would have been copied and widely circulated:

> Since the English yoke bears so heavily upon you as it did recently depress the Scottish people, we intend that by your own efforts and with our irresistible assistance, you will be able to recover your full rights and to possess peacefully your prosperity and inheritance.[26]

The manifesto received a reply from a Welsh magnate, Gruffydd Llwyd, who wrote that if Edward were to come to Wales, or send a representative with even a few men, then all the nobles of Wales would be ready to join him.[27] But this remained in the realm of imagination, for Edward de Bruce never had the chance to extend his activities to Wales. The Welsh rebellion of Llewllyn Bren, who attacked the castle of Caerphilly, is not thought to have owed anything to Scottish encouragement.[28]

However, the threat of Scottish intervention caused Edward II to pour reinforcements into his Welsh castles. Armour for one hundred crossbowmen and twenty footmen was sent from London to Beaumaris; castles were provisioned and coastal defences were repaired.[29] Nothing could have suited King Robert better than that Edward II should deploy his resources against a nebulous pan-Celtic alliance, while he himself was temporarily left free from English interference.

When the fleet that had conveyed Edward de Bruce to Ireland had returned to Ayr, Robert used it for a brief expedition to the Western Isles, to counteract the renewed activities of John of Lorn. From his base in the Isle of Man, John was attempting to reactivate opposition to King Robert in Argyll and the Western Isles. Robert did not attack Man; possibly the Irish expedition had left him too short of resources to be certain of taking it. John of Lorn remained there until the return from Ireland of Thomas Randolph (to whom the King of Scots had previously granted the Isle of Man), who invaded it and drove him out in 1317. In the spring of 1315 Robert concentrated on isolating John of Lorn by reclaiming the loyalty of the chiefs he had been attempting to subvert.

Accompanied by Walter the Stewart, the King sailed his fleet of galleys up the Sound of Bute to the mouth of Loch Fyne, and into East

Loch Tarbert, named after the narrow *tairbeart* (isthmus) that divides it from the long inlet of West Loch Tarbert, leading to open sea. Here he caused pine trees to be felled and a slipway of trunks to be laid across the isthmus. One by one the ships were hauled across, their sails set to take advantage of a strong wind blowing from the east. King Robert was consciously fulfilling a well-known prophecy:

> The man that sails from shore to shore
> At Tarbert with his ships of war
> Shall grasp the Isles within his hand
> By force of arms shall none withstand.[30]

The island chiefs were so utterly overcome ('abaysit sa uterly') by this feat that they hastened to confirm their loyalty to the King. However, Robert did not rely on one spectacular gesture to secure his influence in the area. He founded a new sheriffdom of Argyll with its seat at Tarbert, which over the remaining years of the reign was developed as a castle port and Royal Burgh.[31]

The summer of 1315 was a period of intense activity. The Tarbert expedition was followed immediately by the raid on the bishopric of Durham, from which the King and James Douglas returned with finances for their next project, the siege of Carlisle.

As a target, Carlisle was doubtless chosen for its proximity to the western theatre of war. In Scottish hands it would be a valuable base for attack on Ireland, Man or North Wales, or for raids into unvisited areas of England, and its loss would be a blow to English prestige.

The Scots departed from their well-tested tactics of surprise. On 29 June they approached Carlisle with a large army, and while Douglas burnt the suburbs and surrounding villages, destroyed crops and rounded up herds of cattle to provision the army, the King's forces surrounded the walls and assaulted the city gates for five successive days. On the fifth day of the siege the King brought up a stone-casting machine, which battered the Calden Gate on the west of the city. But the defenders were well prepared and ably commanded by Sir Andrew de Harclay. They had several similar machines with which the attackers' own missiles could be hurled back at them, and also 'other engines of

war which are called springalds, for discharging long darts . . . which
caused great fear and damage to those outside'.[32] The Scots constructed
a tall timber assault tower or 'berefrai' (belfry), whereupon the city car-
penters were immediately put to work on a defensive tower of even
greater height. But the belfry, which was to be dragged up to the wall
on wheels, sank under its own weight in the swampy ground beyond the
moat and remained immovable. Attempts to bridge or fill the moat
were equally unsuccessful.

Finally the Scots reverted to the use of their siege ladders and belatedly attempted a surprise attack. While the King led a massed assault on
the east of the city, hoping to draw all the defenders against him, James
Douglas led a scaling party to climb a particularly high section of wall
on the other side, where it was hoped attack would not be looked for.
But citizens and garrison were too vigilant to fall for such a ruse, and
both attacks were repulsed. On 1 August the Scots abandoned the siege,
and 'marched off in confusion to their own country, leaving behind all
their engines of war'.[33]

Probably Carlisle, set in open country and in enemy territory, had
been deemed impossible to surprise, and a conventional siege had
seemed the only way to take it. It was an experiment that King Robert
did not repeat, and the abandonment of the siege engines seems to
imply an abandonment of faith in them. This humiliating defeat for
Scottish arms seemed to herald a sequence of misfortunes.

Early in 1316 the King and James Douglas turned their attention to
the recapture of Berwick. As the last English outpost in Scotland it was
vigilantly defended, but a surprise attack was planned for the night of
14 January. Presumably, a dark, cloudy night was relied on to conceal a
two-pronged attack by land and sea, but a brilliant moon came out to
reveal the Scots' approach and they were beaten off. James Douglas nar-
rowly escaped in a small boat.[34]

Though this attack failed, pressure on Berwick was kept up. With the
English hold on Northumberland weakened, and Scottish shipping
achieving at least a partial blockade, provisioning Berwick became
increasingly difficult. In February a Gascon knight named Sir Edmund
de Caillan, a kinsman of Piers Gaveston, led a strong foraging party into
Teviotdale, in search of cattle. Word was brought to James Douglas of
the raid, and he led a small band of horsemen to intercept it. Caillan's
force turned out to be twice the size of his own, and he afterwards

admitted that the action was the hardest he had ever fought. But he killed Caillan in hand-to-hand combat, after which the English lost heart and fled.[35]

Shortly afterwards another knight serving in Berwick, Sir Robert Neville – nicknamed 'the peacock of the North' – sent Douglas a personal challenge, which he accepted. They met, each with a retinue of knights, outside the walls of Berwick, and in a hard-fought engagement Sir Robert Neville was killed by Douglas, and his brother Sir Ralph Neville and several other English knights were captured.[36] After these encounters, said Barbour, the English feared Douglas as the 'fell devill of hell'.[37]

The following month tragedy struck the King's family. On 2 March the Lady Marjorie, in the last month of her pregnancy, was thrown from her horse and instantly killed. The child, taken from her body by Caesarian section, miraculously survived, a dearly bought grandson for the King, named Robert after him, and years later to become King Robert III.[38]

At midsummer 1316, after an interval of a year, the Scots raids on England were resumed. Possibly the absence of many Scots in Ireland had curtailed operations in the winter, and during the spring of 1316 another round of abortive peace talks may have been accompanied by a temporary truce.[39]

In June King Robert was reported to be gathering his forces in the Park of Duns, where he was probably joined by knights returned from Ireland. The Scots invaded England on 24 June, advancing down Tynedale and through the bishopric of Durham, which renewed its payment for immunity from destruction. They crossed the Tees at Barnard Castle, and split into three detachments: one turned northwest, and burnt Penrith and Carlatton, and one advanced on Richmond, 'but the nobles of that district took refuge in Richmond Castle . . . and compounded with them for a large sum of money so that they might not burn that town'.[40] The third detachment burnt West Witton in Wensleydale, before moving into Lancashire, having reunited with the force that had threatened Richmond. Bypassing Kirkby Lonsdale and Cartmel, the Scots crossed the sands to Furness,

> and burnt that district whither they had not come before taking away
> with them nearly all the goods of that district, with men and women

as prisoners. Especially were they delighted with the abundance of
iron which they found there, because Scotland is not rich in iron.[41]

They returned home by way of the Cumberland coast, ravaging the district of Copeland as they went.[42]

This profitable and destructive raid brought the first taste of Scottish
terror to the lands of Thomas of Lancaster. His response was to urge
a new invasion of Scotland. But the time was ill chosen, for crop failures in two successive years had led to 'such a mortality of men in
England and Scotland through famine and pestilence as had not been
heard of in our time'.[43] The difficulty of levying and provisioning
troops in these conditions was extreme, but Lancaster, whose influence
was still dominant in England, persisted in his efforts despite the non-
cooperation of the King. According to the *Vita Edwardi Secundi*,
'Whatever pleases the Lord King the Earl's servants try to upset and
whatever pleases the Earl the King's servants call treachery . . .'[44] By the
end of September, Lancaster had managed to gather a force at
Newcastle, where he expected the King to join him; but Edward, avenging himself for Lancaster's refusal to accompany him in the
Bannockburn campaign, did not appear. Lancaster retreated south and
disbanded his force, 'for neither of them put any trust in the other'.[45]

In the face of such disarray it was clear that the Scots had little need
to fear English aggression in the near future. King Robert turned his
attention to the progress of his brother's affairs in Ireland.

The King would have received an authoritative account of events in
Ireland from Thomas Randolph, who had returned to Scotland in the
spring of 1316, and had probably taken part in the midsummer raid.
Edward de Bruce had been inaugurated as High King of Ireland by his
allies, but his title would lack substance unless he won the general
support of the Gaelic Irish. In the meantime Anglo-Irish resistance had
not yet been broken. When Edward landed in Ireland he had besieged
the Earl of Ulster's great stronghold of Carrickfergus, possession of
which would give him dominance over Ulster and command of the
short sea route to western Scotland. The siege had continued as the
background to the campaigns that led to his inauguration as High King.

In September he returned to Scotland to report the fall of

Carrickfergus, and to seek reinforcements, even personal help, from his brother.[46] Probably as a pre-condition, Robert confirmed his earlier grant of the Isle of Man to Thomas Randolph, with the assent of Edward as 'King of Ireland' – perhaps to clear the possibility that Edward might raise some future claim to it.[47] Randolph thus received additional incentive to recover the island at the earliest opportunity.

In January 1317 King Robert, accompanied by Thomas Randolph and an army of veterans, sailed from Loch Ryan to Larne, and at Carrickfergus rejoined Edward de Bruce, who had returned to Ireland before them. James Douglas was appointed Lieutenant of Scotland during the King's absence.[48]

There was an ancient custom that the High King of Ireland should make a progress through the five provinces of Ulster, Meath, Leinster, Munster and Connaught.[49] King Robert's intention was to strengthen his brother's position by accompanying him on this circuit with his army, to crush Anglo-Irish opposition, and if possible to unify the Gaelic Irish in support of the High King. The situation was complicated by the fact that while most of the Anglo-Irish opposed the Bruce brothers (with the exception of the Bissets of Autun, and the Mandevilles and Logans of Ulster, who temporarily joined them),[50] the Gaelic Irish were too preoccupied by their own irreconcilable clan feuds to unite against the English oppressor, while some of them may have regarded Edward de Bruce as a Scottish oppressor who was scarcely preferable.

Robert and Edward advanced southward from Carrickfergus, devastating the Anglo-Irish domains, and by mid-February they had reached Slane. At Ratoath they attacked a manor of the Earl of Ulster, who fled to Dublin. On the approach of the Scots the Mayor of Dublin seized the Earl and imprisoned him in the Castle. Though the Earl had opposed the Bruce invasion, and lost Carrickfergus in the process, he was viewed with suspicion as Robert's father-in-law, and was presumably imprisoned as a hostage.[51]

The citizens of Dublin frantically prepared for a siege, but the Scots judged the city too hard a target, and pushed on south-westward, shadowed by a smaller force under the command of Edmund Butler, Justiciar of Ireland.[52] They were encouraged to advance westward by the promise of the chief of the O'Briens of a general rising of the Gaelic Irish. But instead of meeting the promised Irish army on the River Shannon, they found themselves faced by a hostile force under their ally's clan rival, Muirchertach O'Brien, who had meanwhile defeated him.[53]

With the approach of spring, the expedition faced failure. The conditions of famine and pestilence described in Scotland the previous year now also affected Ireland, and were severest in the south-west. To advance through Munster would be to court starvation. The Scots approached Limerick, but were denied entrance and did not attempt a siege.

The news that Roger Mortimer of Wigmore, a baron from the Welsh marches, lately appointed Lieutenant of Ireland, had sailed from Bristol and landed at Youghal with an English force on 7 April may have clinched the Scots decision to retreat to Ulster. To this retreat belongs one of the most famous personal anecdotes of King Robert recounted by John Barbour. As the army was about to march, the King's attention was caught by a woman's cries, and he demanded to know what had happened to her. He was told that a pregnant laundress had gone into labour, and was crying so piteously because she had been told she would be left behind. The King replied that surely there was no man who would not feel pity for her. He ordered that a tent be put up for her with women to attend her till the child was born. Only then would the army move, and the mother and child should be carried with it.

> This was a full great courtesy
> That a king of such great majesty
> With all his host, delay should make
> For a humble washerwoman's sake.[54]

Barbour's praise of his hero gains additional resonance from the implication that courtesy or humanity to a woman of no importance was a matter of wonder. But, as the example of Edward I had shown in the past, not even a great lady could be confident of receiving humane treatment.

The Scots retreated through Leinster, where they skirmished with Edmund Butler's forces at Eliogarty. But they were in greater danger from famine than from the enemy. Food was unobtainable, and they were reduced to killing and eating their foundering horses. Not until they reached Meath did they find food for themselves, and spring grass on which the surviving horses could graze.[55] Having rested four days at

Trim, they resumed their march, and returned to Ulster as an unde-feated army. But, though Barbour gave a brave account of it, the expedition had undeniably failed: the circuit of the five provinces had not been completed, the Anglo-Irish had suffered no significant defeat, and the Gaelic Irish had not rallied to Edward de Bruce. He still remained in occupation of Ulster, and still held the title of High King of Ireland, but his brother's power had not consolidated his position. However, King Robert could not risk a longer absence from his kingdom. Leaving a proportion of his army to continue to fight for Edward, the King returned to Scotland on 22 May 1317.[56]

During the King's absence there had been two small-scale invasions of Scotland, recounted by Barbour. The Earl of Arundel had brought an English army to the Borders, and a knight named Sir Thomas Richmond led a detachment of it into the forest, in the hope of sur-prising James Douglas at Lintalee, near Jedburgh, where he was reported to have built a hunting lodge at which he was staying.

An attempt to surprise Douglas on familiar ground was surely fore-doomed. The English entered a thickly wooded area of the forest and cleared a broad swathe for their advance with axes.[57] But Douglas had concealed his forest bowmen in a dense grove of birches, their branches interlaced for better camouflage. As the English approached, they loosed their arrows. With shouts of 'Douglas! Douglas!', the Scots burst from their ambush and attacked. In the resulting carnage Sir Thomas Richmond was wounded and Douglas, not in chivalrous vein that day, turned him over and despatched him with a dagger.[58] An English prisoner later confirmed Richmond's identity by recognizing his fur hat, which Douglas had taken for a trophy. After this defeat, according to Barbour, the Earl of Arundel's army retreated from the Borders.

A more serious invasion took place on the east coast. A large gath-ering of men from Humberside (no leader is named), disillusioned by Edward II's failure to protect the North, decided to give the Scots a taste of their own medicine by raiding Fife. They collected a flotilla of ships, sailed from the Humber and entered the Firth of Forth. Warned of their approach, the Earl and the Sheriff of Fife gathered a force, and kept pace with the ships as they sailed close to the north shore. Confident of their strength, the English landed at Inverkeithing, and the Scots, finding themselves outnumbered, fled inland.

Some five miles from the coast they met William Sinclair, Bishop of Dunkeld, at the head of sixty horsemen. He had been staying at the manor of Auchtertool which belonged to the diocese, and hearing that the English were coming, he was preparing to join battle with them. On meeting the retreating Earl and Sheriff and their forces, he poured scorn on them for fleeing from the enemy, pulled off his clerical gown beneath which he was clad in mail, grabbed a spear, and exhorted everyone to follow him to the coast.

By this time the English raiders were busily rounding up animals and collecting booty. At sight of the returning Scots, they fled for their ships, leaving a trail of dead men as the Scots attacked them in the rear. So many fugitives crowded on to one landing craft that it capsized and drowned them all. The rest escaped with ignimony.

When King Robert returned from Ireland, at his first meeting with the warlike bishop he embraced him, and ever afterwards held him in great honour, and called him his 'own bishop'.[59]

In the autumn of 1317 the recently elected Pope John XXII attempted to impose an Anglo-Scottish truce. His ambition was to reconcile the two kingdoms as a preliminary to initiating a new Crusade. But the Scots were determined that any truce with England should be upon their own terms, and the papal initiative was rejected since the King of Scots was not accorded his royal title.

The King's chief objective was the recovery of Berwick, but first he gave Thomas Randolph the opportunity to recover the Isle of Man. The date of his expedition is uncertain. Edward II believed that he still controlled it in October, but shortly after this it was in Randolph's hands.[60] John of Lorn was finally ejected, and he died as a pensioner of England the following year.

In Berwick, partly blockaded though not besieged by the Scots, problems of supply led to ill-feeling between civilians and military. Edward II received complaints of the rapacity of the commander of the garrison. He responded by giving the citizens responsibility for organizing their own defences.

Prominent among them was a man named Peter of Spalding, whose wife was a relative of Sir Robert Keith the Marischal. Peter had been the victim of harassment and insult from the military for being married

Engraving from King Robert I portrait by George Jamesone

Robert I at Bannockburn by Pilkington Jackson (1964)

Cast of the skull of Robert the Bruce

Tomb of Sir James Douglas

Statues of Edward I and Edward II, on the choir screen at York Minster

Coronation of John Balliol,
MS c.1310

John Balliol does
homage to Edward I

Crusader

Robert the Bruce made his last pilgrimage to Whithorn Priory.

to a Scotswoman, and perhaps at her instigation he sent a message to Keith promising that when his turn came to organize the defence of a certain section of the town walls, he would give entry to the Scots.

Keith took the letter to the King, who decided that the offer was genuine ['nae fantis'] and said:

> . . . Thou hast been wise
> That thou hast spoken first to me
> For if thou first had thoughtlessly
> My nephew, Earl of Moray, seen
> Right jealous Douglas would have been
> The same the other way about[61]

These words of Barbour's indicate that their latent rivalry always needed careful handling. Robert told the Marischal to gather a force in the Park of Duns, and he would send Randolph and Douglas to him with a few men each, and they should share the honour of taking the town.

On the night of 1 April 1318 the Scots advanced from Duns and, leaving their horses some distance from Berwick, approached the town as silently as possible. At the place indicated by Peter of Spalding they positioned their scaling ladders and climbed the wall. In possession of a stretch of the fortifications, they awaited the dawn. But daybreak revealed the temptations of an apparently defenceless town, and with unusual indiscipline a large proportion of the Scottish force disappeared to loot. The commanders, with a handful of veterans and a young knight named Sir William Keith of Galston, were left to defend themselves against a crowd of warlike citizens, supported by a sortie of the castle garrison.

After hard fighting the garrison returned and 'barred the gates anew',[62] leaving the Scots still in possession of the wall. Later King Robert arrived with an army of men from the forest, Teviotdale, Lothian and the Mease, and occupied the town. The castle, held by Sir Roger Horsley, resisted for a further eleven weeks, until forced by starvation to surrender on 18 June.[63]

The King rewarded Peter of Spalding with the grant of an estate in Angus.[64] He appointed Walter the Stewart as Governor of Berwick, and provisioned the town and castle for a year. He had little doubt that the

English would attempt to retake Berwick, for he improved the fortifications and hired the services of John Crab, a Flemish engineer and inventor, who constructed a great variety of defensive machines, including 'springalds', the dart-throwing engines which King Robert knew to be effectively injurious from his own experiences at the siege of Carlisle. According to Barbour, writing with knowledge of more advanced military technology later in the century, the only weapons Crab lacked were guns ('gynnys for crakys'), for these had not yet been seen in Scotland.[65]

The capture of Berwick was a great triumph, completing King Robert's reclamation of his kingdom. But he did not rest content with it. He moved southward to capture three castles, Harbottle, Wark and Mitford, and 'subdued nearly the whole of Northumberland as far as the town of Newcastle'.[66] He then launched a particularly savage raid on Yorkshire, led by Douglas and Randolph.

> The Scottish army invaded England further than usual, burning the towns of Northallerton and Boroughbridge and pressing forward as far as the town of Ripon, which town they despoiled of all the goods they could find; and from those who entered the mother church . . . they exacted one thousand marks instead of burning the town itself.[67]

Six burgesses of Ripon were taken as surety for payment. Two years later the wives of these men petitioned Edward II to compel their fellow-citizens to honour the bargain so that their husbands might return.

These men came to no harm, but the Scots left a trail of devastation as they went on to burn Knaresborough and Skipton-in-Craven, before returning home with vast herds of cattle, driven by 'the poor folks' they had taken prisoner.[68]

The year 1318 had been one of success for King Robert, but it turned to tragedy when news was brought that Edward de Bruce had been killed in battle on 14 October, at Fochart near Dundalk, close to where he had been inaugurated as High King of Ireland. According to the Lanercost Chronicle, Edward had recently been reinforced by 'a great army of Scots', and with these and his Irish adherents he had advanced to attack Dundalk.[69] The victor of Fochart was Sir John de

Birmingham, who sent Edward de Bruce's head to Edward II, preserved in a bucket of salt, and had his body quartered and distributed for public display.[70] Edward II rewarded him with the earldom of Louth.

There was lamentation for Edward de Bruce throughout Scotland, but the grief of King Robert himself can only be imagined. In this latest tragedy to strike his family he may have seen the continuing influence of the curse of St Malachy O'Moore, which his grandfather the Competitor had attempted to avert by his pilgrimage and votive offering at the saint's tomb.[71] To Robert, a conventionally religious man, the continuing anger of the saint might well explain the sequence of misfortunes that had befallen his family: the war had claimed the lives of all his brothers, his daughter's life had been cruelly cut short, and his wife remained unable to conceive. Perhaps it was to appease the saint's wrath that on 8 February 1319 the King dedicated a candle and a lamp to burn perpetually before the altar of St Malachy in the Cistercian abbey of Coupar Angus. It was a daughter house of Melrose, the daughter house of Rievaulx, which was in turn the daughter house of Clairvaux, where St Malachy was buried, and where the King's grandfather had made a similar offering.[72]

The death of Edward de Bruce forced the King to readdress the question of the succession, for which there was no longer a mature male candidate. On 3 December 1318 Parliament, assembled at Scone, enacted that failing legitimate male issue to the King, the heir to the throne was the King's grandson, Robert Stewart. Should he succeed as a minor, the Guardian of the Kingdom should be Thomas Randolph, Earl of Moray, and in the event of his death, Sir James, Lord of Douglas.[73] Thus the King provided for the security of the realm under the guardianship of the men in whose ability and judgement he placed most trust, giving precedence, as would have been considered proper, to the one who was his kinsman.

King Robert had been right to anticipate an English attack on Berwick. In August 1318, chiefly through the good offices of the Earl of Pembroke, a rapprochement had been achieved between Edward II and Thomas of Lancaster. To confirm it, the King and his cousin met on a bridge over the River Soar, at Hathern near Loughborough, and

exchanged an insincere kiss of peace.[74] The challenge to English prestige offered by the loss of Berwick checked their perennial hostility long
enough to permit them to go on campaign together.

In readiness for a serious campaign against the Scots, the administration was transferred to York. Queen Isabella accompanied her husband
there, and stayed in a manor outside the city walls, while the King
moved north to Newcastle, where his army began to muster in June
1319.

He gathered a substantial force, variously estimated at eight or twelve
thousand men, and moved up to Berwick in August. The encampment
of the besiegers surrounded the town walls, and was itself strongly
defended against expected attack by the Scots. An English fleet threatened Berwick from the sea. The siege began on 8 September, and
Walter Stewart conducted a vigorous defence, ably assisted by John
Crab's machines.

Robert the Bruce was not in Berwick, and had no intention of risking
his army in attacking the besieging force. He had been told of Queen
Isabella's presence at York, and planned a secret expedition to capture
her. With so important a hostage in his hands, he could demand the
abandonment of the siege, or any other terms. 'Indeed', writes the
author of the *Vita Edwardi Secundi*, 'if the Queen had at that time been
captured, I believe that Scotland would have bought peace for
herself'.[75]

With the utmost secrecy, a force under Douglas and Randolph
entered England by the western route, crossed the Pennines into
Yorkshire, and encamped only a few miles from York near
Boroughbridge. Unfortunately, one of the Scots' agents in York was
captured and brought before Archbishop William Melton, and the
Chancellor, John de Hotham, Bishop of Ely. Threatened with torture,
the man revealed the whereabouts of the Scots, and the plot to seize the
Queen. At first, the story was not believed. It seemed incredible that
two of the Scots' most distinguished commanders should venture a
hundred miles out of their country when the King of England's army
was within it. But the spy, who had bargained for his life with this
information, swore that it was true, saying he was ready to submit to
capital punishment if he lied.[76]

Melton and Hotham assembled an escort of citizens and clerics and
brought the Queen back into the city. Thence she was sent by water to

Nottingham, an inland voyage by way of the Ouse and the Trent, to a city with a strong castle well beyond the reach of the Scots.

Though the Queen had been saved, the danger of a Scottish army close to the city remained. York itself had never been threatened before, and only a few days previously King Edward had ordered the whole of the Yorkshire militia to join him at Berwick.[77]

Archbishop Melton collected an army of citizens, led by the Mayor of York, peasantry from the surrounding countryside and 'a great number of priests and clergy, among whom were sundry religious men, both beneficed and mendicant' (i.e. monks and friars).[78] On 12 September this impromptu army bravely marched out of the city to do battle with the Scots. They had been informed by the spy that they would find the enemy near Boroughbridge, at Myton-on-Swale, about twelve miles north of York,

> but, as men unskilled in war, they marched all scattered through the fields and in no kind of array. When the Scots beheld men . . . they formed up according to their custom in a single schiltrom, and then uttered a tremendous shout to terrify the English, who straightway began to take to their heels at the sound. Then the Scots, breaking up their schiltrom . . . mounted their horses and pursued the English, killing both clergy and laymen . . . among whom fell the mayor of the town, and about one thousand, it was said, were drowned in the water of Swale.[79]

Because of the high proportion of clerics among the slain, this very unequal battle came to be known as 'the Chapter of Myton'.[80]

The news reached the English camp at Berwick two days later. With York defenceless, a multitude of her citizens and clergy dead, and a victorious Scottish army at large in Yorkshire, there were powerful arguments for abandoning the siege. King Edward held a council to decide the issue, and found that magnates from southern England were in favour of persevering with the siege, whereas those from the North wished to disperse to defend their own property. Edward inclined to the former, Thomas of Lancaster to the latter. A quarrel ensued, and Lancaster departed with his following. Since they constituted 'near third part of the host', Edward had no choice but to raise the siege.[81]

Douglas and Randolph, in the meantime, had not wasted their efforts against the walls of York, but reverting to their tactics of terror they recrossed the Pennines, leaving a blaze of destruction in their wake. Edward retreated from Berwick to Newminster Abbey in Northumberland, expecting to intercept the Scots on their homeward way, but their return by the western route completed his humiliation.[82]

A scapegoat was found in the Earl of Lancaster. A murmuring campaign accused him of taking bribes from Robert the Bruce to lend him secret aid, as a result of which the King had been forced to raise the siege, the Scots had known where to attempt to seize the Queen, and had finally been permitted to escape, since 'James Douglas on his way back to Scotland passed through the earl's lines'.[83] Lancaster offered to clear himself of these imputations by undergoing the ordeal of white-hot iron, but since no one openly accused him, he was permitted to clear himself of the rumours by compurgation (i.e. by joint oaths of himself and a group of his peers).[84] But inevitably, relations between him and the King were poisoned anew, and the suspicion of disloyalty still clung to him.

Edward II's position was substantially weakened since Bannockburn: five years on he had definitively lost Berwick; he had almost lost control of Northumberland; and the Scots had demonstrated their power to inflict destruction and extortion on the northern counties without hindrance. Moreover, Edward had now witnessed this devastation for himself.

It was probably in mid-autumn that he received a letter from King Robert, composed in the formal Latin of the King's Chapel (chancery):

> To the most sincere prince, the Lord Edward, by God's grace illustrious King of England, Robert by the same grace King of Scots sends greetings in the name of Him by whom the thrones of rulers are governed.
>
> Since while kindly peace prevails the minds of the faithful are at rest, the Christian way of life is furthered and all the affairs of holy mother church and of all kingdoms are everywhere carried on more prosperously, we in our humility have judged it right to entreat of your highness most earnestly that having before your eyes the righteousness you owe to God and to the people, you desist from persecuting us and disturbing the people of our realm, so that there may be an end of slaughter and shedding of Christian blood. Everything

that we ourselves and our people by their bodily service and contributions of wealth can do, we are now and shall be prepared to do sincerely and honourably for the sake of good peace and to earn perpetual grace for our souls. If it should be agreeable to your will to hold negotiations with us upon these matters, let your royal will be communicated to us in a letter by the hands of the bearer of the present letter.[85]

Edward II, however much Robert's assumption of the kingly title that he refused to acknowledge may have irked him, and however much he may have resented the accusation that he had persecuted the Scots, was in no position to refuse.

At the beginning of November, another raid led by Douglas and Randolph, which brought home cattle, provisions and food supplies from Cumberland, gave Edward an additional reminder of his weakness. But he had accepted the situation, and even before the return of the Scots he had sent Robert Baldock as his representative to Berwick, with proposals for a truce.[86]

The English negotiators included the Earl of Pembroke, and Sir Hugh Despenser the Younger, now King Edward's closest confidant; the Scots included Sir William de Soules, hereditary Seneschal of Scotland, and the deputy Seneschal, Sir Alexander Seton. It was agreed that the truce should last from 21 December 1319 until Christmas 1321. The terms show the Scots' willingness to compromise: English ships, men and goods wrecked on Scottish coasts would be returned; no new fortresses would be built on the Scottish side of the border; and the recently captured Harbottle Castle was put in the hands of the English ambassadors as private persons, on condition that if no permanent peace had been negotiated by Michaelmas (29 September) 1321, it should be returned again, or totally destroyed.[87] Thomas Randolph, Earl of Moray, swore on King Robert's behalf to observe the terms.

King Edward saved face by representing the treaty as a necessary preliminary to his going to France to swear homage to the new King Philip V for his French fiefs.[88] But the clause concerning Harbottle Castle indicates that the truce was really intended as a first step towards a permanent peace.

14

————— |✳|✳|✳| —————

SPIRITUAL WARFARE

'If your Holiness puts too much faith in the tales the
English tell and will not . . . refrain from favouring
them to our prejudice, then the slaughter of bodies, the
perdition of souls, and all the other misfortunes that
will follow . . . will, we believe, be surely laid by the
Most High to your charge . . .'

from the 'Declaration of Arbroath', 1320[1]

ROBERT THE BRUCE might have had less difficulty in forcing Edward II
to negotiate had not the English King been supported by the papacy,
which gave him an internationally recognized position of moral superiority over his enemies.

The pro-English Pope Clement V had died shortly after
Bannockburn, and unfortunately for the Scots, after two years of curial
strife, the pro-English Pope John XXII succeeded him. Jacques Diese,
born in the English fief of Guenne, was over seventy when he was
elected as a stop-gap candidate, but his unexpectedly vigorous and controversial pontificate continued until 1334, when he died aged about
ninety.[2] His supreme ambition to unite the rulers of Christendom to a
new Crusade inspired his attempt to impose an Anglo-Scottish truce. In
the autumn of 1317 he sent Cardinals Gaucelin of SS Marcellinus and
Peter, and Luca of Sta Maria in Via Lota, to England with letters to both
Edward II and Robert the Bruce. The cardinals delegated two envoys to
deliver the letters to Robert who, in deference to Edward II, was not
addressed as King.[3] The report of these envoys on their reception was
described by the Scottish annalist Lord Hailes as 'the best original portrait of Robert the Bruce which has been preserved to our times':

The King graciously received the messengers, and heard them with patient attention. After having consulted his barons he made answer, 'That he mightily desired to procure a good and perpetual peace, either by the mediation of the Cardinals or by other means'. He allowed the open letters from the Pope, which recommended peace, to be read in his presence, and he listened to them with all due respect; but he would not receive the sealed letters addressed to Robert Bruce, governing in Scotland. 'Among my barons', said he, 'there are many of the name of Robert Bruce who share in the government of Scotland; these letters may possibly be addressed to some one of them, but they are not addressed to me, who am King of Scotland; I can receive no letters which are not addressed under that title, unless with the advice and approbation of my Parliament . . .'

The messengers attempted to apologize for the omission of the title of King. They said 'that holy church was not wont, during the dependence of a controversy, to write or say aught which might be interpreted as prejudicial to the claims of contending parties'. 'Since, then', answered the King, 'my spiritual father [the Pope] and my holy mother [the Church] would not prejudice the cause of my adversary, by bestowing on me the appellation of King . . . they ought not to have prejudiced my cause by withdrawing that appellation from me. I am in possession of the kingdom of Scotland; all my people call me king, and foreign princes address me under that title, but it seems that my parents [Pope and Church] are partial to their English son. Had you presumed to present letters with such an address to any other sovereign prince, you might perhaps have been answered in a harsher style; but I reverence you as the messengers of the Holy See'.[4]

The King delivered his ironic reply with 'a mild and pleasant countenance', but the papal envoys received some harsher words from his councillors, who said they knew well enough that the Pope's refusal to address their King by his title was due to English intrigues at the papal court.

The cardinals remained determined to proclaim the papal truce in Scotland, and the unfortunate messenger chosen to deliver it was Adam Newton, superior of the Minorite Friars of Berwick, which was still in English hands. Newton obtained a safe conduct to bring the letters and papal bull enjoining the truce to King Robert at Old Cambus. He did not see the King, but the documents were handed to him by Sir Alexander Seton, and Robert, seeing that they still omitted the title, sent them back to Newton with the message 'I will listen to no bulls until I am treated as King of Scotland and have made myself master of Berwick'. Newton made one more attempt to proclaim the truce in public before he was forced to flee. On his way back to Berwick he was waylaid, stripped and robbed of his documents. He believed that they were taken to King Robert, who was thus enabled to read them while having refused to accept them.[5]

In defiance of the truce the Scots captured Berwick and invaded Yorkshire in 1318, and in response first Archbishop Melton and then the two cardinals on behalf of the Pope pronounced sentence of excommunication against King Robert and his adherents, and placed Scotland under an interdict, which theoretically suspended all aspects of religious life – the celebration of Mass, baptism, marriage, penance and absolution, and burial of the dead. Services of communication were held in churches throughout England, at which Robert the Bruce, Thomas Randolph and James Douglas were solemnly cursed, three times daily.[6]

King Robert could prevent the promulgation of the sentences of excommunication and interdict in Scotland, but he could not prevent the knowledge of them from entering the country. According to an English chronicler, priests were slain throughout Scotland because they 'would sing no mass against the Pope's commandment'.[7] If true, this shows that the interdict had some effect in Scotland, and that there was widespread anger against it. There would also have been fear, for everyone was bred in the belief that the Pope, as the successor of St Peter, by divine ordinance held the keys of heaven and hell. The King and the magnates and ecclesiastics who supported him, though aware that the papal anathemas were politically motivated, still accepted that they defied the Pope at the peril of their souls. Nonetheless, they continued to defy him, and on 18 November 1319 the Pope issued letters summoning the Bishops of St Andrews, Aberdeen, Dunkeld and Moray to appear before the curia and explain the disobedience of Scotland. They ignored the summons, and on 16 June 1320 were excommunicated.[8] The Pope also excommunicated King Robert, although the sentence had already been pronounced by Archbishop Melton and the Cardinals Gaucelin and Luca.

Fortunately the King and his adherents were not obliged to believe the Pope infallible, and the most obvious remedy for his enmity was to induce a change of heart, and persuade him that the Scots were not rebels against Edward II but loyal subjects of their own King, and though devoted to the liberty of their own kingdom, were desirous to be accounted obedient sons of the Church.

The resolution to send an address to the Pope was made at a Great Council held by the King at Newbattle Abbey near Edinburgh, in March 1320.[9] It was recognized that the Pope would be unlikely to accept an address sent by the contumacious clergy of Scotland, so it was agreed that one should be sent in the names of the most influential of the laity, who should speak for the whole community of the realm.

The resulting address, dated 6 April 1320 at Arbroath Abbey, takes its name from it – the 'Declaration of Arbroath' – and its authorship is traditionally attributed to Bernard, Abbot of Arbroath, the Chancellor.[10] He was a distinguished Latinist, and the Declaration was composed in the rhythmic Latin employed by the papal curia for bulls and other papal letters, destined to be read aloud. It was stylistically intended to appeal to the Pope's ears, and its contents were eloquently presented.

The Scots, according to the version of their prehistory which the Declaration recapitulated, came from Greater Scythia and occupied Scotland, and having driven out the Romans and destroyed the Picts, successfully defended it against Danes, Norwegians and English, and held it in freedom under 113 kings of their own royal stock. Before ever they came to Scotland they had been converted to Christianity by the first apostle, St Andrew, brother of St Peter. For his sake the Holy See had extended its special protection to Scotland, until Edward I, at a time when the kingdom had no head and the people were unaccustomed to war, came in the guise of a friend and then revealed himself as an enemy with deeds of massacre, pillage, arson and killing of monks and nuns, such deeds of violence as no one could imagine who had not witnessed them:

But from these countless evils we have been set free, by the help of Him who though He afflicts yet heals and restores, by our most tireless Prince, King and Lord, the Lord Robert. He, that his people and his heritage might be delivered out of the hands of our enemies, met toil and fatigue, hunger and peril, like another Maccabeus or Joshua and bore them cheerfully. Him, too, divine providence, his right of succession according to our laws and customs which we shall maintain to the death, and the due consent and assent of us all, have made our Prince and King. To him, as to the man by whom salvation has been brought into our people, we are bound both by law and by his merits that our freedom may be still maintained, and by him, come what may, we mean to stand.

Yet if he should give up what he has begun, and agree to make us or our kingdom subject to the King of England or the English, we should exert ourselves at once to drive him out as our enemy and a subverter of his own rights and ours, and make some other man who was well able to defend us our King; for, as long as but a hundred of us remain alive, never will we under any conditions be brought under English rule. It is in truth not for glory, nor riches, nor honours that we are fighting, but for freedom – for that alone, which no honest man gives up but with life itself.[11]

The Declaration went on to entreat the Pope to admonish the King of England to be content with his own kingdom and cease from persecuting the Scots. The Christian princes would more readily unite to defend the Holy Land if the stronger among them did not persecute the weaker for motives of profit, and the King of Scots would joyously go on crusade, if only the King of the English would leave him in peace. But if the Pope persisted in believing the English version of events, and favouring them to the prejudice of the Scots, then he would be to blame for all the ensuing miseries and the loss of souls.

The Declaration of Arbroath was not only an ardent and dignified claim to freedom, some passages of which might speak for any country in any century; it was also a skilful exploitation of the Pope's ambition to revive the Crusades and a bold admonition to him to act as an impartial leader of Christendom. The Declaration was issued in the names of eight earls (Duncan, Earl of Fife, Thomas Randolph, Earl of Moray, Patrick, Earl of Dunbar, Malise, Earl of Strathearn, Malcolm, Earl of Lennox, William, Earl of Ross, Magnus, Earl of Caithness and Orkney, and William, Earl of Sutherland), and thirty-one barons 'and the other barons and freeholders and the whole community of the realm of

Scotland'.[12] Among the barons named were James Lord of Douglas, and the hereditary office-holders, Walter the Stewart, Gilbert de la Haye, Constable of Scotland, Robert Keith the Marischal and William de Soules the Seneschal. Though the Declaration purported to speak for the whole community, there was a shortage of names from the Highlands, apart from the earls who held lands beyond the highland line. There was none from the Western Isles, no MacDoualls or MacRuaries, and none from the south-west except Fergus of Ardrossan, who had accompanied Edward de Bruce to Ireland. This suggests that the magnates who had attended the Council in Newbattle and who were conveniently within reach when the Declaration was composed were those whose names were on it, and whose seals were attached.[13]

The Declaration was entrusted to three envoys for delivery to the Pope: Sir Adam Gordon, Sir Odard de Maubisson, and Master Alexander Kinnimonth. Gordon had served as Edward II's Justiciar of Lothian and had transferred his loyalty to Robert the Bruce after Bannockburn;[14] perhaps he was chosen as an example of the effectiveness of Robert's propaganda. Maubisson was a Frenchman who had been captain of Calais and an admiral of the French fleet. That he should be an envoy indicates the sympathy of Philip V for King Robert's diplomacy.[15] Kinnimonth was a church lawyer and papal chaplain with experience of the curia, who would become Bishop of Aberdeen. He has been suggested as a possible alternative to Bernard of Arbroath as the author of the Declaration.[16] But, whether as author or as the Latin scholar of the mission, it would be his task to read the resonant words of the Declaration to the Pope. The envoys reached the papal court at Avignon at the end of June 1320.

Among the barons whose names appeared on the Declaration of Arbroath were some who may have been invited or required to set their seals to it as a test of their loyalty.

In the spring of 1320 there were rumours of a plot against the life of Robert the Bruce, which according to Barbour was revealed by a lady, whom he did not name.[17] According to the *Scotichronicon*, she was the Countess of Strathearn, who confessed to participating in the plot and was imprisoned.[18] Sir Thomas Grey related that the plot was revealed by Murdoch of Menteith, a Scottish nobleman who 'had lived long in England in loyalty to the King', an obscure passage which leaves it unclear whether loyalty to Edward II or a secret sentiment of loyalty to King Robert is meant.[19] He, who may have been approached by the conspirators and feigned to join them in order to betray them, revealed to King Robert a plot to kill him, and enthrone William de Soules as King of Scots. Soules's supporters were named as Sir Patrick Graham, Sir Eustace Maxwell, Sir Roger de Mowbray and Sir David de Brechin, all of whose names had appeared on the Declaration of Arbroath, together with that of Soules himself.[20] The other accused were Sir Walter de Barclay, Sheriff of Aberdeen, Sir Gilbert de Malherbe, Sir John Logie, Eustace de Rattray, Hamelin de Troup and a squire named Richard Brown.[21]

The plot was evidently the last manifestation of the old enmity of the Comyns, for Sir William de Soules's mother was the daughter of Alexander Comyn, Earl of Buchan, and the Countess of Strathearn was her sister. Sir William de Soules's tenuous claim to the throne came through his father, one of the minor Competitors in the Great Cause, who claimed as the son of an illegitimate daughter of Alexander II. The claim was weak, but William de Soules's mother and aunt may have fired his ambition, and instigated his disloyalty to King Robert, who only the previous year had entrusted him with negotiating the truce with England.

It must have been a blow to King Robert that this trust should have been betrayed, and astonishing that Soules should appear in the guise of a rival to the throne, for the obvious choice of the Comyns would have been Edward Balliol, the son of the late King John. But he was an unknown expatriate, and Soules was present in Scotland, and foolish enough to be tempted. Disloyalty is always wounding, but the plot did not come from the very heart of the community of the realm; apart from Soules himself, none of the plotters held high office, none belonged to the highest rank of the nobility and none belonged to the King's intimate circle.

Once denounced, the plotters were speedily arrested, and tried before Parliament which met at Scone on 4 August. According to Barbour, Sir William de Soules confessed to the plot and was sent as a prisoner to Dumbarton Castle, where he died 'in a tower of stone'.[22] Malherbe, Logie and Brown were condemned to death and executed.

Roger de Mowbray had died recently, but his body was brought into Parliament on a litter, for as physical presence was required before a sentence could be pronounced. Mowbray was declared to have been guilty, and the corpse was condemned to be hanged and decapitated. But the King intervened, and ordered that 'it be handed over for a church burial without any kind of mutilation'.[23]

The remaining accused were acquitted, with the exception of Sir David de Brechin. His position was ambiguous because he claimed that the plotters had sworn him to secrecy and had then revealed the plot; he had refused to join them but had felt bound to keep silence. Perhaps he had been required to put his name to the Declaration of Arbroath as a test of loyalty, for his career had shown shifts of allegiance. He had joined King Robert in 1309, returned to the service of Edward II in 1312 and fought on the English side at Bannockburn, after which he had offered his allegiance to King Robert once again. It would have added to the appearance of shiftiness that the seal attached on his behalf to the Declaration of Arbroath was his wife's and not his own.[24] However, since his foreknowledge and concealment of the conspiracy had endangered the King's life, he was condemned to death. He was executed with the severest penalty of Scottish law, being dragged through the streets of Perth at a horse's tail, hanged and beheaded.[25] There was widespread pity for him, probably because 'he was called The Flower of Knighthood by the Christians who knew him when he was fighting the pagans on an expedition to the Holy Land'.[26] It was felt that the King had shown great severity, and the Parliament that had passed sentence on him became known as 'The Black Parliament'.

Barbour seems to have felt that the execution of Sir David de Brechin cast a shadow on the King's reputation, for his account of it is followed by an episode illustrating the King's magnanimity.

Immediately after the execution, Sir Ingram de Umfraville, who had been Brechin's friend, asked the King's leave to give him an honourable burial, which was granted. He next sought the King's permission to dispose of his lands and leave Scotland.

> The King then said to him 'If this
> Be thy desire, so shall it be.
> But tell me, sir, what vexes thee?'

Sir Ingram answered 'By your leave
My answer here shall not deceive.
My heart demands that I should be
No more with you in this country.
Therefore I trust it may not grieve
And beg you dearly, grant me leave.
For seeing that so fine a knight
So chivalrous, so brave in fight
As this Sir David was, so true
So full of manliness all through
With virtue in his every breath
Was put to such a cruel death
My heart will truly not allow
That I should dwell here longer now.'
The King said 'Since thy wish is so
I give consent for thee to go
Whenever it may suit thee, and
To do thy wishes with thy land.'[27]

Umfraville thanked the King courteously, disposed of his lands and
came to take leave of him publicly before departing to England, where
Edward II 'made him right fair welcoming'.[28]

Barbour surely intended the King's generosity to Sir Ingram de
Umfraville to be weighed against his severity to Sir David de Brechin;
if the King could listen to Umfraville's praises of the man he had just
had executed as a traitor, and still let him depart without rancour, he was
demonstrating that though he might be fallible, he was nonetheless
magnanimous. It is the nearest that Barbour ever comes to offering an
excuse for his hero's conduct.

The unhappy episode of the Soules conspiracy was concluded by the
time the envoys returned from Avignon in September 1320.

Pope John XXII, though not entirely persuaded, had been impressed
by the Declaration of Arbroath. His reply was addressed to 'that illustrious man Robert, who assumes the title and position of King of
Scotland',[29] which was deemed sufficiently courteous to be accepted. In
it he promised to exhort the English to make peace, and as a result of
this partial change of heart the most serious peace talks yet undertaken
took place at Newcastle, Berwick and Bamburgh between January and

April 1321, in the presence of three French and two papal representatives, besides the Scots and English negotiators.

Unfortunately the discussions foundered when the 'old, outworn, arrogant terms of English overlordship' proved to be the only basis for negotiation that Edward II would permit.[30] The English negotiators blamed the Scots for the breakdown of their talks, informing their king:

> From the Scots we have heard many declarations that they desire peace above all things, but in practice they have little to say which suggests it, rather the contrary, and finally after they had caused great delays, they would only agree to a long truce, for example of twenty-six years, to which we . . . would not agree without informing you . . .[31]

The excommunication of King Robert, temporarily waived by the Pope under the influence of the Declaration of Arbroath, was pronounced afresh, and it seemed that the Scots' great initiative to woo the papacy had been undertaken in vain. But hostilities with England were not immediately renewed, for the truce negotiated at the end of 1319 would hold until Christmas 1321.

15

———|✳|✳|✳|———

'VANQUISHED IN HIS OWN COUNTRY'

'They worshipped God and gave him praise
That by their prowess and their strength
The King of England had at length
Been vanquished in his own country . . .'

John Barbour, *The Bruce*[1]

EDWARD II, despite his refusal to make peace with the Scots on any but his own impossible terms, needed those remaining months of truce, for once again he faced civil war.

King Edward ill-advisedly permitted the territorial ambitions of Sir Hugh Despenser the Younger, by now so great a favourite that he was said to be 'as it were the King of England's right eye'.[2] Despenser had married one of the three sisters of Gilbert de Clare, the Earl of Gloucester, who had died at Bannockburn, between whom the vast estates of the earldom had been partitioned as co-heiresses. Not content with his wife's portion which had brought him almost all Glamorgan, 'he now put forth all his powers to extend his sway over the neighbouring lands'.[3] Despenser's ambitions provoked a powerful coalition of barons from the Welsh marches, headed by the Earl of Hereford, joined by the Earl of Lancaster, who marched on London and demanded the exile of both Hugh Despenser and his equally unpopular father. Edward II was forced to call a Parliament, and accept its judgement of 19 August 1321 that the Despensers were evil and false counsellors and enemies of the King and kingdom.[4] They were condemned to perpetual exile and disinherited.

As in the past, Edward II showed himself adept at playing off one group of magnates against another. By the end of the year he had won

278

powerful supporters, including his young half-brothers Thomas, Earl of Norfolk, and Edmund, Earl of Kent, and the Earls of Pembroke, Arundel, Richmond and Warenne. The King spent Christmas at Cirencester, and immediately afterwards advanced against the Marcher Lords. In the face of his formidable army, some surrendered, and others led by the Earl of Hereford moved north to join forces with Lancaster, who was now based at Pontefract.

At the beginning of February 1322 Edward was at Gloucester, where he was visited by Sir Andrew de Harclay, who came from Carlisle to tell him that on Epiphany (6 January), the truce having expired, the Scots had crossed the border, and the North was once again ablaze. Since the King was in arms, Harclay urged him to march against the Scots immediately. Edward replied:

> You may know for certain, Andrew, that if Robert Bruce threatens me from behind, and my own men who have committed such enormities against me, should appear in front, I would attack the traitors and leave Robert Bruce alone . . . Return to your own country and keep the strongholds committed to you; I shall pursue my traitors . . . and I shall not turn back until they are brought to naught![5]

Whatever his view of the King's priorities, Harclay obediently returned to his post. Among the traitors the chief object of Edward's vengeance was Thomas of Lancaster, against whom he had a long score to settle: the death of Gaveston, his own humiliation through the Ordinances, Lancaster's refusal to join in the Bannockburn campaign, the recent exile of the Despensers (now recalled) and Lancaster's latest resort to arms.

Lancaster was also guilty of treasonable negotiations with the Scots. Since early December he had been corresponding with Sir James Douglas, using the pseudonym 'King Arthur'.[6] It has been suggested that Lancaster offered the Scots a permanent peace and full recognition of Scottish independence in return for their help in dethroning Edward II.[7] But whatever his offers, King Robert did not regard him as a reliable ally. He is reputed to have said of him 'How will a man who cannot keep faith with his own lord keep faith with me?',[8] echoing the words with which he had dismissed the offers made by Edward II, when he was desperate to save the life of Gaveston. However, Lancaster had his uses in making trouble for Edward II, in which the Scots continued to encourage him.

In January 1322, when King Robert sent Randolph, Douglas and the Stewart to raid northern England, a group of northern knights came to Lancaster at Pontefract to appeal for help against the Scots, but 'he feigned excuse; and no wonder! seeing that he cared not to take up arms in the cause of a king who was ready to attack him'.[9]

On 28 February King Edward mustered his army at Coventry and marched north to do battle with Lancaster and Hereford, who moved south to meet him at Burton-on-Trent, where they assumed the King would use the bridge to take his army across the river. But Edward forded the Trent elsewhere, and got between the enemy forces and their northern base. This manoeuvre drove them into hasty retreat. Avoiding the King's army, by forced marches Lancaster and Hereford reached Pontefract. 'After a short delay there it was decided to press on towards Scotland, because Robert Bruce, as was said, had promised to help against the King.'[10] But at Boroughbridge they were intercepted by Sir Andrew de Harclay, with the levies of Cumberland and Westmorland. Harclay

> posted all his knights and some pikemen on foot at the northern end of the bridge [over the river Ure] and other pikemen he stationed in schiltrom, after the Scottish fashion, opposite the ford . . . to oppose the cavalry . . . Also he dispatched his archers to keep up a hot and constant discharge upon the enemy . . .[11]

Lancaster and Hereford were now in the position they had expected King Edward to be in at Burton-on-Trent, but they found no means to evade it. Hereford led the infantry on to the bridge, and was killed there with his standard-bearer, and his force was repulsed with heavy losses. Lancaster's attempt to ford the Ure with his cavalry was foiled by Harclay's archers. He retreated, and asked for an armistice until the following day. He had intended to resume the battle, but during the night so many of his men had deserted that on the morning of 17 March he was forced to surrender to Sir Andrew de Harclay, who held him prisoner, to wait the King's pleasure.

King Edward occupied Lancaster's castle of Pontefract, and a few days later Lancaster was tried and condemned to death in his own great hall. Not permitted to speak in his own defence, he protested at the illegality of the proceedings without effect. Then, mounted on a 'worthless mule', he was led to a small hillock outside the town, and there beheaded. In its lack of legality, its humiliating circumstances and its method of execution, his death was a re-enactment of that of Gaveston. The author of the *Vita Edwardi Secundi* noted the parallel:

> The Earl of Lancaster once cut off Piers Gaveston's head, and now by the King's command the Earl himself lost his head. Thus, perhaps not unjustly, the Earl received measure for measure . . .[12]

Sir Andrew de Harclay, whose victory at Boroughbridge had delivered Lancaster into Edward's hands, was rewarded with the earldom of Carlisle.

Lancaster's story had a curious conclusion. In his lifetime, though feared as a man of immense power, and viewed with awe as 'the wealthiest earl in the world',[13] he had been devoid of any personal qualities to make him respected or admired. But the manner of his death led him to be regarded as a martyr, and his tomb, before the high altar in Pontefract Priory, became a place of pilgrimage. Though he was never canonized he became an unofficial 'St Thomas of Lancaster', whose sanctity was said to be proved by many miracles.[14] John Barbour referred to both the sanctity and the miracles with a trace of scepticism:

> This Thomas, it was later said,
> That thus had been a martyr made,
> Was holy; miracles he did
> By others' jealousy were hid.
> But whether he was saint or no
> At Pontefract he died, I know.[15]

Thomas of Lancaster had been a tool rather than an ally of the Scots. They had little cause to mourn him, except that his death freed King Edward to lead another campaign against Scotland.

In triumphalist mood King Edward informed the Pope that he intended to impose peace upon Scotland by force of arms.[16] The campaign of 1322 was his last attempt to conquer Scotland, an ambition that a man with a strong grasp of reality would have abandoned some years before.

King Robert's response appeared almost to mock his efforts. Throughout the month of July, Edward's army was massing at Newcastle, in readiness to invade Scotland by the well-trodden eastern route. Ignoring these preparations, on 1 July Robert led a raid across the Solway, and down the coasts of Cumberland and Lancashire, crossing every estuary at low tide:

> [He] plundered the monastery of Holm Cultram, notwithstanding that his father's body was buried there; and thence proceeded to waste and plunder Copeland and so on beyond the sands of Duddon to Furness. But the Abbot of Furness . . . paid ransom for the district . . . Also they [the Scots] went further beyond the sands of Leven to Cartmel, and burnt the lands round the priory . . . and so they crossed the sands of Kent as far as the town of Lancaster, which they burnt . . .[17]

Joined by Randolph and Douglas, the King's force passed Preston and penetrated another fifteen miles into England, before returning with the usual booty of prisoners and cattle. On their way home they paused in the vicinity of Carlisle 'trampling and destroying as much of the crops as they could'.[18] They were back in Scotland by 24 July.

While this raid seemed contemptuously to ignore King Edward's preparations for invasion, effective arrangements were being made for his reception in south-eastern Scotland. There was to be no attempt to repeat Bannockburn, but instead the most thorough application ever attempted of the principles of 'Good King Robert's Testament'.

The main Scottish army retreated beyond the Firth of Forth, and remained encamped near Culross. The populace of Lothian was ordered to evacuate, taking with it all cattle and sheep and as many food supplies as possible, and destroying everything that had to be left behind.

King Edward arrived at Newcastle on 1 August 'and shortly afterwards invaded Scotland with his earls, barons, knights and a very great army'.[19] In addition to the cavalry contributed by his magnates and his household, he had mounted spearmen and crossbowmen from Aquitaine, and every village in England had been required to contribute one fully armed foot-soldier.[20] Edward's infantry totalled some twenty thousand, a larger force than he had led to Bannockburn. A fleet of supply ships sailed up the east coast, escorted by warships under the command of Sir Robert Battaille.[21]

Edward advanced through the frequently devastated countryside of Northumberland, now partly occupied by the Scots, apparently without meeting opposition. He crossed the border into an empty landscape, in which the army became wholly reliant on its own provisions. By 19 August, Edward had reached Musselburgh. The supply ships were expected to put in at the port of Leith, but the army awaited them in vain. The fleet had been attacked by Flemish privateers, allies of the Scots, and then scattered by storms.[22] The English army now faced severe privation, and foraging parties were sent out to scour the countryside. According to Barbour, they found nothing but a lame cow, left behind by the refugees, grazing near Tranent. When the beast was brought into the camp, Earl Warenne exclaimed that it was the dearest beast he ever saw – 'it cost a thousand pound and more!'[23] It also indicated the complete success of King Robert's scorched-earth policy and the necessity for immediate retreat.

Before leaving the vicinity of Edinburgh, the English sacked Holyrood Abbey, and on reaching the Borders set fire to the abbeys of Melrose and Dryburgh. No doubt these acts of sacrilege seemed a satisfactory vengeance on the Scots, though not well calculated to endear Edward II to his ally the Pope. King Robert usually spared religious buildings, though he often exacted a heavy ransom for doing so. At Melrose a force led by James Douglas emerged from the forest to beat off the attack, and continued to harass the retreating English.[24] Starvation and consequent sickness thinned the English ranks, and it was with a greatly depleted army that King Edward returned to his own country at the end of August. The army disbanded at Newcastle.[25]

Edward retreated as far as Durham, and from there at the end of September he wrote to the Governors of four Northumbrian castles, Bamburgh, Warkworth, Dunstanburgh and Alnwick, reproaching them for failure to resist the Scots, who were now besieging Norham.[26] This suggests that he now feared for English possession of Northumberland, whence refugees from the Scots were fleeing into Yorkshire. Edward himself retreated into Yorkshire, and attempted to gather reinforcements.

On 2 October, King Edward summoned the northern magnates to

meet him at 'Blakenumour', probably identifiable as Blackmoor, on the Cleveland Hills. They were to raise levies of able-bodied men between the ages of sixteen and sixty. Edward was indignant that Sir Andrew de Harclay, Earl of Carlisle, did not appear, but Harclay was short of men. The Cumberland and Westmorland levies, who had won the battle of Boroughbridge, would not have served beyond their obligatory duty days. Apart from the garrison at Carlisle, which could not leave the city undefended, he had had a strong cavalry force, which Edward may have expected him to bring to Blackmoor; but as they could not be paid beyond the end of September, they disbanded, and Harclay went to raise levies in Lancashire to obey the King's summons, and missed the ensuing action.[27]

Meanwhile, after Edward's retreat from Scotland, King Robert had moved his army across to the west, and recruited additional forces from Argyll and the Isles of Arran and Bute. On 30 September he crossed the Solway and again ravaged the district round Carlisle. He was still in Cumberland when news was brought to him of King Edward's muster at Blackmoor. North Yorkshire was an area unknown to Robert, 'whither he had never gone before nor laid waste those parts, because of their difficulty of access'.[28] But with the quickness of decision and speed of movement characteristic of him, he saw the opportunity to capture King Edward, and at once struck across the Pennines into Yorkshire in pursuit of him.

On 13 October King Edward was told that the Scots were at Northallerton; for the first time it became obvious that he himself was their quarry. According to Barbour, King Edward's army was now encamped at 'Biland'. His description of the terrain makes perfect sense if this is accepted as being the village of Old Byland near Rievaulx Abbey and not Byland Abbey, which is several miles distant on the other side of Scawton Moor and Wass Moor.[29] Edward's army had moved south from Blackmoor to Old Byland, and the King himself was lodged in greater comfort at Rievaulx Abbey itself. According to Barbour, King Robert was informed of Edward's position and the Scots made a march from Northallerton to surprise him:

> And in the morning ere twas day
> They came upon a field that lay
> From Byland but a little space

But in between them and the place
There stretched a long and rocky brae
Up this there was no other way
Except a pathway steep and wide
To Byland on the further side,
Unless they went a long way round.
And when the English leaders found
That now King Robert was so near
The most part of their forces there
Went to the path and took the brae;
For thus they thought to block the way.[30]

This description of the terrain makes it clear that the 'long and rocky brae' was the escarpment of Scawton Moor, and that the Scots arriving from Northallerton were at the foot of the 'pathway steep' up Sutton Bank, a very considerable barrier, but a shorter route over Scawton Moor to Old Byland and Rievaulx than the 'long way round' by Helmsley.

An English force, commanded by John of Brittany, Earl of Richmond, advanced over Scawton Moor and occupied the edge of the escarpment at the top of Sutton Bank.[31] Sir James Douglas volunteered to dislodge the defenders and, joined by Thomas Randolph, undertook an apparently suicidal attack up Sutton Bank, from the top of which boulders were hurled down at them.

King Robert, watching the attack from below, sent a force of high-landers and islesmen to scale the cliffs further along the escarpment, and take the English by surprise. This ascent could have been made either at Roulston Scar, slightly south of Sutton Bank, or Whitestone Cliff above Gormire Lake, slightly north of it.

The highlanders gained the top of the escarpment and their charge hit John of Brittany's force in the flank. The diversionary tactic enabled Douglas and Moray to gain Sutton Bank and bring their force up on to Scawton Moor. Hard fighting ensued before John of Brittany's men broke ranks. 'But', wrote Sir Thomas Grey, 'the Scots were so fierce and their chiefs so daring, and the English so badly cowed, that it was no otherwise between them than as a hare before greyhounds.'[32] As the English fled across the moor, John of Brittany himself was captured, together with Sir Ralph de Cobham, formerly considered the best knight in England, until his valour was surpassed by that of Sir Thomas Uchtred, who had remained longer at the top of Sutton Bank, resisting the Scots.[33] Sir Henry de Sully, a distinguished French knight, and several compatriots were also taken by the Scots.

Walter the Stewart took a detachment of light horsemen and rode fast to Rievaulx, in the hope of catching Edward II, who had remained at the Abbey. But perhaps warned by the first fugitives from the battlefield, Edward escaped, 'leaving behind in the monastery in his haste his silver plate and much treasure. Then the Scots, arriving immediately after, seized it all and plundered the monastery.'[34]

The Lanercost Chronicler unkindly described his flight as 'chicken hearted', but Edward II had fought bravely enough on many battlefields, and on this occasion he recognized that the aim of the Scots invasion was to capture him and then dictate their peace terms. For this reason he had not led his army on Scawton Moor, and now precipitately fled from the defeat.

Edward's flight took him to Bridlington on the Yorkshire coast, then inland again south to Burstwick-in-Holderness, after which he went by boat to York, up the Humber estuary to the River Ouse, taking in reverse part of Queen Isabella's route when she fled the Scots in 1319.[35] The fact that he made York his refuge instead of fleeing to the south suggests that he had no intention of abandoning his war with the Scots, despite his latest ignominious flight from them. When Edward fled into Holderness, part of the Scots army was not far behind, for they had come 'nearly as far as the town of Beverley, which was held to ransom to escape being burnt by them . . .'[36] According to Barbour, Walter the Stewart pursued Edward 'to the gates of York',[37] but he may have been mistaken, for his lines imply that Stewart pursued him straight from the battlefield, and then returned to Rievaulx.

After the battle, King Robert occupied the Abbey and had the prisoners brought to him there. The first was John of Brittany, who, according to Barbour, was an arrogant man, accustomed to speaking contemptuously of the Scots. Apparently some particularly insulting words had been reported to the King, who ordered him to be kept a close prisoner,

> And said 'If it were not that he
> Were such a caitiff, certainly

His insults should not go unheeded!'
Thereat Sir John for mercy pleaded.[38]

But he remained a prisoner of the Scots for two years before being ransomed for the immense sum of twenty thousand pounds.

By contrast Robert received the French prisoners with the utmost
courtesy, assuring them that he was certain they 'had come to see the
fighting here' because they happened to be in England, and had taken
part as good knights would wish to do from motives of honour, and
not from any ill-will towards himself. He invited them to remain as his
guests for as long as they wished, and returned them to France free of
ransom. As he had intended, his generosity warmed his relations with
France, and in Sir Henry de Sully, the most important of the French
prisoners, he found a useful friend and ally.

The French prisoners had been taken by Sir James Douglas, and the
King recompensed him for the loss of their ransoms by granting him
wide powers of jurisdiction in all his lands, which would certainly bring
him greater profits than he had agreed to forgo. According to legend the
Emerald Charter of 1324 which granted these privileges was so called
because the King took an emerald ring from his own hand and placed it
on that of Douglas in earnest of his promise to issue the Charter.[39]

After his victory parties of Scots collected the spoils of east
Yorkshire. The army was reunited by about 22 October, and returned
to Scotland by 1 November, rejoicing that the King of England had
been 'vanquished in his own country'.[40] Though the battle had been on
a smaller scale than Bannockburn, the fact that it had taken place in
England may have made it seem to the Scots an even greater humiliation of English arms.[41] And though they had failed to capture Edward
II, there seemed little doubt that he must be forced to sue for peace.

Before the Scots left Yorkshire, Andrew de Harclay, Earl of Carlisle,
arrived at York with the Lancashire levies, to join King Edward 'in order
to attack the Scots with him and drive them out of the kingdom; but
when he found the king all in confusion and no army mustered, he disbanded his own forces, allowing every man to go home'.[42]

If it were known what passed between the King and Harclay at York
it would be easier to understand what followed. After Harclay had

visited King Edward at Gloucester in 1322 and been told of his intention to deal with Lancaster and the traitors before the Scots, the King
had empowered him, by letters patent issued on 9 February, 'to treat
with Robert de Bruce and the Scots for peace and truce'.[43] It is possible that Harclay assumed these letters were still in force, or that something the King said to him at York in late October or early November
led him to believe so. Since the King was so evidently unprepared to
continue fighting, the need to treat with the Scots was obvious.

On 3 January 1323 Harclay visited Robert the Bruce at Lochmaben,
and held 'long conference and protracted discussion with him' at which
the main points of a peace treaty were formulated. According to the
Lanercost Chronicler, Harclay visited the King of Scots on his own initiative:

> When the said Earl of Carlisle perceived that the King of England
> neither knew how to rule his realm nor was able to defend it against
> the Scots . . . he feared lest at last he [the King] should lose the entire
> kingdom; so he chose the less of two evils, and considered how much
> better it would be for the community of each realm if each king
> should possess his own kingdom freely and peacefully without any
> homage, instead of so many homicides and arsons, captivities, plun-
> derings and raidings taking place every year . . .[44]

Historians have accepted the view that Harclay acted completely inde-
pendently, which makes his negotiations technically if not intentionally
treasonable.[45] But it is frankly incredible that he should have gone to
Scotland and negotiated with King Robert if he had not believed that
he had some sort of sanction. It is equally incredible that the Scots
could have entered into serious negotiations with him if they had not
accepted him as empowered to negotiate. If they had regarded him
merely as an enterprising English traitor, they would have made use of
him as they had Thomas of Lancaster, and perhaps expressed similar
reservations.

A plausible explanation may be that Harclay, relying on his earlier
commission, exaggerated both to himself and to the Scots the latitude
that it gave him, while the Scots saw Harclay's arrival to treat for peace
as the direct result of their recent victory. The peace talks that had been
held before had always broken down on the basic demands of the Scots

for recognition of Scottish independence and of the kingship of Robert the Bruce. Previous English negotiations, fully in King Edward's confidence, laid down that these demands were totally unacceptable to Edward. Harclay, a northern soldier, recently ennobled but not close to the King, had witnessed the misery of the North year after year, and knew that unless the basic demands of the Scots were met, peace would never come. Thus, with large misapprehensions on both sides, the discussions took place.

The result of the negotiations survives in the form of an agreement between King Robert and Andrew de Harclay, which was to form the basis of a treaty.[46] It was affirmed that both kingdoms had prospered when each had a king for its own ruler and was maintained separately with its own laws and customs, and agreed that this should be re-established. It should be to the common profit of both kingdoms that King Robert should 'hold the realm of Scotland freely, entirely and in liberty'. The common profit of the two realms should be upheld by twelve commissioners, six nominated by the King of Scots and six by Harclay. If King Edward agreed within a year that King Robert should have his realm 'free and quit for himself and his heirs', then Robert should found an abbey in Scotland with a rent of five hundred marks, for the souls of those slain in war, and within ten years should levy King Edward forty thousand marks as tribute of four thousand a year, and should give King Edward the right to choose from his own kindred a wife for King Robert's heir (his grandson, Robert Stewart). If King Edward did not accept the agreement, King Robert should not be bound by it; if he did accept it, neither king would be obliged to 'receive in his realm a man who has been opposed to him, nor to render him the lands that he or his ancestors held in his realm, if he does not wish to do it of his special grace'. This agreement has been rightly described as 'pragmatic, nationalist and statesmanlike'.[47] It would have given the Scots what they wanted (for which generous concessions were offered) and would have done no injury to England. That reference was made to Edward's agreement being obtained within a year, or possibly not obtained, indicates Harclay's awareness that the King of England's reaction was uncertain, but it was far more violent than he could have imagined.

As early as 8 January King Edward was informed that Harclay had gone to Scotland. Immediately he issued orders that no truce should be made without his knowledge, and wrote to Harclay ordering him to

inform him personally regarding the reported truce with the Scots. On
13 January he ordered William Airmyn, Keeper of the Chancery Rolls,
to search them and inform him if Harclay had any commission under
the Great Seal to treat with the Scots, and its endurance.[48] If the search
turned up a copy of the commission issued to Harclay on 9 February the
previous year, it did him no good. According to the Lanercost Chronicle:

> ... after all these things had been made known for certain to the king
> and kingdom of England, the poor folk, middle class and farmers in
> the northern parts were not a little delighted that the King of
> Scotland should freely possess his own kingdom on such terms that
> they themselves might live in peace. But the King [Edward] and his
> council were exceedingly put out, (and no wonder!) because he
> whom the king had made an earl so lately had allied himself to the
> Scots ... to the prejudice of the realm and crown, and would compel
> the lieges of the King of England to rebel.[49]

Edward was still regarding the Scots as his subjects, their claim to independence a rebellion, and recognition of it as treason. Harclay's well-
intentioned but utterly misconceived efforts led to his doom.

On 25 February he was arrested in Carlisle Castle by Sir Anthony de
Lucy, who came to him in the guise of a friend. On 2 March he stood
trial for treason, and on 3 March he was executed with the protracted
pain and ignominy of the English treason sentence. His head was displayed on the Tower of London, the quarters of his body on the gates
of Carlisle, Newcastle, York and Shrewsbury.[50]

Before his death he made a confession to four ecclesiastics separately, all of whom acquitted him of any intention of treason. The
tragedy of his fate seems the greater because the agreement with
Robert the Bruce bears a close resemblance to the Anglo-Scottish peace
treaty of 1328.

One of Harclay's kinsmen took the news of his fate to Scotland,
where the reaction of many must have been to doubt that peace with
England would ever be attained while Edward II lived.

Though King Edward had sacrificed Harclay on the altar of his own
wrath and prejudice, he had not reduced the need to negotiate with the

Scots. If anything he had increased it, for Harclay's execution left Carlisle, long coveted by the Scots, as a vulnerable prey.

Edward reluctantly initiated negotiations for a truce, and Sir Henry de Sully acted as mediator, and visited him on behalf of Robert the Bruce. Having received Edward's unacceptable communications, Robert replied to Sully on 21 March 1323 in a letter which shows that contemptuous amusement rather than anger had been his reaction to Edward's empty posturing:

> Robert, by God's grace King of Scotland, to the most noble Henry, lord of Sully, knight, his good friend, affectionate and loving greeting. You will recall, my lord, how it was stated in our letters sent to the King of England, and how also we informed you by word of mouth, that we desired and still desire at all times to negotiate with the King of England on a good peace between him and us, saving always to us and our heirs our realm free and independent, and also the integrity of our allies. If the English King had been agreeable, we were willing to make a truce until Trinity [22 May]. Regarding this, my lord, we have received your letters, and transcripts of letters from the King of England, declaring that he has 'granted a truce to the people of Scotland who are at war with him'. To us this is a very strange way of speaking. In earlier truces, even though the English King has not deigned to call us King, we have at least been named as the principal on one side, as he has on the other. But it does not seem advisable to us to accept a truce in which no more mention is made of us than of the humblest man in our kingdom, so that we could demand no more than any other if the truce were to be infringed wholly or in part.[51]

On the understanding that Robert should be named as principal on the Scots side, the negotiation proceeded and a truce for thirteen years was concluded at Bishopthorpe near York on 30 May, and ratified by Robert as 'King of Scotland' at Berwick on 7 June. Thus King Edward tacitly accepted the title that officially he still refused to acknowledge.[52]

The unusually long period proposed for the truce probably indicated the intention that it should be converted into a peace before its expiry. But it dealt with none of the basic issues that a peace treaty would be required to address. Under the truce it was agreed that neither country would build new fortifications in the border counties, and that wardens should be appointed to control crossings of the border, to settle disputes, and to report unresolved disputes to the two kings. Ships trading with Scotland, hitherto regarded as enemy shipping by England, should be accorded neutral status. King Edward agreed that he would not oppose the Scots approaching the Pope for the removal of the excommunication and interdict still in force against them. The advantage of the truce was chiefly on the side of the Scots, as was to be expected from the weakness of Edward II's position. But while Edward refused to negotiate on the basic demands of the Scots, peace receded like a mirage.

16

─────|✱|✱|✱|─────

TOWARDS PEACE

'In the course of a twenty years war, the spirit of Scotland
had attained an astonishing ascendant over the English.'

Hailes, *Annals of Scotland*[1]

ON 5 March 1324 the prayers of the King and Queen of Scots were
answered, and they may have believed the displeasure of St Malachy
was finally assuaged. Almost ten years after her return from imprisonment in England the Queen bore her husband a son. They had already
received assurance that she was not barren, for in recent years she had
born two daughters, Matilda and Margaret, whose birth dates were not
recorded.[2] But the birth of a male heir was the Queen's triumph, and a
cause of national rejoicing.

No doubt many people reflected that since the King was in his
fiftieth year, such a late-born son would almost certainly succeed as a
minor, but such anxieties were not publicly expressed. Bernard, Abbot
of Arbroath, celebrated the prince's birth with a Latin poem, in which
he prophesied:

This man will play at combat in the garden of the English
Or else may God make a lasting peace between the kingdoms.[3]

The Scots had already made a move towards peace by seeking the reconciliation with the Church which Edward II had promised not to
impede. Towards the end of 1323 King Robert had appointed Thomas
Randolph to negotiate with the Pope, and he travelled to Avignon
accompanied by Henry de Sully, whose presence would assure the Pope

of French support for the Scots' initiative. The Pope received Randolph and Sully together on 1 January 1324. His own account written to King Edward unconsciously revealed how skilfully Randolph had manipulated him.

Randolph, said the Pope, declared that he had made a vow to go to the Holy Land, and had come to seek the Pope's permission to fulfil it. The Pope replied that his permission could not be granted to an excommunicated person. But he would receive the petition favourably hereafter, if Randolph would do his utmost for the reconciliation of Scotland. Randolph replied that the King would send ambassadors for that very purpose, if the Pope would grant them safe conduct. The Pope replied that he could not grant his safe conduct to excommunicates, but he would request safe conduct from the princes through whose territories they might have to march. Randolph next employed the bait of the Pope's well-known enthusiasm for the Crusade, and said that King Robert desired to join the King of France on his intended expedition to the Holy Land, or if the French expedition failed to take place, to lead a Crusade himself. The Pope replied that until King Robert concluded a peace with England and was reconciled with the Church he could not be accepted as a Crusader. Then Randolph answered that he desired nothing more than peace with England and reconciliation with the Church, and if the Pope would explain his conditions to the King in a bull addressed to him as King of Scots, he had no doubt that it would be reverently received, but if the royal title were withheld, the papal communication would be ignored. It appeared to the Pope that if the reconciliation of Scotland to the Church, peace between Scotland and England and the cause of the Crusade could be advanced by so simple a means, then it was expedient to do as Randolph suggested.

Having related all this to King Edward, the Pope endeavoured to reassure him:

I remember to have told you that my bestowing the title of King on Robert Bruce would neither strengthen his claim nor impair yours. My earnest desires are for reconciliation and peace; and you well know that my Bull, issued for attaining these salutary purposes, will never be received in Scotland, if I address it to Bruce under any other appellation but that of King; I therefore exhort you in royal wisdom that you would be pleased patiently to suffer me to give him that appellation.[4]

This half-apologetic tone scarcely conveyed the authority that should have characterized the head of the Church. Edward's initial response was an angry condemnation of the Pope's concession, followed by the demand that the excommunication and interdict against the Scots should remain in force. In addition he demanded that no Scotsman should be appointed to a Scottish bishopric 'for it is the prelates of Scotland who encourage the nobility, gentry and people in their evil acts'.[5] This demand the Pope refused, pointing out that since no Englishman would be received in Scotland, such a measure would deprive the Scots of bishops altogether, which he could not permit. But he was sufficiently intimidated by Edward to agree to the continuance of the excommunication and interdict, which he justified with the stale excuse that as the Scots had seized Berwick in contravention of a papal truce, the spiritual penalties could not be lifted unless Berwick were returned to England. The Scots preferred to keep Berwick and endure the penalties. However, the Pope did not retract his acknowledgement of Robert the Bruce as King of Scots, which he had already granted. This left King Edward isolated in his refusal to recognize the Scottish monarchy.

Though King Edward had so dishonourably reneged on his undertaking not to oppose the Scots' application to the Pope to be freed from the excommunication and interdict, the Scots persisted in the hope that the truce might be converted into a permanent peace, and new peace talks were proposed.

In November 1324 commissioners from both kingdoms were appointed to meet at York. The Scottish delegation was headed by Bishop Lamberton of St Andrews and Thomas Randolph, Earl of Moray, and the English delegation by Edward's all-powerful advisers the Despensers, father and son. As usual, the talks foundered on Edward's refusal to acknowledge either Scotland's independence or King Robert's title. Despite the fact that Edward no longer occupied a foot of Scottish ground, he declared that to abandon the English claim to overlordship would be 'the manifest disinheritance of our royal crown'.[6]

After the breakdown of the talks there was no resumption of hostil-

ities. Edward II was involved in an escalating quarrel with King Charles
IV of France, and would not undertake a simultaneous campaign
against the Scots; King Robert awaited his opportunity to take advantage of the breach between England and France.

During the next two years the unaccustomed respite from fighting continued, and the King of Scots indulged in the only sustained non-mili-
tary activity of his reign. He built himself a manor house at Cardross,
on the northern shore of the Firth of Clyde, near Dumbarton. The
place was not part of the royal demesne; the King chose the site
because he liked it. He bought part of the manorial estate from the Earl
of Lennox, and acquired part of it from Sir David de Graham, to
whom he gave in exchange the land of Old Montrose in Angus, thus
creating the historic link between the names of Graham and
Montrose.[7]

The King's manor has long since disappeared, and even the site of it
is uncertain, but surviving details of the buildings and materials suggest
that it was of modest size, and designed for comfort and leisure. It had
originally a Hall, a King's Chamber and a Queen's Chamber, a Chapel,
a kitchen and a larder. In 1328 a 'New Chamber' and a 'New Gate' were
added. The walls were whitewashed, the roofs thatched, and there was
glass in the widows, a medieval luxury. Nearby stood a separate building, surrounded by a hedge, to house the King's falcons. The King also
kept a lion, though it was probably a securely caged symbol of royalty
rather than a household pet. The manor house stood in a garden, for
which Gilbert the gardener was given money to buy seeds. Beyond lay
a park for the King's hunting, maintained by three park-keepers;
William, Gilchrist and Gillfillan. Gillies was the King's huntsman;
indoors he was entertained by Patrick the jester.[8]

At anchor in the Clyde lay the King's 'great ship', in which on at least
one occasion he made a voyage to Tarbert, no doubt to oversee
progress on the new royal castle which was under construction there.
When Sir James Douglas and Bishop Lamberton came to visit the
castle, the floors of their chambers were strewn with fresh birchen
boughs.[9] Beside the manor house at Cardross was the mouth of a burn
into which the ship could be hauled up when she needed maintenance.

No doubt as he grew older, and as more peaceful conditions might permit, the King intended to enjoy his leisure at Cardross, but leisure may have been partly enforced, for he began to receive visits from his physician Magister Mabinus, an indication that his health was beginning to deteriorate.[10]

It was natural that King Robert should feel at home in the West of Scotland, for he had spent much of his early life in the West, and probably his earliest memories would have been of his parents' castle of Turnberry on the coast of Carrick. Perhaps it is initially surprising that he did not decide to rebuild one of the actual castles – Turnberry itself, or his grandfather's castle of Lochmaben – which he had destroyed, no doubt reluctantly, in the course of his wars. But Cardross marked a break with the past, and the King was surely building with his son and descendants in mind: kings who, he hoped, would rule a peaceful kingdom and have leisure to entertain their lords and ladies at falconry and the chase, to return to feast in the great hall, and perhaps to listen to the music and song of a bard from the northern Highlands or from Ireland, who would sing the traditional epics of Gaelic heroes, or would improvise the praises of his host.

Cardross was the Gaelic-speaking area of the Lennox, which suggests that King Robert wished to remain in contact with the Gaelic strand in his own ancestry, and wished his successors to do so. It was also well placed for easy contact with his allies in the *Gealtachd* (the Gaelic-speaking area). The Earl of Lennox was one of his oldest associates. Sir Neil Campbell, his brother-in-law, and others of his family controlled much of Argyll; while another brother-in-law, Hugh Earl of Ross, controlled the coast of Western Ross, and Thomas Randolph held lands on the Sound of Sleat. The scattered lordship of Christiana of the Isles was now ruled by her half-brother, Ruairi MacRuarie, and would be inherited by her son, who would marry one of Ruari's daughters. Angus MacDonald of Islay was confirmed in possession of Islay and the MacDonald lands in Kyntyre, and rewarded for his loyalty to King Robert with the forfeited Comyn lordship of Lochaber.[11]

At Cardross many of them could without difficulty come to the King, and from there it was also easy access to Ireland and the Isle of Man. Though the King's new home was not built for defence, it and the western approaches to the King were defended by the stronghold of Dumbarton, the only royal castle King Robert had not demolished, by the castle of Shipness in Kintyre, which he ordered to be repaired, and by the new castle of Tarbert.

Cardross was also sufficiently near the centre of the kingdom for the King to move easily between it and the places at which his peripatetic court and government often stayed: Perth, Dunfermline and Cambuskenneth, where he lodged in monastic buildings which frequently offered greater comfort than the castles, though in most areas King Robert's policy of destroying castles had deprived him of the choice.

On 15 July 1326 Parliament met at Cambuskenneth Abbey to enact a new tailzie of the Crown to the King's son David, giving him precedence over the previous heir, the King's grandson Robert Stewart. David was now two years old, past the most frequent age of infant mortality, which was perhaps why the Parliament was summoned at this time, and the magnates of the realm gathered to swear fealty to the young prince. But, as though to emphasize the uncertainty of royal dynasties, in the same year the Queen bore her last child, a son named John, who was born and died at Dunfermline. If the choice of name seems curious, considering its association with the Bruces' dynastic rival, King John Balliol, the probable explanation is that it was a pious reference to St John the Baptist, later-born son of St Elizabeth, who had long endured the reproach of barrenness, as Queen Elizabeth de Burgh had done.

David, however, survived, and as a modern historian has commented with harsh realism:

> It is surely incontrovertible that the birth of an immediate male heir so late in Robert I's reign was a tragedy for the Scottish kingdom and people . . . If David had not been born or had not survived infancy, his nephew Robert Stewart would have begun to rule at thirteen, on the brink of fourteenth century manhood. It is at least arguable that the situation in Scotland would not in that event have seemed to . . . Edward III . . . so tempting as it did in the 1330's with . . . the throne occupied by a child.[12]

History is haunted by tantalizing alternatives. Another is that the Truce of Bishopthorpe might have run its course until its projected term in 1336, and Edward II continued to reign and reject the Scots' conditions of peace. Ironically, it was the overthrow of Edward II and the accession of Edward III as a minor that gave the Scots the opportunity to take advantage of a kingdom weakened by a royal minority. Edward III would seize a similar chance in the future, but the turn of Robert the Bruce came first.

Edward II's troubles began insignificantly with his apparent reluctance to pay homage to Charles IV for his lands in France. Two years after his accession Charles invited King Edward to meet him at Amiens at Easter 1324 to perform his homage, and subsequently extended his invitation to 1 July. He had some reason to feel exasperated with Edward, aside from the incident that precipitated their quarrel.

King Charles decided to build a *bastide* (fortified town) at Saint Sardos near the border of Gascony. The works were begun when Sir Ralph Basset, the English Senechal of Gascony, attacked Saint Sardos and hanged a Frenchman on a gallows decorated with the arms of France. King Edward insisted that he had known nothing of the outrage committed by his official, and sent his half-brother Edmund, Earl of Kent, to restore good relations. But Kent's diplomatic ineptitude made it appear that Edward II was both condoning the Saint Sardos outrage and withholding his homage, whereupon King Charles declared both Gascony and Ponthieu confiscate to France. Hostilities followed, and Edward II, maintaining his misplaced confidence in his half-brother, appointed Kent to command the English forces in Gascony. When Charles IV invaded, the Earl of Kent retreated to the Castle of La Réole and in September 1324 agreed to a six-month truce.[13]

Edward II, horrified at the deterioration of his relations with France, appointed the Earl of Pembroke to repair the damage. But Pembroke fell ill and died immediately upon his arrival in France. Shortly afterwards the Pope sent nuncios to the French King with the suggestion that Queen Isabella, as wife of King Edward and sister of King Charles, might reconcile the aggrieved monarchs. Edward agreed to the proposal, and on 9 March 1325 Isabella and her household sailed for France.

King Edward assumed the loyalty of his wife, who was secretly but bitterly disaffected. Historians have commented that Isabella had always been generously treated, as though this should compensate for the humiliation of her husband's obvious preference for his favourites, Gaveston at the beginning of his reign and Despenser the Younger towards the end of it. In 1324 even the generosity was withdrawn, when the Despensers advised Edward to sequestrate Isabella's estates, on the grounds that there was danger of invasion from France and the Queen was a Frenchwoman. Isabella was granted an ample allowance, but she was obliged to submit to the appointment of the younger Despenser's wife to oversee her household, including her correspondence.[14] That Edward entrusted this much-injured woman with a delicate diplomatic mission speaks as eloquently for her powers of dissimulation as for his purblind arrogance towards her. At first, despite her ill-usage, Isabella appears to have acted as an honest mediator. By midsummer 1325 she had persuaded her brother Charles IV to restore the English territories he had occupied, on condition that King Edward come in person to pay homage for them. This should have restored happier relations, but the Despensers, whose efficiently rapacious regime had won them wide-spread hatred in England, feared to let Edward quit the country and leave them naked to their enemies.

Queen Isabella suggested that her eldest son Prince Edward should be permitted to do homage in his father's place. King Charles agreed, and young Edward was created Duke of Aquitaine, Count of Ponthieu and Autreil and sent to France, where he performed homage on 21 September 1325. But Charles IV, instead of restoring all the English ter-ritories, insisted on retaining the Agenais in recompense for the losses he had incurred in the earlier hostilities. Edward II, feeling that his son was being taken advantage of, claimed the right to act as 'governor and administrator' of the territories with which he had just endowed young Edward and for which the prince had paid homage. In retaliation Charles IV reoccupied them, and full-scale war between England and France seemed inevitable.

Recently, increasingly friendly relations between Scotland and France led the French to believe that in the event of war with England, the Scots would come to their aid. Early in 1326, with the prospect of war, it seemed appropriate to seek a formal alliance. Early in the spring of 1326 King Robert sent a deputation headed by Thomas Randolph to negotiate an offensive and defensive treaty with France, but in view of the current threat from England 'the initiative may have been as much French as Scottish'.[15] The Treaty of Corbeil, concluded in April 1326, bound both Scotland and France to come to offer aid if the other were attacked by England. It brought King Robert the prestige of alliance with a major power, and he may also have hoped it might assist in forcing Edward II to conclude a formal peace, the chief aim of all his diplomacy.[16] But Edward was now preoccupied with the disturbing transformation in the conduct of his Queen.

Despite the breakdown of Anglo-Frence relations, Isabella refused either to return to England or to send home her son. In France there had gathered around her a group of English malcontents, united by their hatred of the Despensers. They included the King's half-brother, the Earl of Kent, who had turned against the King after his humiliation in Gascony; Edward's cousin John of Brittany, Earl of Richmond, loyal throughout the reign until alienated by the Despensers; Henry de Beaumont, who had also been close to Edward for many years; and the Marcher Lord Roger Mortimer of Wigmore, who had fought against the King with Thomas of Lancaster, and been imprisoned in the Tower of London after the battle of Boroughbridge. He had escaped and taken refuge in France, where he became Queen Isabella's lover. Perhaps this relationship was the catalyst that turned a plot against the Despensers into a plot against Edward II himself.

Isabella's affair alienated her brother King Charles, who required her to leave France. But with as forceful and resourceful a partner as Mortimer she was not dismayed. Accompanied by their allies, they moved to Hainault and bargained with Count William II for military support, to be purchased with the betrothal of Prince Edward to the Count's daughter Philippa. With the prospect of this immensely pres-tigious marriage for her, Count William provided Isabella with a small army commanded by his brother John of Hainault. Isabella's invasion force sailed from Dordrecht on 23 September 1326, and anchored in the Orwell estuary the following day. More influential supporters declared for Isabella, including the King's other half-brother, Thomas, Earl of Norfolk, and Thomas of Lancaster's brother, Henry, Earl of Leicester. The adherence of the Bishops of Norwich, Winchester and Hereford gave the insurgents the added dignity of ecclesiastical support.

Isabella's army advanced on London, the city declared for her, and Edward II's authority crumbled within days. The King, with a handful of supporters, fled westward, and with the younger Despenser made for Wales. The elder Despenser, whom the King had created Earl of Winchester, and Donald, Earl of Mar, attempted to hold Bristol for the King. But there was little support for him there, and the city surrendered to Isabella on 26 October. The Earl of Winchester was captured and suffered a traitor's death the following day.

Donald of Mar, who had refused to return to Scotland after Bannockburn because of his attachment to Edward II, escaped from Bristol and made his way to Scotland, to entreat King Robert's assistance for his lifelong enemy. The King of Scots welcomed Donald and restored him to his earldom. No doubt he was delighted to regain an errant nephew, and to reclaim the loyalty of another leading member of Scotland's nobility, but Donald must have come with full powers to bargain before King Robert would have intervened on behalf of Edward II. According to the Lanercost Chronicler:

> The King [Edward II] had been so ill-advised as to write to the Scots, freely giving up to them the land and realm of Scotland, to be held independently of any King of England, and, which was worse, bestowed upon them with Scotland a great part of the northern lands of England lying next to them, on condition that they should assist him against the Queen, her son, and their confederates.[17]

This statement is not corroborated by any other source, but this does not necessarily invalidate it. Edward had reputedly made desperate offers to Robert the Bruce before, which Robert had spurned because they were desperate, and would have been repudiated by the magnates who opposed the King. But now the situation was different; if Edward's authority were restored with the help of the Scots, Robert could name his own terms, which would have been those that he had always required, with perhaps in addition the cession of Northumberland to Scotland.

While Donald of Mar was making his way to Scotland and reaching an accommodation with his uncle, Edward II was a fugitive in Wales with his remaining supporters. Edward had been at Tintern Abbey before Bristol fell. Thence he fled to Chepstow and attempted to sail with Hugh Despenser the younger to the Isle of Lundy in the Bristol Channel. Despenser was Lord of Lundy, which might have provided a temporary refuge for the King while awaiting a ship to Ireland. Roger

Mortimer, John of Hainault and Henry of Leicester feared that if the King could reach Ireland he might collect an army there and cross over into Scotland, and with the help of the Scots and Irish together attack England.[18] But storms forced Edward's ship back into the harbour of Cardiff, and he and Despenser landed again and wandered Glamorgan, where the pursuit closed around them. On 16 November he was betrayed by Rhys ap Howel at the abbey of Neath, and handed over to Henry of Leicester. Captured with him were Hugh Despenser and his Chancellor, Robert Baldock. Despenser suffered a traitor's death at Hereford, and Baldock, who as a cleric was spared the death sentence, died shortly afterwards as a prisoner in Newgate.[19] King Edward was escorted to Monmouth, where he was forced to surrender the Great Seal of England to the Bishop of Hereford. Thence he was taken to Kenilworth Castle as the prisoner of Henry of Leicester, who proved a humane and courteous gaoler.

The capture of Edward II would not have been good news to the Scots if Edward had indeed offered to surrender his claims on Scotland, and was prepared to negotiate with King Robert through the mediation of Donald of Mar.[20] With Edward II in their hands, the position of Isabella and Mortimer was immeasurably strengthened, and though their intentions for Edward might be foreseeable, their attitude towards Scotland was not. Therefore, at the close of 1326, 'It suited King Robert to give Donald a free hand in his plots to raise English, Scots and Welsh for the release of the captured Edward.'[21]

At the beginning of 1327 the reign of Edward II was brought to a rapid conclusion. On 16 January he was visited by a deputation representing nobility, clergy and commons, which informed him that he was now deposed. He was required to agree to the articles of deposition, to give the new regime some semblance of legality, and when he attempted to resist, the Bishop of Hereford threatened that the kingdom would repudiate not only him but also his son. He then capitulated, and was promised that his elder son would take his place as King, and he himself would be maintained in all appropriate state.[22]

On 24 January the accession of the fourteen-year-old Prince Edward was proclaimed, and the reign of King Edward III was deemed to begin on the following day.[23] To the ageing Robert the Bruce it must have seemed that his enemy was indestructible: when one Edward was gone another took his place, to the third generation. Aware, perhaps, that he had limited time left to complete his life's work, King Robert determined to strike a final blow for victory. Evidently he had received advance notice of events in England, for on the night of 1 February, the date of Edward III's coronation, the Scots attacked Norham Castle.[24] This particular attempt was repulsed, but King Robert 'continued his attacks on border castles, warning the new regime in England that he expected his demands for final settlement to be met'.[25] King Robert's attacks undoubtedly broke the truce, but the Scots argued that it had been broken already by English attacks on Scottish shipping in the course of 1326, against which complaints had been made, but no redress given.

> The English did their villainy
> Whene'er they met them [Scots] on the sea
> He [Robert] then sent word that he felt free
> To give the truce up openly.[26]

The English government declared its intention of maintaining the truce, and once again commissioners were appointed to discuss a final peace. But the English were not yet ready to accept King Robert's terms, and even before the peace talks had broken down, the mobilization of an English army was in hand.[27]

Undoubtedly it would have suited Isabella and Mortimer if the reign of Edward III could have opened with a prestigious victory over the Scots. They had captured Edward II and crowned his son, but their adulterous liaison gave their regime a disreputable character which could bring it into contempt unless they could justify their power by their success. To defeat the Scots would be a spectacular way to do so.

Their motivation would have been obvious to King Robert, who made his own preparations for war. The Scottish army was divided into three brigades, one commanded by Thomas Randolph, one by James Douglas and one by Donald of Mar, who were to invade England. The normally well-informed Lanercost Chronicler explained King Robert's non-participation with the words 'my lord Robert de Brus, who had become leprous, did not invade England on this occasion'.[28] This is the first mention of the disease that the King was erroneously believed to have endured, though the 'fact' that he suffered from and died of leprosy would become an article of faith concerning him.

In fact he did not join in the invasion of England because on 12 April 1327 he had crossed to Ulster, where the affairs of the earldom required his intervention. In 1326 his father-in-law Richard de Burgh, 'the Red Earl', had died, leaving as heir his grandson William, Robert's nephew. But in recent years the old Earl's authority had collapsed, William de Burgh was in England, in the control of Isabella and Mortimer, and the men of Ulster, in despair at the disorder of their country, were ready to choose another lord. There had also been a proposal that English and Welsh settlers might be provided with lands in Ulster. King Robert's arrival in Ulster has been described as 'moving into a power vacuum'.[29] His aim was the establishment of William de Burgh in his earldom as an ally of Scotland; as an interim measure he was determined not to allow Ulster to become an English power-base. By July 1327 he had negotiated with Henry de Mandeville, Seneschal of the earldom, an agreement whereby the people of Ulster bought a truce from the King of Scots to run for one year from 1 August.[30]

Having successfully neutralized Ulster, King Robert seems to have attempted to reach an understanding with the English administration in Dublin:

> [He] sent to the Justiciar of Ireland and to the Council that they should come to Greencastle to draw up a peace between Scotland and Ireland, and because the said Justiciar and Council did not come as he wished . . . he returned to his native land after the feast of the Assumption of the Blessed Virgin [15 August].[31]

The Justiciar was Thomas FitzJohn, Earl of Kildare, who had taken office and proclaimed Edward III as recently as 12 May. His refusal to make peace must have immediately preceded or coincided with the decisive defeat of Edward III's forces in Scotland, where an eventful summer campaign had ended in their complete humiliation on 7 August. News of the Scots triumph would have caused Robert to abandon his negotiations and speed his way back across the Irish Sea to complete his victory.

The King of Scots had shown great faith in his lieutenants, in leaving them to deal with the army amassed by Isabella and Mortimer.

As a preliminary to their campaign against the Scots, they removed Edward II from the custody of Henry of Leicester, whose courtesy to his prisoner may have suggested lack of security, and placed him in the custody of Sir John Maltravers and Thomas, lord of Berkeley, at Berkeley Castle, Gloucestershire.[32] The move from Kenilworth to Berkeley implied a change in Edward's status from that of an ex-king detained with a show of respect to that of a close prisoner whose continued existence might be under threat, especially if the fortunes of war went against his captors.

The English army mustered at York. Its most impressive contingent was a force of 2,500 Flemish cavalry commanded by John of Hainault. Possibly theirs were the helmets decorated with heraldic crests which John Barbour reported that the Scots saw for the first time and admired on this campaign. The English also had another innovation, some small cannons or 'crakys off wer'.[33] But these sinister harbingers of modern warfare gave no hint of their destructive potential, for the summer of 1327 was so wet that the gunpowder became as sodden and useless as the food supplies.

When news arrived of the first Scots incursions on the West March on 15 June, the militias of Yorkshire and Lancashire were ordered to York. The army left York on 10 July, and headed towards Durham, followed by a vast baggage train, but with no clear idea of the whereabouts of the Scots. It is probable that the Scots in their three brigades may have entered England at different points. On 12 July Edward III received a warning that the Scots to the west would either attack Carlisle or make straight for the vicinity of the King himself.[34] This force may have been that commanded by Sir James Douglas, who would shortly attempt to capture the young King. Moray and Mar may have entered England by Kielder Gap and advanced down the valley of the north Tyne.[35] The other force would have crossed the Pennines to converge with them and attempt to meet the English and head off an invasion of Scotland. 'A great deal of risk was involved in this tactic, for King Robert was in Ulster . . . and thus unable to defend Scotland should the English invade.'[36]

On 18 July the English, encamped by Durham, could see smoke billowing from the destructive fires of the invaders. They advanced along

Weardale, which seemed to be in the general direction of the enemy, but never encountered them. The Scots, according to Barbour, were burning 'Cockdale',[37] which has not been identified, but may be the valley of the River Gaunless, in the parish of Cockfield.[38]

The English commanders determined on a forced march to the River Tyne, to cut off the Scots from their own country. On the night of 20 July the cavalry encamped at Haydon Bridge. The baggage train had been left behind, and each man issued with a loaf of bread. That night began the rain which continued to fall for the next eight days, turning the encampment into a swamp. Provisions were hard to obtain, men and horses went hungry and equipment rotted. There was no news of the enemy's expected retreat towards Scotland.

The chronicler Jean le Bel, who was with the Hainaulters on this campaign, wrote a famous description of how the Scots maintained themselves on their raids into England. No doubt they had been doing exactly as he described in all the raids since Bannockburn, which explained their flexibility of movement and their consistent success against larger armies whose provisioning arrangements so frequently broke down:

> These Scots are exceedingly hardy . . . They ride on sturdy horses and bring no wagons with them . . . They need neither pots nor pans for whenever they invade they find plenty of cattle and use the hides of these in which to boil the flesh. Each man carries . . . an iron plate and . . . a little bag of oatmeal. When they have eaten the stewed meat they place the plate on the fire and . . . spread on it a little paste made of oatmeal and water and make a cake in the manner of a biscuit which they eat to comfort their stomachs.[39]

While the English by contrast endeavoured to subsist on their sodden provisions, their commanders had offered a reward of a knighthood and landed endowment to anyone who could locate the Scots. The reward was claimed by a squire named Thomas Rokeby, who had been caught by the Scots and released by Sir James Douglas, chivalrously willing to let him claim it in return for news of Edward III, whom he hoped to capture.

On 1 August the English marched back to the River Wear, and saw the Scots encamped on the south bank of it, strongly positioned on a hill. They contemptuously refused a challenge to come across and fight on equal ground. But during the night of 3 August the Scots, leaving their camp-fires blazing, moved off, crossed the Wear at some distance from the English, and took up another strong position behind the stone walls of Stanhope Park, a hunting preserve enclosed by the Bishop of Durham.[40]

From there, the following night, Sir James Douglas led a raid on the English camp with the intention of capturing the young King. It was, according to Barbour, a massacre:

> Some of the horsemen with him there
> He ordered naked swords to bear,
> And bade them cut the ropes in two
> So that the tents should fall, therethrough
> Upon the men that lay inside.
> The others that were by their side
> Should stab them downward with a spear . . .
> The Scotsmen staked and stabbed and slew,
> And many a tent they overthrew.
> A dreadful slaughter there made they . . .[41]

Of course, there was no intention to kill the young Edward III, though the royal pavilion was tumbled like the rest with the intention of trapping him beneath its folds. But the terrified boy was pulled clear by members of his household, and probably saved from capture by his chaplain, who was killed in defence of him. With the English camp fully aroused, the small party of Scots was forced to withdraw.

There was no more fighting. The English spent the following day loading their dead on to carts and taking them to consecrated ground for burial.[42] The next night the Scots camp appeared to be full of movement, and the English expected another attack. But while horns blared and fires blazed, the Scots army left Stanhope Park in the opposite direction, and moved north across the dangerous marsh beyond it, laying hurdles on the soft ground in front of them and taking them up behind, to impede pursuit.

With the disappearance of the enemy, the English abandoned the campaign. The young King 'shed tears of vexation',[43] weighty tears, since he was old enough to determine to avenge his humiliation. The

English army trailed southwards in a sorry condition, with even the knights of Hainault reduced to retreating on foot, for many of their destriers had died, and others were too starved to bear the weight of their riders. At York the humiliated army disbanded. The total cost of the Weardale campaign has been estimated at seventy thousand pounds.[44] With its failure the prestige of the government and the personal popularity of Isabella and Mortimer sank very low.

King Robert now returned from Ireland to clinch his victory. With a large army which comprised the Scottish forces returned from the Weardale campaign, those that had accompanied the King to Ireland, and all of the fighting men who could be mustered speedily, King Robert invaded Northumberland. His conduct of this final campaign implied not a raid but an occupation. It was described with accuracy and economy by John Barbour.

> The King assembled all his might;
> None left he that were fit to fight.
> A mighty host assembled he,
> That he divided into three.
> To Norham did one part set out
> And laid a siege all round about
> And held the inmates close inside.
> Another part to Alnwick hied . . .
> Since he had many folk, the King
> Left these men to their siege-making
> And with the rest his way he sought
> From park to park, in search of sport,
> As though 'twere all his property!
> To many in his company
> The lands within Northumberland
> That lay the nearest to Scotland
> In fee and heritage gave he
> And for their seals they paid the fee.[45]

The siege of Norham was undertaken with engines designed by the Flemish engineer John Crab, who had proved his worth previously at Berwick. Douglas and Randolph laid siege to both Alnwick and Warkworth, and at Alnwick, as a further display of Scottish confidence, tournaments were held outside the walls. The King's sporting tour and grants of English lands to Scots implied, as Barbour suggested, that the land was already his own. The Scots were also creating a permanent presence in Cumberland, Westmorland and North Yorkshire. 'The threat to dismember the English kingdom had never seemed so real, and the unstable regime of Mortimer and Isabella was in no position to maintain further military catastrophes.'[46]

But at about this time a danger of a different kind threatened. After the Weardale campaign Donald of Mar did not join the invasion of Northumberland, but moved to the Welsh marches, probably to be near Edward II's place of imprisonment at Berkeley Castle.[47] Though the exact dates are uncertain, it was probably in late August or early September that Edward was rescued and spent a brief period at liberty. The deposed King was snatched from Berkeley by the brothers Thomas and Stephen Dunhewed, while Donald of Mar attempted to rouse sympathetic Welsh against Isabella and Mortimer's regime.[48] Had Edward remained at liberty, Donald might well have brought him to Robert the Bruce, to be restored to his throne under the most stringent conditions Robert might choose to impose, or since Edward III was now formally King, as a hostage to exact those terms from the minority government.

As it was, the unfortunate Edward II was recaptured and returned to Berkeley Castle where, it was reported, he died on 21 September 1327 of natural causes.[49] This official statement was not believed. Edward II had been a man of famously good health and strong constitution, and very quickly the rumour was rife that he had been murdered. The public display in Gloucester of his unblemished corpse did nothing to allay the rumour, but merely gave rise to the horrible suggestion that he had been slain with a red-hot iron thrust into the rectum, so that the body would show no visible sign of violence.[50]

Though the death of the deposed King secured Isabella and Mortimer against further plots on his behalf, the accusation of murder caused a strong backlash of public opinion against them, and almost certainly shortened their prospects of remaining in power. They made a final attempt to deflect attention from their troubles and shore up their fading authority by initiating a new campaign against the Scots. But a Parliament summoned at Lincoln at the end of September refused to vote any funds to finance the campaign,[51] and writs for military service issued as late as the first week of October were 'more for form's sake than from any real hope of saving the situation'.[52]

On 9 October 1327 Isabella and Mortimer appointed two envoys, Henry Percy, Lord of Alnwick, and William de Denum, to go to the King of Scots at the siege of Norham, to sue for peace.

17

———— |✳|✳|✳| ————

TREATY AND MARRIAGE

'. . . The envoys worked with speed
And in this manner soon agreed:
That war for ever be renounced;
And that a marriage be announced
Of David, Robert's son and heir . . .
With young Dame Joan of London Tower . . .
Thus peace was made where once was war.
The sieges were pursued no more.'

John Barbour, *The Bruce*[1]

WHEN EDWARD I died King Robert had been overcome with laughter, and had explained to his companions that he was not laughing unchristianly at the death of an enemy, but laughing for joy at Scotland's happier prospects. If Robert remembered that moment of optimism he might have done so with a grim smile, but it is unlikely that the death of Edward II would have seemed an occasion for laughter. The victory that followed it had been too hard-won. The apparently lightweight Edward of Caernarvon had proved an unexpectedly indomitable adversary. Though in many ways stupid, too obstinate and self-willed to command the respect of his magnates, whose final solution was to depose him, yet he had always been able to summon up enough support to campaign against the Scots, had clung to his father's belief that he was the rightful overlord of Scotland, and had held that conviction until death. Now that he was dead and English government was weak, King Robert's long-sought opportunity had come. It was not a moment for the joyous laughter of optimism, but a moment to strike a hard bargain, while Scotland's power was at its zenith, and before the power of

England could begin to revive. Robert, with his long experience of English ambitions and Plantagenet will-power, may well have feared that both would be displayed again when Edward III reached manhood. The aim of his peace process was to secure the independence of Scotland and the sovereignty of his son and his dynasty against all fore-seeable threats.

He responded to the English envoys with a list of six conditions to serve as the bases of peace negotiations, which were issued from Berwick on 18 October 1327. The six requirements were that King Robert should possess the kingdom of Scotland 'free, quit and entire' for himself and his heirs for ever, without the render of any homage; that King Robert's son and heir David should marry Edward III's younger sister, Joan of the Tower (born 1321); that no subject of the King of Scots should claim lands in England, nor any subject of the King of England claim lands in Scotland; that the King of Scots and his heirs would give military aid to the King of England and his heirs saving the alliance between Scotland and France, and that the King of England and his heirs would similarly give military aid to Scotland 'as good allies'; that King Robert would pay twenty thousand pounds within three years of peace being concluded; that King Edward would use his good offices to influence the Pope to release the King of Scots and his subjects from excommunication and interdict.[2]

Whowever drafted the reply on behalf of Edward III assumed the arrogant language of the previous reign, and implied that the Scots were suing for peace by declaring that only the second and fifth condi-tions were acceptable, and the King reserved judgement on the rest. The English were swiftly disabused of these pretentions. When Scots and English negotiators met at Newcastle during November and early December, the six conditions formed the bases of discussion, and other Scottish demands were introduced, including the surrender by England of all documents purporting to show that the English Crown possessed feudal superiority over Scotland.[3]

The negotiations at Newcastle successfully prepared the ground for the peace treaty. In February 1328 Scottish representatives arrived in York, under safe conduct, to be presented with the letters patent issued by the King himself and council in Parliament. This document con-ceded all that King Robert had fought for, and acknowledged his status as unequivocally as he could have desired:

To all Christ's faithful people who shall see these letters, Edward, by the grace of God King of England, Lord of Ireland, Duke of Aquitaine, greeting and peace everlasting in the Lord. Whereas we, and some of our predecessors, Kings of England, have endeavoured to establish rights of rule or dominion or superiority over the realm of Scotland, whence dire conflicts of wars waged have afflicted for a long time the Kingdoms of England and Scotland: we, having regard to the slaughter, disasters, crimes, destruction of churches and evils innumerable which in the course of such wars, have repeatedly befallen the subjects of both realms, and to the wealth with which each realm, if united by the assurance of perpetual peace, might abound to their mutual advantage, thereby rendering them more secure against the hurtful efforts of those conspiring to rebel or attack, whether from within or without; we will and grant by these presents, for us, our heirs and successors whatsoever, with the common advice, assent and consent of the prelates, princes, earls, barons, and the commons of our realm in our parliament, that the Kingdom of Scotland within its own proper marches as they were held and maintained in the time of King Alexander of Scotland, last deceased, of good memory, shall belong to our dearest ally and friend, the magnificent prince Lord Robert, by God's grace illustrious King of Scotland, and to his heirs and successors, separate in all things from the kingdom of England, whole, free and undisturbed in perpetuity, without any kind of subjection, service, claim or demand. And by these presents we denounce and demit to the King of Scotland, his heirs and successors, whatsoever right we or our predecessors have put forward in any way in bygone times to the aforesaid Kingdom of Scotland. And, for ourselves and our heirs and successors, we cancel wholly and utterly all obligations, conventions and compacts undertaken in whatsoever manner with our predecessors, at whatsoever times, by whatsoever Kings or inhabitants, clergy or laity, of the same Kingdom of Scotland, concerning the subjection of the realm of Scotland and its inhabitants. And wheresoever any letters, charters, deeds or instruments may be discovered bearing upon obligations, conventions, or compacts of this nature, we will that they be deemed cancelled, invalid, of no effect and void, and of no value or moment. And for the full peaceful and faithful observance of the foregoing, all and singular for all time we have given full power and special command by our other letters patent to our well-beloved and faithful Henry de Percy our kinsman and William de la Zouche of Ashby and to either of them make oath upon our soul. In testimony whereof we have caused these letters patent to be executed.[4]

As a comprehensive expression of all the Scottish demands, and as a model of lucidity, the document could not be bettered. It was presumably drafted in the course of the discussions at Newcastle, and the suggestion has been made that it could have been the work of the Scottish Chancellor, Bernard, Abbot of Arbroath.[5] Though the terms are too clear to need interpretation, two points of particular interest may be noticed: the juxtaposition of the references to 'King Alexander of Scotland, last deceased' and 'Lord Robert, by God's grace illustrious King of Scotland' implied the Bruce doctrine that Robert was Alexander's lawful successor and the kingship of John Balliol an English-imposed aberration; and the acknowledgement of Scotland's boundaries as being its 'proper marches' in the reign of Alexander III implied that these included the Isle of Man, but excluded the areas of northern England that the Scots had recently occupied.[6]

That the victorious Scots were ready to make such substantial concessions shows the urgency with which the peace process was now being pushed forward. King Robert was clearly desirous to bring it to a conclusion because his health was rapidly failing.

He remained in command of the situation, though he was confined to his bed in the abbey of Holyrood when the English commissioners arrived in Edinburgh on 10 March to conclude the peace. The ascendancy of the Scots was made clear by the fact that the commissioners travelled north to conclude the treaty on Scottish soil, but the Scottish concessions must mirror the King's haste to outwit death in finalizing his victory.

It may seem surprising that the King of Scots, having financed his war in part by exacting extortionate payments for truces from landholders, communities and religious houses in northern England, was now prepared to promise England the very large sum of twenty thousand pounds. This payment was probably to indemnify the King of England and his heirs for their loss of legal title in Scotland,[7] but the popular perception of it was probably as a war indemnity for destruction in northern England. The greater concession made by King Robert, however, was over the question of landholding in two kingdoms. He himself felt strongly that the problems caused by divided loyalties in the past should not be allowed to poison the future. Nonetheless, in the interests of concluding the peace amicably and swiftly, he gave way over the claims of a number of individuals known as 'the disinherited', who had been dispossessed of lands in one or other kingdom as a result of having chosen to support the other during the war, and who wished following the peace to seek reinstatement in their lost estates through the courts. Englishmen eager to take advantage of this concession were Henry de Percy and William de la Zouche, who as negotiators of the peace were strongly placed to press for it, and Henry de Beaumont, who had married the heiress of the earldom of Buchan. The most surprising representative of the disinherited Scots was Sir James Douglas, who claimed some lands in Northumberland.[8] Perhaps the 'disinherited' were displaying some confidence in a peaceful future, as well as covetousness to regain forfeited lands, but the King's preference for exclusive landholding in each kingdom obviously would have been the wiser course.

English eagerness to conclude the treaty amicably was also shown in obliging concessions additional to the original demands. According to the Lanercost Chronicle, King Edward III, 'acting on the pestilent advice of his mother', returned to the Scots the famous Black Rood, or crucifix, which had belonged to St Margaret of Scotland and had been regarded as one of the holiest treasures of the kingdom,[9] 'but the people of London would in no wise allow to be taken away from them the Stone of Scone, whereupon the Kings of Scotland used to be set at their coronation [sic] at Scone'.[10] That the Scots had not asked for it, and are not reported to have cared that its return was promised but not fulfilled, may suggest that it was regarded as a matter of little moment. The King, and the older among his adherents from the beginning of the reign, would have known if Edward I's most prized spoil of war was indeed a supposititious relic.

In the eyes of both English and Scots the most important clause of the treaty concerned the royal marriage, which was seen as the surest guarantee of future peace, a belief given some justification by the past, in which the English marriages of Alexander II and Alexander III were remembered as having kept Anglo-Scottish relations stable and amicable. The English government was particularly anxious that nothing should prevent the marriage from taking place, for if the next King of Scots did not have an English bride, the Franco-Scottish treaty ensured that he would find a wife in France. As an insurance against the Scots discovering a sudden preference for a French Queen, King Robert was asked to guarantee the payment of an indemnity of one hundred thousand pounds if the marriage of David and Joan had not taken place by Michaelmas 1338.[11] By that date David would have reached the age of fourteen, which was the legal age of consent, and therefore also of refusal. The enormous sum mentioned was symbolic of the importance of the match to both kingdoms, but in fact it was intended that the marriage of the two children should be solemnized without any delay.

In spite of the complexity, speed characterized the concluding phase of the treaty negotiations. On 17 March, one week after their arrival in Edinburgh, the English peace commissioners, the Bishops of Lincoln and Norwich, Sir Geoffrey Le Scrope, the English Chief Justice, Henry de Percy and William de la Zouche gathered in King Robert's bedchamber in the abbey of Holyrood, to conclude the treaty with him.

King Robert's moment of triumph was a sombre one. He lay on his bed disfigured by his skin disease and incapable of movement. The previous summer, in Ireland, he had been described as 'so feeble and so weak that . . . he cannot move anything except his tongue',[12] which must have been an exaggeration since he recovered sufficiently to go campaigning and hunting in Northumberland within a few weeks. But it suggests that he could have suffered a stroke and made an unexpectedly good recovery, and had since suffered another. However, his mind remained unimpaired, and no doubt the force of his will dominated the conclusion of the peace, just as his military prowess had dominated the war.

Around him were grouped many of the faithful companions who had fought with him since he claimed the throne, together with a representative gathering of the clergy and magnates of Scotland. James Douglas and Thomas Randolph, Earl of Moray, were beside him, with Sir Gilbert de la Haye, the Constable of Scotland, Sir Robert Keith the Marischal, Bishop Lamberton of St Andrews and Bernard, Abbot of Arbroath, the Chancellor, the group whose combined qualities of military skill, diplomacy and intellect had done so much to win Scotland's independence. Besides Moray, there were five earls: Duncan of Fife, the premier earl of Scotland, Patrick of Dunbar, Hugh of Ross, the King's brother-in-law, Donald of Mar, his nephew, and Murdoch of Menteith, who since revealing the Soules conspiracy had inherited the earldom. In addition to Lamberton there were six other bishops, and among the barons were Sir Andrew de Moray, the son of Wallace's companion in arms, who had lately married the King's widowed sister Christian.[13]

As a gathering, these men showed how conservative a struggle the war of independence had been. This was not a group of revolutionary new men, but of representatives of the old Celtic aristocracy and of the Norman, French and Flemish families established in Scotland since the days of David I and Malcolm IV. They illustrated how successfully Robert the Bruce had held together the society of thirteenth-century Scotland, in spite of the convulsion through which it had passed. In this sense he was indeed the true successor of Alexander III.

The Treaty of Edinburgh sealed in the King's Chamber in the Abbey of Holyrood on 17 March was ratified by King Edward III in Parliament at Northampton on 4 May 1328.

Immediately preparations began for the wedding of the King of Scots' son and the King of England's sister. In the course of the spring and early summer King Robert made a remarkable recovery, and planned to attend the wedding, which was to take place at Berwick in July. Apart from the fur-trimmed robes and the jewels ordered for the principal guests and the four-year-old bridegroom, the King ordered some new finery for himself. It would have been a great grief to him that the Queen would not be at his side to see their son married and, as he hoped, the future of the kingdom secured. Queen Elizabeth had died at the end of the previous October, having lived long enough to see her husband's ambition fulfilled, and to know that the English had sued for peace. Now her body lay beneath the choir of Dunfermline Abbey, in the tomb prepared for her husband and herself.[14]

At the beginning of July Queen Isabella set off for Scotland with her seven-year-old daughter, Joan of the Tower, accompanied by Mortimer, Earl Warenne, the young Earl of Ulster and the Bishops of Lincoln, Ely and Norwich, and a train of 'other English barons'.[15] King Edward III, increasingly restive under his mother's tutelage, and resentful of the influence of Mortimer, did not accompany them, having decided to show his opinion of the peace treaty by refusing to attend his sister's wedding.

No doubt King Robert correctly read this gesture of dissent as an ill-omen for the peaceful future that he was trying to create. But however it may have troubled his mind, he decided to neutralize the effect of the gesture by remaining absent himself. He gave out that he was prevented by illness from attending the wedding, and remained at Cardross. Perhaps, weakened and disfigured as he was, there was relief in being spared appearing before his people beside the young and vigorous King of England.

James Douglas and Thomas Randolph escorted David de Bruce to Berwick, and the marriage of the four-year-old bridegroom and his seven-year-old bride took place on 12 July, in the presence of Queen Isabella, her entourage and a great concourse of the nobility and clergy of Scotland.

John Barbour's account of the wedding concentrated on the festiv-ities that followed it, and the amity that he would have his readers believe had prevailed:

> Then mirth and gladness one might see,
> For joyous feasting made they then.
> The Scottish and the English men
> In joy and fellowship were seen
> With nought of enmity between
> They lingered long with feast and play
> And when twas time to go away
> The good queen left her daughter there
> In rich and royal state to fare.
> I trow, was not in many a day
> A lass so richly given away![16]

When Queen Isabella departed, Douglas and Randolph accompanied her and her escort to the border, before returning to bring David and his bride to visit the King at Cardross.

William de Burgh, Earl of Ulster, had remained in Scotland, and in August 1328 King Robert made his last journey outside his own kingdom to escort the young Earl of Ulster to be installed in his

earldom. Under the terms of the peace treaty, King Robert had undertaken not to assist Edward III's enemies in Ireland, but he was not
infringing the treaty since William de Burgh, like his grandfather,
remained the King of England's liegeman and ally. The King of Scots'
support in helping him to take control of his troubled inheritance could
be seen as an additional gesture of reconciliation, since Earl William in
return might be expected to act as a friendly neighbour to Scotland
when his young cousin David became King.[17]

Edward III, despite his disturbing behaviour in refusing to attend the
royal wedding, also showed apparent goodwill in fulfilling his treaty
obligation to use his influence with the Pope on behalf of Scotland's
reconciliation with the Church. It was a gesture that cost him little and
gratified the Scots to whom, indeed, he would give little cause for complaint until he had received full payment of the twenty thousand
pounds promised by the treaty.[18] In the meantime, on 15 October 1328,
the Pope released King Robert and his subjects from excommunication
and interdict.

The King had long endured his excommunication in the knowledge
that it was politically motivated and unjustly protracted for political
reasons. Yet, given that he was a man of conventional faith and deep
piety, it still could not fail to be an oppressive spiritual burden. The
lifting of the excommunication would have given him a profound sense
of release in the assurance of being at peace with God.

No doubt it was both the desire to give thanks for his spiritual reconciliation and to prepare himself for death that led him to make a
pilgrimage from Cardross to the shrine of St Ninian of Whithorn on
its remote peninsula in Galloway, during the last months of his life. He
had always venerated the saints of Scotland, notably Saints Fillan and
Columba, whose reliquaries had been brought to the field of
Bannockburn, but St Ninian may also have been associated in his mind
with his greatest victory, since St Ninian's kirk stood close to the
battlefield. It is possible, too, that in the early days of the reign, as a fugitive king whose subjects were reduced to a handful of warriors, he may
have visited the shrine to pray for success. Between February and April
1329 he had himself carried south by way of Girvan, Lochinch (then
called Inchmichael, where he paused for more than a month), Glenluce
and Monreith to Whithorn.[19] The slowness of the journey speaks for
the weakness of the King. He remained four or five days at the shrine

in fasting and prayer, before returning, possibly by way of Glen Trool, the site of his earliest victory, and Turnberry Castle, where his son now had an independent household, to Cardross.[20]

After his return, with his death obviously imminent, letters were sent out summoning the magnates of Scotland to his bedside, a summons received and obeyed with universal lamentation. The King of Scots died at Cardross on 7 June 1329.

ROBERT THE BRUCE:
HERO KING AND MYTHIC HERO

'Hic iacet invictus Robertus rex benedictus
Qui sua gesta legit repetet quot bella peregit
Ad libertatem perduxit per probitatem
regnum Scotorum. Nunc vivat in arce polorum.'

('Here lies the blessed invincible King Robert.
Who reads of his deeds will relive his many wars.
By his integrity he led the Kingdom of the Scots
to liberty. Now may he live in Heaven.')

Epitaph of Robert the Bruce[1]

IN THE PERCEPTIVE judgement of a twentieth-century historian of King Robert's reign, 'in the restrained language of Froissart, or the more poignant recital of . . . Barbour, the deathbed scene at Cardross recalls the *Morte d'Arthur*'.[2] Just as the passing of Arthur conveys the British King to a mystic realm of immortal heroes, the passing of Robert the Bruce marks the first phase of his partial metamorphosis from hero king to mythic hero. According to Froissart's narrative:

King Robert of Scotland, who had been a very valiant knight, waxed old, and was attacked with so severe an illness that he saw his end was approaching; he therefore summoned together all the chiefs and barons in whom he most confided, and after having told them that he should never get the better of this sickness, he commanded them, upon their honour and loyalty, to keep and preserve faithfully and entire the kingdom for his son David . . .

He after that called to him the gallant lord James Douglas, and said to him in presence of the others, 'My dear friend lord James Douglas, you know that I have had much to do, and have suffered many troubles, during the time I have lived, to support the rights of my crown: at the time that I was most occupied I made a vow, the non-accomplishment of which gives me much uneasiness – I vowed that if I could finish my wars in such a manner that I might govern peaceably, I would go and make war against the enemies of our Lord Jesus Christ, and the adversaries of the Christian faith. To this point my heart has always leaned; but our Lord was not willing, and gave me so much to do in my lifetime . . . followed by this heavy sickness, that, since my body cannot accomplish what my heart wishes, I will send my heart instead of my body to fulfil my vow. And, as I do not know any one knight so gallant or enterprising, or better formed to complete my intentions than yourself, I beg and entreat of you, dear and special friend, as earnestly as I can, that you would have the goodness to undertake this expedition for the love of me, and to acquit my soul to our Lord and Saviour; for I have that opinion of your nobleness and loyalty, that if you undertake it, it cannot fail of success – and I shall die more contented; but it must be excuted as follows: –

'I will that as soon as I shall be dead, you take my heart from my body, and have it well embalmed . . . you will then deposit your charge at the Holy Sepulchre of our Lord, where he was buried, since my body cannot go there . . . and wherever you pass, you will let it be known that you bear the heart of King Robert of Scotland, which you are carrying beyond the seas by his command, since his body cannot go thither'.

All those present began bewailing bitterly; and when the lord James could speak, he said

'Gallant and noble king, I return you a hundred thousand thanks for the high honour you do me, and for the valuable and dear treasure with which you intrust me; and I will most willingly do all that you command me with the utmost loyalty in my power; never doubt it, however I may feel myself unworthy of such a high distinction.'

The King replied, 'Gallant knight, I thank you – you promise it me then?'

'Certainly, Sir, most willingly,' answered the knight. He then gave his promise upon his knighthood.

The King said 'Thanks be to God! for I shall now die in peace, since I know that the most valiant and accomplished knight of my kingdom will perform that for me which I am unable to do myself'.[3]

John Barbour tells the story with significant differences. The King, having summoned his lords to his bedside, addresses his last request to them collectively:

> He said 'Sirs, such now is my state,
> For me there is but one sure fate,
> And that is death; that I must bear
> As all men must, without a fear.
> I thank my God, that He has sent
> Me time, while living, to repent,
> For through my strife I bear the guilt
> Of blood that has been freely spilt,
> And harmless men that have been slain.
> Therefore this illness and this pain
> My recompense I take to be.
> When I was in prosperity
> Within my heart a vow I made
> Against God's foes to make crusade,
> And thus to expiate my sin.
> But since He now takes me to Him,
> So that my body cannot do
> That which my heart was purposed to,
> I would my heart were thither sent
> Wherein was nurtured that intent.
> Therefore, I pray you, everyone,
> That from yourselves ye choose me one,
> A man of honour, wisdom, might,
> And of his hand a noble knight,
> Against God's foes to bear my heart
> When soul and body death shall part'.[4]

The King does not request that his heart be buried in the Holy Sepulchre, and the choice of the knight who shall carry the King's heart to fight against the enemies of Christ is left to the lords. Barbour goes on to relate that, having heard the King's request, the lords all wept, but the King urged them to calm their grief and come to a speedy decision. So they left the room to confer, and unanimously nominated Sir James Douglas. When they returned to tell him, Robert rejoiced that they had elected the very man he himself would have chosen. Barbour's narrative then concurs with Froissart that Douglas thanked the King for the great honour of entrusting him with his heart, and faithfully promised to fulfil his request.

Though Barbour's historical accuracy seldom falters, Froissart's version seems on the face of it more convincing, since if King Robert desired his dearest friend to fulfil his vow for him, it seems more likely that he would have requested him directly, rather than leaving the matter to the chance of election. However, Barbour's version may be designed to enhance the prestige of Douglas, his secondary hero, by representing him both as the King's choice and the unanimous choice of the magnates. The cynical suggestion of a later historian is that Douglas was entrusted with the King's heart because Thomas Randolph, Earl of Moray, would be Guardian of the Realm for the child King David, and 'the dying King may have reflected that after he should pass away, there would be no-one to keep these fiery spirits in harmony . . . and it might be well that Douglas should have his hands full elsewhere'.[5]

There is also the question of exactly what King Robert desired should be done with his heart: if, as Froissart reported, he asked that it should be buried in the Holy Sepulchre, James Douglas spectacularly failed to fulfil his request; but if, as Barbour reported, he desired that it should be carried into battle against the enemies of Christ, then Douglas faithfully fulfilled his promise. Here Barbour seems likely to be the better guide: fidelity to the King was Douglas's defining characteristic. However, the narratives concur in presenting the King as the would-be Crusader, the repentant Christian hero who bequeaths the fulfilment of his vow to the noblest knight in the kingdom before quitting the world. Both the chivalry-loving prose chronicler and the historically minded epic poet strike the same note of high romance, in which Douglas undertakes to fulfil the King's vow, in the manner of an Arthurian quest.

After the King's death, his heart was taken from his body, embalmed, and given to Sir James Douglas, who had it encased in a casket of silver and enamel, and wore it on a chain around his neck, until his vow should have been fulfilled.

The King's body, also embalmed, was wrapped in a shroud of linen embroidered with gold thread,[6] and carried in procession from Cardross, past the foot of Loch Lomond, by way of Dunipace and Cambuskenneth, to Dunfermline, and there buried in the choir beside the body of his Queen. At about the time of her death he had ordered a black-and-white marble monument, which had been carved in Paris. It was now in place, surrounded by an iron rail, gilded with 1,100 books of gold leaf, bought in York.[7] After the King's interment a 'temporary chapel of baltic timber' was placed over his tomb; this would have been to support the *chapelle ardente* of burning candles at the Requiem Mass.[8]

As news of the death of King Robert spread through the kingdom, it was received with universal grief and extravagant demonstrations of mourning:

> Then might one see men tear their hair,
> And wring their hands in deep despair;
> And knights were seen to weep full sore
> And madly rend the clothes they wore;
> Lamenting for his nobleness,
> His wisdom, honour, manliness,
> Above all for his company
> That he bestowed so courteously.
> 'Alas,' they said, 'our leader just
> Our king in whom was all our trust,
> Our strength, our wisdom in defence
> All these have now been taken hence . . .
> Alas! What shall we say or do?
> For while he was alive 'tis true
> That all our neighbours feared our hand
> In many a far and foreign land
> Our valiant exploits won renown;
> And this was due to him alone!'[9]

They lamented him as a man, for his human qualities and his generosity of spirit, and as a king for his personal renown, which had acted as a rampart for his kingdom. They acknowledged that

> . . . better ruler than was he
> In any country ne'er could be.[10]

They lamented the finality of his loss, for his body had been too decayed and diseased, his death and burial too public, to permit the arising of a myth that like King Arthur he had been taken from the world, and would return at the kingdom's greatest need. Such myths have attached themselves to tangible historical figures, such as Frederick Barbarossa and James IV of Scotland. Even so uninspiring a king as Edward II, because of the mystery surrounding his death, became the subject of a more prosaic survival myth: it began to be said of him that he had never been recaptured and murdered, but had wandered Christendom as a pilgrim and ended his days as a hermit in Lombardy.[11]

In the case of Robert the Bruce, the mythopoeic imagination of his people, limited by the indisputability of his death, concentrated upon inventing stories that seemed characteristic of him in that they illumined his heroic character, and continued to enhance it while remaining within the bounds of the credible.

The adventures of Sir James Douglas with the King's heart blended reality with the making of myth.

Early in 1330 Douglas set sail from Montrose, with a company of knights, including Sir William de St Clair of Roslin, Sir William Keith of Galston, Sir Alan Cathcart and the brothers Sir Robert and Sir Walter Logan, with twenty-six squires attending them. His first port of call was Sluys, where his ship remained twelve days. Douglas stayed the whole time on board 'where he kept a magnificent table, with music of trumpets and drums, as if he had been King of Scotland'.[12] This was to signify that the King was present, in the presence of the heart. From Flanders, Douglas had a stormy voyage to Spain, before entering the Guadalquirin and anchoring in the harbour of Seville. He had letters of safe conduct from Edward III, who had also provided a letter of recommendation to King Alfonso XI of Castile and Leon.[13]

Alfonso was at war with the Moorish Prince of Granada, who had imported reinforcements from Morocco.[14] He welcomed the Scottish knights, and Douglas saw in this campaign an opportunity to fulfil his vow, and carry King Robert's heart into battle against these infidels. King Alfonso gave Douglas command of the foreign knights who had come to Spain to fight against the Moors. They were all willing to serve under a leader of such prowess, and according to Barbour the Englishmen among them showed particular honour to their erstwhile enemy.[15]

On 25 March 1330 the Spanish army went into battle against the Moors at Tebas de Ardales. No doubt Alfonso and his countrymen were accustomed to the tactics of the Moorish cavalry, which would charge, then turn again in apparent flight, before wheeling once more to attack unsuspecting pursuers. Sir James Douglas and the knights under his command had not encountered such fluidity of movement before. They charged the Moors, and continued to pursue a force that had apparently broken before them. Their pursuit carried them far ahead of the main body of King Alfonso's army, when the Moors returned with the force of a whirlwind, and cut them to pieces.

Froissart, shocked that the knights had been isolated among the enemy, wrote:

> He [Douglas] thought that he should be supported by the Spaniards; but in this he was mistaken, for not one that day followed his example. The gallant knight and all his companions were surrounded by the enemy; they performed prodigies of valour, but . . . they were all killed. It was a great misfortune that they were not assisted by the Spaniards.[16]

According to Barbour, Douglas was killed in an attempt to save the life of Sir William de St Clair.[17] When his body was found, the heart of King Robert was still on the chain around his neck. Sir William Keith of Galston, who had been prevented by a previously broken arm from taking part in the battle, took charge of the heart. He carried it back to Scotland, where it was buried in the abbey of Melrose. Possibly, even if Douglas and his companions had intended to travel as far as the Holy Land to fight the infidel, they had known that this was King Robert's desire for the final disposal of his heart.[18] Surely, if he had stated his wish for it to be buried in the Holy Sepulchre, Sir William Keith would have fulfilled Douglas's vow to do as he desired, and taken it there.

Keith and other survivors of Douglas's retinue, in deep grief at his death, disposed of his body in the manner the Teutonic knights had

. devised for those who were slain far from home. The body was boiled until the flesh parted from the bones; the flesh was buried in consecrated ground, and the bones were taken back to Scotland, for burial in the chapel of St Bride at Douglas.[19]

Another version of his death became current in the middle of the following century, the 'Myth of the Thrown Heart', which is thought to have originated in a Scottish vernacular alliterative poem, 'The Buke of the Howlat', by Sir Richard Holland (c. 1420–85), glorifying the deeds of the Douglases. The poem tells that when Douglas and his knights charged the Moors, he threw the heart ahead of him, into their ranks.

> Amang the hethin men the hert hardely he slang,
> Said: 'Wend on as thou was wont,
> Throw the batel in bront,
> Ay formast in the front
> Thy fays amang'.[20]

Douglas then fought on, gaining ground until he reached the heart, and reverently gathered it up again (thus accounting for the fact that it was found on his body after his death).

The story appealed to popular imagination, and won general belief, probably because it enshrined two well-remembered truths: that Douglas (in popular memory 'the good lord James') was recklessly brave, and that Robert the Bruce was always foremost in the fight. It continues to be believed, and is still quite frequently related as a true anecdote, even though it is inherently unlikely, if not impossible. Douglas would not have risked the treasured heart which he had guarded with such reverence. But even had he, in the ardour of battle, hurled it into the mêlée in which he was about to meet his death, his chances of recovering it would have been negligible. Possibility, however, played no part in its mythic appeal.

It is impossible to know whether Sir Richard Holland invented the 'Myth of the Thrown Heart', or whether he incorporated into his poem a myth that was already current. Perhaps one of the essential qualities of a myth is the uncertainty of its origin. But what is certain is that if this myth were already in existence in John Barbour's lifetime, he rejected it.

Barbour's original manuscript has disappeared, and the earliest surviving copies date from 1487 and 1489; the earlier is in the Library of St

John's College Cambridge, the later in the National Library of Scotland.
Both copies were made by a man named John Ramsay, probably
identifiable with a monk of that name who later became Prior of the
Charterhouse, Perth. The first few pages of the Cambridge manuscript
are missing; the Edinburgh manuscript concludes with the statement
that it was 'rapidly written' at the request of Simon Lochmalony of
Ouchtremunsy (Auchter Moonsie), Vicar of Moonsie, Fife.[21] These
two texts are described as being near identical, with line or word vari-
ants probably accounted for by the scribal haste admitted at the end of
the second copy. Neither contains the Myth of the Thrown Heart.

   The first printed edition of 'The Bruce' appeared in Edinburgh in
1570, and there is no known surviving copy. The next edition was
printed by Hart of Edinburgh in 1616, with a further edition in 1620.
Hart's editions contain the Myth of the Thrown Heart in an interpolated passage of twelve lines:

> And as he entered in the fray,
> What Douglas did I now shall say
> The heart that round his neck was hung
> Amidst the battlefield he flung
> A full stone's throw in front, and said:
> 'Brave heart that ever foremost led
> Forward! as thou wast wont. And I
> Shall follow thee, or else shall die!'
> So fought he, and no halt would brook
> Until the heart he overtook,
> And gathered it full reverently
> Thus ever in the field did he.[22]

As a result of its inclusion in the printed editions of Barbour which
made 'The Bruce' known to a wider public, the lines were long accepted
as authentic Barbour, and, with the poet's reputation for accuracy, as
authentic history. It was F.J. Amours, editor of 'The Buke of the
Howlat' (1446), who suggested that this poem was the origin of the
Myth of the Thrown Heart, and source of the interpolated passage in
Barbour. This was accepted by W.M. Mackenzie, whose scholarly
edition of 'The Bruce' long remained definitive.

   A modern biographer of Sir James Douglas has also pointed out that in the interpolation 'Douglas is made to address the heart – and thus, symbolically, Robert – as "thou". But in all conversations between Robert and Douglas related in the manuscripts of The Bruce, Douglas addresses the King as "you" and is addressed as "thou". This supports the assumption that, while Barbour wrote at a time when the correct social uses of the second persons singular and plural were still understood, the interpolated passage was composed at a later date, when they had been forgotten.'[23] It also demonstrates that Barbour, though writing in the Scots vernacular, knew that King Robert and Douglas had spoken French, in which Robert would have *tutoyé* Douglas, and Douglas addressed the King as '*vous*'. By the time Holland wrote 'The Buke of the Howlat' the use of French among the Scots aristocracy had disappeared, and neither he nor the interpolator of Barbour may have known that the King and Douglas had spoken it.

It may disappoint many readers that the story of the throwing of the heart, like the story of King Robert's encounter with the spider, has to be regarded as a myth. These two stories, together with that of his slaying of Sir Henry de Bohun on the eve of Bannockburn, compose a trio of vivid vignettes which stand out from the dense texture of history like manuscript illuminations. If one is true, and two are mythic, this also illustrates how Robert the Bruce is in part a historic and in part a mythic hero. The slaying of Bohun illustrates the historic truth of his prowess as a warrior (also illustrated by many earlier incidents from his fugitive days, which Barbour probably decided to take on trust). The mythic incidents, true to the nature of myth, enshrine a truth about the hero within a fiction: the episode of the spider encapsulates the metamorphosis of the character of Robert the Bruce in adversity; the Myth of the Thrown Heart holds the memory of a war leader who led by example:

> Ay formast in the front
> Thy fays amang.

Robert the Bruce, as the victor of a long war of independence, and the restorer of Scotland's freedom and monarchy, was regarded as a hero in his own lifetime, even before his victory was complete. But ironically, a great contribution to the creation of his mythic status arose from his failure to secure the future independence of his kingdom, despite the careful preparations he had made, and the safeguards that he hoped his peace treaty with England had contained. These hopes proved vain, but King Robert's achievements gained more lustre as his son floundered more and more deeply into difficulty and misfortune.

David II had a difficult inheritance, because it is always difficult to be the child of a great person, and comparisons can be damning. He had a triple disadvantage: firstly, that he succeeded at the age of five, with the inevitability of a long minority; secondly, that this necessitated a regency, leaving Scotland at a disadvantage in dealings with England, which had a strong young king just approaching adulthood; and thirdly that he succeeded with the onset of the sense of anticlimax that follows victory, and leads to post-war malaise and cost-counting. The boy King's first Guardian was Thomas Randolph, Earl of Moray, who died in 1332.[24] He was succeeded by King Robert's nephew Donald, Earl of Mar, whose record of long friendship with Edward II and late reconciliation with Robert led him to be little trusted by the magnates of Scotland. But his tenure of authority was brief, for he was killed in battle at Dupplin Moor, in 1332.

Scotland's new troubles had begun in September 1330, when Edward III overthrew the regime of his mother Queen Isabella and Roger Mortimer, in a coup d'état at Nottingham Castle. Mortimer was executed, and Isabella, to whom Edward's feelings were inevitably ambivalent, was sent to live in retirement.[25] Edward III eased his conscience for the manner of his accession by constructing a magnificent tomb for his father in Gloucester Abbey (now Gloucester Cathedral), which for a time became a place of pilgrimage. Edward III had indicated his resentment of the Treaty of Edinburgh by refusing to attend the wedding of David II and Joan of the Tower. His subjects were now calling it 'the shameful peace', so he had their full support in his decision to repudiate it, in 1332, on the grounds that having been negotiated on his behalf while he was a minor, it was invalid.

He revived the claim to overlordship of Scotland, and in Edward Balliol, the son of the erstwhile King John, found a man who was prepared to become King of Scots on the same terms, as a vassal of England. An invasion of Scotland on his behalf resulted in the defeat of the army of David II at Dupplin Moor in 1332, following which Edward Balliol went through a coronation ceremony at Scone. But the supporters of David II rallied and drove him out of Scotland before the end of the year. Edward III came to his aid, and their combined forces defeated the Scots at Halidon Hill, near Berwick, in July 1333. The situation of Scotland seemed desperate, and King David and his Queen were sent to France for safety, while the King's loyal supporters fought a second War of Independence with all the tenacity King Robert had shown in the earlier years of the century, but without his genius.

By 1341 it was deemed safe for the King and Queen of Scots to return to their kingdom. But it was not long before David was required to repay French hospitality. By now Edward III had advanced his claim to the throne of France,[26] and defeated the French in 1346 at the battle of Crécy. In accordance with the Franco-Scottish alliance, David II, now required to make war on behalf of his ally, invaded England and was defeated and captured at the battle of Neville's Cross, near Durham. He spent the next eleven years at the English court, as a royally entertained prisoner, before being ransomed by his subjects at ruinous expense. He died childless in 1371, to be succeeded by Robert Stewart, now aged fifty-four, the son of King Robert's daughter Marjorie, and the first of the long line of Stewart kings.

David II has had his defenders among modern historians, but whether he was an incompetent king or an underrated one, he was certainly unheroic, and his lack-lustre reign made the heroic reign of his father shine all the more brilliantly in the collective memory of the nation.

Even the darker shadows on the portrait of Robert the Bruce contributed to the development of the heroic myth. The late belief that he had suffered from leprosy also became part of it. In Barbour's words the King confessed that he believed his sickness to be a punishment for his sin – therefore that the sickness should have been leprosy made it an appropriately terrible form of suffering to expiate the murder of Comyn, and the deaths in war of the innocent who burdened the King's conscience. Only the worst of diseases would serve to cleanse the hero.

Barbour himself did not believe that Robert the Bruce had suffered from leprosy; he imputed the breakdown of his health to the long-term effects of his fugitive years and his early campaigns, when he had lived out in all the rigours of the Scottish weather.

Leprosy was first mentioned by the Lanercost Chronicler, and later by Froissart.[27] But descriptions of King Robert's semi-paralysed condition before his death suggest that a stroke or a series of strokes directly caused it. The skin disease from which he was suffering, though painful and disfiguring, does not appear to have been necessarily a contributory cause.

King Robert's own physicians evidently recognised that the disease was not leprosy, even if they were not certain what it was, for he was not segregated from his wife, children, courtiers or diplomatic contacts, which as a leper he would have been. For example, a king who was diagnosed as a leper, Baldwin IV of Jerusalem, though he continued to reign officially, was regarded as unable to rule, and was segregated from his subjects.[28] The fate of the unprivileged leper was to be an outcast from society. A retrospective diagnosis of King Robert's disease is not possible, in the absence of any description of his appearance and symptoms, so suggestions can only be guesswork. Medieval physicians named a skin disease as 'Morphew', sometimes popularly called 'white leprosy', which they recognized as being different and less dangerous than leprosy proper, which did not cause sufferers to be segregated. But what this disease was is not certain. Another possibility is extremely severe psoriasis, which was occasionally mistaken for leprosy, but if it were King Robert's disease, was successfully differentiated.

However, there was a widespread belief in the Middle Ages that disease was a punishment for sin, and leprosy especially was seen as punishment.[29] So King Robert's dying speech in Barbour that he took his sickness as the recompense of his sins would itself contribute to disseminating the belief that he had died a leper, and thus expiated the crimes that might otherwise have detracted from his heroic image. Like the Myth of the Thrown Heart, the myth of Robert the Bruce's leprosy continues to be believed and repeated, and even unofficially confirmed by literature, as in Edwin Muir's poem 'Scotland's Winter', where he writes of

> ... Bruce on his burial bed
> Where he lies white as may
> With wars and leprosy ...[30]

With foundations laid by the memories of his own deeds, built upon by legend, literature and the dispiriting contrast provided by the reign of his son, Robert became both a revered historical figure and a mythic hero. In this he bears less resemblance to the shadowy King Arthur than to other historic figures to whom a mythic dimension has been added. There is an historic Alexander the Great, an historic Charlemagne, an historic King Alfred, whose true achievements and failures have been subjected to scholarly examination and analysis. And there is a mythic Alexander who tames the unmanageable horse Bucephalus, a mythic Charlemagne who hears the horn of Roland from afar, a mythic King Alfred who burns the cakes while planning the liberation of his country from the Danes, just as there is a mythic Robert the Bruce who learns the lesson of perseverance from a spider.

The persistence of these unhistoric legends should not be deplored. For if it is a function of historians to preserve, extend and reinterpret accurate knowledge of the past, it is a function of collective memory to keep alive an imaginative appreciation of a nation's heroes.

NOTES AND SOURCES

ABBREVIATIONS

RBCRS: *Robert Bruce and the Community of the Realm of Scotland*, Prof. G.W.S. Barrow
WB: *The Wars of the Bruces*, Colm MacNamee
VES: *Vita Edwardi Secundi*
APS: *Acts of Parliament of Scotland*, ed. C. Innes.
RRS: *Regesta Regum Scottorum, Vol V*, ed. A.A.M. Duncan.
CDS: *Calendar of Documents relating to Scotland*, ed. J. Bain.

Other works which are abbreviated by author's name (e.g. Stones) can be found in the bibliography, or at first mention in the notes.

INTRODUCTION — HISTORY AND MYTH

1. E.L.G. Stones, *Anglo-Scottish Relations 1174–1328*, Introduction, p. xix.
2. See note 27 for Chapter 1.

PART ONE: A CLAIM TO THE THRONE

Chapter 1 – The Royal Allies

1. E.L.G. Stones, *Anglo-Scottish Relations 1174–1328* p. 85.
2. Lord Cooper, *The numbers and distribution of the population of medieval Scotland*, SHR XXVI, 2–9.
3. Staniland, NAMP – NMS p. 30, 33. These types of fur were the bellies, whole skins, and backs of red squirrels.
4. CCR 1251–3, pp. 12, 14 cit. Staniland NAMP
5. St. Altars Chronicle cit. A.M.M. Duncan *Scotland: the Making of the Kingdom*, p. 560.
6. Ibid., p. 556. Nicholson thinks the motto was chosen simply because it contained the word 'columba' – a reference to Scotland's highly regarded saint, and that otherwise 'the relevance is obscure' loc. cit. ff. But surely it was chosen as a good maxim for a young ruler to learn, and if a play on words was intended, it was appropriate because St Columba had been the advisor of his king, Áedán mac Gábrain, one of the most powerful and successful of early Scottish kings, and 'simple' in the sense of being honest.
7. Staniland, op. cit., p. 33.

8. Ibid., p. 43.

9. Alfonso and Eleanor were both the children of Ferdinand III of Castile, Alfonso by his first wife and Eleanor by his second.

10. Edward heard about the death of his baby son John, and shortly afterwards about the death of his father. He was much more upset about the latter and said 'that it was easy to beget sons, but that the loss of a good father was irreplaceable', Michael Prestwich, *Edward I*, p. 52.

11. Duncan op cit., p. 503. The leading members of the government at this point were William Comyn Earl of Menteith and Robert de Ros, Lord of Wark, who was Henry's representative, but seems to have identified himself with Scottish interests.

12. Nicholson, op. cit., p. 574.

13. David II act. 5, 1329; James II act. 6, 1437; James III act. 8, 1460; James V act. 13 months, 1513; Mary, Queen of Scots act. 1 week, 1542; James VI act. 13 months, 1567.

14. Otherwise they could claim the antithesis of a saintly ancestress by citing the legend of a diabolical ancestress, in Melusin, wife of Falere Nerva, Count of Anjou, who was said to have been the daughter of Satan.

15. M.D. Legge *La Piere D'Escoce* SHR 38 (1959), pp. 109–113.

16. Perhaps this was why Henry III interceded for the imprisoned diplomats. Duncan op cit., p. 577.

17. Ibid., p. 578.

18. Ibid.

19. Ibid., p. 580.

20. Ibid., p. 581. Henry III had attempted to prevent this, by advising Alexander not to undertake the expedition. He would have preferred his son-in-law not to acquire the strategically important Isles, but he could not prevent him.

21. When the estates of the Norwegian Crown were transferred to James III of Scotland, as the dowry of his bride, Margaret of Denmark, [whose father, Christian I, was also King of Norway and Sweden].

22. 'The mood of Edward's troops was one of savage revenge, epitomized by the crude mutilation of Simon de Montfort's corpse. His head and genitals were sent off in triumph to Roger Mortimer's wife at Wigmore, who was no doubt well pleased with the grisly parcel' [Roger Mortimer was Edward's ally in the civil war], Prestwich, *Edward I*, p. 51.

23. Prestwich op. cit., pp. 68–69.

24. Duncan op. cit., pp. 589–590. Edward of Lancaster claimed the right to carry the sword *Curtana* and was refused, as a result of which he seems to have boycotted the ceremony – as his name is not on a list of magnates who attended, Prestwich op. cit., p. 90. Perhaps it was intended that Alexander should carry it.

25. Lanercost, p. 9. He got his information from another Minorite Friar, the

Queen's confessor, who said that after she received the last sacrament she spoke to no-one else 'unless perhaps her husband happened to be present' – which implies that Alexander attended her deathbed.

26. PRO Close Roll 6 Edward I (C 54/95) m.d. 5 (C). Printed in Rymer I ii 563; calendared in Bain II no. 127; parallel text Latin/English in E.L.G. Stones' *Anglo-Scottish Relations 1174–1328*, pp. 78–81.

27. Nat. Lib. Scot. MS Adv. 34. 1. 3a (Cartulary of Dunfermline), f. 39. (N); printed in Registrum de Dunfermelyne ed. Cosmo Innes (1842) p. 217; E.L.G. Stones *Anglo-Scottish Relations 1174–1328*, pp. 80–81.

28. Ibid., pp. 82–83.

29. Lanercost, pp. 22–23.

30. Stones, op cit., pp. 84–85. Edward's words survive because they are quoted in Alexander's letter – in which he is thanked for this message.

31. Ibid.

32. 'Acknowledgement of the Maid of Norway as Heir of Alexander III', 1284, Donaldson (ed.) *Scottish Historical Documents*, pp. 37–38.

33. *Scotichronicon* ed. Watt. Vol. V, Bk. X, Ch. 41, p. 421.

34. Ibid., p. 419.

35. Lanercost, p. 41.

36. Ibid.

37. Historians of Scotland, Vol. II, p. 265. Wyntoun Bk VII, Ch. X, f. 190 of MS.

38. Lanercost, p. 40.

39. Lanercost, pp. 43–44.

Chapter 2 – The Lords of Annandale

1. Motto of the Burgh of Lochmaben.

2. She had been christened Edith, but exchanged this Anglo-Saxon name for a Norman one.

3. '... chiefs relied on the concept of the patriarchal authority of a chief as bestowing a notional fatherhood on them.' And 'in the course of [the 17th] century as surnames replaced patronymics, new clansmen would frequently take the surname of their adoptive chief, with the result that their decendants soon came to believe that they also shared their chief's ancestry.' Bingham, *Beyond the Highland Line*, pp. 95, 96.

4. Kipling, 'Sir Richard's Song', *Puck of Pook's Hill*.

5. Graham Ritchie, *Normans in Scotland*, p. 157 cit. Barrow, *The Kingdom of the Scots*, p. 319.

6. 'The genealogy cannot be accepted' Æneas McKay DNB Vol. III, p. 114. Under Robert de Bruce I (d. 1094?); 'the first Robert Bruce – Robert de Brus – got his name from Brus or Bruis, now Brix, a few miles south of Cherbourg' Barrow, *Robert Bruce and the Community of the Realm of Scotland*, p. 20; 'What I believe is not known is the origin of the Bruce family in

Normandy itself, but the fact that Brix and its forest were important parts of the ducal demesne and the high favour which Robert de Brus I enjoyed with Henry I suggest that the Bruces were closely related to the ducal house, either by blood or service or both', Barrow, *The Kingdom of the Scots*, p. 322.

7. Vide supra [note preceding].

8. R. McN. Scott *Robert the Bruce*, p. 10.

9. Æneas McKay, DNB, Vol. III, p. 114. The third of these four sisters married a distinguished English knight, Sir Marmaduke de Tweng, who fought in the English armies at Stirling Bridge and Bannockburn. J.A. Mackay, *Robert the Bruce* genealogical table, pp. 14–15.

10. RBCRS, p. 20.

11. *Annals of the four masters*, cit. Thomas Hamilton, DNB Vol. XII, p. 838.

12. Lanercost, pp. 112–113.

13. Ibid., p. 112.

14. RBCRS, p. 23.

15. Ibid., p. 25.

16. Lanercost, p. 114.

17. Ibid.

18. RBCRS, pp. 25–6.

19. *Scotichronicon*, Vol. V, Bk. X, Ch. 29, pp. 383–85.

20. Mackay, *Robert Bruce King of Scots*, p. 21.

21. RBCRS, p. 26.

22. Lanercost, pp. 111–12. The monastic chronicler's approval of the man who respected the clergy parallels Wyntoun's approval of Alexander III for the same reason 'relygious men he honoured aye' vide supra Ch. I, p. 19.

23. RBCRS, p. 26 Ch. II, ref. note 30. [note is on p. 332]. There is a contrary statement that King Robert was born within his father's manor of Writtle in Essex. The origin of this is the chronicle of Geoffrey le Baker of Swinbrooke, which is riddled with errors: viz, that Alexander III had no sons but three daughters who married 1) John Balliol, 2) John Comyn, 3) Robert de Bruce (Born at Writtle in Essex) who afterwards became King of Scotland. Such a farrago of nonsense does not encourage belief in any statement about who was born where.

24. RBCRS, p. 26.

25. John Mair [or Mayor] *Historia Majories Brittannias*, cit. Maxwell, *Robert the Bruce*, p. 352.

Chapter 3 – To Choose a King

1. John Barbour, *The Brus* trans. A.A.H. Douglas. In Barbour's original words:
   Qwhen Alexander ye king wes deid
   Yat Scotland haid to steyr and leid
   Ye land [sex] 3er & mayr perfay

Lay desolat eftyr hys day
Til yat ye barnage at ye last
Assemblyt yain and fayndyt fast
To cheys a king yar land to ster
Yat off awncestry cummyn wer
Off kingis yat aucht yat reawte
And mayst had rycht yair king to be.

Barbour's Bruce, ed. McDiarmid & Stevenson [STS Edinburgh, 1980] Vol. II, pp. 2–3.

2. On the name of this dynasty the late Professor Gordon Donaldson wrote: 'Curiously enough there has been no consensus on a suitable label for this dynasty . . . The male progenitor of the dynasty had been Crinan, Abbot of Dunkeld, who married a daughter of Malcolm II, and one would therefore expect the style to derive from him – perhaps "the House of Crinan" . . . or (which sounds better and which I long ago adopted) "The House of Dunkeld".' Donaldson, 'Reflections on the Royal Succession' in *Scotland's History: Approaches and Reflections*, p. 108.

3. Nicholson, *Scotland: The Later Middle Ages*, p. 28.

4. 'Appeal of the Seven Earls' [1251] cit. Stones, p. 91.

5. Ibid., p. 27 words attributed to Walter Comyn, Earl of Menteith, before the inauguration of Alexander III.

6. RBCRS, p. 17, Ch. 1, Ref. note 40.

7. COS II 315, cit. Scott p. 17.

8. The phrase was used to him in a letter addressed to him by the Scottish parliament in 1290.

9. Diplomatarium Norvegium XIX, 230–1, cit. Nicholson, p. 30.

10. 'Treaty of Salisbury 1289' *Scottish Historical Documents*, pp. 38–39.

11. 'Treaty of Birgham 1290', *Scottish Historical Documents*, pp. 40–41.

12. RBCRS, p. 29.

13. COS II, 464, cit. Scott, p. 20. Stevenson, Documents, I nos. xcvi and cxvii, cit. Nicholson, p. 34.

14. Dunbar *Scottish Kings*, p. 106.

15. Ibid., pp. 106, 109; cites Letter of Bishop of Bergen, dated Bergen 1 February 1320, Proceedings of the Society of Antiquaries X. 417, 418 (1874).

16. Ibid. This care in taking note of the identification of the Maid's body should have prevented future imposture, but in 1300 a young German woman arrived from Lübeck and claimed to be Margaret, daughter of King Eric II and Margaret of Scotland. This unfortunate young woman, the 'Anastasia' of her times, was called 'The False Margaret' and having been tried as an impostor and condemned, was burned to death. She claimed to have been kidnapped in Orkney. A church was built on the site of her execution, in memory of 'the martyred Maritte', and became a place of pilgrimage. (Maxwell, *Robert the Bruce*, p. 49).

17. Scott, *Robert the Bruce*, p. 22.

18. Ann. Waverley, cit. Prestwich, Edward I, p. 356. Edward's admirer Sir Maurice Powicke dismissed this passage as 'casual and isolated'. But he also protested that Edward 'respected without question the customs and institutions of Scotland'. loc. cit.

19. *Song of Lewes*, ed. & trans. C.A. Kingsford (1890), p. 42, cit. Scott, op. cit., p. 18.

20. Lady Dervorguilla, as the foundress of Sweetheart Abbey and Balliol College, Oxford, is assured of an honoured place in history.

21. Bishop William Fraser of St Andrews to Edward I of England, 7 October 1290, Nat. MSS Scot i No. IXX, *Scottish Historical Documents*, pp. 42–3.

22. 'Appeal of the Seven Earls', Stones, pp. 89–101.

23. Duncan, op. cit., p. 552.

24. Stones, p. 91.

25. 'The party who were responsible for the document are claiming to speak on behalf of the whole body of earls in Scotland 1290–1'. Ibid, fn. 3.

26. 'There is no evidence of an invitation and he came to *adjudicate*, not *arbitrate*'. Gordon Donaldson 'Errors Old and New – Including my Own' in *Scotland's History – Approaches and Reflections*, p. 30.

27. A precedent had been the crosses set up to mark the journey of St Louis IX's body from Paris to St Denis. Prestwich, *Edward I*, p. 125.

28. It might have been taken as an infringement of the Treaty of Salisbury, being a gathering 'outwith the kingdom'.

29. RBCRS, p. 31.

30. Ibid.

31. Stones, pp. 107, 109, [full parallel text French/English, pp. 106–111]. It could not be said in strict truth that there was no knowledge of the claim; it had been uttered within living memory by Henry III in 1251, and mentioned by the Bishop of Norwich in 1278; but it was certainly true that no one alive had seen it 'used', since it had been abrogated by the Treaty or Quitclaim of Canterbury, 1189, just over a century ago.

32. RBCRS, p. 33.

33. 5 June 1291 'Submission of the Claimants to Edward I', *Scottish Historical Documents*, pp. 43–44.

34. In the case of a disputed succession the King would assert the right to act as 'sovereign lord' to the possessions of the King and make an award of the succession.

35. Florent failed to produce the document, but it was not a simple fabrication on his part. Either he had seen it, or had its existence convincingly reported, or had seen a copy. In mid-November 1291 the Bishop of Moray and the Prior of Pluscarden set their seals to two 'certified copies' of the recognition of Earl David. Professor G.W.S. Barrow refers to the existence of a copy of one of these copies which 'still survives at The Hague,

in what were formerly the Count of Holland's archives'. [RBCRS, p. 46.]
But it is an unsatisfactory document, having no witnesses. When the Court
reconvened and Count Florent could not produce his document, he said
it was being 'wrongfully detained' by the Prior of Pluscarden. Perhaps the
Prior had agreed to provide the document for Count Florent and subsequently fallen out with him. Was there ever an original?

36. This was the usual practice for the husband of a Queen regnant. In
Scotland it would have been the outcome of the marriage of the Maid of
Norway and Edward of Caernarvon. And later it happened when Henry
Stuart Lord Darnley married Mary Queen of Scots, and was recognized as
'King Henry'.

37. Historians differ about this. For a recent and authoritative view see
'Reflections on the Royal Succession' in *Scotland's History – Approaches and
Reflections* by Gordon Donaldson which begins: 'Not many subjects occur
to my mind as often as the succession to the Scottish throne, and I doubt
if there is any subject on which my views have so often changed'. In this
1990 lecture he decided that it did not pass by primogeniture.

38. *Scotichronicon* (Watt) Vol. 6, Bk. XI, Ch. 8, p. 21; Ch. 9, p. 25.

39. Ibid. Vol. 6, Bk. XI, Ch. 11, p. 31.

40. Scott, p. 26. It was somewhat ironic that if this ruling had been applied to
England in the earlier years of the century, Edward I would not have been
king. For his grandfather, King John, had asserted his rights over those of
John's nephew, Arthur of Brittany, [who was later murdered, probably at
John's instigation].

41. 'Grant to the Earl of Carrick' or 'Quitclaim of Robert the Competitor',
Stones, pp. 116–117.

42. *Scotichronicon*, Vol. 6, Bk. XI, Ch. 11, pp. 31, 33.

43. Dunbar, *Scottish Kings*, pp. 108–109. King Eric II married Isabella de Bruce
'before 25 September 1293'. He cites several Norwegian sources including
one which names her as 'Isabell, daughter of Sir Robert, son of Robert Jarl
of Brunsvik' – which, though incorrect, is identified as a quaint garbling
of 'Robert Bruce, Earl of Carrick'.

Chapter 4 – 'Scottorum Malleus'

1. Epitaph of Edward I, on his tomb in Westminster Abbey (not contemporary).

2. *Scotichronicon*, Vol. 5, Bk. X, Ch. 2, p. 295.

3. Rishanger, 371, cit. Scott, p. 30.

4. Lanercost, p. 145. The Lanercost Chronicler opined that John Balliol was
deprived of his kingdom because he was a descendant of Hugh de
Morville, one of the murderers of St Thomas Beckett, and 'there was not

one of his posterity who was not deprived either of his personal dignity or of his landed property'. loc. cit.

5. Bailleul, Dampierre, Hélicourt and Harnoy. J. Pelham Maitland, 'The Early Arms of the Balliols' *Dumfriesshire and Galloway Natural History and Antiquarian Society*, 3rd Series XVIII 235–42, cit. Nicholson SHR Vol. 38, (1959), p. 118.

6. APS 1. 44 7–8, cit. Nicholson, p. 45.

7. RBCRS, p. 54.

8. It could have been argued that as the Treaty of Birgham was a marriage treaty its provisions were *ipso facto* voided by the death of the Maid of Norway. A.M. Mackenzie, *Robert Bruce, King of Scots*, p. 76, remarks that the usually legalistic Edward I did not employ this argument, just stated that he refused to be bound by the treaty or any other promises. This suggests a developing aggression, which Edward made no attempts to camouflage.

9. RBCRS, p. 59, 'presumably Edinburgh, Roxburgh and Berwick'.

10. Dunbar, *Scottish Kings*, p. 72.

11. Dunbar, *Scottish Kings*, p. 118. Edward Balliol died in 1365, without issue.

12. Nicholson, p. 47.

13. Nicholson, 'The Franco-Scottish and Franco-Norwegian Treaties of 1295'; SHR Vol. 38 (1959), p. 118.

14. 'at the least he condoned what had happened', Prestwich, *Edward I*, p. 388.

15. *Scotichronicon*, Vol. 6, Bk. XI, Ch. 11, p. 31.

16. RBCRS, p. 65.

17. Nicholson, p. 46.

18. RBCRS, p. 66.

19. Scott, *Robert the Bruce*, cit. Cal. Docs. Scot. II, p. 675.

20. Ibid.

21. *Scotichronicon*, Vol. 6, Bk. XI. Ch. 18, p. 53, says he made the promise to Robert de Bruce 'the Grandfather', but in Ch. 25, p. 75, Robert de Bruce 'the elder' – i.e. the son of the now deceased grandfather – claims that the promise was made to him.

22. Lanercost, p. 129.

23. RBCRS, p. 67.

24. This popular weapon took its name from its place of origin. By the 17th C it had gained a long hook, mounted on the end of the shaft. In the 18th C it became the ceremonial weapon of the Edinburgh Town Guard. David H. Caldwell, *The Scottish Army*, pp. 19–20, 24.

25. Nicholson, p. 49.

26. 'Song of Lewes', cit. Scott, *Robert the Bruce*, p. 18.

27. 'No fewer than fifteen thousand of both sexes perished, some by the sword, others by fire, in the space of a day and a half, and the survivors, including even little children, were sent into perpetual exile', Lanercost, p. 135.

'In his tyrannous rage he ordered 7500 souls of both sexes to be massacred', *Scotichronicon*, Vol. 6, Bk. XI, Ch. 20, p. 59.

28. Wyntoun, Bk. 8, Ch. XI, II. 1833–38.
29. 'Reddicio Homagii Regis Scocie' [Renunciation of the homage of the King of Scotland] Stones, pp. 141, 143.
30. RBCRS, p. 72.
31. 'Litera Johannis Regis Scocie' [Letter of King John of Scotland], Stones, pp. 147, 149.
32. Nicholson, p. 51.
33. 'Diary of the Expedition of Edward I into Scotland, 1296', *Bannatyne Miscellany*, Vol. I, p. 281. French/Scots parallel text; in orignal French 'e conquise le Roiaume d' Escoce et le sercha . . . dedeinz xxi semaines, sanz plus'.
34. Duncan, p. 557.
35. RBCRS, p. 73.
36. There is no evidence that any king used it for this purpose before the coronation of Henry VI, in 1400.
37. 'La Piere D'Escoce', M. Domenica Legge, SHR Vol. 38 (1959), pp. 109–110.
38. *Political Songs of the English Nation*, ed. T. Wright [Camden Society, 1839], p. 307.
39. Removed in that time during the First World War and the Second World War for safekeeping, and briefly repatriated by Scottish Nationalists in 1952.
40. RBCRS, p. 75. Barrow is careful to stress this distinction.
41. Ibid., p. 77.
42. Ibid.
43. Michael Packe, King Edward III, p. 40. 'an over-rated parchment known as the Ragman Roll (rigmarole?); The curious name is said to derive from the many seals dangling from the roll, giving the appearance of a ragged fringe. Cam, *Hundred and the Hundred Rolls*, p. 45, cit. Prestwich, Edward I, p. 94, fn. 17.
44. 'Letters Patent of Homage and Fealty, Wark, 25 March 1296', Stones, pp. 137, 139.
45. *Scotichronicon*, Vol. 6, Bk. XI, Ch. 25, p. 75.

PART TWO: THE TRIUMPH OF THE KING

Chapter 5 – A Hero and a Man in Perplexity

1. 'Sir William Wallace', traditional ballad.
2. *Scalachronica*, SHR Vol. III, (1906), p. 218.

3. Quote from Hemingburgh, cit. Maxwell, *Robert the Bruce*, p. 92.
4. Wyntoun, Bk. VII, Ch. X, ll. 3619–3626.

> When Alexander our King was dead,
> Who Scotland ruled with love and law,
> Gone was abundance of ale and bread,
> Wine, candlelight and games were fled.
>
> From gold to lead was our alchemy.
> Christ of the Virgin Mary born
> Send Scotland succour and remedy,
> Whose state is in perplexity.
>
> (translation: Caroline Bingham)

5 'Eodem anno inclitus ille Willelmus Wales . . . caput levavit' [In the same year the famous William Wallace . . . raised his head]. *Scotichronicon*, Vol. 6, Bk. VI, Ch. 28, p. 83.
6 Erit enim statura procerus, corpore giganticus, facie serenus, vultu jocunis, ossibus grossus, ventre congruus, lateribus protelus, aspectu gratus sed visu ferus . . . erat enim in donis liberalissimus, in judiciis equissimus, in consolacione tristium compacientiissimus, in consilio peritissimus, in sufferencia pacientissimus. Ibid, loc. cit.
7. John Lase, The Hero: Manhood and Power, (Thames and Hudson, 1995), p. 5.
8. 'Sir William Wallace', traditional ballad.
9. 'Wallace', cit. Peter Reese, *Wallace: A Biography*, p. 43.
10. 'Wallace', op. cit. Reese, p. 45.
11. Lanercost, p. 163.
12. RBCRS, p. 80.
13. Nicholson, p. 52.
14. *Chronicle of Walter of Guisborough*, ed. H. Rothwell (1957), pp. 297–8, cit. Scott, *Robert the Bruce*, pp. 41–42.
15. Nicholson, p. 54.
16. Guisborough, 289–90, cit. Prestwich, *Edward I*, p. 416.
17. Guisborough, 300, cit. Scott, *Robert the Bruce*, p. 46.
18. Hemingburgh, cit. Maxwell, *Robert the Bruce*, p. 92. See also Lanercost, p. 164.
19. RBCRS, p. 90.
20. Knighthood was supposed to convey nobility. A king had to be a knight; there had been controversy as to whether Alexander III could be crowned before he was knighted. In the event he was – but knighthood soon followed.
21. Scott, Robert the Bruce, p. 47, states categorically 'William Wallace was dubbed knight by Robert Bruce, Earl of Carrick'. In note III, p. 241, he states that the Earls of Buchan, Strathearn, Lennox and Carrick were

present, and suggests the Earl of Carrick knighted Wallace because they were related by marriage: William's uncle, Sir Richard Wallace, was married to a Bruce. No doubt this link increases the likelihood – but the matter remains *not proven*.

22. Nicholson, p. 59.
23. Reese, *Wallace*, p. 80.
24. Wyntoun Bk. VIII, Ch. X, ll. 1563–64, Hists. of Scot. Vol. III, p. 324.
25. Cal. Docs, Scot. ii, 1978, cit. Scott, *Robert the Bruce*, p. 54.
26. Ibid., p. 55.
27. 'Roll of Arms of the Princes, Barons and Knights who attended Edward I at the siege of Caerlaverock', trans. Thomas Wright (1864) cit. Bingham, *Life and Times of Edward II*, p. 11.
28. Papal Bulls were named for their opening words 'Scrimus Filii' – 'We know, my son'. What Pope Boniface claimed to know was that Edward I was a devoted son of the Church, and therefore would heed what he had to say.
29. 'The Reply sent by the King of England to the Lord Pope.' *Scotichronicon*, Vol. 6, Bk. XI, Ch. 40, p. 115.
30. 'Baldred's pleading against the fictions of the King of England' Ibid, Ch. 62, p. 183.
31. Wyntoun, Bk. VIII, Ch. XV, ll. 2391–6.
32. Nicholson, op. cit., p. 61.
33. Ibid.
34. RBCRS, p. 119, Nicholson, p. 63.
35. Ibid., cites E.L.G. Stones 'The Submission of Robert the Bruce to Edward I' SHR XXXIV, 122–34 at 132–4.
36. Nicholson, op. cit., p. 63.
37. RBCRS p. 121; E.L.G. Stones 'Submission of Robert the Bruce to Edward I' SHR XXXXIV 122–34 at 125–26.

Chapter 6. *'He Would Be Crown'd'*

1. Shakespeare, *Julius Caesar*, Act Two, Scene One.
2. Stones, op. cit., No. 32, pp. 236–239, [original PRO Duchy of Lancaster, Cartae Miscellaneae (D.L. 36), I, f. I. According to Barrow, RBCRS pp. 122–23, this 'escrit ouvert' should not be described as a 'letter patent' but as an 'open writing' sealed with the privy seal.
3. Stones, op. cit., p. 38, fn 2, doubt that it refers to Bruce's claim to the throne. Barrow, RBCRS, p. 123: 'Ultimately, however, Edward I contemplated enjoying peaceful, unchallenged possession of the Scottish realm, and once that situation was realised Bruce's claims would be maintained by Edward . . .' which appears to be a meaninglessly contradictory state-

ment. Nicholson op. cit., p. 63: 'The word 'right' (le droit) is used with a tantalizing and needless ambiguity that may have suited both Bruce and Edward'.

4. A.M.M. Duncan 'The Community of the Realm of Scotland and Robert Bruce: A Review' SHR XLV, 184–201 at 198.

5. Scott, p. 69, citing CDS II, 1657.

6. 'The Story of England by Robert Manning of Brunne', ed. F.J. Furnival, Rolls Series, i, 12–13, cit. Barrow RBCRS, p. 143.

7. Ibid., Ch. 8, fn. 74.

8. RBCRS, p. 126.

9. Nicholson op. cit. p. 65: John Balliol in 'a last disastrous decision' had given Philip of France a free hand in his negotiations with them.

10. McNamee, *The Wars of the Bruces*, p. 23.

11. RBCRS, p. 128.

12. Palgrave DHS, p. 287; RBCRS, p. 130.

13. Palgrave op. cit. p. 276, 284. Scott, op. cit., p. 65.

14. Scott, op. cit., p. 69.

15. Ibid, Ch. 7, fn 5, citing CDS, II, 1510.

16. Ibid.

17. Prestwich, *Arms and Warfare in the Middle Ages*, p. 287.

18. Scott, p. 71, cit. CDS II, 1817.

19. RBCRS, p. 129.

20. *Scalachronica*, SHR III, (1906), p. 224. The father of the author of the *Scalachronica*, Sir Thomas Grey, was severely wounded in the face at the siege of Stirling. 'the said Thomas was brought in and a party was paraded to bury him, when at that moment he began to move and look about him, and afterwards recovered' [Ibid, loc. cit.]. He lived to be a very good source for his son the chronicler of the history of his times.

21. Nicholson, p. 67.

22. Aeneas Mackay, 'William Wallace', DNB, XX, 570. J.F. Tout 'Sir John de Menteith', DNB, XIII, 256. The chronicler Langtoft said he was taken in bed 'Enpries de sa puteyne' [beside his whore], an example of the use of accusations of misconduct to blacken a man's reputation – *plus ça change*... T. Wright, *Political Songs*, p. 321.

23. T. Wright, Political Songs of England, 'Song on the Execution of Sir Simon Fraser', p. 218. The ensuing verse says that Fraser's garland was of periwinkle.

24. RBCRS, p. 137.

25. Lanercost, p. 176, says that 'his head was exposed upon London Bridge, his right arm on the bridge of Newcastle on Tyne, his left arm at Berwick, his right foot at Perth and his left foot at Aberdeen...'

26. T. Wright, op. cit., p. 213.

27. Blind Harry, *Wallace*, STS pp. 370–2.
28. Nicholson, op. cit., p. 69.
29. '[This commission] was originally meant to consist of two bishops, two abbots, two earls, and two barons, together with one representative of the community north of the Forth and one for the south'. RBCRS, p. 134.
30. Ibid.
31. Ibid, p. 135.
32. M. Prestwich, *Edward I*, p. 132, says Edward in many ways treated John of Brittany as if he were his son.
33. Hutchison, *Edward II*, p. 41.
34. Prestwich, op. cit., p. 3.
35. *Scalachronica*, SHR, p. 329.
36. Ibid, Introd. by Sir Herbert Maxwell, p. 7. Grey begins with the familiar medieval literary device of a dream, in which a Sibyl appears to the author and bids him write his work and call it the 'Scalachronica' [the Ladder Chronicle], the point of this being that the crest of the Grey family was a 'scala' or besiegers' scaling ladder. Grey begins, as do many of the chroniclers, with the creation of the world and a run-through of ancient history, interesting as an evidence of current beliefs.
37. *Scotichronicon*, Vol. 6, Bk. XII, Ch. 5, pp. 304, 305.
38. Ibid., p. 305.
39. Ibid., pp. 305, 307.
40. *Scotichronicon*, Vol. 6, Bk. XII, Ch. 7, p. 311.
41. Barbour's Bruce, ed. McDiarmid and Stevenson, Vol. II, p. 19.
42. Historians of Scotland, Vol. III; Wyntoun, Vol. III, Bk. VIII, Ch. XVIII. p. 367.
43.   The Erle off Glouwerne in that quhylle
       That saw apper and gret peryl
       Tye the Lord the Brews Robert
       The quilk he luvyd wyth all hys hart
       Prevaly hys wardropere
       He gert to this Robert here
       A par off spuris, and wyth tha
       Send twelff pennys wyth hym alsua.
       [The Earl of Gloucester, all this while,
       Saw was threatened great peril
       To the Lord de Bruce, Robert
       Whom he loved with all his heart.
       His wardrober he sent secretly
       To take to Robert privately
       A pair of spurs, and with them too
       Sent twelve silver pence also.]
    Wyntoun, Bk. VIII, Ch. XVIII.

44. Here called 'An ordinance made by the King for the good order of Scotland', text PRO Close Roll 33 Edward I (C 54/122) in 3rd schedule (c). Text and trans. Stones, op. cit. 240–259 at 255.

45. *Scotichronicon*, Vol. 6, Bk. XII, Ch. 7, p. 311.

46. *Scalachronica*, loc. cit. p. 329. Sir Thomas Grey said Robert had told his brothers to kill Comyn, but he had received them so pleasantly they could not bring themselves to do it. Robert replied 'You are right lazy. Let me settle him'.

47. Ibid.

48. 'Male', inquit, 'Quie Johannes Red Comyn ut estimo interfeci': Ibid. A more familiar version of the episode makes Robert say 'I doubt I have slain the Red Comyn', and Kirkpatrick reply 'Doubt you? I'sl mak siccar' [I'll make sure]. In this Robert's curious choice of verb indicates that they were speaking French, so that his 'je doubte' translates as 'I fear I have killed the Red Comyn' and 'You *fear* it? I'll make sure of it'. The essential point seems to be that Bruce struck the first blow, and one of his companions returned to 'mak siccar'.

49. Barbour's Bruce ed. McDiarmid and Stevenson, Vol. II, p. 26; trans. A.A.H. Douglas. Wyntoun, Bk. VIII, Ch. XVIII, p. 368, tells the same tale:

    In the Freris at the hey awtere
    He schawyd him wyth hevy chere
    Hys indenture. Then wuth a kniff
    He renyd him in that sted the lyff.
    [In the Friars' church at the High Altar
    He showed to him with grim laughter
    His indenture. Then with a knife
    He robbed him in that place of life.]

    Trans. Caroline Bingham.

50. A news letter from an unknown author to an unknown recipient, about the ambitions and movements of Robert de Bruce following the murder of Comyn. Stones, op. cit. pp. 260–269 at 266.

51. Ibid., loc. cit.

52. A.A.H. Douglas, p. 70. Barbour, ed. McDiarmid & Stevenson, Vol. II, p. 30:

    Yusgat maid yai yar aquentance
    Yat neuer syne for nakyn chance
    Departyt quhill yai lyffand war,
    Yar frendschip woux ay mar and mar.

53. She is usually said to have been the young earl's elder sister, but she was in fact his aunt. RBCRS, p. 15.

54. The circlet was stolen by a knight called Geoffrey de Conyers.

55. Confession of Bishop Lamberton [having been captured by the English], 9 August 1306. Stones op. cit. pp. 270–279 at 277.

Chapter 7 – The Fugitive

1. *Scotichronicon*, Vol. 6, Bk. XII, Ch. 11, p. 324.
2. Palgrave, Docs & Recs, 'Articles propounded before the Pope against William Lamberton', pp. 331–340 at 335.
3. A.M. Mackenzie, *Robert Bruce King of Scots*, p. 119.
4. Not every young man eligible for knighthood automatically claimed the honour. Some preferred to avoid the expense and the obligations. Hutchison, op. cit. p. 46.
5. Ibid.
6. Scott, op. cit. p. 79.
7. Roger Sherman Loomis, 'Edward I, Arthurian Enthusiast', *Speculum*, Vol. XXVIII (1953), pp. 114–127 at 123.
8. Ibid., p. 125. 'Les Voex de Pao', 'Les Voex de l'Eperrier', 'Les Voex du Heron' and finally 'Le Banquet de Phaisan' – reducto ad absurdam.
9. Hutchison, op. cit., p. 47.
10. RBCRS gives a more detailed analysis of Robert's supporters pp. 154–160. They totalled only 135 knights, before the Battle of Methven.
11. Ibid., p. 183.
12. Prestwich, *Edward I*, p. 506.
13. cit, Scott, *Robert the Bruce*, p. 80.
14. Barbour, McDiarmid & Stevenson, Vol. II, p. 32.
15. RBCRS, p. 153.
16. cit, WB, p. 20.
17. Barbour, McDiarmid & Stevenson, Vol. II, pp. 37, 39.
18. Scott, op. cit., p. 82.
19. Wright, *Political Songs*, p. 217.
20. Barbour, trans. A.A.H. Douglas, p. 81.
21. Barbour, McDiarmid & Stevenson, Vol. II, p. 41.
22. Barbour, trans. Douglas, p. 79.
23. *Scotichronicon*, Vol. 6, Bk. XII, Ch. 11, p. 323.
24. '. . . ye queyn
    And oyir ladis fayr and farand
    Ilkane for luff off yar husband
    Yat for leyle luff and leawte
    Wald partenerys off yar paynys be.'
    Barbour, McDiarmid & Stevenson, Vol. II, p. 42.
25. Barbour, trans. Douglas, p. 81.
    'Yen to ye hill yai raid yar way
    Quhar grete defaut off mete had yai.
    Bot worthy Iames off Dowglas
    Ay trawailland and besy was
    For to purches ye ladyis mete

And on it mony wis wald get,
For quhile he venesoun yaim brocht,
And with his hanys quhile he wrocht,
Gynnys to tak geddis and salmonys
Trowtis elys and als menovyns . . .'
Barbour, McDiarmid & Stevenson, Vol. II, p. 44–45.

26. Barbour, trans. Douglas, p. 50.
'Bot he wes nocht sa fayr yat we
Suld spek gretly off his beaute.
In wysage wes he sumdeill gray
And had blak har as ic hard say,
Bot off lymmys he wes weill maid
With banys gret & schuldrys braid,
His body wes weyll maid and lenze
As yai yat saw hym said to me.
Quhen he wes blyth he wes lufly
And meyk and sweyt in cumpany,
Bot quha in battail mycht him se
All oyir contenance had he.
Barbour, McDiarmid & Stevenson, Vol. II, p. 15–16.

27. I.F. Grant and Hugh Cheape, *Periods in Highland History*, pp. 49–51. A charter of James III (1487) confirmed the office of dewar on one Malise Doine, stating that his family had had hereditarily held the *coigteach* [pastoral staff] of St Fillan since the time of Robert the Bruce and before. Ibid. at 57.

28. Scott, op. cit., p. 83.

29. Barbour, McDiarmid & Stevenson, p. 49–50.

30. Scott, Tales of a Grandfather, Vol. I, pp. 112–13 [ed. of 1828, Cadell & Co., Edinburgh].

31. Scott, *The Lord of the Isles*, canto II, pp. 66–77, Poetical Works of Scott, Cadell & Co., Vol. 10, N.D.

32. Ibid., Appendix note F., 'The Broach of Lorn', p. 297–300 at 298.

33. Ibid.

34. 'The Brooch of Lorn', Iain MacDougall, SHR Vol. III, 1906, pp. 110–115.

35. Ibid., p. 111, fn 3; see also *Brooches in Scotland*, National Museum of Antiquities of Scotland, 2nd ed. 1971, pl. 20, 'Lochbury Brooch'.

36. E.g. as creator of the 'Highland Tradition' of Scotland during the visit of George IV to Edinburgh.

37. The Story of the Brooch of Lorne (sic) is also recounted by Seton Gordon in Highways and Byways in the Central Highlands, pp. 76–77, with the additional local legend that 'when the Bruce, hard pressed, was in retreat, he threw his sword far into Lochawe . . . where it may remain to this day, deeply embedded in the soft peaty bottom', ibid., p. 77.

38. RBCRS, p. 161; Scott, op. cit., p. 84.

39. The traditional date is 11 August, but some historians have suggested this is too late, offering 30 July or 18 July as possible alternatives. Assuming that Barbour's account of Robert's visit to Aberdeen is correct, then 18 July seems too soon – as he had to go to Aberdeen, and then double back through mountainous country after his rendezvous with Sir Neil de Bruce and the ladies. He could have got to 'the head of Tay' by the end of July or beginning of August – but 11 August seems quite a feasible date. His decision to send back the Queen and ladies to Kildrummy seems to argue an ignorance of Pembroke's capture of Aberdeen, anyway.

40. Barbour, McDiarmid & Stevenson, Vol. II, p. 57.

41. Barbour, trans. Douglas, p. 93.
'Men mycht haiff sene quha had bene yar
At leve-takyng ye ladyis gret
And mak yar face with teris wet
And knychtis for yar luffis sak
Bath sich and wep and murnying mak
Yai kyssyt yar luffis at yar partyng.
Barbour, McDiarmid & Stevenson, Vol. II, p. 58.

42. Ibid.

43. Ibid., pp. 75–80; trans. Douglas, pp. 106–111.

44. Ibid.; also *Scotichronicon*, Vol. 6, Bk. XII, Ch. 11, p. 323.

45. Lanercost, p. 179. He remained there from September 1306 to March 1307. (fn).

46. Prestwich, *Edward I*, p. 508.

47. RBCRS, p. 161.

48. *Scalachronica*, SHR III, p. 330.

49. CDS II, 1963.

50. Edward had captured Lochmaben Castle, before joining Pembroke in the capture of Kildrummy. He had also harried and terrorised the countryside:
Ye eldest and aperand ayr
A zoung bacheler and stark and fayr
Schyr Eduuard callyt off Carnauerane
Yat wes ye sterkast man off ane
Yat men fynd mycht in any contre . . .
Barbour, McDiarmid & Stevenson, Vol. II, p. 75.

51. J.S. Hamilton, *Piers Gaveston*, p. 35.

52. He was granted a pension of 100 marks per annum during his absence. Hutchison, *Edward II*, p. 48.

53. Barbour, trans. Douglas, p. 89.
'For disconford, as yen said he,
Is ye werst thing yat may be
For throw mekill disconforting

Men fallis oft in-to disparyng . . .
And fra ye hart be discumfyt
Ye body is nocht worth a myt,.
Barbour, McDiarmid & Stevenson, Vol. II, pp. 52–3.

54. 'innumerabiles angustias . . . leto animo pertulit et invicto', *Scotichronicon*, Vol. 6, Bk. XII, Ch. 9, p. 319.
55. Scott, op. cit., p. 85.
56. Barbour, Douglas, p. 94; 'hunger cauld with schowris snell', McDiarmid & Stevenson, Vol. II, p. 59.
57. Barbour, Douglas, p. 95, McD & S, II, 60.
58. Ibid.;
   Red to yaim yat war him by
   Romanys off worthi Ferambrace
   McD & S, p. 61.
59. 'Fierabras', ll 2805–15, cit. Sarah Kay, *The Chanson de Geste in the Age of Romance*, (Clarendon Press, Oxford, 1995), p. 44; trans. Caroline Bingham.
   'Sire', dist Floripas, 'cel voel quel me donnés'
   'Par mon cief' dist Rollans 'a vostre volentés'
   'Venés avant dan Gui, la mollier recevés'
   'Sire' ce a dit Guis 'ne place a Damedé
   Que j'aie mollier en trestout mon aé
   Se nel me donne Karl, li fors rois couronnés'.
   'Qantl' entent Floripas, tout ot le sanc mué
   Et jure mahomet! Se vous ne me prenés
   Je vous ferai tous prendre et au vent encruer!'
   'Sir Guis', dist Rollans, 'faites nos volentés'
   'Sir', ce respont Guis, 'si soit com vous volés'.
60. Barbour, McD & S, Vol. II, p. 64; Douglas, p. 98. Barbour stresses that there is no disgrace in weeping under such circumstances.
61. Barbour, Douglas, p. 100; McD & S, Vol. II, p. 66, 'ye hyde leve on ye tre'.
62. RBCRS, p. 164.
63. WB, p. 38; RBCRS, p. 169.
64. Ibid.
65. Barbour, McD & S, Vol. II, p. 72; Douglas, p. 104–05.
66. Ibid, McD & S, Vol. II, p. 86; Douglas, p. 117.

Chapter 8 – The Renewal of the War

1. There are several versions of 'Good King Robert's Testament'. This one is quoted by A.M. Mackenzie, *Robert Bruce King of Scots*, p. 220. Another, more fully anglicized, is quoted by Scott, *Robert the Bruce*, p. 242. They are all translations of the Latin verse in the *Scotichronicon*:

Scotica sit guerra pedites mons mossica terra;
silve pro muris sint archus et hasta securis.
Per loca stricta greges minentur, plana per ignes
sic inflammentur ut ab hostibus evacuentur.
Insidie vigiles sint noctu vociferantes.
Sic male turbati redient famis ense fugati
hostes, pro certo sic rege docente Roberto.

Scotichronicon, ed. Watt, Vol. 6, Bk. XII, Ch. 10, p. 320.

2. RBCRS, p. 163.

3. Ibid.

4. WB, p. 36.

5. Text of letter RBCRS, p. 314; suggestion that it belongs to 1306, WB, p. 37. McNamee writes 'The letter survives as an exemplar in a formulary (or copy book for Scottish royal clerks) of the 1320's, preserved in a late fifteenth-century manuscript. In the text the capital letters 'T' and 'A' mark the places where clerks using the exemplar should insert the names of royal envoys . . . these initials could refer to Thomas and Alexander Bruce . . . Not everyone agrees that the letter belongs to this period, but the coincidence is too striking to be ignored.' McNamee cites S. Duffy 'The Bruce Brothers and the Irish Sea World, 1306–29', *Cambridge Medieval Celtic Studies*, (1991), pp. 64–65.

6. *Scotichronicon*, Vol. 6, Bk. XII, Ch. 12, p. 327.

7. RBCRS, p. 170.

8. Nicholson, p. 74, 'By way of Rathlin and Arran slipped unseen to his own earldom of Carrick'; RBCRS, p. 170, Barrow states the crossing was from Kintyre to Arran. But Rathlin, though a longer voyage was involved, seems more likely, as Dunaverty had recently fallen to the English.

9. RBCRS, ibid.

10. WB, pp. 37, 38.

11. Ibid.

12. Ibid.

13. Lanercost, p. 179; RBCRS, p. 169.

14. Lanercost, loc. cit.

15. WB, p. 38.

16. Nicholson, p. 75; WB, p. 38; RBCRS, p. 171.

17. Barbour, McD & S, Vol. II, pp. 92–94; Douglas, pp. 121–22.

18. Douglas, p. 126–27; McD & S, Vol. II, p. 99:
    For in yis land it is nane trewly
    Wate thingis to cum sa weill as I . . .
    With-in schort tyme 3e sall be king
    And haff ye land at 3our liking.

19. Scott, Poetical Works, Vol. X, p. 196 fn.

20. Barbour, Douglas, p. 132; McD & S, Vol. II, p. 107:
    Yan said ye king in full gret ire
    'Tratour quhy mad yow yan ye fyr'.
21. Barbour, McD & S, Vol. II, p. 110, 'with fourty men in company'; Douglas,
    following Skeat's Scottish Text Society edition of 1894, gives her 'fifteen
    men in company', p. 135.
22. Dunbar, Scottish Kings, p. 142, lists six acknowledged illegitimate children:
    Sir Robert – killed at Dupplin 1332
    Walter – predeceased the King
    Nigel of Carrick – killed at Neville's Cross 1346
    Margaret – m. Robert Glen, still living 1364
    Elizabeth – m. Sir Walter Oliphant of Gask
    Christian of Carrick – still living 1329.
23. Paul Hillyard, *The Book of the Spider*, p. 25–6.
24. Ibid., p. 26; Maxwell, *Robert the Bruce*, pp. 14–16, who discusses the myth,
    also cites 'the same venerable fable' in Cornwall, where spiders were held
    sacred because it was believed that one of them wove a web over the infant
    Christ to conceal Him from the soldiers of Herod.
25. Anatole Le Braz, *The Land of Pardons*, (1906), pp. 216–17.
26. Brewer's Dictionary of Phrase and Fable (10th ed. 1968), p. 850. Under
    'spider' Bruce, Frederick the Great, and Mohammed are listed.
27. RBCRS, p. 171–71; Scott, Robert the Bruce, p. 93.
28. With characteristic veracity Barbour said that he did not know the man's
    name, but several informants had said that he had one eye. McD & S, Vol.
    II, pp. 125–26.
    His name can I nocht tell perfay
    Bot ik haff herd syndry men say
    Forsuth yat his ane e ves out
    Bot he sa sturdy was and stout.
    [His name I cannot tell perfay
    But several men have I heard say
    That though he'd had one eye put out
    He was a sturdy man and stout.]
29. This seems the most likely way for John of Lorn to have acquired it,
    though Barbour admitted
    Bot how yat Iohn of Lorn him had
    Ik herd neuer mencion be mad.
    McD & S, II, p. 153.
    [But how it came with John to be
    No mention has been made to me]
30. McD & S, II, p. 171.
    The king went furth way & angri
    Menand his man full tenderly.

31. Ibid., p. 179.
32. Barbour, Douglas, p. 186; McD & S, II, p.180:

> And said 'ʒow aucht to schame perde
> sen ik am ane & ʒe ar thre
> For to schute at me apon fer
> Bot had ʒe hardyment to cum ner
> And with ʒour swordis till assay
> Wyn me upon sic wys giv ʒe may
> ʒe sall wele owte mar prisyt be'.

33. Ibid., p. 182.

> 'I slew but ane forouten ma
> God & my hund has slayn ye twa'.

34. Barbour, Douglas, p. 147; McD & S, II, p. 127:

> Bot on all tym sic hap he had
> Yat quhen men schap yaim to betrais
> He gat witting yaroff all-wayis
> & mony tyme as I herd say
> Throw wemen yet he wyth wald play.

35. Ibid, p. 112: Bath with siluer and with mete.
36. Cit supra, Duncan, *Scottish Kings*, p. 142.
37. Barbour, McD & S, II, p. 173.
38. Maxwell, *Robert the Bruce*, pp. 158–59; Mackay, *Robert Bruce*, pp. 104–5, Scott, *Robert the Bruce*, pp. 99–100. According to Maxwell, the arms of Murdoch are 'two ravens hanging pale-wise *sable*, with an arrow through both their heads fess-wise, *proper*', op. cit., p. 158, fn.
39. Barbour, McD & S, II, p. 173.
40. The attack on him while resting from the hunt occurs after this, but his sequence of increasingly influential minor victories had already begun.
41. WB, p. 41.
42. vide supra, Ch. 8, note 1.
43. WB, pp. 41–42.
44. Following the route of the present Southern Upland Way. Barbour mentions 'Glentrewle', McD & S, II, p. 183.
45. Ibid., p. 185.
46. WB, p. 40. NcNamee states that the Barbour narrative is highly dependent on a Scottish account which exaggerates the extent of Robert's success at Glentrool.
47. Barbour, McD & S, II, p. 187, 'Clyffurd & Waus maid a melle'.
48. CDS II No 1896, Edward I to Aymer de Valance 11 February 1307.
49. Barbour, McD & S, II, p. 197,

> Maid yaim gleterand as yai war lyk
> Tyll angelys hey off hewynnys ryk.

50. Ibid., p. 200.

51. Ibid., p. 201.
... in schort tyme men mycht se ly
At erd ane hunder and wele mar.

52. Ibid., p. 202; Douglas, p. 202.

53. CDS II 1926 (digest); RBCRS, pp. 172–73 (trans).

54. Prestwich, *Edward I*, p. 556–57.

55. Guisborough, p. 379 'intermanus eorum expirauit'.

56. Hailes, Annals of Scotland, Vol. II, p. 26, fn 26–7, cit. Froissart: 'Quand il mourat, il fut appeler son aisne fils, par devent ses barons, et lui fut jurer sur les saints, qu'aussi lésé feroit bouiller en une chaudière faut que le chair se departirent des os, et apres feroit mettre en chair en terre et garderoit les os, et toutes les fois que les Escocois se rebelleroit contre lui, il semier droit ses gens, et porteroit anecques liu les os de son pere'.

57. Binski, *Medieval Death*, p. 64.

58. Lanercost, p. 182; Prestwich, op. cit., p. 557.

59. *Scotichronicon*, Vol. 6, Bk XII, Ch. 14, p. 332, 'Viscera cum cerebro cuius tumulantur in Holmo'; RBCRS, p. 142, Ch. 8, note 63, quotes various sources for burial of Robert the Bruce, father of the King.

60. Lanercost, p. 183.

61. Prestwich, op. cit., p. 566. If Edward II neglected his father's tomb in any way, it was in not commissioning a permanent effigy. But there were frequent orders to the exchequer to pay for 'wax' for the tomb. It was once supposed that this was to renew the waxed 'cerecloths' around the corpse, but this is unlikely. 'Wax' means candlewax, and the normal purpose would have been to maintain a 'Chapelle Ardente' of votive candles over the tomb.

62. Edmund, (d. 1300), was the son of Richard, Earl of Cornwall, younger son of King John.

63. J.S. Hamilton, *Piers Gaveston*, p. 16.

64. Pierre Chaplais, *Piers Gaveston, Edward II's Adoptive Brother*, [the argument of the whole book].

65. Lanercost, p. 184.

66. Vita Edwardi Secundi, p. 15, 'non memini me audisse unum alterum ita dilexisse'; ibid, p. 14.

67. Ibid., p. 17.

68. *Scalachronica*, SHR III, 1957.

Chapter 9 – The War in the North

1. *Scotichronicon*, Vol. 6, Bk. XII, Ch. 16, pp. 338–41. Quique ... a quodam diceretur ... quod ... mortuus fuerat Eadwardus tirannus, in altum resolutus est risum. Quod videntes pauci qui sibi circumsteterant mirabantur, eo quod non perceperunt eum ridere toto anno preterito. 'Letamini',

inquit suis, 'et conridete mecum, quia "Dominus, michi adjutor et amplius non timebo quid faciat michi homo. Dominus michi adjutor et ego despicam inimicos meos . . ." Ut autem, inquit, commilitones mei, sciatis quia non rideo de morte inimici, sed de liberacione gentis et patrie nostre.'

2. *Vita Edwardi Secundi*, p. 18, alluding to Holy Bible (KJV) Kings 12, v. 8, 'But he forsook the counsel of the old men . . . and consulted with the young men that were grown up with him'; Lanercost, p. 183. 'Thus Edward the younger succeeded the elder, but in the same manner as Rehoboam succeeded Solomon'.

3. RBCRS, p. 173.

4. Ibid., p. 174.

5. Ibid., p. 179. Professor Barrow's translation of PRO C41/22/6 No 4; digest in CDS III, no. 80.

6. CDS II 1926.

7. The exact dates of the capture of Inverlochy, Castle Urquhart, Nairn and Inverness are not certain, but they occupied the month of October. According to the letter of Duncan of Frendraugh, on which the chronology of this period is based, Inverlochy fell on the feast of a Virgin Martyr. Those in October were: St Triduana (8th), St Findoca (13th), St Ursula and the 11,000 Virgins (21st), St Kennere (29th), St Begha (31st), RBCRS, Ch. 10, note 47. It would presumably have been on one of the first two that Inverlochy fell.

8. CDS IV, 1837.

9. Barnes & Barrow, 'The Movements of Robert the Bruce between September 1307 and May 1308', SHR 49 (1970) pp. 46–59, at p. 50.

10. Barbour, Douglas, p. 209; McD & S, II, p. 210.

> And yar him tuk sik a seknes
> Yat put him to full hard distres.
> He forbar bath drynk & mete,
> His men na medicyne couth get
> Yat euer mycht to ye king awaile,
> Hys force gan hym halyly faile
> Yat he mycht noyer rid na ga.

11. Ibid., p. 211.

12. Barnes & Barrow op. cit., p. 52, fn 2. In Duncan of Frendraught's letter the Slioch is described as a 'marisca nemorosa'.

13. Barbour, McD & S, II, p. 216.

> And swa lang yar maid soiornyng
> Till he begouth to cowyr & ga.

14. Barnes & Barrow, op. cit., p. 53.

15. *Scotichronicon*, Vol. 6, Bk. XII, Ch. 17, pp. 341, 343. A fragment of a verse chronicle interpolated in the *Scotichronicon* gives the date of the rout of

Inverurie as Ascension Day – *in festo Domini quo scandit sidera celi* [on the feast of the Lord when he rises to the stars of heaven] – which was 23rd May. This is obviously too late, as by that date the King had captured several castles and again besieged Elgin, which he would not have done before settling with the Earl of Buchan. Furthermore, if his illness had lasted so long, he could not have undertaken the attacks on the castles. Barbour tells the same story, but gives the date as Christmas, saying Buchan was at Old Meldrum 'Befoir 3hule ewyn a nycht but mar' [the day preceeding Christmas Eve] McD & S, p. 217, Douglas, p. 215. But the letter of Duncan of Frendraught reports the action at the Slioch as taking place on Christmas Day – and he had witnessed it. Barnes & Barrow op. cit., p. 54. So, given the now established movements of King from Inverurie to the Slioch, from the Slioch to Strathbogie and from Strathbogie back to Inverurie, it seems that the most likely approximate date for the battle is late January or early February 1308.

16. Barnes & Barrow, p. 54. King Edward was evidently in possession only of stale news, for he still assumed he could rely upon Buchan, who was fugitive. He thanked Duncan of Frendraught and John de Mowbray, who had certainly done their best for him, but required more than thanks, if English interests were to be defended.

17. J.S. Hamilton, *Piers Gaveston*, p. 46, cites BL MS Harley 636 f. 232, 'E si haute manere de porture lors emprist, ke les cuntes a li venuz par parler des bosoignes engenulaunt lurs resuns devaunt li mustrer . . .' ref. n. 76, p. 144.

18. Ibid., cit. *Johannis de Trokelowe Annales*, ed. Riley [Rolls Series, London, 1886], p. 65.

19. Ibid., p. 48, ref. n. 90, cit. Annales Paulinus, Chronicles of the Reigns of Edward I and Edward II [Rolls Series, 1882], p. 262.

20. Barnes & Barrow, op. cit., p. 57; Scott, *Robert the Bruce*, p. 111.

21. RBCRS, p. 182.

22. Ibid.

23. W. Stanford Reid, 'Truce, Trades and Scottish Independence', Speculum, Vol. XXIX [1954], pp. 210–221 at 216.

24. Ibid., p. 217. Scots were eventually expelled from Flanders in 1323, when the Scotophile Count was succeeded by a child whose regent succumbed to English pressure. But by that time it was too late to do Edward II any good. Ibid., p. 218.

25. Ibid., p. 214.

26. Scott, op. cit., p. 111.

27. Nicholson, p. 78, acknowledges chronological research of Prof. A.A.M. Duncan, Ibid., fn 57. But McNamee, WB, pp. 40–41, writes that in 1307 'James Douglas of Douglasdale was pursuing his own feud against Robert Clifford, the English lord who had been imposed upon Douglasdale by Edward I'.

28. Barbour, McD & S, II, p. 121.
29. Ibid.

> Yarfor ye men off yat countre . . .
> Callit it 'ye Dowglas lardner'

30. Barbour, McD & S, II, p. 207. This is the central theme of Sir Walter Scott's last novel 'Castle Dangerous' [1832]. It was written after he had suffered a stroke and is a sad testimony to his declining powers; nonetheless it has its moments of inspiration which make the reader regret that he did not choose the subject at the height of his career.

31. Barbour, Douglas, p. 232; McD & S, II, p. 238:

> Ye king off his present wes blyth
> And thankyt him weill fele syth
> And till his nevo gan he say
> 'Yo has ane quhill renyid yi fay
> Bot yow reconsalit now mon be'.
> Yen till ye king ansueryt he
> And said 'ȝe chasty me, but ȝe
> Aucht bettre chastyt for to be,
> For sene ȝe werrayit ye king
> Off Ingland, in playne fechting
> ȝe suld pres to derenȝhe rycht
> And nocht with cowardy na with slycht'.
> Ye king said 'ȝeit may-fall it may
> Cum or oucht lang to sic assay.
> Bot sen yow spekys sa rudly
> It is gret skyll men chasty
> Yai proud wordis till yat yow knaw
> Ye rycht and bow it as yaw aw'.

32. Barbour, McD & S, II, p. 240:

> Crechinben hecht yat montane,
> I trow nocht yat in all Bretane
> Ane heyar hill may fundyn be.
> [I trow, in Britain's land entire
> There cannot be a mountain higher.
> Ben Cruachan 'tis called by name.]
>
>   Douglas, p. 233.

33. *Scotichronicon*, Vol. 6, Bk XII, Ch. 17, p. 345. The battle was fought in the week following the feast of the Assumption of Our Lady, i.e. 15th–22nd August 1305.
34. RBCRS, p. 181.
35. Scott, op. cit., p. 113.
36. *Scotichronicon*, Vol. 6, Bk. XII, Ch. 18, p. 345. Alexander 'de Argyll' 'took refuge in England under safe conduct . . . and there he paid his debt to

nature'. This says he had not paid homage, but surely he had, as he attended Parliament with the King in 1309, before leaving Scotland.

37. RBCRS, p. 182, fn. Ch. 10, note 81, p. 363. Barrow points out that Barbour's siting of the engagement on the Water of Cree is a mistake, as 'The Dee would have been almost in sight of Buittle Castle, the Cree far out of sight' [several miles further away].

38. WB, p. 44.

39. RBCRS, p. 182.

40. Barbour was right that the King 'towart Perth agayne is gane', McD & S, II, p. 244, though he was mistaken in placing the capture of Perth before this date.

41. RBCRS, pp. 182–3.

42. Scott, op. cit., p. 113.

43. Scott, op. cit.; RBCRS, p. 177.

44. APS I, 459.

45. RBCRS, p. 174.

46. Bernard was probably the Tironensian monk who had formerly been Abbot of Kilwinning, and not Bernard de Linton, pastor of Mordington, with whom the Chancellor was quite arbitrarily identified. The confusion has caused the Chancellor to become 'Bernard de Linton' to many historians. RRS V, pp. 198–203.

47. RBCRS, Ch 10, note 106. His seal was on the declaration of the clergy, as was that of Bishop Wishart, which was presumably affixed by a representative from his diocese.

48. APS I, 459.

49. WB, p. 46; text in Stones, *Anglo-Scottish Relations*.

50. APS I, 289; RBCRS, p.185, suggests it may have been identical. It exists only in the form of an 18th C abstract.

Chapter 10 – War with King Edward

1. *Vita Edwardi Secundi*, p. 12.

2. He issued a charter to William Thane of Cawdor on 8 August 1309 at Loch Boon, and to Sir William de Vipont at Dunstaffnage on 20 October 1309. These mark the extremities of the progress. RRS V, Nos 9 & 10, pp. 297–98.

3. WB, p. 46; J.S. Hamilton, *Piers Gaveston*, p. 62.

4. WB, p. 58, citing *Chartulary of St Mary's Abbey, Dublin*, Vol. II, p. 342.

5. Hamilton, op. cit., p. 70. Pope Clement's nephew and namesake Bertrand de Got received the castle and town of Blanquefort, and another nephew, Raymond-Guilliaume de Budos was granted the right of justice in Budos.

6. As is well known, the French King's motive was covetousness of the

Templar's wealth, and the pretext for the suppression of the order was unproven accusations of devil worship and sodomy. It is something in Edward's favour that he did not permit torture to be used to extract confessions in England as it was in France. In 1307 he had written to the Kings of Portugal, Castile, Sicily and Aragon, cautioning them against believing the accusations brought against the knights. Hamilton, op. cit., p. 71.

7. VES, p. 6.

8. Hamilton, op. cit., p. 74; Hutchison, op. cit., p. 63.

9. He exchanged the Gascon and English lands with which he had been compensated the previous year for 'all the lands appurtenant to the earldom', Hamilton, op. cit., p. 75.

10. Hamilton, op. cit., p. 74.

11. Ibid., pp. 75–6.

12. VES, p. 8.

13. Ibid., p. 8. The editor thinks the nickname was Monthemer's, but he had ceased to be Earl of Gloucester in 1307; in any case, it would have had an obvious point if applied to Gilbert de Clare the younger, as his mother Joan of Acre had secretly married Monthemer after the death of her first husband, the elder Gilbert de Clare.

14. Lanercost, p. 194.

15. VES, p. 8. In hoc igitur festa natalitia celebrarunt, cotidie colloquentes ac mutua conuersatione et diu affectata presentia priorem absentiam plene redimentes . . .

16. Ibid., p. 9.

17. WB, p. 47; Hamilton, op. cit., p. 77.

18. The Ordainers chose each other thus: the bishops elected two earls, the earls elected two bishops, then these four elected two barons. The resulting six co-opted fifteen more, bringing the total to twenty-one. Sternly critical of the King were Archbishop Winchelsey and Thomas of Lancaster, but there were friends of the King among the Ordainers, including Richmond and Gloucester, and moderate men such as Lincoln and Pembroke. It was not a body of extremists, however fiercely Edward resented it. Hutchison, op. cit., p. 65.

19. 'the morrow of St Hillary'. The English paid for these truces. Guisborough, p. 384.

20. WB, p. 46.

21. Lanercost, p. 150.

22. Scott, op. cit., p. 121.

23. WB, pp. 48–49.

24. Ibid., p. 51.

25. Ibid., p. 48.

26. Ibid., p. 49.

27. VES, p. 12. The translator and editor of the *Vita Edwardi Secundi*, N. Denholm-Young, doubted the authorship of the 'so-called monk of Malmesbury' to whom it was attributed, and postulated the authorship of the Chancery Clerk, Master John Walwayn, *vide* VES Introd. In February 1311, Walwayn was reported by the Earl of Richmond to have been arrested and imprisoned at Berwick because he had gone towards Perth to speak with Robert Bruce. Dr Colm McNamee comments 'it is tempting to speculate that Walwayn acted as Edward's contact with Robert, imprisoned to appease the outcry when the King's secret contact with the Scots became known. WB, p. 52. If Walwayn was with Edward in Scotland, and wrote the *Vita*, it would account for the vividness of his reportage.

28. Lanercost, p. 191.

29. VES, p. 13.

30. WB, p. 49.

31. Anon letter from someone who came from Newcastle with the Chancery and found the King at Berwick [could this have been Walwayn?]. Dated February 19, 1311. CDS III, no. 197, p. 39.

32. VES, p. 13.

33. Lanercost, p. 191.

34. Lanercost, p. 192.

35. WB, p. 53.

36. Hamilton, op. cit., p. 87.

37. Hutchison, op. cit., p. 67.

38. VES, pp. 13–14.

Chapter 11 – Scotland Reclaimed

1. Sir Walter Scott, *The Lord of the Isles*, canto III.

2. Lanercost, p. 194.

3. Ibid., p. 194–95.

4. Ibid.

5. Ibid. Money forthcoming from these truces helped to finance the siege of Dundee. WB, p. 55, and *vide infra.*

6. T.F. Tout, *Political History of England*, p. 248, cit. Hutchison, op. cit., p. 68.

7. VES, p. 17.

8. Hutchison, op. cit., p. 69.

9. VES, p. 22.

10. Hutchison, op. cit., p. 70. Gaveston was to appear before Parliament, and if no decision as to his future was made, he was to be permitted to return to Scarborough Castle and re-provision it. These generous terms show that Gaveston's captors had no designs on his life.

11. There is a nineteenth century monument to him on the top of this hill,

now concealed by woods. The explanation of the curious story that four cobblers took the corpse to the Earl of Warwick, who refused to receive it, may be that they were members of a Guild dedicated to pious practices and were attempting to perform one of the 'Seven Corporal Works of Mercy', burial of the dead. But Gaveston's body was not buried because he had died excommunicate. It was eventually carried to the Dominicans of Oxford, who kept it above ground unburied and said daily prayers for Gaveston's soul at the King's expense [Lanercost, p. 203]. The burial finally took place in 1314.

12. Lanercost, p. 197.

13. Ibid., p. 199.

14. Ibid., p. 200.

15. Ibid.

16. RBCRS, p. 198.

17. Lanercost, p. 205.

18. WB, p. 57.

19. WB, p. 59, and note 124, p. 70.

20. Ibid., p. 55.

21. Lanercost, pp. 201–02.

22. Scott, op. cit., p. 131.

23. RBCRS, p. 201.

24. RRS V nos 24 (renewal of Treaty of Perth) and 25 (settlement of disputes), pp. 307–14.

25. Ibid., p. 308. The treaty refers to the 'most serene Prince Haakon V by the grace of God King of Norway' and the 'magnificent Prince Lord Robert by the same grace King of Scots'.

26. Lanercost, p. 201, 202.

27. Barbour gives the length of time as six weeks, but the date of the capture of Perth does not allow for this, Douglas, p. 220–21. He was placing it wrongly chronologically, as he recounts it as following the battle of Inverurie.

28. Ibid., Douglas, p. 221.

> And his ledder in hand gan ta
> Ensample till his men to ma,
> Arayit weill in all his ger
> Schot in ye dik and with his sper
> Taistyt till he it our-woud
> Bot till his throt ye watyr stud

McD & S, II, p. 224.

29. Scott, op. cit. p. 135. Scott also says Dalswinton surrendered at this time, but it had probably fallen as much as two years earlier, vide supra p. 205.

30. Hutchison, op. cit., p. 75.

31. *Chronicon Manniae*, p. III, cit. Arthur W. Moore, 'The Connexion between Scotland and Man', SHR Vol. III, p. 405.
32. Chartulary of St Mary's Abbey, Dublin, ed. T.S. Gilbert, Vol. II, p. 34, cit. WB, p. 58.
33. RBCRS, p. 193.
34. Barbour, Douglas, p. 260.

> Ye king said quhen he hard ye day
> 'Yat was wnwisely doyn perfay.
> Ik herd neuer quhar sa lang warnyng
> Wes gevyn to sa mychty a king
> As is ye king off Ingland
> For he has now in-till hand
> Ingland Ireland and Walis alsua
> And Aquitayngne ʒeit with all ya
> & off Scotland ʒeit a party
> Duelles under his senʒowry
> And off tresour sua stuffyt is he
> Yat he may wageouris haiff plente,
> And we ar quhoyne agayne sa fele.
> God may rycht weill oure werdys dele,
> Bot we are set in iuperty
> To tyne or wyn yen hastily'.

McD & S, III, p. 2.
35. Lanercost, p. 195.
36. RBCRS, p. 188.
37. Barbour, Douglas, p. 237–240.
38. Ibid., Douglas, p. 244; McD & S, II, p. 253 'a crafty man and a curious'. Sim may have taken his name from 'the Ledows' near Crossford in the parish of Lesmahagow, the next parish north of Douglas. RBCRS, Ch. 14, note 45, p. 365.
39. Barbour, Douglas, p. 246; McD & S, 'stekyt him wpwart with a knyff', II, p. 255.
40. Ibid., Douglas, p. 248; McD & S, II, p. 257.
41. Barbour, Douglas, p. 250; McD & S, II, p. 260, 'lovyt a wench her in y toun' ... 'se newyr sa myrk ye nycht'.
42. Ibid.; McD & S, II, p. 262, 'Away, I se ʒow weill'.
43. RBCRS, p. 196.

Chapter 12 – The Year of Victory 1314

1. Lanercost, p. 210.
2. Scott, op. cit., p. 143; Hutchison, op. cit., p. 75.

3. RBCRS, p. 203. Text of Edward's letter *Rotuti Scotiae* I, 114 G.

4. Writs of Summons, Ibid, I, 118, 119, etc.

5. The *Scotichronicon*, Vol. 6, Bk. XII., Ch. 20, p. 353, says that John of Brittany, Earl of Richmond, was captured at Bannockburn. But it is doubtful if he was present, as the other statements about him are incorrect: 1) That he was exchanged after the battle for Bruce's Queen, as it was not Richmond but Hereford; 2) That he was ransomed for a huge sum – this happened later, after the Battle of Byland, 1322.

6. I. Lubimenko, *Jean de Bretagne*, p. 61.

7. Barbour, Douglas, p. 307:

> 'The third best knight was he, they say.
> Of all men living in his day'.

Scotichronicon, Vol. 7, Bk. XIII, Ch. 15 & 16, pp. 51–57, tells how the English King-of-Arms, asked by Edward II who were the three best knights living, named the Emperor, Sir Giles d'Argentan, and King Robert. There was loud protest at his naming an enemy, but having demanded a hearing he defended himself, and eloquently argued that King Robert was the best of the three.

8. RBCRS, p. 207; Prestwich, *Armies and Warfare in the Middle Ages*, pp. 234–35, for a sketch of Sir Giles d'Argentan's career. He was a great jouster, and was crowned 'King of the Greenwood' in a tournament held at Stepney in 1309.

9. Friar Baston's poem 'The Battle of Bannockburn', quoted in extensio in the *Scotichronicon*:

> Bis duo Theutonici veniunt ad prelia gratis
> (Thrice two Teutonic [knights] came freely to the fight)

op. cit. Vol. 6, Bk. XIII, Ch. 23, p. 368.

10. Barbour, Douglas, p. 263; McD & S, III, pp. 6–7:

> He wes rycht ioyful in his thocht
> & weile supposyt yat yar wes nocht
> In warld a king mycht him withstand
> Him thocht all wonnyn till his hand
> And largly amang his men
> Ye land of Scotland delt he yen
> Off oyer mennys thing larg wes he.

11. WB, p. 61. Professor Mary McKisack seems to doubt the participation of the Irish at all, in describing the gathering of Edward II's infantry in the north of England prior to the campaign she refers to the coming of 'possibly, some Irish'. *The Fourteenth Century*, p. 35.

12. Barbour, McD & S, 'Ane hunder thowsand men & ma', III, p. 5.

13. RBCRS, p. 204.

14. Ibid., pp. 204, 206; Prestwich, *Armies & Warfare*, p. 117.

15. Prestwich, *Armies & Warfare*, p. 40.

16. RBCRS, p. 207.

17. WB, p. 62.

18. RBCRS, p. 204.

19. Scott, op. cit., p. 144.

20. *Scotichronicon*, Vol. 6, Bk. XII, Ch. 22, p. 363.

21. Ibid., p. 367.

22. For the arguments in favour of this site see RBCRS, pp. 209–16.

23. *Scalachronica*, SHR, Vol. III, p. 460.

24. Barbour, Douglas, p. 267.

25. Ibid., p. 269.

26. RBCRS, p. 210; Scott, op. cit., p. 146. The latter suggests that Edward de Bruce's division contained men from Buchan, Mar, Angus, the Mearns, Menteith, Strathearn and Lennox, with only a small contingent from Galloway.

27. Having said that King Edward had 'a hundred thousand men and more' of King Robert's army he says 'Of fighting men I trow the score Was thirty thousand, something more'. Barbour, A.A.H. Douglas, p. 266. McD & S, III, p. 10:

    > Off fechtand men I trow ye war
    > Thretty thowsand & sum-dele mar.

28. RBCRS, p. 209.

29. Barbour, McD & S, III, p. 12:

    > 'For in ye park amang ye tres
    > Ye hors-men alwayis cummerit beis,
    > And ye sykis als-sua yat ar yar-doun
    > Sall put yaim to confusione'.

30. Barbour, McD & S, III, p. 16.

31. Ibid., III, p. 19.

    > Bot lat yaim in-to comowne say
    > Yat yai cum in-till ewyll aray

32. RBCRS, p. 217.

33. *Scalachronica*, SHR III, pp. 456–59.

34. Ibid., p. 459.

35. RBCRS, p. 217. Professor Barrow mentions that Gloucester and Hereford were also rivals as Lords of Glamorgan and Brecknock respectively, where their families harboured an old quarrel.

36. *Scalachronica*, SHR III, p. 459; Barbour, McD & S, III, p. 21:

    > 'Ye New park all eschewit yai'.

37. Ibid:

    > To ye castell yai thocht to far
    > For giff yat yai weill mycht cum yar
    > Yai thocht it suld reskewit be.

38. Ibid., p. 27:

And on his bassynet he bar
Ane hat off qwyrbolle ay-quhar
And yar-wpon in-to taknyng
Ane hey croune yat he wes king.

'Qwyrbolle' was 'cuir bouillé', or boiled leather. It was moulded when wet
into pieces of armour, and was both light and strong. Prestwich, *Armies &
Warfare*, pp. 21–22.

39. Barbour, A.A.H. Douglas, p. 281; McD & S, III, p. 28–9:
Sprent yai samyn in-till a ling
Schyr Henry myssit ye noble king
And he yat in his sterapys stud
With ye ax yat wes hard & gud
With sua gret mayne raucht him a dynt
Yat noyer hat na helm mycht stynt
Ye hewy dusche yat he him gave
Yat ner ye heid till ye harnys clave.
Ye hand-ax schaft fruschit in twa,
And he doune to ye erd gan ga
All flatlynys for him faillit mycht.
Yis wes ye fryst strak off ye fycht . . .

In the *Scalachronica* Sir Thomas Grey tells the story, but incorrectly gives
the name of the English Knight as Sir Pieris de Mountforth.

40. Barbour, McD & S, III, p. 30; A.A.H. Douglas, p. 282.
41. Ibid., Douglas, p. 274; McD & S, II, p. 22.
42. *Scalachronica*, SHR III, p. 141.
43. Barbour, Douglas, p. 284; McD & S, III, p. 33.
And glaidsome cher to yaim mad
For yai sa weile yaim borne had.
44. Lanercost, p. 207.'From that moment began a panic among the English
and the Scots grew bolder'.
45. Barbour, Douglas, p. 286; McD & S, III, p. 35:
In hart gret glaidschip can he ta.
46. *Scalachronica*, SHR III, p. 142.
47. Barbour, Douglas, p. 290; McD & S, III, p. 41.
48. Friar Barton in *Scotichronican*, Vol. 6, Bk. XII, Ch. 23, p. 369:
Dum se sic jactant cum bacho nocte jocando
Scocia, te mactant, verbis vanis reprobando.
[While they spend the night in braggartry and revelry with Bacchus
They wrong you, Scotland, by reviling you with empty words.]
49. Barbour, Douglas, pp. 291–92; McD & S, III, p. 42.
50. Ibid. And ye hard feld on hors has tane.
51. *Scotichronicon*, Vol. 6, Bk. XII, Ch. 22, p. 365.
52. Ibid, pp. 363, 365. Abbot Bernard set it down in Latin verse.

53. Barbour, Douglas, p. 289; McD & S, III, p. 39. Barbour gave Robert the Bruce a more pugnaciously patriotic speech; but the simple words of patriotism and devoutness reported by Abbot Bernard are most likely to represent what he said. Barbour's speech includes a caution against taking prisoners for ransom, or plundering, until victory was certain. But this message had probably been reiterated many times before.

54. Scott, op. cit., p. 157. The idea may have arisen from Barbour's saying that the King created the knights 'ilkane in yar degre'.

55. RRS V, no. 7, p. 295, (and see p. 111–12).

56. *Scotichronicon*, loc. cit.

57. Barbour, Douglas, p. 293; McD & S, III, p. 45: 'In plane hard feild to giff bataile'.

58. Ibid., p. 46:

    Schyr Ingrahame said '3e say soth now
    Yai ask mercy bot nane at 3ow
    For yar trespas to God yai cry.
    I tell 3ow a thing sekerly
    Yat 3one men will all wyn or de . . .'

59. VES, p. 52.

60. Lanercost, p. 208. 'This account I had from a trustworthy person who was present as eyewitness'.

61. Ibid; VES, p. 52–54.

62. Barbour, A.A.H. Douglas, p. 299; McD & S, III, p. 53:

    And woundis wid to yaim yai maid
    And slew of yaim a full gret dele.

63. Scott, op. cit., p. 159.

64. *Scalachronica*, SHR III, pp. 460–61.

65. Barbour, McD & S, III, p. 57:

    'On yaim on yaim on yaim yai faile'.

66. Ibid., p. 59.

67. Lanercost, p. 208.

68. Barbour, McD & S, III, p. 63:

    And Bannokburne betuix ye brays
    Off men and hors swa stekyt wais
    Yat apon drownyt hors and men
    Men mycht pas dry owt-our it yen.

69. Ibid, A.A.H. Douglas, p. 308; McD & S, III, p. 63.

    Ran amang yaim and swa gan sla
    As folk yat na defens mycht ma
    Yat war pitte for to se.

70. *Scalachronica*, p. 461.

71. Ibid.; also Barbour, A.A.H. Douglas, p. 307; McD & S, III, p. 61–62.

72. Ibid., A.A.H. Douglas, pp. 308–9; McD & S, III, p. 64.

73. Ibid., A.A.H. Douglas, p. 315; McD & S, III, p. 71.

74. Lanercost, p. 209.

75. WB, p. 66. McNamee makes this point à propos Mowbray; RBCRS, p. 232, Professor Barrow makes the point à propos Dunbar.

76. Barbour, A.A.H. Douglas, p. 310, 319; McD & S, III, pp. 65, 76–76.

77. Lanercost, p. 209; Barbour, A.A.H. Douglas, p. 310; McD & S, III, p. 66. Barbour attributes this feat of chivalric leadership to Maurice, Lord of Berkley.

78. RBCRS, pp. 231–2, and Ch. 12, note 160, on p. 370.

79. Barbour, A.A.H. Douglas, pp. 321–13, McD & S, III, pp. 68–9. Barbour mistakenly says that Atholl's sister 'dame Isabel' was Edward de Bruce's wife, but in fact he was unmarried.

80. RBCRS, p. 275.

81. Barbour, A.A.H. Douglas, p. 321; McD & S, III, p. 67:
    Twa hunder payr off spuris reid
    War tane of knychtis yat war deid.

82. *Scotichronicon*, Vol. 6, Bk. XII, Ch. 21, p. 359. Anonymous verses on the battle: Bannok habet limus quorum nec nomina scimus [The muddy Bannock holds those whose names we do not know].

83. Barbour, A.A.H. Douglas, pp. 313–14; McD & S, III, p. 70.

84. *Scotichronicon*, Vol. 6, Bk XII, Ch. 23, pp. 367–375, at 374–5.
    Sum Carmelita Baston cognomine dictus.
    Qui doleo vita in tali strage relictus.
    Si quid deliqui, si que recitanda reliqui,
    hec addant hii qui non sunt sermonis iniqui.

85. CDS III, no. 393.

86. RBCRS, p. 162. Beaumont had married her husband's niece.

87. Ibid., p. 274.

88. Ibid., p. 278; see also RRS V, no. 72, pp. 354–60.

89. Barbour, A.A.H. Douglas, p. 314; McD & S, III, p. 70:
    Quhill ye last end off his lyf-day.

90. Ibid., Douglas, p. 320, McD & S, III, pp. 77–8:
    In ser townys gert cry on hycht
    That quha-sa clemyt till haf rycht
    To hald in Scotland land or fe
    yat in yai tuelf moneth suld he
    Cum and clam yt and yarfor do
    To ye king yat pertenyt yarto
    And giff yao come nocht in yat ȝer
    Yan suld yai wit with-owtyn wer
    Yat hard yar-eftre nane suld be.

91. RRS V, no 41, p. 330. It disinherited them from the date of issue, but in fact the year's grace operated.

92. Scott, op. cit., p. 169.
93. Lanercost, p. 210.

Chapter 13 – Terror and Truce

1. From a letter of Robert I King of Scots to Edward II King of England, date unknown. RBCRS, p. 314; RRS V, no. 569, p. 698.
2. VES, p. 54; the Lanercost chronicle also called the day of Bannockburn 'an evil, miserable and calamitous day for the English' [Lanercost, p. 207], and considered that King Edward was to blame for failing to honour the saints as Edward I had done before going on campaign, [Ibid., p. 206]; The author of the Scotichronicon reported that two heavenly visitors to Glastonbury Abbey on Midsummer's Eve 1314 told how the next day they were going to fight for the Scots in a battle at Bannockburn to avenge the unjust death of Simon de Montfort at the battle of Evesham fifty years earlier. An old Scottish religious was able to tell the Abbot of Glastonbury, who had never heard of the place, that Bannockburn was 'beside the royal burgh of Stirling in Scotland, lying on the boundary of Britain', *Scotichronicon*, Vol. 6, Bk XII, Ch. 20, p. 355.
3. Lanercost, p. 210. The chronicler says John de Soules, but this is almost certainly a mistake for William, who was the great-nephew of Sir John de Soules, the sometime Guardian of Scotland, and son of the Competitor Nicholas de Soules.
4. Lanercost, p. 210–11.
5. WB, p. 72.
6. Ibid., p. 77; RRS V, no. 40, pp. 328–30.
7. Lanercost, p. 210.
8. Hutchison, op. cit., p. 89.
9. VES, p. 57.
10. WB, p. 77.
11. Lanercost, p. 211.
12. WB, p. 78, suggests that the talks broke down 'as soon as they proceeded to the substantiative issue of Scottish kingship'.
13. WB, p. 79, cit. V.H. Galbraith, 'Extracts from the Historia Aurea and a French Brut', EHR XLIII (1928), p. 209.
14. Ibid., p. 79. McNamee considers that 'These grants are not proof that Robert was thinking in terms of permanent conquest; it is rather the sort of aggressive posturing that might be expected'.
15. Ibid., p. 78.
16. Guisborough, p. 396; Lanercost, p. 213.

17. WB, p. 76.
18. Barbour, A.A.H. Douglas, p. 322; McD & S, III, p. 79:
    Ye erle off Carrick schyr Eduuard
    Yat stoutar wes yan a libard
    And had na will to be in pes
    Thocht yat Scotland to litill wes
    Till his broyer and him alsua,
    Yarfor to purpos gan he ta
    Yat he off Irland wald be king.
19. Curiously enough, there was another 'Maid of Norway' waiting in the wings, should all the other Bruce heirs die out. King Robert's sister, Queen Isabel, was the mother of Princess Ingeborg of Norway.
20. RBCRS, p. 293.
21. RBCRS, p. 323, n. 31, citing M. McKisack, *The Fourteenth Century*, p. 42. Edward de Bruce was educated with an Irish potentate, probably Domhnall Ua Neill, King of Tyrone, (1283–1325).
22. Barbour, A.A.H. Douglas, p. 42; McD & S, III, p. 80: 'And oyer knychtis mony ane'.
23. Ibid., Douglas, p. 323; McD & S, III, p. 80.
24. Lanercost, pp. 212–13.
25. VES, p. 61.
26. Extract from manifesto cit., McNamee, WB, p. 192; RRS V, no. 571, pp. 700–701.
27. WB, p. 194.
28. Ibid.; Hutchison, *Edward II*, p. 91.
29. WB, p. 191.
30. Barbour, A.A.H. Douglas, p. 349; McD & S, III, p. 111:
    . . . he yat suld ger schippis sua
    Betruix yai seis with saillis ga
    Suld wyne ye Ilis sua till hand
    Yat nane with strenth suld him withstand.
31. RBCRS, pp. 291–2, 295, 321.
32. Lanercost, p. 213.
33. Ibid., p. 215.
34. Ibid., p. 216.
35. Barbour, A.A.H. Douglas, p. 350–52; McD & S, III, pp. 112–116.
36. Ibid., Douglas, pp. 353–56; McD & S, III, pp. 116–19.
37. Ibid., p. 120.
38. Scott, op. cit., p. 177, says the child was saved for the sake of the succession, but no alteration was made to the 'tailzie' until after the death of Edward de Bruce in 1318.
39. WB, p. 81.
40. Lanercost, p. 216.

41. Ibid., pp. 215–16.
42. WB, pp. 82, 84, account of raid here based on reassessment of parish valuations for ecclesiastical taxation in the archdeanery of Richmond, the *Prima Nova Taxatio*. By detailing the parishes most affected by the Scots raid, this supplements the Lanercost narrative.
43. Lanercost, p. 217.
44. VES, p. 75.
45. Lanercost, p. 217.
46. RRS V, no. 101, pp. 378–79.
47. WB, p. 180, cites the Irish Laud annalist recording under 1316 that news came to Dublin that Robert Bruce King of Scotland entered Ireland to help his brother Edward and that the castle of Carrickfergus was besieged by the said Scots, so Carrickfergus may have surrendered not to Edward but to Robert himself. But it seems unlikely that Robert would have left Scotland just when Lancaster's invasion was threatened. In any case he was in Scotland on 30 September, so the visit would have been very brief. It seems more likely that the annalist has just pre-dated his expedition.
48. RBCRS, p. 238.
49. Nicholson, op. cit., p. 94.
50. RBCRS, p. 316.
51. WB, p. 182.
52. Ibid. Butler had 220 men-at-arms, 300 light horse and 400 foot. The Bruces' army, for which there are no numbers, must have been considerably larger.
53. Scott, op. cit., p. 179; RBCRS, p. 316.
54. Barbour, A.A.H. Douglas, p. 367; McD & S, III, p. 133:
    Yis wes a full gret curtasy
    Yat swilk a king and sa mychty
    Gert his men duell on yis maner
    Bot for a pouer lauender.
55. Scott, op. cit., p. 180.
56. Lanercost, p. 218.
57. Barbour, McD & S, III, p. 136, says the intention of the English was:
    To hew Iedwort forrst sa clene
    Yat ne tre suld yar-in be sene
    – which is surely irony, in the spirit of 'seven maids with seven mops'.
58. Ibid., p. 138:
    And him reuersyt and with a knyff
    Rycht in yat place reft him ye lyff.
59. Ibid., p. 148:
    Him luffyt and prisyt and honoryt ay
    And held him in sulk daynte
    Yat his awne bischop him callit he.

60. RRS V, p. 379.

61. Barbour, A.A.H. Douglas, p. 382; McD & S, III, p. 152:

> He said him 'Certes yow wrocht as wis
> Yat has discoweryt ye fyrst to me
> For giff yow had discoueryt ye
> To my newo ye erle Thomas
> Yow suld disples ye lord Douglas
> And him alsua in ye contrer . . .

62. Barbour, Douglas, p. 385; McD & S, III, p. 156: 'Sparyt yar ʒattis hastily'.

63. WB, p. 85.

64. RBCRS, p. 281. This, says Professor Barrow, raised him to the knightly class; RRS V, no. 150. Lanercost tells the same story as Barbour of the capture of Berwick, but says that Peter of Spalding was 'bribed by a great sum of money received from them [the Scots] and by the promise of land', p. 219.

65. Barbour, McD & S, III, p. 159.

66. Lanercost, p. 220.

67. Ibid., p. 221.

68. Ibid.

69. Ibid., p. 225.

70. Ibid., p. 225–6; Barbour has a curious story that the beheaded and quartered body belonged to one Gib Harper who was wearing Sir Edward de Bruce's armour. Barbour, A.A.H. Douglas, p. 413; McD & S, III, pp. 189, 192, 194.

71. WB, p. 186.

72. RBCRS, p. 318, and Ch. 15, n. 25, p. 380, cit. *Coupar Angus Chrs.*, no. 100, (February 8th 1319).

73. *Scotichronicon*, Vol. 7, Bk. XIII, Ch. 12, or 'King Robert Bruce's second tailzie', pp. 39–43; APS Vol. I, pp. 465–6.

74. Hutchison, op. cit., p. 99.

75. VES, p. 95.

76. Ibid., pp. 95–6.

77. WB, p. 94.

78. Lanercost, p. 226.

79. Lanercost, pp. 226–27; also VES, pp. 96–7.

80. Barbour, A.A.H. Douglas, p. 398; McD & S, III, p. 172.

81. Ibid., Douglas, p. 407; McD & S, III, pp. 181–2: 'Yat off ye ost ner thrid part was'.

82. WB, pp. 94–5.

83. VES, p. 97.

84. Ibid., p. 102.

85. RRS V, no. 569, p. 698, [undated] original Latin text; RBCRS, p. 314;

Scott, op. cit., pp. 194–95, same trans. The date of this letter is controversial. Professor Duncan in RRS suggests April–May 1320; Professor Barrow in RBCRS does not commit himself; Scott suggests the date I have followed.

86. WB, p. 95.
87. RRS V, no 162, pp. 433–37.
88. VES, pp. 102–03.

Chapter 14 – Spiritual Warfare

1. Sir James Fergusson, 'The Declaration of Arbroath', p. 11, (Fergusson's translation).
2. Enc. Brit.
3. Scott, op. cit., p. 182, says the envoys were the Bishop of Corbeil and the Archdeacon of Perpignan; R. Hill, 'An English Archbishop and the Scottish War of Independence', [Innes Review, Vol. 1971], pp. 59–71 at p. 66, says they were Peter of Bologna, one of Archbishop Melton's suffragans with a title *'in publicus instrumentus'*, and Master Gerard, Archdeacon of Ely.
4. Hailes, *Annals of Scotland*, Vol. II, pp. 93–4.
5. Ibid., pp. 95–6; Scott, op. cit., pp. 183–84; R. Hill, op. cit., pp. 67–8.
6. Scott, p. 186; Nicholson, p. 99.
7. Ibid.
8. RBCRS, p. 302; Nicholson, pp. 99–100.
9. RBCRS, p. 304.
10. Fergusson, op. cit., p. 29, 'For two and a half centuries it has been generally agreed that Bernard de Linton was probably the actual composer of the Declaration' [though it now seems that this Bernard was not 'de Linton', vide supra]; Nicholson, op. cit. p. 101.
11. Fergusson, 'The Declaration of Arbroath', p. 9, (Fergusson's translation).
12. Ibid., p. 5.
13. RBCRS, pp. 308–09. Whether they actually went to Arbroath is a matter of controversy. Ibid., p. 304; Fergusson, op. cit., pp. 16–18. This can only be a matter of opinion.
14. Nicholson, p. 101.
15. RBCRS, p. 305.
16. Ibid., p. 308.
17. Barbour, Douglas, p. 429.
18. *Scotichronicon*, Vol. 7, Bk. XIII, Ch. 1, p. 3.
19. *Scalachronica*, SHR III, p. 463 and fn 3.
20. Fergusson, op. cit., p. 5.
21. *Scotichronicon*, loc. cit.

22. Barbour, A.A.H. Douglas, p. 430; McD & S, III, p. 209–10:
    Ye lord ye Sowllis has grantyt yar
    Ye deid in-to plane parleament
    Till his pennance to Dunbertane
    And deit yar in a tour off stane.
    Douglas, a normally very accurate translator, has him condemned to death, but the original lines do not necessarily have this sense, I think.
23. *Scotichronicon*, loc. cit.
24. Fergusson, op. cit., p. 4. 'David, Lord of Brechin, having perhaps mislaid his own seal, used that of Mary Ramsay, his second wife'.
25. His condemnation for foreknowledge and concealment of the plot is reminiscent of that of the Regent Morton, executed in 1581 for foreknowledge and concealment of the plot against the life of Darnley.
26. *Scotichronicon*, loc. cit.
27. Barbour, A.A.H. Douglas, pp. 431–32; McD & S, III, pp. 211–12.
    Ye king yan sone has said him till
    'I will wele graunt yat it sua be,
    Bot tell me quhat amowis ye'.
    He said agane 'Schyr graunt mercy
    And I sall ell ʒow it planely
    Myne hart giffis me na mar to be
    With ʒow duelland in yis countre,
    Yarfor bot yat it nocht ʒow grewe
    I pray ʒow hartly of ʒour leve.
    For quhar swa rycht worthi a knycht
    And sa chewalrous and sa wicht
    And sa renownyt off worchip syne
    As gude schyr Dauid off Brechyn
    And sa fullfillyt off all manheid
    Was put to sa welanys a ded
    Myn hart forsuth may nocht gif me
    To duell for na thing yat may be'.
    Ye king said 'Sen yat ya will sua
    Quhen-euer ye likys yow may ga
    And yow sall haiff gud leve yar-to
    Yi liking off yi land to do'.
28. Ibid.
29. Nicholson, p. 103; G. Donaldson, 'The Pope's Reply to the Scottish Barons in 1320', SHR XXIX, pp. 119–20.
30. RBCRS, p. 240.
31. Report of the Ambassadors to Edward II, written from Woodham, near Bishop Auckland, County Durham, 8 April 1321. Stones, *Anglo-Scottish Relations*, p. 305.

Chapter 15 – 'Vanquished in His Own Country'

1. Barbour, A.A.H. Douglas, p. 428.
2. Lanercost, p. 229.
3. VES, p. 108.
4. Ibid., p. 114.
5. Ibid., pp. 120, 121.
6. CDS III, no 746, p. 139.
7. Scott, op. cit., p. 200.
8. RBCRS, p. 242.
9. Lanercost, pp. 230–31.
10. VES, p. 123.
11. Lanercost, p. 232.
12. VES, p. 126; The Lanercost Chronicler disagreed with this return of justice, and wrote 'O The excessive cruelty of the King and his friends!', Lanercost, p. 235.
13. Ibid., p. 234.
14. Ibid., pp. 234–5; *Scotichronicon*, Vol. 7, Bk. XIII, Ch. 4, p. 11.
15. Barbour, A.A.H. Douglas, p. 408; McD & S, III, p. 182:
    Men said syne efter yis Thomas
    Yat on yis wis maid marter was
    Was saynct and myrakillis did,
    Bot enwy syne gert yaim be hid
    Bot quhgeyer he haly wes or nane
    At Pomfret yus was he slane.
16. Scott, op. cit., p. 201.
17. Lanercost, p. 238.
18. Ibid.
19. Ibid.
20. Scott, op. cit., p. 201.
21. CDS III, no. 752, p. 140.
22. WB, p. 99.
23. Barbour, A.A.H. Douglas, p. 420; McD & S, III, p. 196; also *Scotichronicon*, Vol. 7, Bk XII, Ch. 4, p. 11.
24. Ibid., Douglas, p. 421; McD & S, III, pp. 197–8; *Scotichronicon*, loc. cit. pp. 11, 13, mentions the sack of Melrose Abbey but not the attack by Douglas.
25. *Scalachronica*, SHR III, p. 471.
26. WB, p. 99.
27. Ibid., p. 100.
28. Lanercost, p. 239.
29. Barbour, A.A.H. Douglas, p. 422; McD & S, III, p. 199; Lanercost, p. 240; RBCRS, p. 243 and Ch. 13, note 46, pp. 371–2. 'The account in the text [RBCRS] is based on the assumption that when contemporary sources use

the name Byland they mean Old Byland; and that in Barbour 'Bilandis abbay' is a mistake arising from confusion between Old Byland (close to Rievaulx Abbey) and [New] Byland Abbey.' From my own acquaintance with the area I agree with Professor Barrow's conclusion.

30. Barbour, A.A.H. Douglas, pp. 422–23; McD & S, III, pp. 199–200:

> King Robert yat had witteryng yen
> Yat he lay yar with mekill mycht
> Tranounyt swa on him a nycht
> Yat be ye morn yat it wes day
> Cummyn in a plane feld war yai
> Fra Biland bot a litill space,
> Bot betuix yaim and it yar was
> A craggy bra strekyt weill lang
> And a gret peth wp for to gang,
> Oyer-wayis mycht yai nocht away
> To pas to Bilandis abbay°
> Bot gif yai passyt fer about.
> And quhen ye mekill Inglis rout
> Hard yat ye king Robert wes sa ner
> Ye mast part of yaim yat yar wer
> Went to ye peth and tuk ye bra,
> Yai thocht yar defens to ma . . .

This is the erroneous reference to Byland Abbey; otherwise Barbour's narrative refers to 'Biland', and makes complete sense so long as 'Old Byland' is intended.

31. RBCRS, p. 243, and Ch. 13, note 47, p. 372. Barbour and Lanercost 'agree on the nature of the terrain, and their accounts will fit only Sutton Bank and Roulston Scar'. Lanercost, p. 240, says that John of Brittany took possession of the ridge and rolled boulders down.

32. *Scalachronica*, SHR III, p. 470.

33. Barbour, A.A.H. Douglas, p. 424; McD & S, III, pp. 201–2.

34. Lanercost, p. 240.

35. WB, p. 101.

36. Lanercost, p. 240.

37. Barbour, A.A.H. Douglas, p. 426; McD & S, III, p. 204: 'Till ʒorkis ʒettis'.

38. Ibid, Douglas, pp. 426–27; McD & S, III, p. 205:

> And said war it nocht yat he war
> Sic a catyve he suld be sar
> Hys wordys yat war war swa angry
> And he humbly criyt him mercy.

39. RBCRS, p. 284.

40. Barbour, A.A.H. Douglas, p. 428; McD & S, II, p. 207: 'Discumfyt in his awne countre'.

41. Barbour's prose translator, George Eyre Todd writes 'Had the Battle of Byland [sic] been described [by Barbour] with the same detail and spirit as the Battle of Bannockburn, it might have held almost as great a place in history'. Eyre Todd, *The Bruce*, preface, p. XIII, fn.

42. Lanercost, pp. 240–41.

43. CDS III, no. 745, p. 139.

44. Lanercost, p. 241.

45. RBCRS, p. 248: Harclay's negotiations 'were a piece of private enterprise, undertaken without Edward II's knowledge. Consequently, they were held to be as treasonable as those of Lancaster . . .'; WB, p. 104: 'Harclay . . . made a unilateral peace with the Scots'; Hutchison, op. cit., p. 120: 'Harclay's action was completely 'ultra vires', and an insult to his King . . . Harclay's negotiations with Bruce were clearly traitorous . . .'; Nicholson, op. cit., p. 104: 'Harclay, who found him [Edward II] confused . . . returned to Carlisle ready to take an initiative of his own . . .'

46. Stones, Anglo-Scottish Relations, text of agreement, pp. 308–15, and details of other versions, in note on text fn, p. 308; CDS III, no. 803, pp. 148–9, (resumé of text).

47. Nicholson, p. 105.

48. CDS III, nos 800, 801, 802, p. 148.

49. Lanercost, pp. 242–3.

50. Ibid., pp. 243–5, and 245 fn 1.

51. RBCRS, pp. 244–5, [trans. of full text, cit. Faedora II, 511]; CDS III, no. 807, p. 149, [resumé]; Hailes, Annals II, pp. 134–5.

52. Hailes, II, p. 136; Scott, op. cit., p. 207.

Chapter 16 – Towards Peace

1. Hailes, Annals of Scotland II, p. 162.

2. Dunbar, *Scottish Kings*, pp. 141–2, *Handbook of British Chronology*, p. 59.

3. *Scotichronicon*, Vol. 7, Bk. XIII, Ch. 5, p. 15:
   Iste manu fortis Anglorum ludet in ortis / vel faciat pacem Deus inter regns tenacem.
   An English poet wrote less pleasant verses, deriding the fact that when Prince David was christened immersion in cold water loosened the unfortunate baby's bowels and he defecated in the font. Instead of being regarded simply as a mishap, in a period of superstitious piety it would have been regarded as sacriligious and ill-omened. The event made an unpleasant canard which David's enemies revived from time to time throughout his life. Lanercost, p. 333, fn 1; and Maxwell, *Robert the Bruce*, p. 296, fn.

4. Hailes, II, pp. 138–40.

5. RBCRS, p. 250.

6. Ibid.; Hailes, II, p. 143, fn.

7. RBCRS, p. 319, cit. RRS V, no 294, pp. 553–4.

8. RBCRS, pp. 319–21; Scott, op. cit., pp. 210–11; Maxwell, op. cit., p. 301–2.

9. Ibid., pp. 300–01.

10. Ibid., pp. 302–3.

11. RBCRS, p. 291.

12. Ibid., p. 294.

13. Hutchison, op. cit., pp. 124–5.

14. Ibid., p. 129.

15. RBCRS, p. 251.

16. WB, p. 239.

17. Lanercost, p. 253.

18. Ibid.

19. Hutchison, op. cit., p. 137, for Edward's wanderings he cites *Edward II in Glamorgan*, John Griffiths, (London, 1904), pp. 192–231. The King's remaining supporters were Arundel and Surrey, who were shortly captured. Arundel was sent to Hereford to share Despenser's fate; Surrey was inexplicably pardoned by Isabella.

20. WB, pp. 239–40, discusses the possibility.

21. Nicholson, p. 118.

22. Hutchison, p. 139. Translation of the articles of deposition, Ibid., appendix V, pp. 169–70. The King was accused of incompetence, of being controlled by others who have given him evil counsel, of having lost the realm of Scotland, and other territories and lordships in Ireland and Gascony left him by his father, and of having lost the friendship of the King of France.

23. Ibid., p. 140.

24. Lanercost, p. 256.

25. WB, p. 240.

26. Barbour, A.A.H. Douglas, p. 436.

27. Nicholson, p. 118: Scott, p. 217: 'It must be assumed that they [the English] were playing for time' by holding talks at all when they were mobilizing.

28. Lanercost, p. 257.

29. WB, p. 242.

30. Ibid., p. 243; Nicholson, p. 118.

31. WB, p. 244, cit. Chartulary of St Mary's, Dublin, II, p. 367.

32. Hutchison, p. 140.

33. Barbour, A.A.H. Douglas, p. 441; McD & S, III, p. 223.

34. WB, p. 241.

35. RBCRS, p. 252.

36. WB, loc. cit.

37. Barbour, A.A.H. Douglas, p. 437.

38. RBCRS, p. 253.

39. Le Bel/Froissart, cit. Scott, p. 218.

40. Barbour, A.A.H. Douglas, p. 444; RBCRS, p. 253 and Ch. 13, note 83, p. 373; Lanercost, p. 257.

41. Barbour, Douglas, p. 446.

42. Ibid., p. 452.

43. Lanercost, p. 258.

44. Nicholson, p. 119.

45. Barbour, A.A.H. Douglas, pp. 454–5; McD & S, III, pp. 239–40.

46. WB, p. 245; RBCRS, p. 254. Barrow thinks it 'more likely that Bruce meant only to terrorize the enemy into agreeing to make permanent peace.'

47. Ibid., p. 240

48. Ibid.; Lanercost, p. 258, says Thomas Dunheved had previously gone on an abortive mission from Edward II to the Pope to obtain a divorce between Edward and Isabella.

49. Lanercost, p. 259 and fn 1; Hutchison, p. 141.

50. T.F. Tout, *The Captivity and Death of Edward of Caernarvon*, (Manchester, 1920); Hutchison, op. cit., pp. 141–2; Bingham, op. cit., pp. 196–7.

51. Scott, p. 221.

52. RBCRS, p. 254.

Chapter 17 – Treaty and Marriage

1. Barbour, A.A.H. Douglas, pp. 456–7.

2. Stones, Anglo-Scottish Relations, pp. 316–21; RBCRS, pp. 254–5; Scott, p. 221.

3. RBCRS, p. 255.

4. Scott, pp. 222–3; Stones, pp. 323–5; Lanercost, pp. 261–2.

5. Scott, p. 223.

6. Though Alexander III had held the honours of Tyndale and Penrith from the English Crown, Robert would presumably have preferred to forgo these, since his preference was for the integrity of both kingdoms, no-one else holding lands of both kings.

7. WB, p. 245.

8. WB, p. 246; Nicholson, p. 121; RBCRS, p. 259 and chapter 13, note 102, makes the point that no-one had been under the threat of total disinheritance. The choice before each man had been to swear allegiance to the King of England and retain his English lands *or* to the King of Scots and retain his Scottish lands. The problem of the disinherited arose from preferring covetousness to loyalty.

9. It would be recaptured from the Scots again at the Battle of Neville's Cross. 1346. WB, p. 246.

10. Lanercost, p. 259, 260.
11. RBCRS, p. 260.
12. WB, p. 243.
13. RBCRS, pp. 257–58.
14. She had died at Callen, in Banffshire, and was evidently embalmed there in preparation for the return of her body to Dunfermline, for her entrails were buried ['bowallis erdit'] in the Lady Kirk of Cullen. Had she, perhaps, gone there on pilgrimage, and died suddenly? The King founded a chaplaincy in the Lady Kirk, to pray for her soul. Maxwell, op. cit., p. 331.
15. Lanercost, p. 260.
16. Barbour, A.A.H. Douglas, pp. 457–8; McD & S, III, 242–3.
17. WB, p. 253; Scott, p. 224. Unfortunately William de Burgh, known as 'the Brown Earl', was murdered in 1333.
18. Nicholson, op. cit., 124.
19. RBCRS, p. 319.
20. Scott, p. 225.

EPILOGUE – Robert the Bruce: Hero King and Mythic Hero

1. *Scotichronicon*, Vol. 7, Bk. XIII, Ch. 14, p. 50.
2. Nicholson, p. 122.
3. Froissart, *Chronicles*, ed. and trans. Thomas Johnes (2 Vols, London, 1839) Vol. I, pp. 26–7.
4. Barbour, A.A.H. Douglas, pp. 460–1; McD & S, III, pp. 245–6:

> He said 'Lordingis swa it is gayn
> With me yat yar is nocht bot ane
> Yat is ye dede with-outyn drede
> Yat ilke man mon thole off nede.
> And I thank God yat has me sent
> Space in yis lyve me to repent,
> For throwch me and my werraying
> Off blud has bene rycht grete spilling
> Quhar mony sakles men war slayn,
> Yarfor yis seknes and yis payn
> I tak in thank for my trespas.
> And myn hart fichyt sekerly was
> Quhen I wes in prosperite
> Off my synnys to sauffyt be
> To trawaill apon Goddis fayyis,
> & sen he now me till him tayis
> Swa yat ye body may na wys
> Fullfill yat ye hart gan dewis

> I wald ye hart war yidder sent
> Quhar-in consawyt wes yat entent.
> Yarfor i pray ʒow euerilkan
> Yat ʒe among ʒow ches me ane
> Yat be honest wis and wicht
> And off his hand a noble knycht
> On Goddis fayis my hart to ber
> Quhen saule and cors disseueryt er . . .'

5. Maxwell, op. cit., p. 358.

6. Ibid., p. 343.

7. Ibid., p. 341.

8. The tomb of Robert the Bruce and Elizabeth de Burgh did not survive the iconoclasm of the Reformation. 'On 28 march 1560, the choir, transepts and belfry, as well as the monastery of Dunfermline were razed by the Reformers, and the nave was refitted four years later to serve as a parish church. Ruin – senseless ruin – fell upon the monument of Scotland's greatest ruler . . .' ibid., p. 342.

9. Barbour, A.A.H. Douglas, p. 463; McD & S, III, p. 249:

> Yar mycht men se men ryve yar har
> And comounly knychttis gret full sar
> And yar newffys oft samyn dryve
> And as woud men yar clathis ryve
> Regretand his worthi bounte
> His wyt his strenth his honeste
> And our-all ye gret company
> Yat he maid yaim oft curtasly.
> 'All our defens', yai said, 'allace
> And he yat all our comford was
> Our wit and all out gouernyng
> Allace is brocht her till ending . . .
> Allace quhat sall we do or say
> For on lyff quhill he lestyt ay
> With all our nychtbowris dred war we,
> And in-till mony ser countre
> Off our worschip sprang ye renoun
> And yat wes all for his persoune'.

10. Ibid., Douglas, p. 463; McD & S, III, p. 249:

> '. . . better gouernour yan he
> Mycht in na countre fundyn be'.

11. Bingham, *Life and Times of Edward II*, p. 212–5.

12. Froissart, Chronicles, I, p. 28.

13. Maxwell, op. cit., p. 359; CDS III, nos 990. 991, p. 179.

14. RBCRS, p. 323.

15. Barbour, A.A.H. Douglas, p. 466; McD & S, III, p. 253.

16. Froissart, Chronicles, I, p. 28.

17. Barbour, A.A.H. Douglas, pp. 469–70; McD & S, III, pp. 256–7.

18. Dunbar, *Scottish Kings*, p. 141.

19. Barbour, A.A.H. Douglas, p. 474; McD & S, III, pp. 261–2. Douglas had not married, but he had an illegitimate son, Archibald the Grim, eventually acknowledged as his heir, who set up a magnificent tomb for him. Unlike King Robert's tomb, that of Douglas survives. It is curious to reflect that the body of Douglas received the same treatment as that of Edward I, but it adds emphasis to the point that Edward's wishes were not macabre by the standards of the time. It was a practical way of dealing with the dead, though it now seems gruesome.

20. 'Buke of the Howlat', *Oxford Book of Scottish Verse*, pp. 36–8, at 38.

21. A.A.H. Douglas, 'Foreword' to The Bruce, p. 23.

22. Barbour, Douglas, p. 468; McD & S, III, p. 244, fn. In his Introduction A.A.H. Douglas reluctantly admits 'It is believed that, in the description of Douglas's death, the twelve lines beginning "and as he entered in the fray" were not written by Barbour himself.'

23. I.M. Davis, *The Black Douglas*, Appendix I, 'The Myth of the Thrown Heart', p. 168.

24. There were rumours of poison, but he appears to have died of natural causes, and been greatly lamented.

25. She spent much of her time at Castle Rising, Norfolk.

26. The male line of the Capetians had died out with the last of Philip IV's sons. The King's cousin Charles de Valois succeeded, but Edward III claimed through his mother, Queen Isabella.

27. Lanercost, p. 264; Froissart, p. 26, fn.

28. Runciman, History of the Crusades, pp. 392–3, Vol. II.

29. Jacques le Goff, The Medieval Imagination, p. 84.

30. Edwin Muir, Collected Poems, p. 229.

SELECT BIBLIOGRAPHY

PRIMARY SOURCES (PRINTED)

Acts of Parliament of Scotland, ed. Thomson and Innes, 1814–75.
Barbour's Bruce, ed. McDiarmid & Stevenson, 3 Vols., Edinburgh 1981.
John Barbour, *The Bruce*, trans. A.A.H. Douglas, 1964.
Walter Bower, *Scotichronicon*, gen. ed. D.E.R. Watt, 1991.
Calendar of Documents relating to Scotland, ed. J. Bain, 1881–8.
Declaration of Arbroath, 1320, ed. & trans. Sir James Fergusson, 1970.
Foedera, Conventiones, Litterae, ed. T. Rymer, 1816.
Froissart, *Chronicles of England, France and Spain*, trans. T. Johnes, 1839.
Sir Thomas Grey, *Scalachronica*, trans. Sir Herbert Maxwell, 1907.
The Chronicle of Walter of Guisborough, ed. H. Rothwell, 1957.
The Chronicle of Lanercost, trans. Sir Herbert Maxwell, 1913.
Jehan Le Bel, *Les Vraies Chroniques*, ed. M.L. Poulain, 1863.
Song of Lewes, ed. & trans. C.A. Kingsford, 1890.
Malmesbury, *Vita Edwardi Secundi*, ed. & trans. N. Denholm-Young, 1957.
Documents and Records illustrating the history of Scotland, ed. F. Palgrave, 1837.
The Book of Pluscarden, ed. F.H. Skene, 1880.
The Chronicle of William Rishanger, ed. H.T. Riley, 1865.
Anglo-Scottish Relations 1174–1328, ed. E.L.G. Stones, 1964.
Regesta Regum Scotorum V, The Acts of Robert I, ed. Archibald A.M. Duncan, 1988.
Johannis de Trekelowe, *Annales*, ed. H.T. Riley, 1886.
Thomas Walsingham, *Historia Anglicana*, ed. H.T. Riley, 1863.
Andrew Wyntoun, *Orygynale Chronykil of Scotland*, ed. D. Laing, 1872.

SECONDARY SOURCES

Joseph Bain, *The Edwards in Scotland: 1296–1377*, [The Rhind Lectures] 1901.
Richard Barber, *The Knight and Chivalry*, 1995.

E.M. Barron, *The Scottish War of Independence*, 1934.

G.W.S. Barrow, *Robert Bruce and the Community of the Realm of Scotland, 1988.*
   The Kingdom of the Scots, 1973.

Caroline Bingham, *The Life and Times of Edward II*, 1973.

David H. Caldwell, *The Scottish Army.*

John Chancellor, *The Life and Times of Edward I*, 1981.

Pierre Chaplais, *Piers Gaveston: Edward II's Adoptive Brother*, 1994.

I.M. Davis, *The Black Douglas*, 1974.

Gordon Donaldson, *Scotland's History: Approaches and Reflections*, 1995.

A.H. Dunbar, *Scottish Kings*, 1906.

A.A.M. Duncan, *The Nation of Scots and the Declaration of Arbroath*, 1970.

— *Scotland: The Making of the Kingdom*, 1975.

W. Fraser, *Douglas Book*, 1885.

Lord Hailes, *Annals of Scotland*, 1819.

J.S. Hamilton, *Piers Gaveston Earl of Cornwall 1307–1312*, 1988.

Paul Hillyard, *The Book of the Spider.*

Harold F. Hutchison, *Edward II*, 1971.

Sarah Kay, *The Chanson de Geste in the Age of Romance*, 1995.

John Lase, *The Hero: Manhood and Power*, 1995.

I. Lubimenko, *Jean de Bretagne*, 1908.

J.A. Mackay, *Robert the Bruce*, 1974.

Sir Herbert Maxwell, *Robert the Bruce and the Struggle for Scottish Independence*, 1897.

Sir Herbert Maxwell, *A History of the house of Douglas*, 1902.

Agnes Mure Mackenzie, *Robert Bruce King of Scots*, 1956.

May McKisack, *The Fourteenth Century: 1307–1399*, 1966.

Colm McNamee, *The Wars of the Bruces*, 1997.

Ranald Nicholson, *Scotland: The Later Middle Ages*, 1974.

Michael Packe, *King Edward III.*

Michael Prestwich, *Arms and Warfare.*

Sir Maurice Powicke, *The Thirteenth Century 1216–1307*, 1953.

Michael Prestwich, *Edward I*, 1988.

Peter Reese, *Wallace: A Biography.*

Graham Ritchie, *The Normans in Scotland.*

John Barbour, The Buik of Alexander, ed. R.L. Ritchie, 1925.

L.F. Salzman, *Edward I*, 1968.

Ronald McNair Scott, *Robert the Bruce King of Scots*, 1982.

Sir Walter Scott, *Tales of a Grandfather*, 1828.

— *The Lord of the Isles*, N.D.

T.F. Tout, *Edward I*, 1872.

— *The Captivity and Death of Edward of Caernarvon*, 1920.

T. Wright (ed.), *Political Songs of England*, 1839.

INDEX